COFRESTRI PLWYF CYMRU

PARISH REGISTERS OF WALES

COFRESTRI PLWYF CYMRU
PARISH REGISTERS OF WALES

Cynullwyd gan : Compiled by

C. J. Williams
&
J. Watts-Williams

LLYFRGELL GENEDLAETHOL CYMRU
a GRŴP ARCHIFYDDION SIROL CYMRU
mewn cydweithrediad â
CHYMDEITHAS YR ACHYDDWYR

NATIONAL LIBRARY OF WALES &
WELSH COUNTY ARCHIVISTS' GROUP
in association with the
SOCIETY OF GENEALOGISTS

1986

Mabwysiadwyd y llyfr hwn gan Gymdeithas yr Achyddwyr fel rhif 13 yn y gyfres *National Index of Parish Registers.*

This book has been adopted by the Society of Genealogists as volume 13 of the *National Index of Parish Registers.*

Cofrestri plwyf Cymru = Parish registers of Wales.
  1. Church records and registers—Wales—Bibliography   2. Wales—Genealogy—Bibliography   I. Williams, C.J.   II. Watts-Williams, J.   III. National Library of Wales   IV. Welsh County Archivists' Group   V. Society of Genealogists
  016.929'3429   Z5313.G7W3

ISBN 0-907158-14-5

Argraffwyd ar wasg breifat Llyfrgell Genedlaethol Cymru, Aberystwyth
Printed at the private press of the National Library of Wales, Aberystwyth

RHAGAIR

Pleser arbennig yw cael croesawu ymddangosiad y gyfrol hon, sef blaenffrwyth y cydweithredu a fu'n ddiweddar rhwng Grŵp Archifyddion Sirol Cymru a Llyfrgell Genedlaethol Cymru. Bydd y gyfrol yn amlwg o'r gwerth mwyaf i bawb a fo'n ymwneud â hanes diweddar Cymru ac yn arbennig efallai â hanes ei theuluoedd, maes a welodd flodeuo mawr yn ystod y blynyddoedd diwethaf. Diolchaf yn gynnes i bawb a fu â rhan yn nwyn y gyfrol i fodolaeth, yn enwedig ei golygyddion Mr. John Watts-Williams, Ceidwad Cynorthwyol yn Adran Lawysgrifau a Chofysgrifau Llyfrgell Genedlaethol Cymru, a Mr. Christopher Williams, Dirprwy Archifydd Sirol Clwyd; rhaid diolch hefyd i Isadran Argraffu'r Llyfrgell Genedlaethol am waith nodweddiadol lân.

R. GERAINT GRUFFYDD
Llyfrgellydd
Medi 1985

FOREWORD

It is a particular pleasure to be able to welcome the appearance of this volume, the first-fruit of the recent co-operation between the Welsh County Archivists' Group and the National Library of Wales. The volume will clearly be a most helpful aid to all who study modern Welsh history, particularly perhaps those who study Welsh family history, a field that has burgeoned mightily during the last few years. I thank warmly all those who had a part in the bringing of the project to fruition, especially its editors Mr. John Watts-Williams, an Assistant Keeper in the Department of Manuscripts and Records of the National Library of Wales, and Mr. Christopher Williams, Deputy County Archivist of Clwyd; I have to thank also the Printing Section of the National Library for characteristically skilful work.

R. GERAINT GRUFFYDD
Librarian
September 1985

CYMRU
WALES

YR HEN SIROEDD A'R NEWYDD
THE OLD AND NEW COUNTIES

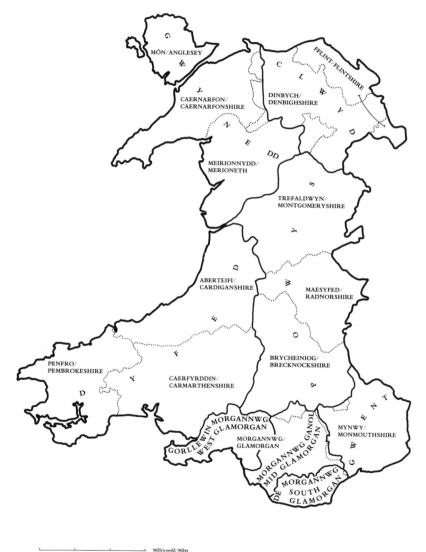

MÔN/ANGLESEY

FFLINT/FLINTSHIRE

CAERNARFON/
CAERNARFONSHIRE

DINBYCH/
DENBIGHSHIRE

MEIRIONNYDD/
MERIONETH

TREFALDWYN/
MONTGOMERYSHIRE

ABERTEIFI/
CARDIGANSHIRE

MAESYFED/
RADNORSHIRE

PENFRO/
PEMBROKESHIRE

BRYCHEINIOG/
BRECKNOCKSHIRE

CAERFYRDDIN/
CARMARTHENSHIRE

GORLLEWIN MORGANNWG
WEST GLAMORGAN

MORGANNWG/
GLAMORGAN

MORGANNWG GANOL
MID GLAMORGAN

MYNWY/
MONMOUTHSHIRE

DE MORGANNWG
SOUTH GLAMORGAN

Milltiroedd/Miles
0   10   20   30

....   YR HEN SIROEDD/THE OLD COUNTIES
——————   Y SIROEDD NEWYDD/THE NEW COUNTIES

CYNNWYS   CONTENTS

LLUNIAU

ILLUSTRATIONS

Cydnabyddiaeth/Acknowledgements

Archifdy Clwyd/Clwyd Record Office 1 & 8; Gwasanaeth Archifau Gwynedd/Gwynedd Archive Service 2 & 7; Archifdy Sirol Gwent/Gwent County Record Office 3; Gwasanaeth Archifau Morgannwg/Glamorgan Archive Service 6 & 11; Gwasanaeth Archifau Dyfed/Dyfed Archive Service 9; Llyfrgell Genedlaethol Cymru/National Library of Wales 4-5, 10, 12.

CYDNABYDDIAETH

Mae'r golygyddion yn ddyledus i staff yr archifdai sydd â gofal dros y cofnodion a ddisgrifir yn y gyfrol hon am ddarparu rhestrau ac am ateb eu hymholiadau mor amyneddgar; i Mrs. D. M. Rowland o Archifdy Clwyd a Mrs. M. Wendy Jenkins a Mrs. Ann Evans o'r Llyfrgell Genedlaethol am deipio'r drafftiau; i Ambrose Roberts ac aelodau eraill o isadrannau Argraffu a Ffotograffiaeth y Llyfrgell Genedlaethol am baratoi'r testun a'i argraffu; i Dafydd Ifans am gywiro'r Gymraeg; i Gareth Lloyd Hughes am ei help gyda'r mapiau; ac i Caroline Williams a Doreen Watts-Williams am eu cymorth wrth ddarllen y proflenni.

Dylid diolch i Fainc Esgobion yr Eglwys yng Nghymru ac i swyddogion ei Chorff Llywodraethol am gymeradwyo'r egwyddor o ddiogelu cofnodion plwyfol, ac i'r ymgynghorwyr ar archifau ymhob esgobaeth am eu hymdrech i'w wireddu. Ond ni allesid bod wedi cyflawni dim heb gydweithrediad yr offeiriaid. Rydym yn hynod ddiolchgar iddynt hwy am roi hen gofrestri plwyf Cymru ar gadw yn ddiogel mewn archifdai a, thrwy hynny, wneud y gyfrol hon yn bosibl.

Hydref 1985

ACKNOWLEDGEMENTS

The editors are grateful to the staffs of the repositories which hold the records described in this volume for supplying lists and patiently answering enquiries; to Mrs. D. M. Rowland of the Clwyd Record Office and Mrs. M. Wendy Jenkins and Mrs. Ann Evans of the National Library of Wales, who typed the drafts; to Ambrose Roberts and the staff of the Printing & Photographic Sections of the National Library, who prepared and printed the text; to Gareth Lloyd Hughes for his help with the maps; and to Caroline Williams and Doreen Watts-Williams for their assistance with proof reading.

Thanks are due to the Bench of Bishops of the Church in Wales, and the officials of the Governing Body, who approved the proposals for the preservation of parish records, and to the advisers on archives in each diocese who encouraged their deposit. However, little could have been achieved without the co-operation of incumbents; particular thanks are due to them for depositing the ancient parish registers of Wales in safe custody in record repositories, so making the present volume possible.

October 1985

RHAGYMADRODD

Cofrestri plwyf ar adnau

Rhydd y gyfrol hon fanylion am gofrestri plwyf gwreiddiol ac adysgrifau'r esgob, ac am feicroffilmiau, adluniadau, a chopïau eraill ohonynt a gedwir gan archifdai yng Nghymru a'r gororau, a chan Gymdeithas yr Achyddwyr. Mae'n cynnwys y tair ar ddeg o hen siroedd y dywysogaeth, gan ddisgrifio cofrestri tros fil o blwyfi a chapeli anwes a oedd mewn bodolaeth cyn 1812, a chofrestri tua 200 o eglwysi a godwyd wedi 1812 y mae eu cofnodion ar adnau mewn rhyw archifdy neu'i gilydd.

Yn 1944 arwyddwyd cytundeb rhwng Llyfrgell Genedlaethol Cymru a Chorff Cynrychiolwyr yr Eglwys yng Nghymru i roddi cofnodion esgobol, cabidylaidd, esgobaethol, ac eglwysig eraill ar adnau yn y llyfrgell.[1] Yn unol ag estyniad i'r cytundeb hwnnw, dechreuodd y Llyfrgell ar y dasg o gasglu'r cofrestri plwyf a chofnodion plwyfol eraill yn 1950. Trwy gytundeb pellach yn 1976 rhwng y Corff Cynrychiolwyr a phob un o gynghorau sir Cymru (ac eithrio Powys) penodwyd yr archifdai sirol hefyd yn gadwrfeydd addas ar gyfer cofnodion plwyfol eglwysig.[2] Mewn cylchlythyr a ddosbarthwyd yr un flwyddyn yn enw Cofrestrydd Archesgob Cymru anogwyd pob periglor i roi ei gofnodion eglwysig ar adnau mewn lle diogel, a phenodwyd ymgynghorydd archifol ymhob esgobaeth i arolygu'r gwaith. Mae llwyddiant y mesurau hyn yn amlwg pan sylweddolir nad oes erbyn hyn ond ychydig iawn o hen blwyfi Cymru sydd heb roi eu cofrestri ar adnau naill ai yn y Llyfrgell Genedlaethol neu yn un o archifdai sirol Cymru. Staff y sefydliadau hyn sydd wedi paratoi'r arolwg hwn.

Terfynau'r esgobaethau

Tan ei datgysylltu yn 1920 roedd yr eglwys Gymreig yn rhan annatod o Eglwys Loegr. Anwybyddid ffiniau Cymru a Lloegr gan yr esgobaethau (a oedd yn wir yn eu rhagflaenu). Ymestynnai'r pedair esgobaeth Gymreig hynafol ar draws ffiniau'r siroedd fel a ganlyn:

Llanelwy	y rhan fwyaf o siroedd y Fflint a Dinbych, ynghyd â rhannau o siroedd Caernarfon, Meirionnydd, Trefaldwyn, a'r Amwythig.
Bangor	Môn, y rhan helaethaf o sir Gaernarfon, rhannau o Feirionnydd a Threfaldwyn, ynghyd â deoniaeth Dyffryn Clwyd yng nghanolbarth sir Ddinbych.
Tyddewi	siroedd Caerfyrddin, Aberteifi, Penfro, Brycheiniog, y rhan fwyaf o Faesyfed, a rhannau o Drefaldwyn, Morgannwg, Mynwy, a Henffordd.
Llandaf	y rhan fwyaf o siroedd Morgannwg a Mynwy.

Nid oedd yng Nghymru ond un priodoriaeth yn rhydd oddi wrth awdurdod esgobaethol, sef Penarlâg yn sir y Fflint.

Roedd hefyd rannau o Gymru yn perthyn i esgobaethau Seisnig:

Caer   rhannau o siroedd y Fflint a Dinbych

Caerlwytgoed   plwyf Llannerch Banna, sir y Fflint

Henffordd   rhannau o siroedd Trefaldwyn, Maesyfed, a Mynwy.

Trosglwyddwyd amryw o'r plwyfi hyn o'u hesgobaethau Seisnig i rai Cymreig yn 1849. Bu cryn newid yn y ffin rhwng esgobaethau Bangor a Llanelwy yn 1859 pan roddwyd deoniaeth Dyffryn Clwyd i Lanelwy yn gyfnewid am ddeoniaeth Cyfeiliog a Mawddwy. A chafwyd ad-drefnu pellach ar y gororau yn sgîl Deddf Eglwys Cymru 1914 a ddaeth i rym yn 1920. Roedd y plwyfi a arferai berthyn i esgobaethau Cymreig ond a safai yn gyfan gwbl ar dir Lloegr i'w trosglwyddo i esgobaethau Seisnig, ac i'r gwrthwyneb. Roedd pob un ond dau o'r pedwar plwyf ar bymtheg a safai yn rhannol ar dir Cymru ac yn rhannol ar dir Lloegr, i'w trin 'yn unol â dymuniad cyffredinol eu plwyfolion,' fel petaent yn Lloegr. Yn y ddau achos arall, bu'n rhaid cynnal pleidlais, a dewisodd pobl Llansilin fod yn rhan o Gymru. (Mae cofrestri'r plwyfi Cymreig sydd yn dal i berthyn i Eglwys Loegr wedi eu rhoi ar adnau yn yr archifdy sirol priodol dros Glawdd Offa - Caer, Amwythig, neu Henffordd). Crewyd dwy esgobaeth newydd yng Nghymru - Mynwy o esgobaeth Llandaf yn 1921, ac Abertawe ac Aberhonddu o esgobaeth Tyddewi yn 1923.

Terfynau'r siroedd

Mae testun y gyfrol hon wedi ei drefnu yn ôl hen siroedd Cymru fel yr oeddent cyn eu diddymu gan y mesur ad-drefniant llywodraeth leol yn 1974. Y pryd hwnnw rhannwyd y tair sir ar ddeg yn wyth o siroedd newydd fel a ganlyn:

Clwyd   sir y Fflint, y rhan fwyaf o sir Ddinbych, a rhan o sir Feirionnydd.

Gwynedd   sir Gaernarfon, Môn, y rhan fwyaf o Feirionnydd, ac ychydig o sir Ddinbych.

Dyfed   siroedd Aberteifi, Caerfyrddin, a Phenfro.

Powys   sir Drefaldwyn, Maesyfed, a'r rhan fwyaf o sir Frycheiniog.

Morgannwg   yr hen sir, ynghyd â chyfran fechan o siroedd Brycheiniog a Mynwy, wedi ei rhannu'n dair sir newydd, sef Gorllewin, Canol, a De Morgannwg.

Gwent   y rhan fwyaf o Sir Fynwy ac ychydig o sir Frycheiniog.

Defnyddir y siroedd newydd wrth gyfeirio at y plwyfi ym mynegai'r llyfr hwn.

Cofrestri plwyf

Hyd yn oed yn y siroedd lle y maent wedi goroesi yn well na'r cyffredin, nid yw cofrestri Cymru i'w cymharu ag eiddo'r siroedd Seisnig ar y gororau. Thomas Cromwell yn 1538 a orchmynnodd gyntaf y dylid cadw cofrestri plwyf, ond un gofrestr yn unig sydd ar gael heddiw yng Nghymru yn dyddio yn ôl i 1538, sef cofrestr Gwaunysgor, sir y Fflint. Nid y gofrestr bapur wreiddiol mo honno ond copi memrwn a wnaethpwyd ar ryw adeg wedi'r cadarnhad yn 1598 o gyfansoddiad y flwyddyn flaenorol a orchmynnai gadw'r cofrestri plwyf yn fwy gofalus. Eithr y mae gan sir Amwythig bump o gofrestri yn dechrau yn 1538, a chan swydd Henffordd saith.[3] O'r ychydig dros fil o blwyfi a chapeli anwes hynafol sydd yng Nghymru, nid oes ond saith deg â chofrestr yn cychwyn cyn 1600 ac y mae ymhell dros eu hanner hwy heb gofrestr cyn 1700. Yn wir, mewn llawer o blwyfi, yn enwedig yn ne Cymru, nid oes cofrestr cyn 1754 pan ddechreuwyd cadw cofnodion priodas ar wahân, neu hyd yn oed 1813, pryd y defnyddiwyd y cyfrolau printiedig ar gyfer bedydd a chladdu am y tro cyntaf ar eu gwedd bresennol. Yn y plwyfi hyn, mae'r cofrestri cynharaf (o femrwn fel rheol) a gynhwysai gofnodion bedydd, priodas, a chladdu rhwng yr un cloriau, wedi diflannu'n llwyr.

Mae'r cofrestri wedi goroesi yn well mewn ambell esgobaeth na'i gilydd. Llanelwy sydd â'r cyfartaledd uchaf o gofrestri cynnar, a chan Dyddewi (lle y mae dros hanner y plwyfi heb gofrestr gynharach na 1754) mae'r isaf. Yn gyffredinol, mae cofrestri gogledd Cymru yn fwy cynnar na rhai'r de. O ran siroedd, y Fflint sy'n rhagori. Mae ganddi'r unig gofrestr sy'n dechrau yn 1538; mae deunaw o'i naw ar hugain o blwyfi hynafol (62%) yn meddu ar gofrestr sy'n dechrau cyn 1660, ac mae gan bob un o'i phlwyfi gofrestr cyn 1754. O'u trefnu yn ôl cyfartaledd y plwyfi sydd â chofrestr cyn 1660, siroedd gogleddol Trefaldwyn (49%), Dinbych (33%), a Meirionnydd (29%) ddaw nesaf i'r Fflint. Yn ne Cymru, sir Fynwy (20%) sydd agosaf at y cyfartaledd a geir yn y gogledd. Ar waelod y rhestr gwelir Aberteifi (4%) heb un gofrestr gynharach na 1653; bron dwy ran o dair o'i phlwyfi heb gofrestr cyn 1754; a chynifer â thri ar ddeg ohonynt heb gofrestr cyn 1813.

Dengys manylion dau arolwg arall a wnaethpwyd pan oedd y cofrestri yn dal i fod yn y plwyfi, pa gyfrolau sydd wedi eu colli yn ystod y can mlynedd a hanner diwethaf. Seiliwyd y cyntaf ar atebion clerigwyr i holiadur a ddosbarthwyd yn adeg Cyfrifiad 1831.[4] Cafwyd manylion, gyfrol wrth gyfrol gan amlaf, am y cofrestri cyn-1813 a oedd ar gael y pryd hwnnw, ac ambell waith cynigiwyd rheswm da am golledion diweddar o'u plith. (Mewn ambell esgobaeth, mae'r atebion gofwyol tua diwedd y ddeunawfed ganrif a dechrau'r bedwaredd ar bymtheg yn cynnig manylion am oed cofrestri hefyd.) Er gwaethaf ei aml feflau a'i ambell wall dybryd, bu arolwg 1831 yn ffynhonell werthfawr i awduron.[5] Yn nes at ein dyddiau ni, gwnaeth y Llyfrgell Genedlaethol arolwg o gofnodion plwyfol fesul esgobaeth rhwng 1933 a 1940.[6] Ar ffurf holiadur i'r clerigwr y lluniwyd yr arolwg hwn hefyd, ond fel rheol mae'r atebion yn ddigon manwl i hwyluso cymhariaeth bellach. Yn fwy diweddar fyth gwnaeth rhai o'r archifdai arolwg o'r sefyllfa yn eu siroedd gan archwilio'r cofrestri eu hunain. Mae'r wybodaeth am unrhyw gofrestr sydd wedi mynd ar goll ers ei gofnodi gan y naill arolwg neu'r llall wedi ei hymgorffori yn y testun.

Collodd 144 o blwyfi o leiaf un o'u cofrestri ers 1831, ac mewn 74 o achosion eraill mae cofrestri a nodwyd yn y 1930au wedi diflannu erbyn hyn. (Ar y llaw arall, mewn ambell blwyf daeth i glawr gofrestr gynharach na'r rhai a nodwyd ar ei gyfer gan y naill arolwg a'r llall). Bu'r colledion yn drymach yn ne Cymru; mae tua un o bob pedwar o blwyfi Caerfyrddin a Phenfro wedi colli cofrestr ers 1831, a thua un o bob tri o blwyfi Aberteifi, Brycheiniog, Maesyfed, a Morgannwg.

Collwyd cofrestri yn ddamweiniol trwy dân (Llanddeusant, Llangynog, a Phentywyn, sir Gaerfyrddin; Llansanffraid Glan Conwy, sir Ddinbych; Hanmer a Llanfynydd, sir y Fflint; Diserth a Phyllalai, sir Faesyfed; Rhodogeidio, sir Fôn; Eglwys y Drindod a Saint Arvans, sir Fynwy; Angle a Chastellmartin, sir Benfro); a thrwy lifogydd (Llechryd, sir Aberteifi). Yng Nghilymaenllwyd, sir Gaerfyrddin, a Llangatwg, sir Forgannwg, fe'u rhoddwyd o bwrpas ar y tân er mwyn cynhesu trigolion y persondy. Fe'u dygwyd gan swyddogion y plwyf (Nantglyn, sir Ddinbych), gan offeiriaid (Caerau a Threlái, sir Forgannwg), a chan ladron (Trefesgob, sir Fynwy). Yn sir Gaerfyrddin, cyhuddwyd curad Llan-gain o werthu'r gofrestr am ddeugain punt; yn sir Aberteifi, haerir bod cofrestr gynnar Llanfihangel Genau'r-glyn wedi ei dwyn ymaith i'w harddangos mewn llys barn ac na ddychwelwyd mohoni; ac yn sir Benfro tybir bod y Ffrancod wedi difa cofrestri Llanwnda a Threletert yn adeg y glaniad yn 1797. Fe sonnir hefyd am fuwch yn cnoi cil ar gofrestr plwyf (nas enwir) ym Mon.[7]

Ychydig sy'n rhaid ei ddweud am gynnwys y cofrestri, oherwydd yr un yw eu hanes â rhai Lloegr sydd wedi cael sylw tra helaeth.[8] Yn Lladin mae'r cofnodion, gan fwyaf, tan tua 1732. Mae cofnodion Cymraeg yn hynod o brin, ond fe'u gwelir o bryd i'w gilydd yn ystod y ddeunawfed ganrif mewn cylch cyfyng iawn o blwyfi. Ambell waith gwelir plwyf tlawd yng nghefn gwlad yn ymwrthod yn llwyr â'r gorchwyl o gadw cofrestr ei hun gan roi'r cofnodion yng nghofrestr y plwyf agosaf ato. Er enghraifft ni cheir cofrestr ar wahân ar gyfer plwyf Llanfaelrhys, sir Gaernarfon, tan 1811, ond ceir y cofnodion perthnasol am y cyfnod cyn hynny yng nghofrestr Aberdaron. Rhoddir croesgyfeiriad at achosion o'r fath yn nhestun y llyfr hwn. Mae amryw o blwyfi bychain yn dal i ddefnyddio'r un gofrestr brintiedig ar gyfer bedydd neu gladdedigaeth ag a ddechreuwyd yn 1813, ac oherwydd hynny mae'r cofrestri a roddwyd ar adnau ganddynt yn gorffen gyda'r flwyddyn 1812. Caewyd yr hen gofrestri priodas trwy orchymyn y Cofrestrydd Cyffredinol yn 1971 pan ddaeth y cyfrolau dwyieithog i gymryd eu lle, gyda'r canlyniad fod y cofrestri priodas a roddwyd ar adnau gan blwyfi gwledig yn fynych yn llawer mwy diweddar eu cynnwys na'r rhai bedydd a chladdu. Dewiswyd y lluniau i'r gyfrol hon gyda'r bwriad o ddangos cynifer â phosibl o'r amrywiol fathau o gofrestri gan gynnwys enghreifftiau o'r cofrestri priodasau a ddefnyddiwyd ar wahanol adegau er 1754, ac o'r cofrestri bedyddiadau a chladdedigaethau er 1813.

Adysgrifau'r esgob

Mesur 1597 oedd man cychwyn effeithiol y drefn yn Eglwys Loegr o yrru bob blwyddyn at yr esgob gopi o'r cofnodion a roddwyd yn y gofrestr plwyf yn ystod y deuddeg mis blaenorol - copi a adwaenir wrth yr enw adysgrif yr esgob, neu yn fyr A.E. (B.T. - bishop's transcript). Cadarnhawyd y mesur gan ganon 1603.[9] Er bod gan lawer o blwyfi Lloegr adysgrifau sy'n mynd yn ôl mor bell â 1597 a chyn hynny, nid oes gan blwyfi Cymru nemor ddim ohonynt cyn 1660. Yn hynny o beth cydymffurfiant â phatrwm cyffredinol cofysgrifau'r esgobaethau Cymreig. Yn wir, yr unig blwyfi Cymreig sydd ag adysgrifau'r esgob cyn 1660 yw'r dwsin neu ragor ar y gororau a arferai berthyn i esgobaeth Caer neu Henffordd.[10] Hyd yn oed wedi 1660, nid yw adysgrifau esgobion Cymru wedi eu cadw'n gyflawn a pharchus bob amser. Yn achos Tyddewi, er enghraifft, daeth rhai o adysgrifau coll y ddeunawfed ganrif i'r golwg yn gymharol ddiweddar fel labedi ar fwndeli o ewyllysiau sydd yn awr yn y Llyfrgell Genedlaethol.

Gellir crynhoi dyddiadau adysgrifau'r esgobion Cymreig fel a ganlyn fesul esgobaeth:

Bangor	1662-1917	(1675-1880 gan fwyaf)
Llandaf	1696-1916	(1725-1870 gan fwyaf)
Llanelwy	1661-1898	(1661-1850 gan fwyaf)
Tyddewi	1671-1911	
archddeoniaethau:		
Aberhonddu	1685-1874	(1700-1850 gan fwyaf)
Aberteifi a Thyddewi	1673-1911	(1799-1880 gan fwyaf)
Caerfyrddin	1671-1902	(1671-1870 gan fwyaf)
Gŵyr	1671-1910	(1671-1880 gan fwyaf)

Sylwer bod prif gorff yr adysgrifau ar gyfer y rhan fwyaf o esgobaethau Cymru yn fwy cyfyng eu cyfnod nag y mae'r terfynau eithaf yn ei awgrymu. Tua naw deg o blwyfi oedd yn parhau i anfon eu hadysgrifau at yr esgob wedi 1900; un Llangoed, Môn, am y flwyddyn 1917 yw'r diweddaraf ohonynt i gyd, mae'n debyg. Mae dyddiad rhoi'r gorau i'r arfer yn amrywio'n fawr o ardal i ardal. Cystal ychwanegu na cheir gan unrhyw blwyf gyfres gyflawn o adysgrifau'r esgob sydd yn cyfateb yn union i'r terfynau eithaf a nodir uchod.

Mae'r trwch pennaf o adysgrifau i'w cael ymhlith yr archifau esgobaethol a roddwyd ar adnau yn y Llyfrgell Genedlaethol yn 1944.[11] Yn swyddfeydd y cofrestryddion esgobaethol y cedwid hwy gynt, ac roeddent, gydag un eithriad, wedi eu trefnu y pryd hwnnw mewn bwndeli fesul blwyddyn. Yn ystod y cyfnod rhwng tua 1870 a'r dyddiad y trosglwyddwyd yr archifau esgobaethol i'r Llyfrgell, rhoddwyd adysgrifau archddeoniaeth Aberhonddu yn nhrefn y plwyfi a'u rhwymo'n gyfrolau. Aildrefnwyd adysgrifau gweddill Cymru yn yr un modd wedi iddynt gyrraedd Aberystwyth, a'u cadw'n rhydd mewn bocsys. Yn ddiweddar ffeiliwyd adysgrifau Llanelwy a'r gweddill o rai Tyddewi rhwng cloriau caled. Aros yn eu bocsys mae adysgrifau Bangor a Llandaf am y tro. Rhestrwyd yr adysgrifau yn rhan o'r archifau esgobaethol y maent yn perthyn iddynt. Mae'r rhestrau i'w gweld yng nghatalogau teipysgrif Cofysgrifau'r Eglwys yng Nghymru sydd ar gael yn y Llyfrgell Genedlaethol a'r archifdai sirol, sef: Bangor, cyf. 2, 1-58; Llandaf, 3, 1-29; Llanelwy, 1, 312-335; a Thyddewi, 2, 162-252. Ar y rhestrau hynny y seiliwyd y wybodaeth a geir yn y gyfrol hon gyferbyn â'r pennawd BT.

Nid oes cysondeb nac unffurfiaeth yng nghofnod cyfrif yr adysgrifau esgobol cyn 1812. Amrywia o blwyf i blwyf, ac o adeg i adeg mewn llawer plwyf unigol. Gall y dyddiad olaf fod yn sefydlog - Gŵyl Fair (25 Mawrth) neu'n symudol - Y Pasg, neu ddyddiad llys yr esgob (neu'r archddiacon). Hyd yn oed wedi mabwysiad swyddogol y calendr Gregoraidd yn 1752, ni ollyngwyd yr hen arferion gan nifer fawr o blwyfi hyd nes i Ddeddf Rose ddod i rym ar Ddydd Calan 1813. Wedi hynny, mae'r adysgrifau, bron heb eithriad, yn rhedeg yn rheolaidd o 1 Ionawr hyd 31 Rhagfyr. At ddibenion yr arolwg hwn, ac er dangos yn eglur y bylchau mewn cyfres o adysgrifau, dynodir pob un sydd ar gael gan ddyddiad ei flwyddyn gychwynnol, hyd yn oed pan fo'n cynnwys misoedd cyntaf y flwyddyn ganlynol. Er enghraifft, mae adysgrif Abergele, sy'n cynnwys cofnodion am y cyfnod o 7 Ebrill 1670 hyd 21 Mai 1671 wedi ei restru yn syml fel 1670.

Dogfennau memrwn yw'r rhan fwyaf o'r adysgrifau, rai ohonynt wedi eu defnyddio cyn hynny i bwrpas arall, e.e. adysgrifau Llanddoged, sir Ddinbych 1702-3 a ysgrifennwyd ar ddail a dorrwyd o'r gofrestr wreiddiol gyda chofnodion bedydd a chladdu tua 1638 braidd yn aneglur weladwy arnynt o hyd. Yn aml bydd yr adysgrif yn cynnig gwybodaeth ychwanegol i'r hyn a geir gan y gofrestr wreiddiol.[12] Fel rheol ni chofnodir priodasau yn adysgrifau'r esgob wedi dechrau cofrestru sifil ym mis Gorffennaf 1837.

Ceir rhai o adysgrifau'r esgob mewn archifdai heblaw'r Llyfrgell Genedlaethol, sef a) ambell strae ymhlith y cofnodion plwyfol a roddwyd ar adnau mewn archifdy lleol (pob un ohonynt yn fwy diweddar nag 1820, mae'n ymddangos); b) y rhai sy'n perthyn i'r eglwysi ym mhriodoriaeth Penarlâg; ac c) y rhai sy'n perthyn i'r plwyfi sydd neu a fu ar un adeg mewn esgobaeth Seisnig, lle y mae'r adysgrifau yn rhan o'r archif esgobaethol a roddwyd ar adnau yn yr archifdy sirol priodol dros y ffin, Caer, Henffordd, neu Gaerlwytgoed. Am yr un rheswm, ceir yn y Llyfrgell Genedlaethol nifer fechan o adysgrifau sy'n perthyn i ambell blwyf Seisnig a fu ar un adeg mewn esgobaeth Gymreig.[13]

Copïau meicroffilm o adysgrifau'r esgob

Ffilmiwyd adysgrifau pob un o esgobaethau Cymru gan Eglwys Iesu Grist Seintiau'r Dyddiau Diwethaf yn y 1950au cynnar. Ond ni ffilmiwyd yr adysgrifau cynharaf oll yn eu cyfanrwydd oherwydd nad oedd y dogfennau wedi eu llwyr drefnu yr adeg honno. Mae copïau o'r meicroffilmiau hyn ar gyfer esgobaeth Llanelwy ar gael gan archifdai Clwyd ym Mhenarlâg a'r Rhuthun.

Meicroffilmiau ac adluniadau o'r cofrestri plwyf

Paratoir adlun rhwymedig o bob cofrestr plwyf a ddaw i ofal yr archifdai. Trosglwyddir yr adlun i'r periglor i'w gadw yn y plwyf. Ambell waith pan fo'r gofrestr yn dal i gael ei defnyddio fe geidw'r archifdy'r adlun ac anfonir y gwreiddiol yn ôl i'r plwyf. Dyna oedd y drefn yn y 1930au pan anfonwyd nifer o gofrestri cynnar i'r Llyfrgell Genedlaethol i'w hatgyweirio a'u hail-rwymo. Tra oeddent yn y Llyfrgell copïwyd y mwyafrif ohonynt ar feicroffilm neu ffotostat. Doeth o beth oedd hynny, oherwydd mae'n ymddangos fod rhai o'r cofrestri gwreiddiol hynny wedi diflannu ers eu hanfon yn ôl i'r plwyfi: e.e. Bodedern, Diserth (Maesyfed), Llandanwg, Llandeilo Fawr, Llandysul (Aberteifi), a Llanwenog.

Bu'r archifdai yn cydweithio fwyfwy yn ddiweddar i gyfnewid meicroffilmiau ac adluniadau. Mae llawer wedi ei gyflawni yn y cyswllt hwn yn barod ac mae'r gwaith yn mynd rhagddo wrth i'r gyfrol hon fynd i'r wasg. Mae ambell archifdy yn cymell darllenwyr i ddefnyddio meicroffilm neu adlun er mwyn arbed traul ar y gofrestr wreiddiol, mesur sy'n debyg o gael ei fabwysiadu gan eraill yn y dyfodol agos.

Copïau

Defnyddir yr ymadrodd 'copïau' er mwyn gwahaniaethu rhwng adysgrifau cyffredin ag adysgrifau'r esgob. Ceisiwyd nodi hefyd pa gopi sydd yn bigion (*extracts*) o'r cofnodion gwreiddiol yn hytrach na chopi cyflawn, ond y mae'n bosibl mai pigion yw rhai o'r copïau cynharaf e.e. y rhai a ddelir gan Gymdeithas yr Achyddwyr. Mae rhai o'r cymdeithasau hanes teulu a sefydlwyd yn ddiweddar yng Nghymru wedi dechrau ar y gwaith o adysgrifo'n systematig gofrestri eu hardaloedd, ond nid yw ffrwyth eu llafur wedi ymddangos mewn pryd i'w gynnwys yn y gyfrol hon. Serch hynny, gwnaethpwyd cryn ymdrech i grybwyll pob copi lled helaeth ei gynnwys y gwyddys amdano, heb anghofio'r ychydig a gyhoeddwyd a'r llawer a gopïwyd mewn llawysgrifen a theip gan selogion yn ystod y can mlynedd diwethaf. Maent oll ar gael i ddarllenwyr naill ai gan un o'r archifdai yng Nghymru neu gan Gymdeithas yr Achyddwyr.

Nodiadau

[1] J. Conway Davies, 'The Records of the Church in Wales', *Cylchgrawn Llyfrgell Genedlaethol Cymru*, IV (1945-6), 1.

[2] A. G. Veysey, 'Ecclesiastical Parish Records in Wales', *Journal of the Society of Archivists*, VI (1978-81), 31-3. Yn 1976 Powys oedd yr unig sir yng Nghymru heb archifdy sirol. Penodwyd archifydd sirol yno yn 1984. Gwasanaethir siroedd newydd Gorllewin, Canol, a De Morgannwg gan Wasanaeth Archifau Morgannwg sydd â'i brif swyddfa yng Nghaerdydd. Yn y pen draw, bwriedir trosglwyddo cofrestri Gorllewin Morgannwg i'r swyddfa ranbarthol yn Abertawe, lle y mae eisoes ar gael i chwilotwyr ddyblygion o adluniadau'r rhan fwyaf o'r cofrestri sydd ar gadw yn y brif swyddfa. Nid yw'r Mesur Cofrestri a Chofysgrifau Plwyfol 1978, sydd yn rheoli diogelwch cofnodion plwyfol yn Lloegr, yn weithredol yng nghyswllt Eglwys ddadsefydliedig Cymru.

[3] D. J. Steel, *National Index of Parish Registers*, V: *South Midlands and Welsh Border Counties*, 3ydd arg. (Llundain, 1976), 75-92 *passim*, 146.

[4] *Abstract of the Answers and Returns made pursuant to an Act...for taking an Account of the Population of Great Britain...: Parish Register Abstract* (Llundain, 1833), 198-203, 416-85.

[5] e.e. A. M. Burke, *Key to the Ancient Parish Registers of England and Wales* (Llundain, 1908).

[6] Cedwir yr atebion gwreiddiol mewn cyfrolau rhwymedig, fesul esgobaeth, ymhlith papurau'r Eglwys yng Nghymru yn Llyfrgell Genedlaethol Cymru. Mae copiau serocs rhwymedig ohonynt ar gael yn Ystafell Ddarllen y Llawysgrifau yn y llyfrgell.

[7] R. M. & G. A. Benwell, 'Interpreting the Parish Registers and Bishop's Transcripts for Anglesey and Llŷn', *Trafodion Cymdeithas Hynafiaethwyr a Naturiaethwyr Môn* (1975), 77.

[8] Y mwyaf cynhwysfawr yw D. J. Steel, *National Index of Parish Registers*, I (Llundain, 1968). Ceir astudiaeth fanwl ynghyd â dyfyniadau o gofrestri o bob rhan o Gymru gan R. W. McDonald, 'Cofrestri Plwyf Cymru', *Cylchgrawn Llyfrgell Genedlaethol Cymru*, XIX (1975-6). Sonnir am gofnodion plwyfol yn gyffredinol yn ogystal â'r cofrestri gan W.E. Tate, *The Parish Chest*, 3ydd arg. (Caergrawnt, 1969). Rhydd J.C. Cox, *The Parish Registers of England* (Llundain, 1910) lu o enghreifftiau, ond o Loegr yn unig.

[9] Dorothy M. Owen, *The Records of the Established Church in England* (British Records Association, 1970), 26-7.

[10] Daeth adysgrif strae o blwyf Nyfer, sir Benfro, 1634 i'r golwg yn gynharach y ganrif hon mewn bwndel o bapurau yng nghofrestrfa brofeb Caerfyrddin (Llsgr. Francis Green, cyf. 8, t. 175). Ffeiliwyd ef gyda'r adysgrifau eraill yn y Llyfrgell Genedlaethol erbyn hyn.

[11] *Adroddiad Blynyddol Llyfrgell Genedlaethol Cymru 1944*, 32-4; *1945*, 34.

[12] Benwell, *op. cit.*, 87-9.

[13] Steel, *op. cit.*, V. 65-92 *passim*, 143-83 *passim*.

FFURF Y COFNOD

Plwyf neu eglwys

Trefnir enwau'r plwyfi a'r eglwysi yn ôl yr wyddor o dan yr hen siroedd. Defnyddir y ffurfiau Cymraeg gan ddilyn sillafiad Elwyn Davies, *Rhestr o Enwau Lleoedd* (Caerdydd, 1967). Os oes enw Saesneg cyfatebol neu fersiwn Saesneg o'r enw, fe'i rhoddir ochr yn ochr â'r enw Cymraeg gyda strôc letraws rhyngddynt. Rhoddir ffurfiau hynafol neu amrywiol mewn cromfachau. Lle bo gwahaniaeth mawr rhwng y ddau enw, ceir ail gofnod o dan yr enw Saesneg hefyd, a dynodir mai ail gofnod ydyw trwy roi seren o flaen yr enw.

Dilynir enw'r eglwys gan fyrfodd sy'n dynodi'r esgobaeth *fodern* y perthyn yr eglwys iddi. Yn achos y pedair hen esgobaeth, dynoda hefyd ym mha archif esgobaethol y ffeiliwyd adysgrifau'r esgob ar gyfer yr eglwys honno. Yn achos y ddwy esgobaeth newydd, ceir adysgrifau Mynwy ymhlith papurau Llandaf, a rhai Abertawe ac Aberhonddu ymhlith papurau Tyddewi.

Lle bo'r plwyf neu'r eglwys yn sefydliad modern, rhoddir ar linell nesaf y cofnod enw'r hen blwyf y tardd ohono, gyda'r symbol ‹ yn dynodi'r ymadrodd 'a ffurfiwyd o'. Rhoddir hefyd, pan ellir, ddyddiad codi'r eglwys neu flwyddyn creu'r plwyf newydd, pa un bynnag sy'n ymddangos yn fwyaf priodol, er mwyn cynorthwyo'r darllenydd i chwilio cofrestr am y cyfnod cyn sefydlu'r eglwys fodern.

Cofrestri

Cymharwyd pob cofnod â'r atebion i Gyfrifiad 1831, ag arolwg y Llyfrgell Genedlaethol yn y 1930au, ac ag archwiliadau mwy diweddar yr archifdai lleol, a nodwyd pob cofrestr a aeth ar goll ers hynny.

Sylfaen y wybodaeth a roddir ar gyfer bedyddiadau (C), priodasau (M), a chladdedigaethau (B) yw catalogau'r archifdai o'r cofrestri sydd o dan eu gofal. Gan amlaf, dyddiad cyntaf ac olaf pob cyfrol a geir yn y catalogau hynny. Felly oni bai bod catalog yr archifdy'n manylu ynglŷn â bylchau oddi mewn i gyfrol, ni noda'r llyfr hwn ddim ond y bylchau sydd rhwng y naill gyfrol a'r llall. Yn y mannau priodol nodir pa gofrestri sydd yn dal ym meddiant yr offeiriad.

Adysgrifau'r esgob

Nodir pob bwlch yng nghyfresi adysgrifau'r esgob. Adlewyrchiad yw hynny o'r ffaith fod yr archifdai sydd â'r cyfryw ddogfennau yn eu gofal wedi eu rhestru'n fanwl. Cofier yr hyn a esbonnir uchod am anghyfatebiaeth yr adysgrifau cynnar i'r flwyddyn galendr.

Adlun, meicroffilm, a chopi

Ar ddiwedd y llinell sy'n rhestru dyddiadau'r cofrestri gwreiddiol neu adysgrifau'r esgob, nodir pa adlun (Fac), boed ffotostat, ffotogopi, neu feicroprint, neu ba gopi meicroffilm (Mf) o'r deunydd sydd ar gael. Ym mharagraff olaf pob cofnod y dylid chwilio'r manylion am gopïau printiedig, teipysgrif (ts), neu lawysgrif (ms).

BYRFODDAU

B	claddedigaethau	Mf	meicroffilm
BT	adysgrifau'r esgob	ms	llawysgrif
C	bedyddiadau	nd	heb ddyddiad arno
Cop	copi	PR	cofrestr plwyf
Fac	adlun	ts	teipysgrif
M	priodasau		

ESGOBAETHAU

B	Bangor	*M*	Mynwy
C	Caer	*SA*	Llanelwy
H	Henffordd	*SB*	Abertawe ac Aberhonddu
L	Caerlwytgoed	*SD*	Tyddewi
LL	Llandaf		

YR ARCHIFDAI

Carm RO — Gwasanaeth Archifau Dyfed, Archifdy Sir Gaerfyrddin, Neuadd y Sir, Caerfyrddin, Dyfed SA31 1JP. Tel: 0267 233333 est. 4182

Cer RO — Gwasanaeth Archifau Dyfed, Archifdy Ceredigion, Swyddfa'r Sir, Aberystwyth, Dyfed, SY23 2DE. Tel: 0970 617581 est. 2120

Ches RO — Cheshire Record Office, Duke Street, Chester, CH1 1RL. Tel: 0244 602574

CROH — Archifdy Clwyd, Yr Hen Reithordy, Penarlâg, Glannau Dyfrdwy, Clwyd, CH5 3NR. Tel: 0244 532364

CROR — Archifdy Clwyd, 46 Heol Clwyd, Rhuthun, Clwyd, LL15 1HP. Tel: 08242 3077

GASC — Gwasanaeth Archifau Gwynedd, Archifdy Caernarfon, Doc Fictoria, Caernarfon, Gwynedd (llythyrau i'w cyfeirio at: Swyddfa'r Sir, Stryd y Jêl, Caernarfon, Gwynedd, LL55 1SH). Tel: 0286 4121 est. 2095

GASD — Gwasanaeth Archifau Gwynedd, Archifdy Dolgellau, Cae Penarlâg, Dolgellau, Gwynedd, LL40 2YB. Tel: 0341 422341 est. 260

GASL — Gwasanaeth Archifau Gwynedd, Archifdy Llangefni, Neuadd y Sir, Llangefni, Gwynedd, LL77 7TW. Tel: 0248 723262 est. 269

Glam RO — Gwasanaeth Archifau Morgannwg, Neuadd y Sir, Parc Cathays, Caerdydd, CF1 3NE. Tel: 0222 820282

Gwent RO — Archifdy Sirol Gwent, Neuadd y Sir, Cwmbran, Gwent, NP44 2XH. Tel: 06333 67711 est. 214

HRO — Hereford Record Office, The Old Barracks, Harold Street, Hereford, HR1 2QX. Tel: 0432 265441

Lichfield JRO — Lichfield Joint Record Office, Lichfield Library, Bird Street, Lichfield, WS13 6PN. Tel: 0543 256787

NLW — Llyfrgell Genedlaethol Cymru, Aberystwyth SY23 3BU. Tel: 0970 3816 est. 216

Pemb RO — Gwasanaeth Archifau Dyfed, Archifdy Sir Benfro, Y Castell, Hwlffordd, Dyfed, SA61 2EF. Tel: 0437 3707

Soc Gen — Society of Genealogists (Cymdeithas yr Achyddwyr), 14 Charterhouse Buildings, London EC1M 7BA. Tel: 01 251 8799

SRO — Shropshire Record Office, Shirehall, Abbey Foregate, Shrewsbury, SY2 6ND. Tel: 0743 252851

INTRODUCTION

The deposit of parish registers

This volume provides details of original parish registers and bishop's transcripts, and of microfilm, facsimile, and other copies of them held by record repositories in Wales and adjoining border counties, and by the Society of Genealogists. It covers all thirteen ancient counties in the principality, describing the registers of over 1,000 parishes and chapelries in existence by 1812, and of about 200 post-1812 churches for which records are held by a repository.

The task of collecting parish registers and other records into safe custody was begun in 1950 by the National Library of Wales under an extension of an agreement made in 1944 between the library and the Representative Body of the Church in Wales, by which episcopal, capitular, diocesan registry and other records of the church were deposited in the library.[1] In 1976 agreements between the Representative Body and all the Welsh county councils (with the exception of Powys) designated county record offices as additional repositories for ecclesiastical parish records.[2] In the same year a circular letter to incumbents from the Registrar of the Archbishop of Wales urged the deposit of ecclesiastical records in safe custody, and diocesan advisers on archives were appointed to supervise this work. The success of these measures is evident from the fact that the registers of all but a few ancient parishes have now been deposited either in the National Library or in one of the Welsh county record offices, and it is the staff of these institutions who have been responsible for this survey.

Diocesan boundaries

The Welsh church was, until its disestablishment in 1920, an integral part of the Church of England. The diocesan boundaries disregarded (and indeed pre-dated) those of England and Wales. The four ancient Welsh dioceses covered the following areas:

St. Asaph	most of Flintshire and Denbighshire, with parts of Caernarfonshire, Merioneth, Montgomeryshire and Shropshire
Bangor	Anglesey, most of Caernarfonshire, parts of Merioneth and Montgomeryshire, and the deanery of Dyffryn Clwyd in central Denbighshire
St. David's	Carmarthenshire, Cardiganshire, Pembrokeshire, Breconshire, most of Radnorshire, and parts of Montgomeryshire, Glamorgan, Monmouthshire and Herefordshire
Llandaff	Most of Glamorgan and Monmouthshire

There was only one peculiar exempt from episcopal jurisdiction - Hawarden in Flintshire.

English dioceses also included parts of Wales:

Chester	parts of Flintshire and Denbighshire
Lichfield	parish of Penley in Flintshire
Hereford	parts of Montgomeryshire, Radnorshire and Monmouthshire

Some of these parishes in English dioceses were transferred to Welsh ones in 1849. A substantial exchange of parishes was effected in 1859 between the dioceses of Bangor and St. Asaph, the deanery of Dyffryn Clwyd being transferred to St. Asaph in exchange for the deanery of Cyfeiliog and Mawddwy. A further transfer of border parishes followed the Welsh Church Act of 1914, which took effect in 1920. Parishes belonging to Welsh dioceses, but lying wholly in England, were transferred to English dioceses, and vice versa. Of nineteen parishes situated partly in Wales and partly in England, seventeen were, 'with reference to the general wishes of the parishioners', treated as being in England, while in the remaining two parishes the choice was put to the vote, and one, Llansilin, opted for inclusion in Wales. (The registers of Welsh parishes remaining in the Church of England have been deposited in the appropriate county record office over the border - Cheshire, Shropshire, or Hereford.) Two new Welsh dioceses were created - Monmouth out of Llandaff in 1921, and Swansea and Brecon out of St. David's in 1923.

County boundaries

The text of this volume is arranged by the historic counties of Wales as they were at the time of their disappearance under the reorganization of local government in 1974. The thirteen ancient counties were then divided or amalgamated into eight modern ones, made up as follows:

Clwyd	Flintshire, most of Denbighshire, and part of Merioneth
Gwynedd	Caernarfonshire, Anglesey, most of Merioneth, and part of Denbighshire
Dyfed	Cardiganshire, Carmarthenshire and Pembrokeshire
Powys	Montgomeryshire, Radnorshire, and most of Breconshire
Glamorgan	Divided into the three modern counties of West, Mid and South Glamorgan, with the addition of small parts of Breconshire and Monmouthshire
Gwent	Most of Monmouthshire and a small part of Breconshire

The modern county is used to identify parishes in the index to this work.

Parish registers

Registers in Wales, even in counties where their survival has been better than average, do not match those of English border counties. The keeping of registers was ordered by Thomas Cromwell in 1538, but in only one parish (Gwaenysgor, co. Flint) is there a 1538 register in existence. Even this is not an original paper volume, but a parchment copy made at some time after the confirmation in 1598 of a constitution of the previous year which ordered a more careful keeping of parish registers. By contrast, Shropshire has five registers dating from 1538, and Herefordshire seven.[3] Of just over a thousand ancient parishes and chapelries in Wales, only seventy have registers which begin before 1600; far more than half have registers which start only in the eighteenth century. Indeed, many parishes, particularly in south Wales, have no registers earlier than 1754, when separate marriage registers begin, or even 1813, when printed volumes for baptisms and burials were introduced. In such parishes the earlier registers (usually of parchment), including baptisms, marriages and burials in one volume, have entirely disappeared.

The registers have survived better in some dioceses than others. St. Asaph has the highest proportion of early registers, and St. David's (where over half of the parishes have no registers earlier than 1754) the lowest. Generally, north Wales has earlier registers than the south. On a county basis, the registers of Flintshire come first. It has the only 1538 register; eighteen out of the twenty-nine ancient parishes (62%) have registers starting before 1660, and every parish has registers which begin before 1754. In a hierarchy based on the percentage of parishes with pre-1660 registers, the north Wales counties of Montgomery (49%), Denbigh (33%) and Merioneth (29%) follow. In south Wales only Monmouthshire (20%) comes near to the survival rate in the north. At the bottom end of the scale, Cardiganshire (4%) has no registers earlier than 1653; nearly two thirds of the parishes have no registers dating before 1754, and as many as thirteen have no registers before 1813.

Two earlier detailed surveys of parish registers in Wales, compiled when the records remained in the churches, reveal what volumes have been lost in the last hundred and fifty years. The first was based on enquiries made of clergymen at the time of the 1831 census.[4] The returns gave details, usually volume by volume, of registers prior to 1813, and sometimes gave reasons for recent losses. (For some dioceses, visitation returns of the late eighteenth and early nineteenth centuries also give dates of registers.) The 1831 survey has been much used as a source for later writers,[5] although the returns are often inaccurate - sometimes wildly so. More recent surveys were carried out, diocese by diocese, by the National Library of Wales between 1933 and 1940.[6] Again, the survey was based on a questionnaire rather than examination of the registers, but the results are usually sufficiently detailed to allow further comparisons. Some subsequent surveys, based on inspection, were made by county record offices. Details of registers lost since these surveys were carried out have been incorporated into the text.

144 parishes have lost one or more registers since 1831, and in 74 other cases registers noted in the 1930s have disappeared. (In a few parishes, registers earlier than those noted in either survey have come to light, however.) The losses have been

heavier in south Wales; about a third of the ancient parishes in the counties of Brecon, Cardigan, Glamorgan and Radnor, and about a quarter of those in Carmarthen and Pembroke, have lost registers since 1831.

Registers have been accidentally lost in fires (Llanddeusant, Llangynog, and Pendine, co. Carmarthen; Llansanffraid Glan Conwy, co. Denbigh; Hanmer and Llanfynydd, co. Flint; Diserth and Pilleth, co. Radnor; Rhodogeidio in Anglesey; Christchurch and St. Arvans, co. Monmouth; Angle and Castlemartin, co. Pembroke); and floods (Llechryd, co. Cardigan). At Cilymaenllwyd, co. Carmarthen, and Cadoxton-juxta-Neath, co. Glamorgan, they were deliberately used to stoke the parsonage fire. They have been taken by parish officials (Nantglyn, co. Denbigh), incumbents (Caerau with Ely, co. Glamorgan), and thieves (Bishton, co. Monmouth). In Carmarthenshire, a curate of Llan-gain is alleged to have sold a register for £40; in Cardiganshire, an early register of Llanfihangel Genau'r-glyn is supposed to have been taken away to be produced in a court of law and never returned; and in Pembrokeshire the early registers of Llanwnda and Letterston were reputedly destroyed at the time of the French invasion of 1797. The register of one unidentified Anglesey parish is said to have been eaten by a cow.[7]

Little need be said of the content of the registers, for their history is the same as those of England, which has received extensive treatment.[8] Most entries were made in Latin until about 1732. The use of Welsh is very rare and is restricted to a few parishes for short periods in the seventeenth and eighteenth centuries. It occasionally happened that in very poor, rural parishes no separate registers were kept before 1813, but entries were made in the registers of an adjoining parish. For example, in the parish of Llanfaelrhys, co. Caernarfon, there are no registers before 1811, but entries for the earlier period are to be found in the registers of Aberdaron. Cross-references are provided in the text of this volume where necessary. Some small parishes are still using the printed registers of baptisms and burials introduced in 1813, and so the registers deposited end in 1812. Marriage registers in Wales were all closed by direction of the Registrar General in 1971, when bilingual volumes were substituted, so that in rural parishes the marriage registers deposited are often later in date than baptismal and burial ones. The illustrations in this volume have been selected with the aim of illustrating as wide a range of registers as possible, including examples of the separate registers of marriages introduced, from 1754, and of baptisms and burials, from 1813.

Bishop's transcripts

The annual return to the bishop of a copy of the register entries for the year - known as a bishop's transcript, or BT - was effectively established in the Church of England by a constitution of 1597, the procedure being codified by a canon of 1603.[9] Whereas many parishes in England have transcripts going back to the 1597 injunction and beyond, those of Wales have virtually no transcripts dated earlier than 1660. This conforms with the general pattern of Welsh diocesan records. Indeed the only Welsh parishes which do have pre-1660 transcripts are the dozen or so along the border which belonged to the dioceses of Chester and Hereford.[10] Even after 1660, the transcripts have not always been well kept. For instance, some bundles of wills now in the National Library of Wales were found to have parchment labels made from eighteenth-century transcripts belonging to the diocese of St. David's.

The dates of the Welsh transcripts may be summarised by diocese as follows:

Bangor	1662-1917	(mostly 1675-1880)
Llandaff	1696-1916	(mostly 1725-1870)
St. Asaph	1661-1898	(mostly 1661-1850)
St. David's	1671-1911	
archdeaconry of:		
Brecon	1685-1874	(mostly 1700-1850)
Cardigan & St. David's	1673-1911	(mostly 1799-1880)
Carmarthen	1671-1902	(mostly 1671-1870)
Gower	1671-1910	(mostly 1671-1880)

As can be seen, the dates of the main body of transcripts for most Welsh dioceses are somewhat shorter than the outside dates given. The terminal dates vary considerably. Some ninety parishes continued to send in returns after 1900; the 1917 transcript for Llangoed in Anglesey seems to be the latest of all. It may be added that there is no parish with a full set of transcripts corresponding to the outside dates shown above.

Nearly all the existing transcripts for Wales are housed at the National Library, to which they were transferred with the other diocesan archives in 1944.[11] Originally they were kept in annual bundles at the diocesan registries. Between about 1870 and the time of their deposit at the Library, the transcripts of the archdeaconry of Brecon were re-arranged and bound in volumes by parish. The other transcripts have been re-arranged in a similar way since their transfer to Aberystwyth. Those of St. Asaph and the archdeaconries of the diocese of St. David's other than Brecon have in recent years been filed between hinged boards. For the time being the transcripts of Bangor and Llandaff are kept loose in boxes. All the transcripts were listed as integral parts of their respective diocesan records, and the lists may be consulted in the typescript schedules of the Church in Wales records available at NLW and the various county record offices, viz.: Bangor, vol. 2, pp. 1-58; Llandaff, vol. 3, pp. 1-29; St. Asaph, vol. 1, pp. 312-335; and St. David's, vol. 2, pp. 162-252. These lists form the basis of the BT entries in the present volume.

The dates covered annually by the transcripts before 1812 vary from parish to parish, and from time to time within each parish. Before the adoption of the Gregorian calendar in 1752, Ladyday (25 March), Easter, or the date of the bishop's (or archdeacon's) visitation were the customary dividing lines between one return and the next; and they remained in common, if gradually declining, use in many Welsh parishes until the provisions of Rose's Act became effective on 1 January 1813. From then on, virtually all the transcripts run from 1 January to 31 December. For the purposes of this survey, and in order that the gaps in the sequence of returns may be shown more clearly, each transcript has been given a single-year value, irrespective of its inclusion of entries for the first few months of the following year. For example, the Abergele transcript for the period from 7 April 1670 to 21 May 1671 is simply listed as 1670.

Most of the transcripts are on parchment, some of which may have been used previously for other purposes. For example, the Llanddoget, co. Denbigh, transcripts for 1702-3 were entered on leaves cut out of the earliest register of the parish, on which entries dated 1638 or thereabouts are still faintly discernible. The transcripts often supplement the entries given in the original registers.[12] Marriages are not as a rule included in the bishop's transcripts after the commencement of civil registration in July 1837.

Bishop's transcripts to be found at repositories other than the National Library of Wales include a) odd strays which occasionally turn up among parish records deposited at local record offices (all apparently post-1820); b) those belonging to churches in the peculiar of Hawarden; and c) those from parishes which used to or still do belong to English dioceses, in which cases the transcripts remain with the diocesan records at the appropriate county record office at Chester, Hereford, or Lichfield. In like manner, a few English parishes which were at one time in Welsh dioceses have some of their transcripts located at the National Library.[13]

Microfilm copies of bishop's transcripts

The transcripts for all the Welsh dioceses were microfilmed in the early 1950s by the Church of Jesus Christ of Latter-Day Saints. However, many of the early returns went unfilmed, because the records had not been fully sorted at that stage. Copies of these microfilms for the diocese of St. Asaph are held by the Clwyd Record Office at Hawarden and at Ruthin.

Microfilms and facsimiles of parish registers

Each repository prepares bound facsimiles of the registers placed in its care. These facsimiles are handed over to the incumbents to be kept in their respective parishes. In some instances where the register may still be in current use at the parish church, the repository may have made a facsimile copy for its own use and returned the original to the parish. Such was also the procedure in the 1930s when a number of parishes sent their earliest registers to be repaired and rebound at the National Library. During their stay at the library, most of them were copied on microfilm or photostat. The wisdom of that course is shown by the fact that some of the originals which were returned to their parishes have subsequently disappeared: Bodedern, Diserth (co. Radnor), Llandanwg, Llandeilo Fawr, Llandysul (co. Cardigan), and Llanwenog.

The exchange of microfilms and facsimiles between repositories is a growing trend. Much has been done already, and work was continuing as the volume went to press. To save wear and tear, some repositories ask readers to use facsimiles or microfilms in place of the original registers, a practice which is likely to be adopted by others in the not-too-distant future.

Copies

The term 'copies' rather than 'transcripts' has been adopted to avoid confusion with the BTs. Every effort has been made to distinguish between full copies and extracts, but some early copies may in fact be extracts, e.g. those held by the Society of Genealogists. Some of the family history societies recently established in all parts of Wales are actively engaged in the systematic transcription of registers in their respective areas, but the fruits of their labours have not appeared in time for their inclusion in this volume. An attempt has been made, however, to include details of every known copy of an extensive nature, including the few which have been published, and the many which have been transcribed by enthusiasts during the last hundred years or so in manuscript and typescript. All of these are available for consultation by readers at one or other of the Welsh repositories or the Society of Genealogists.

Notes

[1] J. Conway Davies, 'The Records of the Church in Wales', *National Library of Wales Journal*, IV (1945-6), 1.

[2] A. G. Veysey, 'Ecclesiastical Parish Records in Wales', *Journal of the Society of Archivists*, VI (1978-81), 31-3. Powys was the only Welsh county which, in 1976, had no county record office. An archivist was appointed in 1984. The new counties of West, Mid, and South Glamorgan are served by Glamorgan Archive Service from its main office at Cardiff. It is intended that the registers of West Glamorgan will eventually be transferred to the area office at Swansea, where searchers may already consult duplicate facsimiles of most of the registers held at the main office. The Parochial Registers and Records Measure 1978, which regulates the care of parish records in England, does not apply to the disestablished Church in Wales.

[3] D. J. Steel, *National Index of Parish Registers*, V: *South Midlands and Welsh Border Counties*, 3rd ed. (London, 1976), 75-92 *passim*, 146.

[4] *Abstract of the Answers and Returns made pursuant to an Act... for taking an Account of the Population of Great Britain... : Parish Register Abstract* (London, 1833), 198-203, 416-85.

[5] e.g. A. M. Burke, *Key to the Ancient Parish Registers of England and Wales* (London, 1908).

[6] The replies are preserved as bound volumes, arranged by diocese, among the records of the Church in Wales in the NLW. Bound facsimiles are available in the Manuscript Reading Room of the library.

[7] R. M. & G. A. Benwell, 'Interpreting the Parish Registers and Bishop's Transcripts for Anglesey and Llŷn', *Anglesey Antiquarian Society and Field Club Transactions* (1975), 77.

[8] Most comprehensive is D. J. Steel, *National Index of Parish Registers*, I (London, 1968). R. W. McDonald, 'The Parish Registers of Wales', *National Library of Wales Journal*, xix (1975-6), is a detailed account, providing extracts from registers from all parts of Wales. W.E. Tate, *The Parish Chest*, 3rd ed. (Cambridge, 1969) covers parish records in general as well as registers. J. C. Cox, *The Parish Registers of England* (London, 1910), gives many examples, although for England alone.

[9] Dorothy M. Owen, *The Records of the Established Church in England* (British Records Association, 1970), 26-7.

[10] A stray transcript for Nevern, co. Pembroke, for the year 1634, now at the National Library, came to light earlier this century among a bundle of papers at the Carmarthen probate registry (Francis Green MSS., vol. 8, p. 175).

[11] *N.L.W. Annual Report 1944*, 32-4; *1945*, 34.

[12] Benwell, *op. cit.*, 87-9.

[13] Steel, *op cit.*, V, 65-92 *passim*, 143-83 *passim*.

FORM OF ENTRY

Parish or Church

Entries are arranged under the old counties, and then alphabetically by name of parish or church. The arrangement is by the Welsh form of the name, using the spelling given in Elwyn Davies, *Gazetteer of Welsh Place-Names* (Cardiff, 1967). The Welsh form is followed, after an oblique stroke, by the English name, or an Anglicized version of the Welsh name, and obsolete forms are given in round brackets. Where the English name is greatly different from the Welsh, a second entry is provided under that name, preceded by an asterisk.

The name of the church is followed by an abbreviation indicating the *modern* diocese in which it is found. For the four ancient dioceses, this provides a guide to the diocese under which the bishop's transcripts for the church are filed. In the case of the new dioceses, the transcripts for Monmouth will be found among the records of the ancient diocese of Llandaff, and for Swansea and Brecon among those of St. David's.

For modern parishes and chapelries, the next line of the entry gives the names of the older parish or parishes from which it was formed, the symbol ‹ being used to denote 'formed out of '. Where known, the date that follows is either the date of construction of the church or the creation of the new parish, whichever seems more appropriate. The aim is to indicate to the reader where to look for registers for the earlier period.

Registers

Each entry has been checked against the returns made in the census of 1831, the surveys carried out by the National Library in the 1930s, and later surveys by record offices, and any registers which have disappeared are noted.

The dates of the registers of christenings (C), marriages (M) and burials (B) are based on the outside dates of each volume, given in the list compiled by the repository where it is held. The entry will therefore note gaps between volumes, but not gaps within a volume unless they were of sufficient length to have been noted in the list. Where appropriate, dates of registers retained by incumbents are given.

Bishop's transcripts

Since all repositories holding bishop's transcripts for Welsh parishes have now listed them in detail, the entry notes any break in the series. It should be remembered that, as explained above, the early transcripts do not normally cover a calendar year.

Facsimiles, microfilms and copies

Facsimiles (Fac), whether photostats, photocopies, or printout from microfilm, and microfilms (Mf) of registers and bishop's transcripts are noted at the end of each entry. Details of copies - printed, typescript (ts) or manuscript (ms) - are given in the final paragraph.

ABBREVIATIONS

B	burials	Mf	microfilm
BT	bishop's transcript	ms	manuscripts
C	christenings	nd	no date
Cop	copy	PR	parish register
Fac	facsimile	ts	typescript
M	marriages		

DIOCESES

B	Bangor	M	Monmouth
C	Chester	SA	Saint Asaph
H	Hereford	SB	Swansea and Brecon
L	Lichfield	SD	Saint David's
LL	Llandaff		

REPOSITORIES

Carm RO	Dyfed Archive Service, Carmarthenshire Record Office, County Hall, Carmarthen, Dyfed, SA31 1JP. Tel: 0267 233333 ext. 4182
Cer RO	Dyfed Archive Service, Ceredigion Record Office, Swyddfa'r Sir, Aberystwyth, Dyfed, SY23 2DE. Tel: 0970 617581 ext. 2120
Ches RO	Cheshire Record Office, Duke Street, Chester, CH1 1RL. Tel: 0244 602574
CROH	Clwyd Record Office, The Old Rectory, Hawarden, Deeside, Clwyd, CH5 3NR. Tel: 0244 532364
CROR	Clwyd Record Office, 46 Clwyd Street, Ruthin, Clwyd, LL15 1HP. Tel: 08242 3077
GASC	Gwynedd Archives Service, Caernarfon Record Office, Victoria Dock, Caernarfon (letters to be addressed to County Offices, Shirehall Street, Caernarfon, Gwynedd, LL55 1SH). Tel: 0286 4121 ext. 2095
GASD	Gwynedd Archives Service, Dolgellau Record Office, Cae Penarlâg, Dolgellau, Gwynedd, LL40 2YB. Tel: 0341 422341 ext. 260
GASL	Gwynedd Archives Service, Llangefni Record Office, Shirehall, Llangefni, Gwynedd, LL77 7TW. Tel: 0248 723262 ext. 269
Glam RO	Glamorgan Archive Service, County Hall, Cathays Park, Cardiff, CF1 3NE. Tel: 0222 820282
Gwent RO	Gwent County Record Office, County Hall, Cwmbran, Gwent, NP44 2XH. Tel: 06333 67711 ext. 214
HRO	Hereford Record Office, The Old Barracks, Harold Street, Hereford, HR1 2QX. Tel: 0432 265441
Lichfield JRO	Lichfield Joint Record Office, Lichfield Library, Bird Street, Lichfield, WS13 6PN. Tel: 0543 256787
NLW	National Library of Wales, Aberystwyth, SY23 3BU. Tel: 0970 3816 ext. 216
Pemb RO	Dyfed Archive Service, Pembrokeshire Record Office, The Castle, Haverfordwest, Dyfed, SA61 2EF. Tel: 0437 3707
Soc Gen	Society of Genealogists, 14 Charterhouse Buildings, London EC1M 7BA. Tel: 01 251 8799
SRO	Shropshire Record Office, Shirehall, Abbey Foregate, Shrewsbury, SY2 6ND. Tel: 0743 252851

1 Tudalen cyntaf cofrestr plwyf Gwaunysgor, sir y Fflint - yr unig gofrestr sydd ar gael yng Nghymru yn dyddio yn ôl i 1538.
The first page of the parish register of Gwaenysgor, co. Flint - the only 1538 register surviving in Wales.

2 Cofrestr Penrhosllugwy, sir Fôn - enghraifft brin o gofrestr gyda chofnodion Cymraeg o'r ail ganrif ar bymtheg.
Register of Penrhosllugwy, co. Anglesey - a rare example of a register kept in Welsh in the seventeenth century.

Newport

Births in 1785

1785

Feb 4th — John son of John Morgan and Sarah his wife — baptized

March 5 — Rebekah daughter of Mr Charles Price and Elizabeth his wife bap.

25 — Thomas son of Thomas Edmunds and Elisabeth his wife baptized

June 5 — Elisabeth daughter of John Thomas and Susanna his wife bap.

26 — Rees son of David Jenkins and Mary his wife — — baptized

July 3rd — John son of John Frost and Sarah his wife — — — baptized

11 — John son of William Morgan Harry and Elisabeth his wife baptized

August — John son of Thomas Morgan and Margaret his wife — — baptized

Septem 4th — Margaret daughter of William Lewis and Sarah his wife baptized

18 — Elisabeth daughter of David Morgan and Sarah his wife baptized

22 — Charlotte daughter of William Edmunds and Elisabeth his wife baptized

Octobr 2 — Charlotte daughter of John Charles and Elisabeth his wife — baptized

30 — Elisabeth daughter of Thomas Hookwood and Margaret his wife baptized

30 — William, and Thomas, sons of William Keene and Sarah his wife baptized

Novem 30th — Elisabeth daughter of Richard Hopkins and Anne his wife baptized

Decem 4th — Edward the illegitimate son of Thomas Tamplin and Anne Evans bap

11 — Sarah daughter of Edmund Thomas and Anne his wife baptized

25 — Mary daughter of William George and Jane his wife — baptized

This Page contains a true entry of all Baptisms
in the town of Newport in A.D. 1785.

John Evans Vicar of Newport.

3 Cofrestr S. Woolos, Casnewydd, sir Fynwy, yn cofnodi bedydd John Frost, arweinydd y Siartwyr, ar 3 Gorffennaf 1785.
Register of St. Woolos, Newport, co. Monmouth, recording the baptism on 3 July 1785 of the Chartist leader, John Frost.

BAPTISMS.

Date.	Aged.	Name of the Child.	Names of the Father and Mother.
178*. May the 4th	— Days.	John Smith, Son of	John Smith, Labourer, and Mary his Wife, formerly Mary Evans.
1783 August 25.	26 Years	Elizabeth Fiddis, Daughter of	John Fiddis, Barber, and Martha his Wife, formerly Martha Shim
July 24th	10 Days	William Sidall, Son of	Thomas Peregrine, Surveyor, and Hannah his Wife, formerly Hannah Sidall.
August 24th	2 Weeks	L.d Phillips, Son of	William Phillips, Crafter, and Mary his Wife, formerly Mary Martha.
September 28th	2 Weeks	Charles Thomas, Son of	David Thomas, Labourer, and Margaret his Wife, formerly Margaret Morgan
October 12th	two Weeks	Mary James, Daughter of	Michael James, & Mary his Wife, formerly Mary George.

The above is the first Christening since Duty commenced on Baptisms, Marriages, and Burials, the 29 Day of September 1783.

4 Enghraifft brin o'r gofrestr argraffedig, *Proposed Form of Register for Baptisms,* a gyhoeddwyd yn 1781. Plwyf Hubberston, sir Benfro, biau hon. Mae ail hanner y gyfrol wedi ei dudalennu â fformat cyfatebol ar gyfer claddedigaethau.
A rare example of the printed register, *Proposed Form of Register for Baptisms,* published in 1781. This one belongs to the parish of Hubberston, co. Pembroke. The other half of the volume has a similar format for burial entries.

Page 74

BAPTISMS solemnized in the Parish of _Clyro_
in the County of _Radnor_ in the Year 18**66** and 18**67**

When Baptised.	Child's Christian Name.	Parent's Name. Christian.	Surname.	Abode.	Quality, Trade, or Profession.	By whom the Ceremony was performed.
1866 October 7th No. 585	Eliza daughter of	Samuel & Jane	Collett	Lower Cabalva	Land Steward	R.L.Venable
1866 November 29th No. 586	Kate daughter of	James and Catherine	Handley	Grafton Villa nr Hereford	Gentleman's Servant	R. F. Kilvert Curate
1866 December 16th No. 587	George son of	John and Elizabeth	Harris	Village	Carpenter	R. F. Kilvert Curate
1866 December 23rd No. 588	Alfred son of	Henry and Anne	Perkins	Village	Mason	R. F. Kilvert Curate
1867 January 19th No. 589	William son of	William and Mary	Phillips	Pentley	Farmer	R. F. Kilvert Curate
1867 February 3rd No. 590	Herbert son of	Henry & Ann	Batts	Village	Coal Agent late Butler	R.L.Venable
1867 February 3rd No. 591	Sarah daughter of	Frederick & Sarah	Dance	Cwm. Clyro	Game keeper	R.L.Venable
1867 March 12th No. 592	Arthur Frederick son of	Charles James & Elizabeth	Partridge	Clyro Court Farm	Farmer	R. F. Kilvert Curate

5 Cofrestr bedyddiadau Cleirwy, sir Faesyfed, yn cynnwys cofnodion gan y curad, Francis Kilvert y dyddiadurwr, 1866-7. Defnyddiwyd y patrwm printiedig hwn am y tro cyntaf yn 1813.
Baptismal register of Clyro, co. Radnor, with entries by the curate, the diarist Francis Kilvert, 1866-7. This printed format was used from 1813.

THE

Register-Book

OF

MARRIAGES

IN ALL

Parish Churches & Chapels,

Conformable to an Act of the Twenty Sixth of King
GEORGE II. Intitled,

AN ACT FOR THE BETTER PREVENTING ALL
CLANDESTINE MARRIAGES.

PUBLISHED ACCORDING TO ACT OF PARLIAMENT.

MERTHYR TYDFIL:
PRINTED BY WILLIAM WILLIAMS.

1811.

6 Cofrestr priodasau Aberdâr, sir Forgannwg, 1811 - enghraifft o gofrestr a argraffwyd yn lleol cyn dyfodiad
cyfrolau safonol 1813.
Marriage register of Aberdare, co. Glamorgan, 1811 - an example of a locally-printed register which pre-dates the
standard volumes of 1813.

MARRIAGES folemnized in the Parifh of _Clynnog_
in the County of _Caernarvon_ in the Year 18_30_

Ebenezer Thomas of _this_ Parifh
Bachelor
and _Mary Williams_ of _this_ Parifh
Spinster
were married in this _Church_ by _Banns_ with Confent of
this _twenty third_ Day of
December in the Year One thoufand eight hundred and _thirty_
By me _Hugh Williams Vicar_
This Marriage was folemnized between us { _Ebenezer Thomas_
Williams Jones { _Mary Williams_
In the Prefence of { _Richard Evans_

No. 196.

Hugh Roberts of _this_ Parifh
Bachelor
and _Catharine Griffith_ of _this_ Parifh
Spinster
were married in this _Church_ by _Banns_ with Confent of
this _eleventh_ Day of
December in the Year One thoufand eight hundred and _thirty_
By me _Hugh Williams Vicar_
This Marriage was folemnized between us { _Hugh Roberts_
{ The mark of Catharine Griffith
In the Prefence of { _John Roberts_
{ _William Roberts_
No. 197.

Evan Jones of _the_ Parifh
of Llanfihangel in the County of Merioneth Bachelor
and _Mary Roberts_ of _this_ Parifh
Spinster
were married in this _Church_ by _Licence_ with Confent of
this _thirty first_ Day of
December in the Year One thoufand eight hundred and _thirty_
By me _Hugh Williams Vicar_
This Marriage was folemnized between us { _Evan Jones_
{ _David Owen_ } The mark of Mary Roberts
In the Prefence of { _Owen Owen_
No. 198.

Hugh Williams Vicar
David Williams Churwardens

7   Cofrestr priodasau Clynnog Fawr, sir Gaernarfon, 1830 gyda chofnod o briodas Mary Williams ac
    Ebenezer Thomas (*Eben Fardd*). Defnyddiwyd cofrestri safonol ar wahân i gofnodi priodasau am y
    tro cyntaf yn 1754. Dyma'r patrwm (yn cynnwys mân newidiadau 1812) a barhaodd hyd 1837.
    Marriage register of Clynnog Fawr, co. Caernarfon, 1830. The first entry records the marriage of
    Mary Williams and Ebenezer Thomas (the poet *Eben Fardd*). Separate standard registers for marriages
    were kept from 1754 and these continued in use (with minor changes in 1812) until 1837.

Page 27.

18 3 9. Marriage solemnized _in the parochin church_ in the _Parish_ of _Gwaentun_ in the County of _Flint_.

No.	When Married.	Name and Surname.	Age.	Condition.	Rank or Profession.	Residence at the Time of Marriage.	Father's Name and Surname.	Rank or Profession of Father.
53	June 25	Peter Hughes & Elizabeth Edwards	full age	Bachelor Spinster	Laborer Servant	Gwaentun	Thomas Hughes John Edwards	Laborer Laborer

Married in the _parochin church_ according to the Rites and Ceremonies of the _established church_ by me,

This Marriage was solemnized between us, Peter Hughes / The mark X of Elizabeth Edwards in the Presence of us, Hugh Probert / Griff. I. Probert

18 3 9. Marriage solemnized _in the church_ in the _Parish_ of _Hawarden_ in the County of _Flint_.

No.	When Married.	Name and Surname.	Age.	Condition.	Rank or Profession.	Residence at the Time of Marriage.	Father's Name and Surname.	Rank or Profession of Father.
54	July 25	William Ewart Gladstone & Catherine Glynne	full age full age	Bachelor Spinster	Member of Parliament	Hawarden Castle	John Gladstone Stephen Richard Glynne	Esquire, Merchant of Portland Bart

Married in the _parish church_ according to the Rites and Ceremonies of the _established church_ by me,

This Marriage was solemnized between us, William Ewart Gladstone / Catherine Glynne in the Presence of us,

8   Cofrestr priodasau Penarlâg, sir y Fflint, lle y cofnodir priodas W. E. Gladstone a Catherine Glynne, 1839. Sefydlwyd patrwm y math hwn o gofrestr pan ddaeth cofrestru sifil i fodolaeth yn 1837, ac fe'i defnyddiwyd gyda dim ond ambell fân amrywiad hyd ei ddisodli gan y patrwm dwyieithog yn 1971. Marriage register of Hawarden, co. Flint. The lower entry records the marriage of W. E. Gladstone and Catherine Glynne of Hawarden Castle, 1839. Registers in this format, introduced when civil registration began in 1837, were used with only minor alterations until bilingual volumes were substituted for them in 1971.

No. _110_ *

Banns of Marriage between _David Davies and Margaret Parry both of this Parish_ were published on the Three Sundays underwritten;

That is to say, On Sunday the _11 January_

On Sunday the _18 Do_

1829. On Sunday the _25 Do by me Thomas Rees_

No. _111_

Banns of Marriage between _Roger Roger and Ann Williams both of this Parish_ were published on the Three Sundays underwritten;

That is to say, On Sunday the _25 January_

On Sunday the _1 February_

1829. On Sunday the _8 Do by me Thomas Rees_

No. _112_

Banns of Marriage between _William Davies and Elizabeth Rees both of this Parish_ were published on the Three Sundays underwritten;

That is to say, On Sunday the _22 February_

On Sunday the _1 March_

1829. On Sunday the _8 Do by me Thomas Rees_

No. _113_

Banns of Marriage between _Francis Hall of this Parish and Elizabeth Howell of the Parish of Llanelly in the county_ were published on the Three Sundays underwritten;

That is to say, On Sunday the _22 February_

On Sunday the _1 March_

1829. On Sunday the _8 Do by me Thomas Rees_

No. _114_

Banns of Marriage between _John Thomas and Hannah John both of this Parish_ were published on the Three Sundays underwritten;

That is to say, On Sunday the _1 March_

On Sunday the _8 Do_

1829. On Sunday the _15 Do by me Thomas Rees_

* D. Davies alias Salmon was by order of sessions transported for felony for the period of seven years, which prevented his Marriage with the said Mar. Parry. No 100. ... ...

9 Cofrestr gostegion Pen-bre, sir Gaerfyrddin, 1829. Nodir ar waelod y ddalen sut na bu modd i David Davies (y cofnod uchaf) briodi oherwydd y cafwyd ef yn euog o ffeloniaeth a'i drawsgludo am saith mlynedd.

Banns register for Pembrey, co. Carmarthen, 1829. A note at the foot records that the marriage of David Davies (first entry) was prevented by his being transported for seven years for felony.

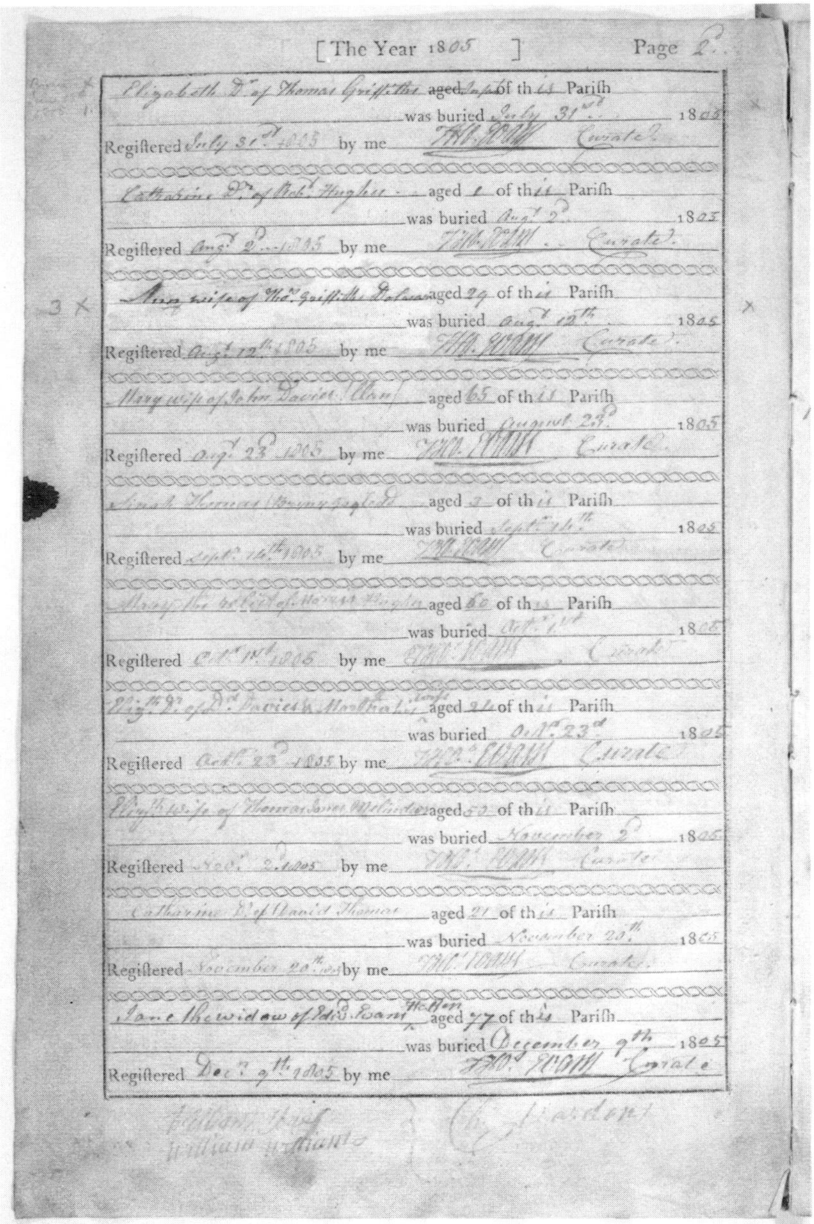

10 Patrwm cofrestr brintiedig a luniwyd i gydymffurfio â Deddf Stamp 1783. Dangosir yma'r tudalen yng nghofrestr Llanfihangel-yng-Ngwynfa, sir Drefaldwyn, sy'n cofnodi claddu Ann Griffiths yr emynyddes ar 12 Awst 1805.

A sample of the printed register designed to comply with the provisions of the Stamp Act 1783. The page shown here from the register of Llanfihangel-yng-Ngwynfa, co. Montgomery, records the burial of Ann Griffiths, the hymn-writer, on 12 August 1805.

BURIALS in the Parish of *Aberavon*
in the County of *Glamorgan* in the Year 1830-1

Name.	Abode.	When buried.	Age.	By whom the Ceremony was performed.
Elizabeth Bradley No. 185 (Illegitimate)	Aberavon	22nd Decbr	2 wks	E. Thomas Curate of Aberavon with Baglan & Pistill Curate of Britton
1831 Lemuel Hopkin No. 186.	Aberavon	14th Feby	1yr & 3 mts	E. Thomas Curate
Edward David No. 187 (Illegitimate)	Corlanna Aberavon	22rd Feby	1½ yrs	E. Thomas Curate
Leina Lawrence No. 188.	Aberavon	14th March	6 yrs	E. Thomas Curate
Mary Thomas No. 189.	Cwm Avon	5th April	28 yrs	E. Thomas Curate
John Rowland No. 190.	Cwcu Cribbur Tythegstone	11th April	65 yrs	E. Thomas Curate
Richard Jeffreys No. 191.	Aberavon	26th May	39 yrs	E. Thomas Curate
Richard Lewis No. 192.	Merthyr Tydfil	14th Augst	23 yrs	E. Thomas Curate

The above unfortunate man was Executed at Cardiff on the 13th August 1831, for Stabbing Donald Black, one of the 93rd Highlanders while Stationed on duty at Merthyr, during the Riots on the 3rd of June last. He was indicted under 9 Geo: IV cap: 31. s. 12.

---

11 Cofrestr claddedigaethau Aberafan, sir Forgannwg, 1830-1 - y math o gofrestr argraffedig sydd mewn bodolaeth er 1813. Ar 14 Awst 1831 cofnodir claddu Dic Penderyn (Richard Lewis) a ddienyddiwyd am anafu milwr ar ddyletswydd ym Merthyr yn ystod terfysgoedd Mehefin 1831.
Burial register of Aberavon, co. Glamorgan, 1830-1 - a printed register of the type used from 1813. The entry for 14 August 1831 records the burial of Dic Penderyn (Richard Lewis) who was executed for wounding a soldier stationed in Merthyr during the riots of June 1831.

A Coppy of Llanvronach Register from march 2.5.1714.
to march 2.5.1715.

Edward son to Lewis John. by maud his wife. Buried. Apr. 3. 1714.

Joan Reavans widdow was Buried. April. 6. 1714.

Thomas son to David Thomas by mary his wife. Bapt. may 6. 1714.

Thomas son to Evan John. DD by Eliz: his wife. Buried. July 1. 1714.

Thomas son to David Thomas by mary his wife. Buried. July 2. 1714.

mary daughter to Wm Hughes by Rachel his wife. Bapt. July 23.

Rachel, an illegitimate daughr to Cathrin John. widd: Bapt. July 29.

Rice Herbert of Llanvygan & Gwen: Watkins of ye Parish of St.
Davids. married. Oct. 19. 1714. Banns being first Published.

Edward James of Tregars Esqr. Buried. Decber 6. 1714.

Peter son to Peter Jones by Jonnett his wife. Bapt. Jan: 1. 1714.

Lewis son to Wm John by Margarett his wife. Bapt. Jan: 24.

Phillip son to Lewis John by maud his wife. Bapt. march 13.

Evan Thomas was Buried. march 24. 1714.

Registered by

Jeff: Coke Rect.

the mark of

John F Pugh.

the mark of   Ch: wardens.

Thomas X Jones

12   Adysgrif yr esgob ar gyfer Llanfrynach, sir Frycheiniog, am y cyfnod 25 Mawrth 1714 - 25 Mawrth 1715.
The bishop's transcript for Llanfrynach, co. Brecknock, for the period 25 March 1714 - 25 March 1715.

ABERTEIFI
CARDIGANSHIRE

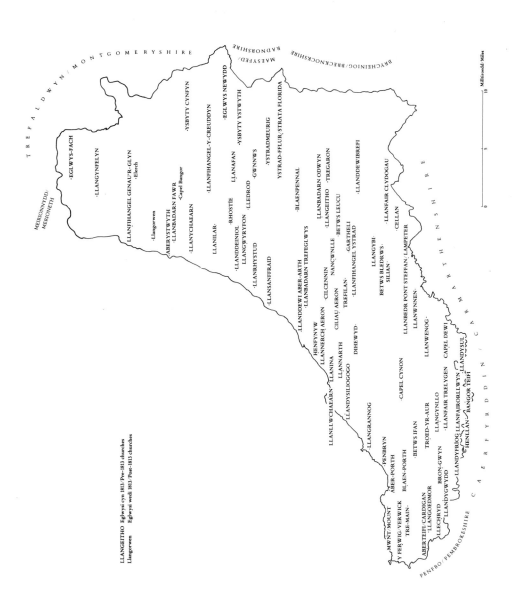

ABERTEIFI/CARDIGANSHIRE

ABER-PORTH   *SD*
C 1662-1970   M 1662-1971 (Banns 1824-1956)   B 1662-1929 **NLW**
BT 1674-6, 1678-81, 1683-6, 1689, 1799-1804, 1806-71, 1874 **NLW**

ABERTEIFI/CARDIGAN   *SD*
C 1653-1959   M 1653-1971 (Banns 1823-75)   B 1653-1911 **NLW**
BT 1675-6, 1678-83, 1685-6, 1688, 1701, 1799-1801, 1803, 1806-10, 1812-75 **NLW**
Cop ts PR CMB 1669-97, 1700 **NLW**

ABERYSTWYTH St. Michael   *SD*
‹Llanbadarn Fawr 1787
C 1788-1933   M 1804-6, 1861-1953   B 1791-1906, 1911-20 **NLW**
BT 1811, 1813-14, 1816-19, 1822-74, 1876, 1878-80, 1882, 1885-7 **NLW**

ABERYSTWYTH Holy Trinity   *SD*
‹Llanbadarn Fawr 1886
C 1886-1976   M 1887-1974   B 1886-1928 **NLW**

BANGOR TEIFI   *SD*
Diocesan records suggest that *c.* 1790 this parish had registers going back 'about 60 years'
C 1802-11   M 1804-1970 **NLW**   CB 1813- incumbent
BT 1676, 1683-6, 1688-9, 1706, 1711, 1799-1811, 1813-80, 1882 **NLW**

BETWS BLEDRWS   *SD*
PR CMB 1775-1812 recorded in 1831 apparently lost
CB 1813-1984   M 1813-1970 **NLW**
BT 1801-2, 1804-8, 1810-14, 1816-17, 1819-20, 1822-9, 1831-8, 1840-2, 1844-5, 1847-55, 1857-80
  NLW

BETWS IFAN   *SD*
CB 1726-1835   M 1726-1813, 1816-37 **NLW**
BT 1678, 1680-1, 1688, 1703, 1799, 1801-3, 1806, 1808-63, 1865-6, 1873-8, 1882-3, 1885-8, 1890-3,
  1896-7 **NLW**
Cop ms PR (extracts) CMB 1792-1832 **NLW**

BETWS LEUCU   *SD*
CMB 1813- incumbent   M 1837-1971 **NLW**
BT 1813-15, 1825-9, 1832-4, 1840-1, 1846-8, 1853-8, 1860-1, 1863-72, 1876-9, 1882, 1885-8, 1890-9,
  1902, 1905-9, 1911 **NLW**

BLAENPENNAL   *SD*
PR CM 1797-1812 recorded in 1831 apparently lost
C 1813-1977   M 1837-1971 **NLW**   B 1830- incumbent
BT 1813-19, 1823-35, 1850-77, 1879, 1882, 1885-7 **NLW**

BLAEN-PORTH   *SD*
CB 1716-1812   M 1716-53, 1767-1812 **NLW**
BT 1674-6, 1678, 1680-9, 1700, 1702, 1704-5?, 1802-60, 1862, 1865-6 **NLW**
Cop ts PR CB 1716-1812 M 1716-53 **NLW**

BORTH, Y gweler/see LLANFIHANGEL GENAU'R-GLYN

BRON-GWYN   SD
CB 1726-1812   M 1726-99, 1803-37   Fac C 1813-1965   B 1813-1966 **NLW**
BT 1678, 1680-1, 1688, 1703, 1803-52, 1858-9, 1876, 1886, 1891-3 **NLW**
Cop ms PR (extracts) CMB 1788-1809 **NLW**

CAPEL BANGOR (MELINDWR)   SD
‹Llanbadarn Fawr 1839
CB 1839-   M 1846- incumbent
BT 1847-63, 1865-80, 1888 **NLW**

CAPEL CYNON   SD
‹Llandysiliogogo. Not in use *c.* 1790 'for want of endowment'. Rebuilt chapel consecrated 1822
C 1822-1978   M 1824-1971 (Banns 1826-1931) Talgarreg 1930-71   B 1824-1971 **NLW**
BT 1824-45, 1847-50, 1852-5, 1857-9, 1861-72 **NLW**

CAPEL DEWI   SD
‹Llandysul
CB 1843-1932   M 1843-1971 **NLW**

*CARDIGAN/ABERTEIFI   SD
C 1653-1959   M 1653-1971 (Banns 1823-75)   B 1653-1911 **NLW**
BT 1675-6, 1678-83, 1685-6, 1688, 1701, 1799-1801, 1803, 1806-10, 1812-75 **NLW**
Cop ts PR CMB 1669-97, 1700 **NLW**

CELLAN   SD
PR C 1779- MB 1780- recorded as being on loose leaves in 1933 apparently lost
CMB 1813- incumbent
BT 1674, 1676, 1678-82, 1684, 1687, 1689, 1705, 1711, 1799, 1803-38, 1840, 1842, 1844-5, 1847,
    1849, 1852-4, 1857, 1863-73, 1875-82 **NLW**
Cop ms PR C 1779-1812 MB 1780-1812 **NLW**

CILCENNIN   SD
Entries of CMB 1724-33 included in PR Llanbadarn Trefeglwys
C 1734-1812   M 1734-1837   B 1734-1895 **NLW**   Mf M 1837-1951 **CerRO**
BT 1678, 1681-3, 1685, 1811-39, 1841-57, 1863-73 **NLW**
Cop ms PR CB 1734-51 M 1734-51, 1754-83 **NLW**

CILIAU AERON   SD
PR CB 1715-[74] M 1715-73 recorded in 1831 apparently lost
C 1775-1960   M 1806-37 (Banns 1823-34)   B 1775-1812 **NLW**
BT 1678-83, 1685-6, 1705, 1711, 1799-1839, 1841, 1843-65, 1867-75 **NLW**

DIHEWYD   SD
PR CMB 1718-1807 recorded in 1831 apparently lost. A description of it, with extracts, appears in
    G. Eyre Evans, *Cardiganshire and Its Antiquities* (1903), 217
C 1807-1953   M 1807-1970 (Banns 1828-71)   B 1807-80 **NLW**
BT 1676, 1678-81, 1683, 1685-6, 1705, 1800-3, 1806-15, 1818-78 **NLW**

EGLWYS-FACH (YSGUBOR-Y-COED)   SD
‹Llanfihangel Genau'r-glyn 1855. In 1814 the minister wrote, 'This chapel was built in the year
    1623 and they say they baptized, married, and buried here since the said date. Therefore, the old
    registers have been lost here as in all other churches in the neighbourhood' (SD/Misc/873)
C 1774-1931   M 1754-1837   B 1784-1878 **NLW**
BT 1813-69, 1877-8 **NLW**

EGLWYS NEWYDD (HAFOD)   SD
C 1773-1892   M 1774-89   B 1773-1914 **NLW**
BT 1811-61, 1863-79, 1882, 1885, 1887-8 **NLW**

ELERCH   SD
'Llanbadarn Fawr & Llanfihangel Genau'r-glyn 1868
C 1865-   B 1868- incumbent   M 1868-1970 **NLW**
BT 1869-79, 1882, 1885 **NLW**

FERWIG, Y/VERWICK   SD
Diocesan records suggest that *c.* 1790 this parish had PR going back 30 years
C 1813- incumbent   M 1769-1970   B 1813-1955 **NLW**
BT 1674-5, 1679-84, 1686-7, 1699-1700, 1799, 1801, 1803-7, 1810-55, 1865-6 **NLW**

GARTHELI   SD
Entries for CMB before 1812 in PR for Llanddewibrefi
C 1813-   M 1813-38   B 1871- incumbent   M 1839-1971 **NLW**
BT 1813-15, 1821-3, 1827-37, 1850-79, 1885-8, 1890-2, 1894-9, 1901-2, 1905-6, 1908-11 **NLW**

GWENLLI gweler/see LLANDYSILIOGOGO St. Mark

GWNNWS (LLANWNNWS)   SD
PR C 1760-1810 M 1754-1803 B 1789-1810 recorded in 1831 apparently lost
C 1811-64   M 1805-37 (Banns 1823-81)   B 1812-1968 **NLW**
BT 1811, 1813-62, 1864-78 **NLW**

HAFOD gweler/see EGLWYS NEWYDD

HENFYNYW   SD
PR CB 1718-1812 M 1718-72 recorded in 1831 apparently lost
C 1813-99   M 1772-1971 (Banns 1824-42, 1900-2)   B 1813-1939 **NLW**   Fac C 1813-99
    M 1772-1877 (Banns 1824-42, 1900-2)   B 1813-1939 **CerRO**
BT 1674, 1679-80, 1682, 1684, 1799, 1802, 1804, 1806-68 **NLW**

HENLLAN   SD
C 1798-1812   M 1780-1970 **NLW**   CB 1813- incumbent
BT 1676, 1683-6, 1688-9, 1706, 1711, 1799-1811, 1813-80, 1882 **NLW**

*LAMPETER/LLANBEDR PONT STEFFAN   SD
C 1695-1805, 1813-1937 Maestir 1869-85   M 1739-44, 1746-1970 (Banns 1824-57)   B 1695-1805,
    1813-1968 **NLW**
BT 1799-1808, 1811-17, 1823-37, 1839-80 **NLW**
Cop ms PR CB 1695-1745 M 1739-44 **NLW**   CB 1695-1734 *Welsh Gazette* (1903-5)

LLANAFAN   SD
PR CB 1772-1812 M 1767-1812 recorded in 1831 and CB 1750-1811 M 1802-13 in 1933 apparently
    lost. They were described as 'several loose leaves of three different books' by G. Eyre Evans in
    Cardiganshire and Its Antiquities (1903), 24
C 1813-80   M 1815-37   B 1813-1947 **NLW**
BT 1811, 1813, 1815, 1818, 1820-78 **NLW**

LLANBADARN FAWR   *SD*
C 1678-1736, 1752, 1766-1837   M 1695-1736, 1754-1837 (Banns 1849-52 Penrhyn-coch 1937-55)
    B 1678-1736, 1752, 1766-1841 **NLW**
BT 1678, 1680-1, 1703, 1773, 1811-79, 1882, 1885-92 **NLW**
Cop ts PR (extracts) CMB 1678-1736 **NLW**   ts PR CB 1830-79 with index **NLW & CerRO**

LLANBADARN ODWYN   *SD*
PR CMB 1777-1812 recorded in 1831 apparently lost
C 1815-1956   M 1813-37 (Banns 1823-36, 1913) **NLW**   B 1813- incumbent
BT 1683-5, 1811, 1813-35, 1841-56, 1866, 1871, 1873, 1875, 1877 **NLW**

LLANBADARN TREFEGLWYS   *SD*
PR CB 1789-1813 M 1798-9, 1805-12 recorded in 1933 apparently lost
C 1724-88, 1813-1978   M 1724-88, 1813-37   B 1724-88, 1813-72 **NLW**   Mf C 1789-1817
    M 1837-1959   B 1789-1817, 1872-1960 **CerRO**
BT see Cilcennin
Cop ms PR CMB 1724-85 **NLW**

LLANBEDR PONT STEFFAN/LAMPETER   *SD*
C 1695-1805, 1813-1937 Maestir 1869-85   M 1739-44, 1746-1970 (Banns 1824-57)   B 1695-
    1805, 1813-1968 **NLW**
BT 1799-1808, 1811-17, 1823-37, 1839-80 **NLW**
Cop ms PR CB 1695-1745 M 1739-44 **NLW**   CB 1695-1734 *Welsh Gazette* (1903-5)

LLANDDEINIOL   *SD*
C 1776-7, 1780-1978   M 1754-1811, 1814-1971 (Banns 1825-1965)   B 1776-7, 1780-1977 **NLW**
BT 1811, 1813-16, 1820, 1822-5, 1827-79, 1882, 1885-91 **NLW**

LLANDDEWI ABER-ARTH   *SD*
C 1737-1841   M 1737-1809, 1813-1970   B 1737-1868 **NLW**   Fac C 1737-1841   M 1737-
    1809, 1813-37   B 1737-1868 **CerRO**
BT 1811-18, 1821-57, 1859-63, 1865-72 **NLW**
Cop ms PR CB 1737-1812 M 1737-1801 **NLW**

LLANDDEWIBREFI   *SD*
C 1775-1859   M 1775-1837   B 1775-1886 **NLW**
BT 1683-5, 1702-3, 1811-59, 1861-7, 1871, 1873, 1875-9, 1882, 1885-6 **NLW**
Cop ms PR C 1776-1812 M 1776-1807 B 1776-1835 **NLW**

LLANDYFRÏOG   *SD*
C 1725-1812 with gaps   M 1725-1971   B 1725-1869 with gaps, 1869-1955 **NLW**
BT 1676, 1680, 1682, 1686, 1703, 1799-1803, 1805-12, 1819-20, 1823-58, 1861-74 **NLW**
Cop ts PR CB 1725-1812 M 1725-1837 **NLW**

LLANDYGWYDD   *SD*
PR CMB 1677-1740 recorded in 1933 apparently lost
C 1745-1812   M 1745-1837 (Banns 1839-44, 1868)   B 1745-1909 **NLW**
BT 1674-6, 1678-85, 1687, 1699-1702, 1704-5, 1711, 1799-1865, 1867, 1874-5 **NLW**
Cop ts PR CMB 1677-1802 **NLW**

LLANDYSILIOGOGO   *SD*
C 1727-52, 1765-1923   M 1727-52, 1765-1970 (Banns 1823-64) St. Mark 1942-70   B 1727-1752,
    1765-1860 **NLW**
BT 1679-81, 1683-9, 1702-3, 1706, 1799-1880 **NLW**
Cop ms PR (extracts) CMB 1738-45 **NLW**

LLANDYSUL   *SD*
PR CMB 1722-65 recorded in 1933 apparently lost. Diocesan records suggest that *c*. 1790 this parish
   had registers going back to 1680
C 1798-1914   M 1755-1885   B 1798-1925   Fac CMB 1722-65 **NLW**
BT 1675, 1681-6, 1688-9, 1693, 1705, 1799, 1801-11, 1813-51, 1853-4, 1856-7, 1868-70, 1872-3,
   1876-9 **NLW**
Cop ts PR (extracts) CMB 1727-85 **NLW**

LLANFAIR CLYDOGAU   *SD*
PR C 1817-[1910] M 1817-[37] B 1817-1934 recorded in 1934 apparently lost
C 1748-1810, 1910-   M 1748-1810, 1838-   B 1748-1810, 1965- incumbent
BT 1676, 1678-9, 1684, 1686, 1799, 1806, 1808-9, 1811-16, 1818-34, 1836, 1838-40, 1853-4, 1859-80,
   1882 **NLW**

LLANFAIRORLLWYN   *SD*
PR CMB 1768-1812 recorded in 1831 as being bound up 'in great confusion' apparently lost. For a
   description of it see G. Eyre Evans, *Cardiganshire and Its Antiquities* (1903), 139
C 1813- incumbent   M 1813-1970   B 1813-1963 **NLW**
BT 1676, 1679-87, 1700-1, 1703, 1799-1814, 1816, 1818-28, 1830-67, 1874-5, 1878-9 **NLW**

LLANFAIR TRELYGEN   *SD*
Church disused since the beginning of the nineteenth century. PR & BT included in those of
   Llandyfrïog

LLANFIHANGEL GENAU'R-GLYN   *SD*
'Earlier registers are known to have once been in existence, but, it is said, were taken away to
   Shrewsbury to be produced at some trial, and were never returned to the parish' (G. Eyre Evans,
   Cardiganshire and Its Antiquities, 207)
C 1736-73, 1779-1847   M 1736-1861 (Banns 1823-44) Y Borth 1887-1907   B 1736-73, 1783-
   1927 **NLW**
BT 1675, 1680-3, 1686, 1688-9, 1692, 1699, 1702-3, 1811, 1813-15, 1823-74, 1876-80, 1882 **NLW**

LLANFIHANGEL-Y-CREUDDYN   *SD*
C 1791-1890   M 1786-1970 (Banns 1786-1812, 1823-1900)   B 1781-1909 **NLW**
BT 1674-5, 1680-2, 1686, 1701, 1811, 1813-16, 1820, 1822-37, 1839-66, 1869-72, 1874-6 **NLW**

LLANFIHANGEL YSTRAD   *SD*
PR CMB 1748-1812 recorded in 1933 apparently lost
C 1712-46, 1813-69   M 1712-46, 1812-1970 (Banns 1823-92)   B 1712-46, 1813-1915 **NLW**
BT 1676, 1678-9, 1681-3, 1689, 1799-1867, 1869-82, 1885-8, 1890 **NLW**

LLANGEITHO   *SD*
C 1769-1950   M 1761, 1770-1971   B 1769-1858 **NLW**
BT 1811, 1813-35, 1840-1, 1846-8, 1852-8, 1860-79, 1882, 1885-8 **NLW**
Cop ms PR C 1769-1832 M 1761-1812 B 1769-1812 **NLW**

LLANGOEDMOR   *SD*
PR CMB 1725-63 recorded in 1831 apparently lost. Diocesan records suggest that *c*. 1790 this parish
   had registers going back to 1684
C 1764-1812   M 1754-1837 (Banns 1754-1804, 1823-44)   B 1764-1938 **NLW**
BT 1674-5, 1678, 1680-1, 1683-6, 1689, 1705, 1710, 1799-1861, 1863-80 **NLW**

LLANGORWEN   *SD*
‹Llanbadarn Fawr 1842
CMB 1842- incumbent
BT 1841-67, 1869-72, 1874, 1878-82, 1885-7 **NLW**

LLANGRANNOG   *SD*
PR CB 1763-1812 recorded in 1831 apparently lost
C 1813-1922   M 1762-1836 (Banns 1824-1923)   B 1813-1914 **NLW**
BT 1679-81, 1683-9, 1702-3, 1706, 1799-1880 **NLW**

LLANGWYRYFON   *SD*
C 1729-1883   M 1729-1837   B 1729-1929 **NLW**
BT 1674-5, 1678, 1680-1, 1683-5, 1687, 1699, 1811-66, 1868-79, 1887-90 **NLW**

LLANGYBI   *SD*
Entries of CMB 1748-1812 included in PR Llanfair Clydogau
CB 1813- incumbent   M 1813-1970   Fac CB 1813-1984 **NLW**
BT 1678, 1683-4, 1799-1806, 1808-16, 1818-40, 1859-80, 1882 **NLW**

LLANGYNFELYN   *SD*
C 1770-1861   M 1754-1970   B 1772-1870 **NLW**
BT 1675, 1678-9, 1681-3, 1687-9, 1691, 1699, 1701-3, 1705, 1803, 1811-53, 1855-63, 1865-71,
   1873-80, 1882, 1885-6 **NLW**

LLANGYNLLO   *SD*
PR CB 1784-1812 recorded in 1831 apparently lost. Diocesan records suggest that *c.* 1790 this parish
   had registers going back to 1724
C 1756-83, 1813-1957   M 1755-1837   B 1756-83, 1813-1958 **NLW**
BT 1675-6, 1679, 1681, 1683-8, 1690, 1702-3, 1705, 1799-1804, 1806-11, 1813-14, 1816, 1818-72,
   1875, 1885-6 **NLW**

LLANILAR   *SD*
C 1685-1844   M 1685-1970 (Banns 1823-51)   B 1685-1869 **NLW**
BT 1675-6, 1678-9, 1682-3, 1688, 1699, 1702-3, 1705, 1811-72, 1874-6 **NLW**

LLANINA   *SD*
PR earliest entries in Llannarth PR. Entirely separate PR begins 1781
CB 1688-1813   M 1688-1754, 1781-1970 **NLW**
BT see Llannarth

LLANLLWCHAEARN   *SD*
C 1720-1913   M 1720-1837 (Banns 1823-70)   B 1720-1898 **NLW**
BT 1674, 1678, 1680-1, 1684-8, 1699-1700, 1702, 1799-1800, 1802-4, 1806-74 **NLW**

LLANNARTH   *SD*
C 1688-1855   M 1688-1969 (Banns 1824-57) Mydroilyn 1928-64   B 1688-1864 **NLW**
BT 1674, 1679, 1681, 1683-5, 1688-9, 1799-1800, 1802-6, 1808-80, 1882, 1885-8, 1890-2 **NLW**

LLANNERCH AERON   *SD*
PR CB 1730-1812 [M 1730-54?] recorded in 1831 apparently lost
CB 1813- incumbent   M 1754-1970 **NLW**
BT 1705, 1799-1802, 1804-5, 1807-9, 1811-78 **NLW**

LLAN-NON gweler/see LLANSANFFRAID

LLANRHYSTUD   *SD*
C 1738-97, 1800-1977   M 1738-1971 (Banns 1823-37)   B 1738-97, 1800-1978 **NLW**
BT 1676, 1678, 1699, 1703, 1811, 1813-74, 1876-8 **NLW**
Cop ms PR C 1738-59, 1800-1900 M 1738-54, 1801-1950 B 1738-59, 1800-1953 **NLW**

LLANSANFFRAID   *SD*
Diocesan records suggest that *c.* 1790 this parish had registers going back to 1696
C 1796-1842   M 1754-1812   B 1796-1860 **NLW**
BT 1678, 1681, 1811-65, 1870-80, 1882 **NLW**

LLANWENOG   *SD*
PR CMB 1722-1812 photocopied *c.* 1930-40 apparently lost
C 1813-54   M 1813-37   B 1813-50   Fac CMB 1722-1812 (Banns 1855-1942) **NLW**
BT 1676, 1681, 1799-1845, 1847-9, 1855-6, 1865-6, 1892 **NLW**
Cop ms PR (extracts) CMB 1722-1812 **NLW**

LLANWNNEN   *SD*
PR C 1799-1812 B 1796-1812 recorded in 1831 apparently lost. CB 1776-95 included in PR Llan-
    wenog CMB 1722-1812
M 1765-1801   Fac CB 1776-95, 1813-1944   M 1813-36 **NLW**
BT 1684-6, 1689, 1702, 1705, 1799-1803, 1807, 1811, 1813-36, 1840-7, 1849-80, 1882, 1885-8 **NLW**

LLANWNNWS gweler/see GWNNWS

LLANYCHAEARN   *SD*
Diocesan records suggest that *c.* 1790 this parish had PR going back 'about 40 years'
C 1803-82   M 1754-1971 (Banns 1825-86)   B 1803-78 **NLW**
BT 1689, 1702-3, 1811-19, 1823-5, 1827-48, 1850-80, 1882, 1893 **NLW**

LLECHRYD   *SD*
PR CB 1787-1812 M 1787-1804 recorded in 1831 apparently lost in the floods of 1861 (G. Eyre
    Evans, *Cardiganshire and Its Antiquities,* 251)
C 1813- incumbent   M 1805-37   B 1813-1939 **NLW**
BT 1799-1855, 1862-3, 1876-7 **NLW**

LLEDROD   *SD*
PR M 1804-12 recorded as missing in 1831
C 1770-2, 1778-1850   M 1766-1804, 1813-37   B 1770-2, 1778-1945 **NLW**
BT 1674-5, 1678-80, 1682, 1684, 1687, 1699-1700, 1703, 1811-17, 1819-29, 1831-75, 1880 **NLW**

MAESTIR gweler/see LLANBEDR PONT STEFFAN/LAMPETER

MELINDWR gweler/see CAPEL BANGOR

MWNT/MOUNT   *SD*
PR CMB 1778-1810 recorded as being on loose and imperfect leaves in 1831 apparently lost
CB 1813- incumbent   M 1813-1971 **NLW**
BT 1674, 1676, 1679-85, 1799-1800, 1802-3, 1805, 1808-13, 1815-29, 1831-7, 1839-40, 1842-54, 1865,
    1867, 1871-5 **NLW**

MYDROILYN gweler/see LLANNARTH

NANCWNLLE   *SD*
PR C 1768-1811 M 1763-1809 B 1771-1811 microfilmed in 1960 apparently lost
C 1813-1968   M 1813-1971   B 1813-57 **NLW**   Mf CMB 1768-1809 **CerRO**
BT 1675, 1799, 1811, 1813, 1815-17, 1820, 1822-43, 1845-72, 1874-80, 1882, 1885-8 **NLW**

PENBRYN   *SD*
CB 1726-1813   M 1726-1837 **NLW**
BT 1678, 1680-3, 1685, 1687-8, 1703, 1799, 1801-3, 1805-11, 1813-18, 1820-63, 1865-6, 1870-4,
    1876-7 **NLW**
Cop ms PR (extracts) CMB 1796-1812 **NLW**

PENRHYN-COCH gweler/see LLANBADARN FAWR

RHOSTÏE   *SD*
The church was a ruin at visitation in 1755. Rebuilt *c.* 1815. United with Llanilar 1875. Try Llanilar
or Llangwyryfon for records before 1815
C 1815-1920   M 1822-1925   B 1824-54 **NLW**
BT 1816, 1821-4, 1828-49, 1851-63, 1865-71, 1873-5 **NLW**

SILIAN   *SD*
CM 1792-1812 in churchwardens' account book 1792-1852 recorded in 1933 apparently lost. Some
entries CB 1776-91 in PR Llanwenog 1722-1812
C 1813-1964   M 1813-1970 (Banns 1830-48)   B 1813-1984   Fac CB 1776-91 **NLW**
BT 1683-6, 1689, 1702, 1705, 1802, 1811, 1813-16, 1820, 1823-37, 1840-72, 1874-80, 1882, 1885-8
NLW

*STRATA FLORIDA/YSTRAD-FFLUR   *SD*
C 1750-1873   M 1750-1971   B 1750-1940 **NLW**
BT 1811-13, 1823, 1825-35, 1837-51, 1853-60, 1864-5, 1867-72, 1874-5, 1877-8, 1885-99, 1901-2
NLW

TALGARREG gweler/see CAPEL CYNON

TREFILAN   *SD*
PR M 1757-1811 recorded in 1831 apparently lost
CB 1705-1800   M 1705-53, 1813-37 **NLW**
BT 1678, 1684, 1811-38, 1840-71, 1873-83 **NLW**

TREGARON   *SD*
C 1653-1931   M 1653-1919 (Banns 1830-1915)   B 1653-1937 **NLW**
BT 1678, 1680, 1700, 1811-17, 1828-9, 1831-9, 1841-66, 1869-79, 1882 **NLW**

TRE-MAIN   *SD*
CB 1763-1812   M 1763-1971 **NLW**
BT 1676, 1678-84, 1686-9, 1700-1, 1705, 1799, 1801-3, 1806-66 **NLW**

TROED-YR-AUR   *SD*
C 1655-1812   M 1655-1837   B 1655-1875 **NLW**
BT 1674, 1678-81, 1683-9, 1702-3, 1705, 1799, 1801-53, 1855-83 **NLW**
Cop ms PR (extracts) C 1814-75 **NLW**

*VERWICK/Y FERWIG   *SD*
Diocesan records suggest that *c.* 1790 this parish had registers going back 30 years
C 1813- incumbent   M 1769-1970   B 1813-1955 **NLW**
BT 1674-5, 1679-84, 1686-7, 1699-1700, 1799, 1801, 1803-7, 1810-55, 1865-6 **NLW**

YSBYTY CYNFYN   *SD*
Diocesan records suggest that *c.* 1790 this chapel of ease to Llanbadarn Fawr had 'a register which
goes back 20 years'
C 1789-1852   M 1762-1837   B 1787-1863 **NLW**
BT 1813, 1815, 1819-20, 1822-67, 1870-6, 1878-81 **NLW**

YSBYTY YSTWYTH   *SD*
C 1781-1915   M 1781-1837   B 1781-1886 **NLW**
BT 1682, 1811, 1813-53, 1858-79, 1884-93 **NLW**

YSTRAD gweler/see LLANFIHANGEL YSTRAD

YSTRAD-FFLUR/STRATA FLORIDA *SD*
C 1750-1873   M 1750-1971   B 1750-1940 **NLW**
BT 1811-13, 1823, 1825-35, 1837-51, 1853-60, 1864-5, 1867-72, 1874-5, 1877-8, 1885-99, 1901-2
   NLW

YSTRADMEURIG *SD*
C 1798-1916   M 1798-1836   B 1799-1812 **NLW**
BT 1682, 1813, 1823, 1825-80, 1885-90 **NLW**

BRYCHEINIOG
BRECKNOCKSHIRE

YSTRADGYNLAIS Eglwysi cyn 1813/Pre-1813 churches
Cefncoedycymer Eglwysi wedi 1813/Post-1813 churches

LLANWRTHWL·

MAESYFED

ABERTEIFI / CARDIGANSHIRE

RADNOR SHIRE

LLANFIHANGEL BRYNPABUAN·
LLANAFAN FAWR ·

LLANFIHANGEL ABERGWESYN
LLANDDEWI ABERGWESYN
LLANGANTEN
LLANFAIR-YM-MUALLT/BUILTH·
LLANAFAN FECHAN· ·LLANYNYS
LLANLLYWENFEL/LLANLLEONFEL ·MAESMYNYS
LLANDDEWI'R-CWM·
LLANGAMARCH ALLT-MAWR·
LLANWRTYD·
LLANGYNOG·

HENFFORDD / HEREFORDSHIRE

GWENDDWR·
CRUCADARN/CRICKADARN·
TIRABAD· DYFFRYN HONDDU·
Y GELLI/HAY
·LLANIGON
Y CLAS-AR-WY/GLASBURY
LLYS-WEN·

MERTHYR CYNOG·
LLANFIHANGEL FECHAN·
LLANDYFALLE·
LLANDEILO'R-FÂN· LLANFIHANGEL NANT BRÂN· ·BRONLLYS
GARTHBRENGI· LLANFILO ·LLANELEU/LLANELIEU
LLANDYFAELOG FACH· TALACH-DDU ·TALGARTH
Y BATEL/BATTLE· CAPEL-Y-FFIN·
LLYWEL· ·LLAN-DDEW LLANDYFAELOG TRE'R-GRAIG
TRALLWNG/TRALLONG· ABERYSGIR/ABERYSCIR·
RHYD-Y-BRYW· ABERHONDDU/BRECON· ·LLAN-Y-WERN
PEN-PONT· ·LLANFIHANGEL TAL-Y-LLYN
DEFYNNOG· ·LLANSBYDDYD ·LLAN-GORS/LLANGORSE
LLANHAMLACH·
CAPEL ILLTUD· LLANFRYNACH· ·LLANGASTY TAL-Y-LLYN
CANTREF· ·CATHEDIN
CRAI/CRAY· LLANFEUGAN·
LLANSANFFRAID· ·LLANFIHANGEL CWM DU
PATRISIO/PARTRISHOW·

TRETŴR/TRETOWER·
CALLWEN· LLANDDETI/LLANTHETTY· LLANBEDR YSTRAD YW·
LLANGYNIDR· CRUCYWEL/CRICKHOWELL·
GLYNCOLLEN· LLANGATWG/LLANGATTOCK· LLANGENNI/
LLANGENNY
LLANELLI/LLANELLY·

CAPEL NANT-DDU·
YSTRADFELLTE· ·CAPEL TAF FECHAN
Y COELBREN· Bryn-mawr·
·YSTRADGYNLAIS Y FAENOR/VAYNOR·
PENDERYN· Cefncoedycymer·

CAERFYRDDIN / CARMARTHENSHIRE

MORGANNWG / GLAMORGAN

MYNWY

MONMOUTHSHIRE

Milltiroedd/Miles
0   5   10

BRYCHEINIOG/BRECKNOCKSHIRE

ABER-CRAF/ABERCRAVE gweler/see YSTRADGYNLAIS

ABERHONDDU/BRECON St. David (LLAN-FAES)   *SB*
C 1730-63, 1768-1944   M 1730-1837 (Banns 1823-51, 1904-65)   B 1730-63, 1768-1895 **NLW**
BT 1715-31, 1733-97, 1799-1809, 1813-14, 1817, 1823-44 **NLW**
Cop PR CB 1730-63, 1768-1810 M 1730-53 in Edwin Davies, *Parochial Registers and Records,* 1
   (Brecon, 1906), 20-72

ABERHONDDU/BRECON St. John Evangelist   *SB*
C 1727-1924   M 1727-1927 (Banns 1787-1823, 1870-1921)   B 1727-1851 **NLW**
BT 1716, 1720-2, 1724-46, 1748-53, 1755-1809, 1813-37, 1840, 1864-5 **NLW**

ABERHONDDU/BRECON St. Mary   *SB*
C 1684-1900   M 1684-1920 (Banns 1883-1913)   B 1684-6, 1693 (see St. John for later B) **NLW**
   Fac CMB 1706-33   Mf CB 1813-52   M 1787-1875 **NLW**
BT 1701, 1713, 1716-21, 1724-30, 1735-41, 1743-55, 1757-65, 1767-71, 1774-82, 1786, 1789, 1791-5,
   1797-1809, 1813-40, 1864-6 **NLW**

ABERYSGIR/ABERYSCIR   *SB*
Diocesan records suggest that *c.* 1790 this parish had PR beginning in 1720
CB 1813- incumbent   M 1755-1833   Fac CB 1813-1981 **NLW**
BT 1715-17, 1721, 1723-6, 1729-43, 1745-53, 1755-61, 1763-9, 1771-82, 1784, 1786-95, 1797-1809,
   1813-19, 1821-48, 1865-6, 1869-71 **NLW**

ALLT-MAWR   *SB*
Pre-1813 entries included in PR Llanafan Fawr (1831 survey); the only nineteenth-century records
   extant in 1935, but now apparently lost, were eight entries of M 1813-37 on 'three sheets
   mounted on gauze' and four entries of M 1842-93 in 'a portion of a register'
C 1915- incumbent   M 1912-70 **NLW**   B 1914- incumbent
BT 1713, 1720, 1729-30, 1738, 1741, 1751, 1756-60, 1762-9, 1771, 1773-5, 1777-83, 1785-9, 1793-
   1809, 1813-16, 1819-37, 1839-40, 1843 **NLW**

BATEL, Y/BATTLE   *SB*
C 1720-79, 1785-1807   M 1720-50, 1754-1812   B 1778-9, 1785-1807 **NLW**
BT 1714-15, 1717-18, 1720-1, 1724-50, 1753-4, 1756-75, 1777-8, 1780-1809, 1813-19, 1821-5, 1827,
   1829-33, 1835-41 **NLW**

BETWS PEN-PONT gweler/see PEN-PONT

*BRECON/ABERHONDDU St. David (LLAN-FAES)   *SB*
C 1730-63, 1768-1944   M 1730-1837 (Banns 1823-51, 1904-65)   B 1730-63, 1768-1895 **NLW**
BT 1715-31, 1733-97, 1799-1809, 1813-14, 1817, 1823-44 **NLW**
Cop PR CB 1730-63, 1768-1810 M 1730-53 in Edwin Davies, *Parochial Registers and Records,* 1
   (Brecon, 1906), 20-72

*BRECON/ABERHONDDU St. John Evangelist   *SB*
C 1727-1924   M 1727-1927 (Banns 1787-1823, 1870-1921)   B 1727-1851 **NLW**
BT 1716, 1720-2, 1724-46, 1748-53, 1755-1809, 1813-37, 1840, 1864-5 **NLW**

*BRECON/ABERHONDDU St. Mary   *SB*
C 1684-1900   M 1684-1920 (Banns 1883-1913)   B 1684-6, 1693 (see St. John for later B) **NLW**
   Fac CMB 1706-33   Mf CB 1813-52   M 1787-1875 **NLW**
BT 1701, 1713, 1716-21, 1724-30, 1735-41, 1743-55, 1757-65, 1767-71, 1774-82, 1786, 1789, 1791-5,
   1797-1809, 1813-40, 1864-6 **NLW**

BRONLLYS   *SB*
Diocesan records suggest that *c.* 1790 this parish had registers going back to 1759
C 1813- incumbent   M 1755-1837   B 1813-1939   Fac C 1813-1982 **NLW**
BT 1713, 1715-16, 1719-25, 1727, 1729-30, 1733-5, 1737-52, 1754-1809, 1813, 1818-41, 1845-8, 1865,
   1871-2 **NLW**

BRYN-MAWR   *SB*
‹Llangatwg/Llangattock
C 1850-1954   M 1873-1977 (Banns 1943-53)   B 1888-1943 **Gwent RO**

*BUILTH/LLANFAIR-YM-MUALLT   *SB*
C 1681-1730, 1750-1848   M 1681-1730, 1750-65, 1770-1837   B 1681-1730, 1750-1859 **NLW**
BT 1687, 1713-16, 1719-21, 1723-5, 1728-42, 1744-95, 1797-1804, 1806-9, 1813-22, 1824-31, 1836-41
   NLW

CALLWEN (GLYNTAWE)   *SB*
C 1685-94, 1760-1958   M 1685-94, 1760-1808, 1840-1922, 1924-39 (Banns 1833-1977)   B 1685-
   1694, 1778-1958 **Glam RO**   Fac 1685-94, 1760-1808 **NLW**
BT 1775, 1777, 1783-95, 1797-8, 1800, 1802-9, 1813-38, 1840 **NLW**

CANTREF   *SB*
C 1779-1812   M 1754-1971   B 1784-1811 **NLW**
BT 1714-15, 1719-20, 1723-5, 1729-42, 1745, 1747-78, 1780-8, 1790, 1792-4, 1797-1809, 1813-41,
   1864-5, 1871 **NLW**

CAPEL COELBREN gweler/see **COELBREN, Y**

CAPEL GLYN COLLWYN gweler/see **GLYNCOLLEN**

CAPEL ILLTUD (LLANILLTUD)   *SB*
A chapel of ease to Defynnog without its own PR before 1776. Separate parish 1887
C 1776-1983   M 1776-1817   B 1776-1945 **NLW**
BT 1776, 1783-4, 1787-92, 1795, 1797-1800, 1802-9, 1813-39, 1842-5, 1847, 1864, 1871 **NLW**

CAPEL NANT-DDU   *SB*
C 1779-1808, 1813-1967   M 1813-14, 1858-1971   B 1779-1930 **NLW**
BT see Cantref

CAPEL TAF FECHAN   *SB*
‹Llanddeti/Llanthetty. CMB 1772-1812 recorded in 1831 apparently lost
C 1813-1981   M 1891-1925 **NLW**

CAPEL-Y-FFIN   *SB*
‹Llanigon
M 1845-1907 **NLW**
BT see Llanigon

CATHEDIN   *SB*
C 1732-1812   M 1732-1971   B 1732-1812 **NLW**
BT 1687, 1713-16, 1718, 1720-6, 1728-65, 1767-8, 1770-6, 1778-83, 1785-90, 1794-7, 1799-1809,
   1813-15, 1821-41, 1865, 1867 **NLW**

CEFNCOEDYCYMER   *SB*
‹Y Faenor/Vaynor
C 1877-1910, 1924-50   M 1883-1973 (Banns 1926-51) **NLW**

CLAS-AR-WY, Y/GLASBURY St. Peter   *SB*
The Radnorshire portion of this parish has been served since 1882 by the church of All Saints (see
    under Maesyfed/Radnorshire)
C 1660-1955   M 1660-1976 (Banns 1823-1940)   B 1660-1929 **NLW**
BT 1715-16, 1719-69, 1771-4, 1776-1808, 1810, 1813-38, 1873-4 **NLW**
Cop printed PR CMB 1660-1837 with index (ed. T. Wood, 1904)

COELBREN, Y   *SB*
An ancient chapelry of Ystradgynlais. Earlier CMB in PR of the mother church
CB 1902-25   M 1863-1923 **Glam RO**

CRAI/CRAY   *SB*
An ancient chapelry in the parish of Defynnog possibly without its own PR before 1813
C 1820-   M 1884-   B 1885- incumbent

CRICKADARN gweler/see CRUCADARN

CRICKHOWELL gweler/see CRUCYWEL

CROSS OAK gweler/see LLANFEUGAN

CRUCADARN/CRICKADARN   *SB*
Diocesan records suggest that *c.* 1790 this parish had registers going back to 1705
CB 1734-56, 1775-82   M 1734-1970 **NLW**
BT 1705-8, 1710, 1713, 1720-60, 1762-75, 1777-1809, 1813-38, 1841, 1844-7, 1865-73 **NLW**

CRUCYWEL/CRICKHOWELL   *SB*
C 1633-84 with gaps, 1700-20, 1726-1936   M 1633-84 with gaps, 1700-20, 1754-1944 (Banns 1824-
    1971)   B 1633-84 with gaps, 1700-20, 1726-1941 **NLW**
BT 1714-21, 1723-5, 1728-95, 1797-1809, 1813, 1815, 1821-9, 1835-6 **NLW**

DEFYNNOG   *SB*
C 1695-1939   M 1695-1983   B 1695-1984 **NLW**
BT 1713-14, 1717-21, 1723-68, 1771-88, 1790, 1792, 1795, 1797-1809, 1813-36, 1839-48, 1864-73
    NLW

DYFFRYN HONDDU (UPPER CHAPEL)   *SB*
‹Merthyr Cynog. Diocesan records suggest that *c.* 1790 this chapel had registers beginning in 1716
C 1825-44   M 1826-32, 1855-1970 **NLW**

FAENOR, Y/VAYNOR   *SB*
PR 1759-1812 recorded in 1935 apparently lost. M 1868-92 recorded in 1900 parish inventory
    (NLW, SD/Misc. B/102) was missing in 1935 and has not been recovered
C 1813-1923   M 1755-1868, 1892-1975 (Banns 1823-1903)   B 1813-1905, 1923-50 **NLW**
BT 1714-15, 1717-47, 1749-62, 1764-95, 1797-1809, 1813-23, 1825-37, 1840-2 **NLW**

GARTHBRENGI   *SB*
Diocesan records suggest that *c.* 1790 this parish had registers going back to 1653
C 1733-52, 1758-63, 1766-86, 1804, 1813-1978   M 1733-52, 1758-63, 1767, 1776-9, 1789-99,
    1803-4, 1813-1971   B 1733-52, 1758-63, 1766-86, 1804, 1813-1982 **NLW**
BT 1687, 1707-8, 1712-41, 1744-95, 1797-1809, 1813-31, 1833-52, 1854 **NLW**

GELLI, Y/HAY   *SB*
C 1688-1895   M 1688-1890 (Banns 1841-1949)   B 1688-1856 **NLW**
BT 1687, 1713-14, 1720, 1723-52, 1756-95, 1797-1809, 1813, 1815-55, 1867 **NLW**

*GLASBURY/Y CLAS-AR-WY St. Peter   *SB*
The Radnorshire portion of this parish has been served since 1882 by the church of All Saints (see
    under Maesyfed/Radnorshire)
C 1660-1955   M 1660-1976 (Banns 1823-1940)   B 1660-1929 **NLW**
BT 1715-16, 1719-69, 1771-4, 1776-1808, 1810, 1813-38, 1873-4 **NLW**
Cop printed PR CMB 1660-1837 with index (ed. T. Wood, 1904)

GLYNCOLLEN   *SB*
An ancient chapelry in the parish of Llanfeugan
C 1914-25 **NLW**

GLYNTAWE gweler/see CALLWEN

GWENDDWR   *SB*
CB 1752-3, 1798-1813   M 1752-3, 1766-1801, 1812-1966 **NLW**
BT 1713-18, 1721-34, 1736-56, 1758-67, 1769-95, 1797-1809, 1813-17, 1819-20, 1822-35, 1837-8,
    1841, 1844-58, 1865-73 **NLW**

*HAY/Y GELLI   *SB*
C 1688-1895   M 1688-1890 (Banns 1841-1949)   B 1688-1856 **NLW**
BT 1687, 1713-14, 1720, 1723-52, 1756-95, 1797-1809, 1813, 1815-55, 1867 **NLW**

LLANAFAN FAWR   *SB*
PR M 1771-1812 recorded in 1935 apparently lost
CB 1720-59, 1762-1812   M 1723-70, 1813-1971 (Banns 1790-1840) **NLW**
BT 1708, 1710, 1714-23, 1730, 1736-63, 1765-95, 1797-1809, 1813-42, 1844 **NLW**

LLANAFAN FECHAN (LLANFECHAN)   *SB*
CB 1745-52, 1762-1812   M 1745-52, 1755-97, 1801-11, 1813-1970 **NLW**
BT 1701, 1713-16, 1719-31, 1733-8, 1740-51, 1753-4, 1756-64, 1766-95, 1797-1809, 1813-30, 1832-6,
    1839-40, 1842 **NLW**

LLANBEDR YSTRAD YW   *SB*
C 1675-1708, 1712-1812   M 1675-1708, 1712-1841   B 1675-1708, 1712-1894 **NLW**
BT 1713-19, 1721-7, 1730, 1732-47, 1749-59, 1761-92, 1794-5, 1798, 1800-9, 1813-15, 1817, 1819-36
    NLW

LLANDDETI/LLANTHETTY   *SB*
PR 1693-1812 recorded in 1831 apparently lost, except for the cover of one volume with entries of
    CB 1740-1
C 1740-1, 1813-1975   M 1813-1970 (Banns 1962-70)   B 1740-1, 1813-1974 **NLW**
BT 1708, 1714-95, 1797-1809, 1813-34, 1836, 1839-44 **NLW**

LLAN-DDEW   *SB*
PR 1709-1805 recorded in 1831 apparently lost
CB 1813-   M 1837- incumbent
BT 1687, 1698, 1707-8, 1712-58, 1761-95, 1797-1809, 1813-31, 1833-8 **NLW**

LLANDDEWI ABERGWESYN   *SB*
PR 1738-1812 recorded in 1831 and M 1754-79 recorded in 1935 apparently lost
CB 1813- incumbent   M 1813-62 (Banns 1957-9) **NLW**
BT 1714-51, 1753-60, 1762-95, 1797-1809, 1813-44 **NLW**
Cop ms PR CB 1738-1812 M 1738-56, 1765-1812 **Cardiff Central Library & NLW**

LLANDDEWI'R-CWM   *SB*
CB 1765-1810   M 1754-1837 **NLW**
BT 1716-17, 1719-25, 1727, 1729-32, 1734-71, 1773-85, 1787-95, 1797-1809, 1813-23, 1825-31, 1836-
   41 **NLW**

LLANDDULAS gweler/see TIRABAD

LLANDEFAELOG gweler/see LLANDYFAELOG

LLANDEFALLE gweler/see LLANDYFALLE

LLANDEILO'R-FÂN   *SB*
PR CMB 1770- recorded in 1831 apparently lost
C 1809-1949   M 1813-1966   B 1809-1918 **NLW**
BT 1714-16, 1719-95, 1797-1809, 1813-38, 1840, 1843-4 **NLW**

LLANDYFAELOG FACH   *SB*
CB 1715-54, 1762-79, 1783-1980   M 1715-54, 1783-1971 (Banns 1787-1812, 1865, 1910, 1938-79)
   NLW
BT 1712-25, 1727-56, 1759-95, 1797-1809, 1813-15, 1817-29, 1831-2, 1834-8, 1866, 1872-3 **NLW**

LLANDYFAELOG TRE'R-GRAIG   *SB*
Some entries of CMB in PR Llanfilo
C 1786-98   M 1755-1827   B 1782-99 **NLW**
BT 1710-17, 1729-30, 1732, 1740, 1743, 1746, 1749, 1752, 1754, 1765, 1774, 1786-9, 1791, 1795,
   1797-1809, 1820-1, 1823-30, 1832-9, 1842 **NLW**

LLANDYFALLE   *SB*
PR CMB 1720-1812 recorded in 1935 apparently lost
C 1813-1930   M 1813-1970   B 1813-1981 **NLW**
BT 1705-8, 1710, 1713, 1715, 1719-38, 1740-65, 1767-8, 1771-84, 1786-95, 1797-1809, 1813-47
   NLW

LLANELEU/LLANELIEU   *SB*
PR CB 1746-1812 M 1746-53 recorded in 1831 apparently lost
C 1813-1964   M 1754-1811, 1814-36   B 1813-1943 **NLW**
BT 1713-16, 1718-21, 1724-5, 1727-33, 1735-6, 1739-50, 1752-5, 1757-1809, 1813, 1817-32, 1834-6,
   1838-9, 1848-50 **NLW**

LLANELLI/LLANELLY   *SB*
C 1708-1924   M 1701-1933 (Banns 1842-1921)   B 1708-1925 **Gwent RO**   Fac C 1708-1811
   M 1701-1809, 1847-74   B 1701-1847 **NLW**
BT 1712-13, 1715-18, 1720, 1722-35, 1737-95, 1797-1809, 1812-37 **NLW**

LLAN-FAES gweler/see ABERHONDDU/BRECON St. David

LLANFAIR-YM-MUALLT/BUILTH   *SB*
C 1681-1730, 1750-1848   M 1681-1730, 1750-65, 1770-1837   B 1681-1730, 1750-1859 **NLW**
BT 1687, 1713-16, 1719-21, 1723-5, 1728-42, 1744-95, 1797-1804, 1806-9, 1813-22, 1824-31, 1836-41
   NLW

LLANFECHAN gweler/see LLANAFAN FECHAN

LLANFEUGAN   *SB*
C 1747-1976   M 1747-1970 (Banns 1754-1818, 1892-4, 1918) Cross Oak 1890-1953   B 1747-1812 **NLW**
BT 1687, 1714, 1717-21, 1723-37, 1739-64, 1766, 1768-95, 1797-1809, 1813-36, 1865-7 **NLW**

LLANFIHANGEL ABERGWESYN   *SB*
CB 1730-1812   M 1730-1837 (Banns 1825-63, 1897) **NLW**
BT 1713-25, 1727-42, 1744, 1747-74, 1776-95, 1797-1809, 1813-38, 1840, 1842-4 **NLW**

LLANFIHANGEL BRYNPABUAN   *SB*
PR CB 1722-1812 M 1723-54 recorded in 1935 apparently lost
CB 1762-1804   M 1755-93, 1813-37 **NLW**
BT 1698, 1708, 1710, 1713-20, 1723, 1726, 1728-39, 1741-50, 1752-7, 1760-95, 1797-1809, 1813-36, 1839-42, 1844 **NLW**

LLANFIHANGEL CWM DU (ST. MICHAEL CWMDU)   *SB*
C 1734-1922   M 1734-1971 (Banns 1802-1968)   B 1734-1875 **NLW**
BT 1688, 1714-15, 1719-21, 1725, 1729-95, 1797-1809, 1813-38, 1840 **NLW**

LLANFIHANGEL FECHAN   *SB*
‹Llandyfaelog Fach. Diocesan records suggest that *c*. 1790 this chapel had no PR of its own
C 1819-1979   M 1872-1971   B 1819-1981 **NLW**
BT 1765, 1819-27, 1830-1, 1833-52, 1854 **NLW**

LLANFIHANGEL NANT BRÂN   *SB*
PR CMB 1758-1812 recorded in 1831 apparently lost
CB 1813- incumbent   M 1813-19, 1835-7   Fac CB 1813-1981 **NLW**
BT 1714-15, 1719-1809, 1813-38, 1840-4 **NLW**

LLANFIHANGEL TAL-Y-LLYN   *SB*
PR CB 1700-13 M 1750 recorded in 1831 and CB 1785-1812 recorded in 1935 apparently lost
CB 1813-   M 1813-37 incumbent   M 1767-1810, 1837-1971 **NLW**
BT 1714-17, 1720-1, 1723-33, 1735-88, 1790-1809, 1813-16, 1818-19, 1821-34, 1837-8, 1843, 1845-8, 1865, 1871, 1873 **NLW**
Cop ms PR CB 1785-1812 M 1767-1810 **NLW**

LLANFILO (LLANFILLO)   *SB*
C 1680-1739, 1786-1812   M 1680-1739, 1755-1836   B 1680-1739, 1782-1967   Fac C 1813-1981 **NLW**
BT 1687, 1713, 1717, 1719-21, 1723, 1725-7, 1729-35, 1737-95, 1797-1809, 1813-45, 1864-73 **NLW**

LLANFRYNACH   *SB*
PR CB 1695-1776 M 1695-1754 recorded in 1831 and M 1754-1812 recorded in 1935 apparently lost
C 1776-1935   M 1813-37 (Banns 1823-1961)   B 1776-1912 **NLW**
BT 1707, 1713-16, 1718-22, 1725-7, 1729-32, 1734-57, 1759-64, 1767-1809, 1813-14, 1820-40 **NLW**

LLANGAMARCH   *SB*
C 1764-1918   M 1767-1970 (Banns 1782-1854)   B 1764-1955 **NLW**
BT 1713, 1715-30, 1732-4, 1736-1809, 1813-44, 1864-8 **NLW**

LLANGANTEN   *SB*
PR CMB 1738-50 recorded in 1831 and CB 1769-1812 recorded in 1935 apparently lost
C 1792-5   M 1754-1812, 1837-1971   B 1792-5, 1813-1984 **NLW**
BT 1714, 1720, 1723-38, 1740-54, 1756-95, 1797-1809, 1813-33, 1835-53 **NLW**

LLANGASTY TAL-Y-LLYN *SB*
CB 1718-68, 1770-1812   M 1718-1971 **NLW**
BT 1685, 1714-17, 1719, 1721-45, 1747, 1749-66, 1772-6, 1778-84, 1786-9, 1791-5, 1797-1809, 1813-15, 1821-40, 1842-52, 1865-6 **NLW**

LLANGATWG/LLANGATTOCK *SB*
C 1703-1961   M 1703-1979 (Banns 1823-48)   B 1703-1881 **NLW**
BT 1714-32, 1734-94, 1797-1809, 1812-37 **NLW**

LLANGENNI/LLANGENNY *SB*
C 1695-1891   M 1695-1809, 1813-38   B 1695-1911 **NLW**
BT 1687, 1714, 1716-97, 1799-1809, 1813-32, 1834-5, 1838-9 **NLW**

LLAN-GORS/LLANGORSE *SB*
C 1693-1965   M 1693-1971   B 1693-1927 **NLW**
BT 1714-17, 1720, 1723-34, 1736-8, 1740-58, 1760-83, 1785-91, 1793-5, 1797-1809, 1813-30, 1832-43, 1865-8 **NLW**
Cop ms PR CB 1695-1790 M 1695-1753 **NLW**

LLANGYNIDR *SB*
PR CB 1736-81 M 1736-54 recorded in 1831 apparently lost
C 1783-1868   M 1754-1980 (Banns 1852-1939)   B 1783-1879 **NLW**
BT 1707-8, 1713-27, 1729-95, 1797-1808, 1813-36, 1838-41 **NLW**

LLANGYNOG *SB*
C 1745-1934   M 1746-71, 1801-37, 1844-1929   B 1745-1932 **NLW**
BT 1717, 1722, 1730, 1732, 1736-41, 1743-9, 1751, 1753-4, 1757-89, 1791-3, 1795-9, 1801-9, 1813-33, 1835-40, 1843-6 **NLW**

LLANHAMLACH *SB*
C 1717-46, 1755-1812   M 1717-46, 1754-1971   B 1717-46, 1755-1930 **NLW**
BT 1716-38, 1741, 1744-6, 1749-51, 1753-8, 1760, 1762-5, 1769-72, 1774-95, 1797-1809, 1813-29, 1831, 1834 **NLW**

LLANIGON *SB*
C 1712-85, 1788-1906   M 1712-1837 (Banns 1824-1976)   B 1712-53, 1783-1953 **NLW**
BT 1720-1, 1723-82, 1784-95, 1797-1809, 1813-52 **NLW**

LLANILID/LLANULID gweler/see CRAI/CRAY

LLANILLTUD gweler/see CAPEL ILLTUD

LLANLLYWENFEL/LLANLLEONFEL *SB*
PR CB 1764-1812 M 1755-94 recorded in 1831 apparently lost
CB 1813- incumbent   M 1794-1970 **NLW**
BT 1714, 1716, 1718-24, 1726-33, 1735-67, 1769-83, 1785-95, 1797-1809, 1813-29, 1831-5, 1837-47 **NLW**

LLANSANFFRAID (-AR-WYSG) *SB*
CB 1718-47, 1749-1813   M 1718-47, 1749-1837 **NLW**
BT 1716-19, 1721-4, 1726-95, 1797-1809, 1814-30, 1832-6, 1838-68 **NLW**

LLANSBYDDYD/LLANSPYTHID   *SB*
C 1699-1811, 1813-1983   M 1699-1836   B 1699-1811, 1813-1909 **NLW**
BT 1687, 1713-14, 1717, 1719-35, 1737-1809, 1813-42, 1845-6, 1864, 1871 **NLW**

*LLANTHETTY/LLANDDETI   *SB*
PR 1693-1812 recorded in 1831 apparently lost, except for the cover of one volume with entries of
   CB 1740-1
C 1740-1, 1813-1975   M 1813-1970 (Banns 1962-70)   B 1740-1, 1813-1974 **NLW**
BT 1708, 1714-95, 1797-1809, 1813-34, 1836, 1839-44 **NLW**

LLANWRTHWL   *SB*
PR CMB 1713-1812 recorded in 1935 apparently lost
C 1813-1922   M 1813-1971 **NLW**   B 1813- incumbent
BT 1696, 1713, 1715-95, 1797-1809, 1813-41, 1865 **NLW**

LLANWRTYD   *SB*
C 1748-1812   M 1748-57, 1772-1837   B 1748-1915 **NLW**
BT 1713, 1715-26, 1728-31, 1733-5, 1737-71, 1773-4, 1776-95, 1797-1809, 1813-44, 1864-8 **NLW**

LLANYNYS   *SB*
CB 1731-1812   M 1733-1970 (Banns 1805-50) **NLW**
BT 1713-17, 1719-95, 1797-1809, 1813-17, 1819-42, 1844-5, 1847-8 **NLW**

LLAN-Y-WERN   *SB*
CB 1653-9, 1664, 1666, 1674, 1688-9, 1695-1708, 1711-15, 1717-1800   M as CB & 1801-12, 1847-
   1971 **NLW**
BT 1713-14, 1718-19, 1724-7, 1729-33, 1735-47, 1749-58, 1760-83, 1785-95, 1797-1809, 1813-40,
   1842-5, 1847-50, 1871 **NLW**
Cop ms PR CB 1653-1800 M 1656-1812 **NLW**

LLYS-WEN   *SB*
C 1718-1981   M 1718-94, 1813-36, 1839-1971   B 1718-1980 **NLW**
BT 1716, 1718-21, 1723-70, 1772-95, 1797-1809, 1813-30, 1833-5, 1837-8, 1842-6, 1853 **NLW**

LLYWEL   *SB*
C 1694-1730, 1733-1938   M 1694-1730, 1733-53, 1782-1809, 1813-37   B 1694-1730, 1733-1900
   NLW
BT 1708, 1713-19, 1721-31, 1733-49, 1751-1809, 1813-54, 1856-8 **NLW**

MAESMYNYS   *SB*
C 1684-1713, 1743-80   M 1684-1971 (Banns 1754-1850)   B 1684-1812 **NLW**
BT 1687, 1690, 1705, 1707, 1714-16, 1718-95, 1797-1804, 1806-9, 1813-42, 1844-5, 1847-8 **NLW**

MERTHYR CYNOG   *SB*
PR CB 1681-1768, 1782-1804 M 1681-1755 recorded in 1831 apparently lost
C 1813-1981   M 1756-66, 1777-1800, 1803-1971 (Banns 1803-1979)   B 1813-1951 **NLW**
BT 1713-95, 1797-1809, 1813-50, 1864, 1866-7, 1871 **NLW**

NANT-DDU gweler/see CAPEL NANT-DDU

PATRISIO/PARTRISHOW   *SB*
PR CB 1793-1812 M 1750-1812 recorded in 1831 apparently lost
CB 1728-92   M 1728-49, 1813-43 **NLW**
BT 1713-17, 1719, 1721-30, 1732-64, 1766-95, 1797-1809, 1813-15, 1817-19, 1821-36 **NLW**

PENDERYN   *SB*
CB 1762-1805, 1807-12   M 1754-1813 **NLW**
BT 1713-14, 1717-21, 1723-5, 1727-95, 1797-1809, 1813-17, 1819-32, 1835-6 **NLW**

PEN-PONT (BETWS PEN-PONT)   *SB*
‹Llansbyddyd/Llanspythid
CB 1813- incumbent   M 1835-6   Fac C 1813-1978   B 1814-1981 **NLW**
BT 1803-4, 1814, 1817, 1821, 1824-5, 1827-9, 1831-6, 1842-4, 1866-9, 1871-2 **NLW**

RHYD-Y-BRYW   *SB*
‹Llywel 1861. Diocesan records suggest that *c.* 1790 this chapel had no PR of its own
C 1813-1985   M 1852-1954   B 1813-1983 **NLW**
BT 1803, 1813-32, 1834-54, 1857-8, 1864 **NLW**

TAF FECHAN gweler/see CAPEL TAF FECHAN

TALACH-DDU   *SB*
PR CMB 1640-79 transcribed by John Lloyd *c.* 1904 apparently lost
CB 1601-40, 1725-1812   M 1601-40, 1725-1837 **NLW**
BT 1708, 1713-56, 1758-62, 1764-8, 1770-4, 1776-95, 1797-1801, 1803-9, 1813, 1815-33, 1835, 1837-8 **NLW**
Cop PR CMB 1600-79 in J. Lloyd, *Historical Memoranda of Breconshire* 2 (1904), 84-118

TALGARTH   *SB*
C 1695-1957   M 1695-1837 (Banns 1823-1914)   B 1695-1905 **NLW**
BT 1686, 1708, 1714-23, 1725, 1731, 1734, 1736-95, 1797-1809, 1813-14, 1817-32, 1834-8, 1840 **NLW**

TIRABAD (LLANDDULAS)   *SB*
This chapel in the parish of Llangamarch was built at the expense of Sackville Gwynne, and consecrated in 1726 (SD/Misc. B/41). PR CMB 1729-1812 recorded in 1831 apparently lost
CB 1813- incumbent   M 1814-36 **NLW**
BT 1807-9, 1813-38, 1840, 1842-8 **NLW**

TRALLWNG/TRALLONG   *SB*
PR M 1752-1812 recorded in 1831 apparently lost. Diocesan records suggest that *c.* 1790 this parish had ‘imperfect’ PR back to 1700
C 1752-6, 1771-1804   M 1813-37   B 1771-1804   Fac C 1813-1980   B 1813-1981 **NLW**
BT 1687, 1712-14, 1737-8, 1740-2, 1744-5, 1747, 1749-51, 1772-95, 1797-1809, 1813, 1815-36, 1870 **NLW**

TRETŴR/TRETOWER   *SB*
‹Llanfihangel Cwm Du
C 1813-75   B 1813-70 **NLW**   M 1877- incumbent
BT see Llanfihangel Cwm Du

*VAYNOR/Y FAENOR   *SB*
PR 1759-1812 recorded in 1935 apparently lost. M 1868-92 recorded in 1900 parish inventory (NLW, SD/Misc. B/102) was missing in 1935 and has not been recovered
C 1813-1923   M 1755-1868, 1892-1975 (Banns 1823-1903)   B 1813-1905, 1923-50 **NLW**
BT 1714-15, 1717-47, 1749-62, 1764-95, 1797-1809, 1813-23, 1825-37, 1840-2 **NLW**

YSTRADFELLTE   *SB*
PR CB 1737-58 **M** 1737-53 recorded in 1831 apparently lost
C 1759-1959   M 1754-1970   B 1759-1811, 1815-82 **Glam RO**
BT 1713, 1715-62, 1764-95, 1797-1809, 1813-36, 1871-3 **NLW**

YSTRADGYNLAIS   *SB*
C 1721-1916   M 1721-1856 (Banns 1823-1913) Aber-craf/Abercrave 1912-30   B 1721-1902
  Glam RO
BT 1713-1804, 1806, 1808-9, 1813-16, 1819, 1822-34, 1836 **NLW**

CAERFYRDDIN
CARMARTHENSHIRE

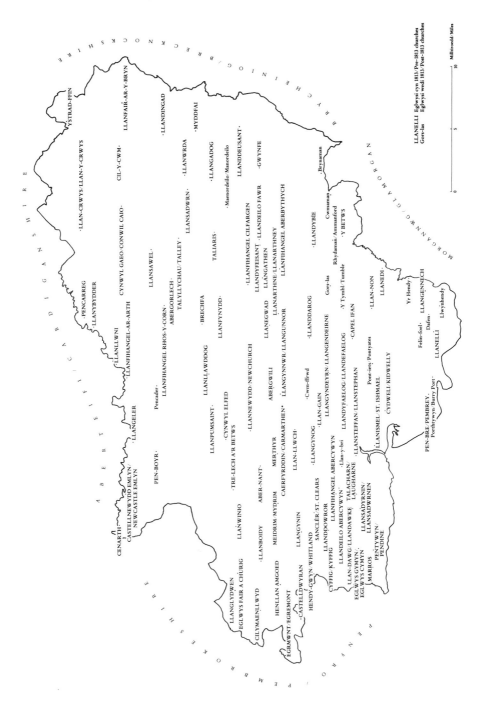

CAERFYRDDIN/CARMARTHENSHIRE

ABERGORLECH   *SD*
An ancient chapelry. CMB prior to 1813 included in PR Llanybydder
M 1901-69   B 1813-71 **Carm RO**   C 1883- incumbent
BT see Llanybydder & Talyllychau/Talley

ABERGWILI   *SD*
CB 1661-1902   M 1661-1934 **NLW**
BT 1672, 1674-6, 1680, 1684, 1694, 1698, 1703-5, 1717-18, 1721, 1724-5, 1727-41, 1743-59, 1763,
    1765-1800, 1802-35, 1837-52, 1856-82, 1884-91, 1893-4 **NLW**
Cop ts PR CB 1813-75 M 1661-1875 with index **Soc Gen**

ABER-NANT   *SD*
CMB 1763-1812 **NLW**   M 1754-1965 **Carm RO**
BT 1672, 1675-7, 1679, 1681-4, 1686-7, 1690-1, 1693-5, 1697-9, 1701, 1703-4, 1707-11, 1717, 1721,
    1724-40, 1742-6, 1748-68, 1770, 1773, 1775, 1778-9, 1781-5, 1800, 1802, 1804-64 **NLW**

ALLTYFERIN gweler/see LLANEGWAD

*AMMANFORD/RHYDAMAN All Saints   *SD*
    C 1915-40   M 1915-23, 1935-43, 1953-71 (Banns 1915-73) **Carm RO**

*AMMANFORD/RHYDAMAN St. Michael   *SD*
    ‹Llandybïe & Y Betws 1903
    M 1893-1971 (Banns 1892-1964)   B 1885-1958 **Carm RO**

BETWS, Y   *SD*
CM 1706-1973 (Banns 1823-1964)   B 1706-1909 **Carm RO**
BT 1702, 1707-8, 1716-22, 1728-84, 1786-7, 1789-90, 1793-6, 1798, 1800, 1802-3, 1805-65 **NLW**

BRECHFA   *SD*
C 1780-1881   M 1806-1970 (Banns 1831-1976)   B 1780-1915 **Carm RO**
BT 1800, 1808-35, 1880-3 **NLW**

BRYNAMAN   *SD*
‹Llangadog 1889
C 1881-1928   M 1889-1980 (Banns 1924-61)   B 1882-1950 **Carm RO**

*BURRY PORT/PORTHTYWYN   *SD*
‹Pen-bre/Pembrey
C 1903-79 Pwll 1924-76   M 1902-76 **Carm RO**

CAERFYRDDIN/CARMARTHEN St. Peter   *SD*
C 1671-1923   M 1671-1916 (Banns 1823-1915)   B 1671-1885 **Carm RO**
BT 1675-6, 1678, 1682-3, 1686, 1691-4, 1701, 1704, 1707, 1712-13, 1719-22, 1728-36, 1739-40,
    1742-3, 1749-63, 1767-93, 1796-1800, 1802-58, 1860, 1862-1901 **NLW**
Cop PR/BT C 1671-94, 1699-1746, 1748-99 M 1671-94, 1699-1745, 1748-99 B 1671-94, 1699-1745,
    1748-99 *West Wales Historical Records*, 7-14 (1918-29) ms PR CB 1671-90, 1699-1812 M 1671-90,
    1699-1754 **NLW**

CAERFYRDDIN/CARMARTHEN St. David   *SD*
‹St. Peter 1844
C 1841-1965   M 1842-1976 Christ Church 1873-1971   B 1841-1952 **Carm RO**
BT 1841-5 **NLW**

CAPEL IFAN gweler/see PONTYBEREM

CARMARTHEN gweler/see CAERFYRDDIN

CASTELLDWYRAN   SD
M 1754-82, 1837-1926 **NLW**
BT see Cilymaenllwyd

CASTELLNEWYDD EMLYN/NEWCASTLE EMLYN   SD
The chapel of ease to Cenarth built here *c.* 1780 seems to have been without separate PRs until the
   late 1830s. District assigned to new church 1843
C 1839-1915   B 1842-1957 **NLW**   M 1838- incumbent
BT 1874, 1885-8, 1890, 1898 **NLW**

CENARTH   SD
C 1701-68, 1775-1909   M 1701-1837 (Banns 1824-60, 1934-5)   B 1701-68, 1775-1844 **NLW**
BT 1676, 1678, 1680, 1682, 1684-9, 1699, 1704, 1799-1806, 1808-58, 1860-1 **NLW**

CIL-Y-CWM   SD
C 1701-1882   M 1701-1970 (Banns 1755-1885)   B 1701-1876 **Carm RO**
BT 1673, 1677-9, 1684, 1690-1, 1693-5, 1703, 1707-8, 1711, 1713, 1716-18, 1720-7, 1729-68, 1780-2,
   1784-94, 1796-1800, 1802-4, 1806-48, 1850-80, 1882, 1887-1900, 1902 **NLW**

CILYMAENLLWYD   SD
PR earliest reputedly used to stoke parsonage fire *c.* 1765 (NLW Facs. 75, p.7)
C 1742-1956   M 1742-1836   B 1742-1812 **NLW**   M 1837-1947   B 1813-1977   Fac C
   1742-1956   M 1742-1947   B 1742-1972 **Carm RO**
BT 1671-2, 1675, 1677-9, 1681-7, 1690-1, 1693-9, 1711, 1713, 1715-18, 1720-2, 1724-92, 1794-1800,
   1802-3, 1805-41 **NLW**
Cop ts PR CMB 1742-1812 **NLW & Carm RO**

*CONWIL CAIO/CYNWYL GAEO   SD
PR M 1754-83 recorded as being 'supposed lost' in 1831
CB 1698-1979   M 1698-1754, 1783-1970 (Banns 1783-1806, 1850-73) **NLW**
BT 1672, 1677-9, 1681-3, 1693, 1695, 1702-3, 1705, 1707-9, 1713, 1718-27, 1729-45, 1747-90, 1792-4,
   1796-1800, 1802, 1804-36, 1838-40, 1855-6 **NLW**

CROSS HANDS gweler/see GORS-LAS

CWMAMAN   SD
‹Y Betws, Llandybïe, Llandeilo Fawr, & Llan-giwg/Llanguicke 1843
C 1840-1930   M 1842-1948 (Banns 1842-67, 1887-1949)   B 1842-1959 **Carm RO**
BT 1840-52, 1854-67, 1869-74 **NLW**

CWM-FFRWD gweler/see LLANDYFAELOG/LLANDEFAELOG

CYDWELI/KIDWELLY   SD
C 1626-1809, 1813-1962   M 1626-1971 (Banns 1754-1809, 1823-71)   B 1626-1809, 1813-1947
   Carm RO
BT 1672, 1677-8, 1681-4, 1686-7, 1690-1, 1693-6, 1699, 1705, 1715, 1717-21, 1724-5, 1727-33, 1735,
   1737-59, 1761-80, 1782-1800, 1802-82, 1884-5 **NLW**
Cop ts PR CB (extracts) 1765-1809 M 1627-1753 with index **Soc Gen**

CYFFIG/KIFFIG   *SD*
PR CMB 1725-1812 recorded in 1831 apparently lost
CB 1813-1979   M 1813-1931 **Carm RO**
BT 1675, 1677-9, 1682-7, 1690, 1693-1702, 1707-8, 1711, 1715-21, 1724-31, 1733-59, 1761-75, 1777-81, 1784-9, 1791-8, 1802-40, 1842-81 **NLW**

CYNWYL ELFED   *SD*
C 1743-1968   M 1743-1896 (Banns 1842-94)   B 1743-1982 **NLW**
BT 1672-3, 1676, 1681-2, 1684, 1686, 1689-91, 1693-8, 1700-3, 1707-8, 1711, 1713, 1716-18, 1720-1, 1724-6, 1728-34, 1736-40, 1742-6, 1748-68, 1770, 1772-4, 1779, 1783-4, 1799-1800, 1802, 1805-64 **NLW**
Cop ts PR C 1813-75 **Soc Gen**

CYNWYL GAEO/CONWIL CAIO   *SD*
PR M 1754-83 recorded as being 'supposed lost' in 1831
CB 1698-1979   M 1698-1754, 1783-1970 (Banns 1783-1806, 1850-73) **NLW**
BT 1672, 1677-9, 1681-3, 1693, 1695, 1702-3, 1705, 1707-9, 1713, 1718-27, 1729-45, 1747-90, 1792-4, 1796-1800, 1802, 1804-36, 1838-40, 1855-6 **NLW**

DAFEN   *SD*
‹Llanelli 1879
C 1874-1947   M 1874-1959 (Banns 1874-1963) **Carm RO**   B 1878- incumbent

EGLWYS FAIR A CHURIG   *SD*
PR CMB 1761-1812, recorded in 1831 as being 'much decayed and very imperfect until 1805', apparently lost
M 1813-1941 **Carm RO**   CB 1813- incumbent
BT see Henllan Amgoed

EGLWYS FAIR GLYN TAF gweler/see HENDY-GWYN/WHITLAND

EGLWYS GYMYN/EGLWYS CYMYN   *SD*
PR M 1754-1812 recorded in 1831 apparently lost
C 1731-1982   M 1731-51, 1838-1970   B 1731-1984 **Carm RO**
BT 1690, 1693-6, 1698-9, 1701-3, 1705, 1707-8, 1716, 1720-2, 1725-7, 1729-30, 1733, 1739-41, 1744-51, 1753-1800, 1802-16, 1818-67, 1869 **NLW**
Cop PR C 1732-1812 M 1732-51 B 1731-1812 *Transactions of the Carmarthenshire Antiquarian Society,* 5 & 8 (1909-10)

EGRMWNT/EGREMONT   *SD*
PR all prior to 1813 recorded as lost in 1831. Diocesan records suggest that *c.* 1790 they went back only to 1778
C 1813-1968   M 1813-65 **Carm RO**   B 1813- incumbent
BT 1671, 1677-9, 1683-4, 1686, 1699, 1703, 1794, 1796-1800, 1802-3, 1805-7, 1809-10, 1812-37, 1851-2, 1863-5, 1870, 1875-6 **NLW**

FELIN-FOEL   *SD*
‹Llanelli 1879
C 1858-1948   M 1858-1976 (Banns 1858-1963)   B 1858-1956 **Carm RO**

GORS-LAS   *SD*
‹Llanarthne/Llanarthney, Llandybïe, Llanfihangel Aberbythych 1879
C 1880-1951   M 1880-1982 Cross Hands 1959-79   B 1881-1945 **Carm RO**

GWYNFE *SD*
An ancient chapelry, with CMB prior to 1812 entered in PR Llangadog
M 1837-1970 **Carm RO** CB 1862- incumbent
BT see Llangadog

HENDY, YR *SD*
‹Llanedi
C 1911-77 M 1892-1977 (Banns 1925-74) **Carm RO**

HENDY-GWYN/WHITLAND (EGLWYS FAIR GLYN TAF) *SD*
Formerly a chapelry to Llanboidy. Ecclesiastical parish ‹Cyffig/Kiffig, Llanboidy, Llan-gan, and
   Llanbedr Felffre/Lampeter Velfrey 1910. PR CB 1783-1807 M 1765-1812 recorded in 1831
   apparently lost
C 1813-1932 M 1813-1952 B 1813-1913 **Carm RO**
BT see Llanboidy

HENLLAN AMGOED *SD*
PR CMB prior to 1812 were reported in 1831 to be ‘completely decayed’ by dampness, whereas the
   imprecise return of 1933 suggests there were then extant records beginning in 1787 now
   apparently lost. Diocesan records suggest that *c.* 1790 the registers went back to 1754
M 1826-1969 **Carm RO**
BT 1671-2, 1675, 1678-84, 1686-7, 1693, 1695, 1697-9, 1702-3, 1707-8, 1713, 1716-18, 1720-2,
   1724-30, 1732-59, 1762-3, 1768-70, 1772-7, 1780-1800, 1802-16, 1818-21, 1824-5, 1827-33, 1835-9,
   1846-7, 1849, 1855, 1864, 1866-7 **NLW**

*KIDWELLY/CYDWELI *SD*
C 1626-1809, 1813-1962 M 1626-1971 (Banns 1754-1809, 1823-71) B 1626-1809, 1813-1947
   Carm RO
BT 1672, 1677-8, 1681-4, 1686-7, 1690-1, 1693-6, 1699, 1705, 1715, 1717-21, 1724-5, 1727-33, 1735,
   1737-59, 1761-80, 1782-1800, 1802-82, 1884-5 **NLW**
Cop ts PR CB (extracts) 1765-1809 M 1627-1753 with index **Soc Gen**

*KIFFIG/CYFFIG *SD*
PR CMB 1725-1812 recorded in 1831 apparently lost
CB 1813-1979 M 1813-1931 **Carm RO**
BT 1675, 1677-9, 1682-7, 1690, 1693-1702, 1707-8, 1711, 1715-21, 1724-31, 1733-59, 1761-75, 1777-
   1781, 1784-9, 1791-8, 1802-40, 1842-81 **NLW**

*LAUGHARNE/TALACHARN *SD*
C 1651-1974 M 1639-1971 (Banns 1801-47, 1857-1907) B 1645-1972 **Carm RO** Fac C
   1651-1812 M 1639-1800 B 1645-1812 **NLW & Soc Gen**
BT 1672, 1677-9, 1681-2, 1686, 1704-5, 1711, 1715, 1717, 1721, 1725-1800, 1802-39, 1841, 1854-5,
   1857, 1859-61, 1864, 1868-82, 1884-5, 1887-9 **NLW**
Cop ts PR C (extracts) 1646-1749 M 1639-1747 B (extracts) 1646-1749 with index **Soc Gen**

LLANARTHNE/LLANARTHNEY *SD*
C 1720-1891 M 1720-1909 (Banns 1754-96, 1829-47) B 1720-1953 **Carm RO** Fac CB
   1720-1812 M 1720-1811 **NLW**
BT 1672-3, 1678, 1681, 1707, 1717, 1720, 1725, 1727, 1730-46, 1748-53, 1755-89, 1791-1800,
   1802-67, 1871-81 **NLW**

LLANBOIDY *SD*
Diocesan records suggest that *c.* 1790 the PR began in 1694
CB 1751-1812   M 1751-1837 **Carm RO**
BT 1672, 1679, 1681-4, 1687, 1690-1, 1694-9, ?1703, 1707-8, 1711, 1714-20, 1722, 1724-56, 1758-74,
    1776-8, 1780-91, 1794-5, 1798, 1802, 1804, 1806-9, 1811-13, 1815, 1817-41, 1843-4, 1849, 1852,
    1864-6 **NLW**

LLAN-CRWYS/LLAN-Y-CRWYS   *SD*
PR CB 1720-1812 M 1746-1812 recorded in 1831 apparently lost
CB 1813- incumbent   M 1813-85 **NLW**
BT 1677-9, 1681, 1684, 1686-7, 1690, 1693-4, 1696-9, 1703, 1708-9, 1716, 1718, 1720-2, 1724-8,
    1730-46, 1750-1, 1754-70, 1772-9, 1781-6, 1788-9, 1791, 1794, 1809-11, 1813-39, 1841-2, 1852-5,
    1874-6 **NLW**

LLAN-DAWG/LLANDAWKE   *SD*
Diocesan records suggest that *c.* 1790 the PR went back to 1754
C 1771-1812, 1832-1963   M 1771-1812, 1815-29, 1846-1958   B 1771-1812, 1822-1962 **Carm
RO**
BT see Pentywyn/Pendine

LLANDDAROG   *SD*
C 1736-1869   M 1736-1919   B 1736-1944 **Carm RO**
BT 1671-2, 1677-9, 1681-7, 1690, 1693-7, 1701-3, 1705, 1707, 1713, 1716-22, 1726-30, 1732-80,
    1782-4, 1786-93, 1796-1800, 1802-41, 1843-65, 1867, 1869-70, 1872 **NLW**

LLANDDEUSANT   *SD*
PR prior to 1813 were reported in 1831 to have been 'partially destroyed by fire', leaving only a
    few very imperfect loose leaves 1784-1809 then extant and now apparently lost. Diocesan records
    suggest that *c.* 1790 there was here a PR going back 40 years
M 1813-1924 (Banns 1824-1966)   B 1816-81 **Carm RO**   C 1816- incumbent
BT 1677-8, 1681-7, 1690, 1693, 1697-9, 1702-3, 1707, 1716, 1719, 1721, 1724-8, 1730-1, 1735-6,
    1738-40, 1742, 1744-51, 1753-80, 1782-3, 1785-1800, 1802-6, 1809-12, 1814-67, 1871 **NLW**

LLANDDOWROR   *SD*
Diocesan records suggest that *c.* 1790 the earliest PR went back to 1694
CB 1726-1979   M 1726-1812, 1837-1969 **Carm RO**   Fac CB 1813-1957 **NLW**
BT 1671-2, 1677-9, 1681-4, 1686-7, 1698-9, 1708, 1713, 1717-18, 1720-2, 1724-30, 1732-6, 1738,
    1740-51, 1759-1800, 1802-6, 1808, 1810-35, 1837-42, 1844-56 **NLW**

LLANDEBIE gweler/see LLANDYBÏE

*LLANDEFAELOG/LLANDYFAELOG   *SD*
C 1695-1966   M 1695-1805, 1808-1970 Cwm-ffrwd 1877-1970   B 1695-1911 **NLW**
BT 1672, 1679-80, 1684-8, 1690-1, 1693-4, 1697-1704, 1707-14, 1717-51, 1753-66, 1768-99, 1802-52,
    1854-62 **NLW**

LLANDEILO ABERCYWYN   *SD*
PR CMB 1807-12 recorded in 1831 apparently lost
CB 1707-1806   M 1707-84 **NLW**   C 1813-88   M 1819-64, 1928-47   B 1813-95   Fac CB
    1707-1806   M 1707-84 **Carm RO**
BT 1672, 1675, 1677-9, 1681, 1691, 1695-7, 1699, 1702, 1715-18, 1720-2, 1724-6, 1728-30, 1732,
    1734, 1736-8, 1740-5, 1748-54, 1757-8, 1761-2, 1764, 1766-71, 1773-9, 1781-1800, 1803-6, 1808-9,
    1811, 1813-19, 1821-6, 1836, 1844-7, 1865-6, 1871, 1881 **NLW**

LLANDEILO FAWR   *SD*
PR 1679-1724 transcribed in 1955 apparently lost
C 1732-1937   M 1732-95, 1822-1961 (Banns 1754-69, 1823-1956)   B 1732-1966 **Carm RO**
   Fac C 1720-4   M 1683-1722, 1754-69   B 1679-1723
BT 1679, 1681-2, 1684, 1686-7, 1730, 1732-7, 1739-71, 1773-1800, 1802-11, 1813-38, 1840, 1842-68,
   1873-6 **NLW**
Cop ts PR/BT C 1679-1776 M 1683-1769 B 1679-1779 **Soc Gen**

LLANDINGAD (LLANYMDDYFRI/LLANDOVERY)   *SD*
Diocesan records suggest that *c.* 1790 the earliest PR here went back to 1660
C 1733-1909   M 1733-1904, 1907-65 (Banns 1823-1905)   B 1733-1911 **NLW**   Fac **Carm RO**
BT 1672, 1677-9, 1681-4, 1686-7, 1711, 1715-16, 1718, 1721-2, 1724, 1728-31, 1733-45, 1748-83,
   1785-94, 1796-1800, 1802-54, 1856-7, 1859-60, 1865 **NLW**

LLANDOVERY gweler/see LLANDINGAD

LLANDYBÏE   *SD*
C 1695-1765, 1778-1919   M 1695-1925 (Banns 1823-63, 1866-1962)   B 1695-1765, 1778-1948
   Carm RO
BT 1672, 1677-8, 1681-2, 1711, 1713, 1717-22, 1724-5, 1730-3, 1735-7, 1739-57, 1761, 1763, 1767-73,
   1776-84, 1787-99, 1802-70 **NLW**

LLANDYFAELOG/LLANDEFAELOG   *SD*
C 1695-1966   M 1695-1805, 1808-1970 Cwm-ffrwd 1877-1970   B 1695-1911 **NLW**
BT 1672, 1679, 1683-4, 1686-7, 1690, 1693, 1697-1701, 1703, 1707-8, ?1710, 1711, 1713, 1717-20,
   1722, 1724-31, 1733-51, 1753-66, 1768-99, 1802-52, 1854-62 **NLW**

LLANDYFEISANT   *SD*
PR CMB 1755-82 recorded in 1933 apparently lost
C 1784-1946   M 1784-1953 (Banns 1784-1902)   B 1813-1970 **Carm RO**
BT 1813-22, 1824-7, 1832-5, 1838-46, 1850-1, 1853-8, 1860, 1862, 1864, 1869-71 **NLW**

LLANEDI   *SD*
C 1708-1977   M 1708-1973 (Banns 1790-1913, 1932-69)   B 1708-1976 **Carm RO**   Mf CB
   1708-83   M 1708-1812 **NLW**
BT 1679, 1690, 1698-9, 1702, 1707-8, 1717-22, 1724-33, 1735-1800, 1802-56, 1858-62 **NLW**

LLANEGWAD   *SD*
C 1701-1901   M 1701-1953 Alltyferin 1900-70 St. John 1901-70   B 1701-1905 **NLW**
BT 1679, 1681-2, 1686-7, 1690, 1701-3, 1707, 1716-20, 1725-31, 1733-62, 1764-91, 1793-1800,
   1802-81 **NLW**

LLANELLI All Saints   *SD*
‹St. Elli
C 1874-1927   M 1874-1974   B 1878-94, 1930-53 **Carm RO**

LLANELLI Christ Church   *SD*
‹St. Paul
C 1898-1954   M 1887-1973 (Banns 1893-1961) **Carm RO**

LLANELLI St. Alban   *SD*
‹St. Elli
C 1912-65   M 1915-70 **Carm RO**

LLANELLI St. David *SD*
'Christ Church
C 1890-1951   M 1901-70 (Banns 1901-66) **Carm RO**

LLANELLI St. Elli *SD*
C 1684-1923   M 1684-1971 (Banns 1754-1940)   B 1684-1930 **Carm RO**
BT 1686, 1703, 1711, ?1718, 1724-8, 1730-2, 1735-1800, 1802-55, 1862-89 **NLW**
Cop M 1685-1837 in A. Mee, *Llanelly Parish Church* (1888)

LLANFAIR-AR-Y-BRYN *SD*
Diocesan records suggest that *c.* 1790 the earliest PR here went back to 1660 'but not entire'
C 1735-90, 1796-1865   M 1736-1837 (Banns 1823-1905)   B 1735-90, 1796-1844 **NLW**   Mf
  CB 1735-90   M 1736-65 **Carm RO**
BT 1675, 1677-9, 1681-3, 1685-8, 1690-1, 1693-8, 1701-2, 1708, 1711, 1713, 1716-18, 1721-2, 1725,
  1727-36, 1738-83, 1785-94, 1796-1800, 1802-60, 1865 **NLW**

LLANFAIR CWM-GORS gweler/see GWAUNCAEGURWEN (Morgannwg/Glamorgan)

LLANFIHANGEL ABERBYTHYCH *SD*
C 1674-83, 1695-1922   M 1674-83, 1695-1970 (Banns 1755-1959) St. Mary 1959-69   B
  1674-83, 1695-1904 **Carm RO**
BT 1679, 1681-4, 1686, 1707-8, 1710-11, 1717, 1719-22, 1724-30, 1735, 1739-45, 1747-59, 1761,
  1763-1800, 1802-37, 1839-66 **NLW**
Cop ts PR CMB 1675-1758 **Soc Gen**

LLANFIHANGEL ABERCYWYN *SD*
PR C 1759-1812 recorded in 1831 apparently lost. It would be reasonable to suppose that the said
  register contained B 1759-1812 although the return reported that no register of burials could be
  found. Diocesan records suggest that *c.* 1790 there was here a PR going back to 1665
M 1754-1970 **Carm RO**   CB 1813- incumbent
BT 1672, 1676-8, 1681, 1683-4, 1686-7, 1690-1, 1693-7, 1705, 1708, ?1715, 1717-18, 1721-2, 1724,
  1726-45, 1747-82, 1784-91, 1793-7, 1803-4, 1806-41, 1844, 1846, 1848-57 **NLW**

LLANFIHANGEL-AR-ARTH *SD*
C 1787-1977   M 1756-1971 (Banns 1878-1959)   B 1787-1896 **Carm RO**   Fac CB 1787-1812
  M 1813-37 **NLW**
BT 1672, 1678, 1694, 1697-1700, 1711, 1713, 1716-17, 1719-22, 1724-9, 1731, 1733-4, 1736-43,
  1745-9, 1752-62, 1764-7, 1769-72, 1775-8, 1780, 1782-3, 1785, 1787-1800, 1802-12, 1814-33,
  1835-53, 1855, 1871-3, 1875-6 **NLW**

LLANFIHANGEL CILFARGEN *SD*
C 1746-1934   M 1746-1838   B 1746-1812 **Carm RO**
BT 1672, 1677-9, 1683-4, 1693, 1757-62, 1764, 1767-81, 1783-1800, 1802-15, 1817-32, 1834, 1837-43,
  1846-62, 1866-72 **NLW**

LLANFIHANGEL RHOS-Y-CORN *SD*
C 1768-1932   M 1754-1967 (Banns 1823-1937)   B 1768-1812   Fac B 1813-1975 **Carm RO**
BT 1672, 1677-9, 1682-6, 1690-1, 1694-6, 1698-9, 1702-4, 1707, 1711, 1713, 1716-17, 1719-20, 1722,
  1724-34, 1737, 1739, 1741-2, 1744-51, 1754-6, 1758-64, 1768, 1770-2, 1774-6, 1778, 1780-1, 1785-
  1800, 1802-35, 1853-5, 1865-7, 1872 **NLW**

LLANFYNYDD *SD*
C 1692-1812   M 1692-1782, 1797-1967 (Banns 1823-78)   B 1692-1940 **Carm RO**
BT 1672, 1678-9, 1681, 1683-4, 1686-7, 1693, 1696-8, 1701-3, 1707, 1716-17, 1719-22, 1725-31,
  1733-57, 1759-73, 1775-82, 1786-1800, 1802-56 **NLW**

LLANGADOG   *SD*
C 1708-1878   M 1708-1970 (Banns 1823-50)   B 1708-1959 **Carm RO**
BT 1677-9, 1681-7, 1690, 1693-6, 1698, 1702, 1704, 1710-11, 1716-17, 1720-1, 1724-6, 1728-9,
    1735-41, 1745-84, 1787-96, 1798-1800, 1802-7, 1809-60, 1862-7, 1871 **NLW**

LLAN-GAIN   *SD*
PR CB 1772-1812 recorded in 1831 and 1760-1806 in 1933 apparently lost. A former curate of this
    parish is alleged to have given an earlier PR of unknown extent to a Carmarthen solicitor who
    had offered him £40 for it (NLW, Cwmgwili Document 638 dated 1753). PR going back 'about
    50 years' recorded *c.* 1790
C 1807-9   M 1772-1837 (Banns 1825-45) **Carm RO**
BT ?1672, 1679, 1681-3, 1694, 1696-9, 1701, 1703, 1707-8, 1711, 1713, 1717-18, 1720-7, 1729-47,
    1749-62, 1765-70, 1772-88, 1790-1800, 1802-12, 1814-37, 1842-7, 1849-56, 1858-65 **NLW**

LLANGATHEN   *SD*
C 1747-1972   M 1747-1969   B 1747-1965 **Carm RO**
BT 1678-9, 1682, 1684, 1696, 1715, 1717-22, 1725-31, 1738-45, 1753-6, 1758-91, 1794-8, 1800,
    1802-38, 1844-60, 1865 **NLW**

LLANGELER   *SD*
PR B 1805-12 recorded in 1831 apparently lost
C 1704-1877   M 1704-1801, 1813-1921 (Banns 1795-1833)   B 1704-1804, 1813-1900 **NLW**
BT 1674, 1678-9, 1681-3, 1685, 1687, 1689, 1705, 1799, 1801-11, 1813-63, 1865, 1874 **NLW**

*LLANGENDEIRNE/LLANGYNDEYRN   *SD*
PR 1665-1700 recorded in 1933 apparently lost
C 1813-58   M 1754-1960   B 1813-37   Fac CB 1735-1812, 1837-1972   M 1735-1812, 1963-
    1971 **Carm RO**
BT 1671, 1677-9, 1681-7, 1690, 1692-6, 1700-4, 1707-8, 1711, 1717-21, 1724-43, 1746-7, 1749-51,
    1753-67, 1769-94, 1796-1800, 1802-52, 1854-7, 1859-66 **NLW**
Cop ts PR C (extracts) 1665-1811 M 1671-1754 B (extracts) 1668-1807 **Soc Gen**

LLANGENNECH   *SD*
C 1742-1960   M 1742-1970   B 1742-1875 **Carm RO**
BT 1678, 1703, 1707-8, 1711, 1713, 1717, 1719, 1721, 1724-32, 1736-40, 1742-64, 1766-95, 1797-
    1800, 1802-37, 1839-40, 1842-4, 1850-3 **NLW**

LLANGLYDWEN   *SD*
CB 1765-84, 1793-1810   M 1755-1811, 1814-36 **NLW**   M 1837-1968 **Carm RO**
BT 1671-2, 1675, 1678-9, 1681, 1683-4, 1686-7, 1690-1, 1693-9, 1708-11, 1713, 1715-22, 1724-37,
    1739-47, 1749, 1752-7, 1759-90, 1793-5, 1797-1800, 1802-6, 1808-22, 1824-37, 1859, 1867-70,
    1872-7 **NLW**
Cop ts PR CMB 1755-1837 **Carm RO**

*LLANGUNNOR/LLANGYNNWR   *SD*
C 1678-1817   M 1678-1938, 1956-75 (Banns 1854-1949)   B 1678-1926 **Carm RO**   Fac
    CB 1727-1817   M 1727-54 **NLW**
BT 1675, 1677-8, 1681-4, 1686, 1693-9, 1702-4, 1708, 1712, 1717-22, 1724-36, 1738-41, 1744-1800,
    1802-11, 1813-20, 1822-64, 1866-7 **NLW**
Cop ts PR CB 1678-1726 (& extracts to 1784) M 1675-1754 **Soc Gen**

LLANGYNDEYRN/LLANGENDEIRNE   *SD*

PR 1665-1700 recorded in 1933 apparently lost

C 1813-58   M 1754-1960   B 1813-37   Fac CB 1735-1812, 1837-1972   M 1735-1812, 1963-71
Carm RO

BT 1671, 1677-9, 1681-7, 1690, 1692-6, 1700-4, 1707-8, 1711, 1717-21, 1724-43, 1746-7, 1749-51,
1753-67, 1769-94, 1796-1800, 1802-52, 1854-7, 1859-66 **NLW**

Cop ts PR C (extracts) 1665-1811 M 1671-1754 B (extracts) 1668-1807 **Soc Gen**

LLANGYNIN   *SD*

C 1736-1975   M 1756-1970   B 1736-1977 **Carm RO**

BT 1679, 1681-4, 1697, 1729, 1731-4, 1736, 1738, 1740-5, 1747-53, 1755-81, 1783-93, 1798-9,
1805-10, 1812-16, 1818-23, 1825-31, 1833, 1835, 1837, 1843, 1854-5 **NLW**

LLANGYNNWR/LLANGUNNOR   *SD*

C 1678-1817   M 1678-1938, 1956-75 (Banns 1854-1949)   B 1678-1926 **Carm RO**   Fac CB
1727-1817   M 1727-54 **NLW**

BT 1675, 1677-8, 1681-4, 1686, 1693-9, 1702-4, 1708, 1712, 1717-22, 1724-36, 1738-41, 1744-1800,
1802-11, 1813-20, 1822-64, 1866-7 **NLW**

Cop ts PR CB 1678-1726 (& extracts to 1784) M 1675-1754 **Soc Gen**

LLANGYNOG   *SD*

PR prior to 1775 'destroyed by fire' according to 1831 survey

M 1768-75, 1783-1834 **NLW**

BT 1693-1700, 1703, 1707-8, 1711, 1713, 1716-18, 1720, 1722, 1724-30, 1732-51, 1753-67, 1769-76,
1778-9, 1781-1800, 1802-12, 1814-55, 1857-67, 1870-2, 1876-8, 1880-1 **NLW**

LLANISMEL/ST. ISHMAEL   *SD*

C 1560-1890   M 1561-1920 (Banns 1929-71)   B 1560-1900 **Carm RO**   Fac CMB 1560-1761
NLW

BT 1671-2, 1675, 1677-9, 1681-4, 1686-7, 1690, 1693-4, 1696-9, 1701-3, 1707-8, 1710-11, 1713,
1716-58, 1760-1800, 1802-40, 1842-6, 1848-50, 1853-5, 1879 **NLW**

Cop ts PR M 1561-1640, 1678-1753 **Soc Gen**

LLANLLAWDDOG   *SD*

PR 1689-[1717] recorded in 1933 apparently lost

C 1718-1941   M 1718-1969   B 1718-1923 **Carm RO**

BT 1671, 1673, 1678, 1682-7, 1691, 1693, 1695, 1697-9, 1702-3, 1707, 1712, 1714, 1716-22, 1724-41,
1750, 1754-5, 1757, 1759-60, 1763-7, 1787-91, 1793-1800, 1802-12, 1814-82, 1887-94 **NLW**

Cop ts PR CB 1813-75 M 1695-1875 with index **Soc Gen**

LLAN-LLWCH   *SD*

PR CB 1779-[95] recorded in 1831 apparently lost

C 1800-59   M 1754-1970 (Banns 1824-33)   B 1796-1943 **Carm RO**

BT 1802-3, 1815-18, 1826-31, 1833-6, 1838-58 **NLW**

LLANLLWNI   *SD*

PR M 1755-1812 recorded in 1831 as being in poor condition now apparently lost

C 1739-58, 1787-1923   M 1739-58, 1813-1971   B 1739-58, 1787-1910 **NLW**

BT 1671, 1677, 1679, 1681, 1684, 1690-1, 1699, 1710-11, 1717, 1719-22, 1724-8, 1730, 1733-4, 1737,
1739-65, 1770-87, 1789-90, 1792-3, 1795-1800, 1802-17, 1819-38, 1840-59, 1864-7, 1871-2 **NLW**

LLANNEWYDD/NEWCHURCH   *SD*
PR 1719-38 recorded in 1933 apparently lost
C 1742-1980   M 1742-1970   B 1742-1975 **Carm RO**
BT 1675-7, 1681-2, 1686-7, 1690, 1693, 1696-8, 1702-3, 1705, 1707-8, 1711, 1713, 1716-18, 1720-1, 1724-40, 1743-59, 1762-70, 1773, 1775-85, 1787-99, 1802-58, 1878 **NLW**
Cop ms PR CB 1719-38, 1742-1812 M 1720-38, 1742-1838 **NLW**

LLAN-NON   *SD*
C 1679-1738, 1741-1913   M 1679-1738, 1741-1978 (Banns 1823-1945)   B 1679-1738, 1741-1971 **NLW**
BT 1681-4, 1686-7, 1690, 1693, 1695-9, 1703-4, 1716-18, 1720-5, 1727-70, 1772-1800, 1802-35, 1844-5, 1850-2 **NLW**

LLANPUMSAINT   *SD*
C 1775-1896   M 1755-1971 (Banns 1823-1953)   B 1775-1866 **Carm RO**
BT 1675, 1677-9, 1681-2, 1685-7, 1690, 1693, 1695-7, 1699, 1702, 1707-8, ?1711-12, 1715-22, 1724-41, 1750-1, 1754-5, 1757, 1759, 1763, 1765-7, 1787-91, 1793-1800, 1802-82, 1884-5, 1887 **NLW**
Cop ts PR CB 1813-75 M 1695-1875 with index **Soc Gen**

LLANSADWRN   *SD*
C 1739-1847   M 1739-1812 (Banns 1823-74)   B 1739-1812 **NLW**
BT 1673, 1678-9, 1681-4, 1686-7, 1690-1, 1693, 1695-9, 1702-4, 1707, 1709, ?1711, 1713-18, 1720-2, 1724-38, 1740-7, 1749-52, 1755-60, 1762-1800, 1802-57 **NLW**

LLANSADYRNIN/LLANSADWRNEN   *SD*
CB 1663-1812   M 1667-1969   Mf CB 1813-1972 **Carm RO**   Fac CMB 1663-1812 **NLW & Soc Gen**
BT 1677-8, 1682, 1684, 1686, 1691, 1716-21, 1727-33, 1735-44, 1746-8, 1750-95, 1797-1800, 1802-12, 1814-39, 1849-51, 1854-5, 1857-64, 1868, 1871-2, 1880, 1884-5, 1888 **NLW**

LLANSAWEL   *SD*
C 1751-1979   M 1751-1970 (Banns 1823-1919)   B 1751-1980 **NLW**
BT 1675-9, 1682, 1693-5, 1702, 1705, 1707, 1724, 1726-9, 1731, 1733-7, 1739, 1741-4, 1746-7, 1749-54, 1756-60, 1762-5, 1767-88, 1790, 1792-4, 1796-1800, 1802-12, 1814-35, 1838-40, 1849, 1855-7 **NLW**

LLANSTEFFAN/LLANSTEPHAN   *SD*
CB 1762-1812   M 1756-1812 **NLW**   C 1697-1762, 1813-88   MB 1697-1762, 1813-1971 **Carm RO**   Fac CMB 1697-1762 **NLW**   Fac CB 1762-1812   M 1756-1812 **Carm RO**
BT 1671, 1677, 1680, 1682, 1684, 1687, 1690, 1693, 1695-8, 1703, 1707-8, 1711, 1713-18, 1720, 1724-62, 1764-1800, 1802-81, 1884 **NLW**
Cop ts PR (extracts) C 1677-1753 M 1697-1739 B 1714-58 with index **Soc Gen**

LLANWINIO   *SD*
PR 1729-[66] recorded in 1831 apparently lost
C 1767-1812   M 1767-1967 (Banns 1824-75)   B 1767-1910 **Carm RO**
BT 1672, 1678, 1681-8, 1691, 1694, 1696-9, 1702, 1707-8, 1711, 1715-18, 1720, 1724-48, 1751-72, 1774-81, 1784-90, 1792-8, 1802-8, 1810-58, 1860-77 **NLW**

LLANWRDA   *SD*
PR CB 1772-1812 M 1762-1812 recorded in 1933 apparently lost
C 1689-1767, 1813-1916   M 1689-1767 (Banns 1824-70)   B 1689-1767 **NLW**
BT 1673, 1677-9, 1681-7, 1690-1, 1693, 1695-9, 1701, 1703, 1707-8, 1716-22, 1724-43, 1745-7, 1749-52, 1755-1800, 1802-57 **NLW**

LLAN-Y-BRI SD
‹Llansteffan/Llanstephan 1863. The ancient chapel here passed in the seventeenth century into the
hands of the Independents. The present church and parish are of mid-nineteenth century origin
CB 1861- incumbent   M 1863-1970 **Carm RO**
BT 1861-81 **NLW**

LLANYBYDDER SD
C 1783-1972   M 1754-1970   B 1783-1812   Fac B 1813-1984 **Carm RO**
BT 1679, 1694, 1696, 1699, 1705, 1711, 1719-21, 1723, 1728-34, 1737, 1739, 1741, 1743-4, 1748-50,
1752-5, 1757, 1761, 1763, 1767, 1770, 1772-3, 1789-90, 1793-1800, 1802-44, 1847-9, 1851, 1854-6,
1880, 1892 **NLW**

*LLAN-Y-CRWYS/LLAN-CRWYS SD
PR CB 1720-1812 M 1746-1812 recorded in 1831 apparently lost
CB 1813- incumbent   M 1813-85 **NLW**
BT 1677-9, 1681, 1684, 1686-7, 1690, 1693-4, 1696-9, 1703, 1708-9, 1716, 1718, 1720-2, 1724-8,
1730-46, 1750-1, 1754-70, 1772-9, 1781-6, 1788-9, 1791, 1794, 1809-11, 1813-39, 1841-2, 1852-5,
1874-6 **NLW**

LLANYMDDYFRI gweler/see LLANDINGAD

LLWYNHENDY SD
‹Dafen
C 1882-1946   M 1939-71 **Carm RO**

MAENORDEILO/MANORDEILO SD
‹Llandeilo Fawr 1905
C 1860-1939   M 1861-1970 **Carm RO**

MARROS SD
CB 1738-1984   M 1738-1962 **Carm RO**
BT 1813-80 **NLW**

MEIDRIM/MYDRIM SD
C 1653-1921   M 1653-1971   B 1653-1882 **Carm RO**
BT 1671-2, 1675-8, 1681, 1683-7, 1690-1, 1693-5, 1698-1700, 1703, 1705, 1708-9, 1715, 1717-19,
1721, 1724-96, 1803-57 **NLW**

MERTHYR SD
CB 1681-1980   M 1681-1970 **Carm RO**
BT 1672-3, 1677-9, 1682, 1686, 1690-1, 1694-9, 1702-3, 1707-8, 1711, 1713, 1715-18, 1720-1,
1723-36, 1738-1800, 1802-39, 1841-2 **NLW**

MYDDFAI SD
C 1653-1853   M 1653-1971 (Banns 1823-1925)   B 1653-1851 **NLW**   Fac **Carm RO**
BT 1671-3, 1677-9, 1681-4, 1686, 1690, 1693-4, 1696-9, 1703, 1707, 1709, 1718-22, 1724-88, 1790-4,
1796-1800, 1802-6, 1808-68 **NLW**

MYDRIM gweler/see MEIDRIM

*NEWCASTLE EMLYN/CASTELLNEWYDD EMLYN SD
The chapel of ease to Cenarth built here $c.$ 1780 seems to have been without separate PRs until the
late 1830s. District assigned to new church 1843
C 1839-1915   B 1842-1957 **NLW**   M 1838- incumbent
BT 1874, 1885-8, 1890, 1898 **NLW**

*NEWCHURCH/LLANNEWYDD   *SD*
PR 1719-38 recorded in 1933 apparently lost
C 1742-1980   M 1742-1970   B 1742-1975 **Carm RO**
BT 1675-7, 1681-2, 1686-7, 1690, 1693, 1696-8, 1702-3, 1705, 1707-8, 1711, 1713, 1716-18, 1720-1,
    1724-40, 1743-59, 1762-70, 1773, 1775-85, 1787-99, 1802-58, 1878 **NLW**
Cop ms PR CB 1719-38, 1742-1812 M 1720-38, 1742-1838 **NLW**

PEMBREY gweler/see PEN-BRE

PEN-BOYR   *SD*
C 1752-1901   M 1752-1970 St. Barnabas 1907-64   B 1752-1947 **NLW**
BT 1674-6, 1678-89, 1701, 1703, 1799-1812, 1819, 1823-6, 1828-80, 1882 **NLW**

PEN-BRE/PEMBREY   *SD*
C 1700-1921   M 1700-1964 (Banns 1823-1973)   B 1700-1965 **Carm RO**
BT 1671-2, 1675, 1677-8, 1681-3, 1686-7, 1690-1, 1693, 1695-6, 1698-9, 1702-3, 1707-8, 1711,
    1715-23, 1725-64, 1766-1800, 1802-15, 1817-67 **NLW**

PENCADER   *SD*
‹Llanfihangel-ar-arth
C 1883-1952   M 1886-1969   B 1883-1935 **Carm RO**

PENCARREG   *SD*
CB 1789- incumbent   M 1754-1968 **NLW**
BT 1679, 1696-7, 1699, 1702-3, 1720-1, 1728-31, 1737-41, 1743, 1756-7, 1761, 1763, 1767, 1772-3,
    1789-90, 1793-1800, 1802-11, 1813-32, 1834-64, 1867-72, 1874-5 **NLW**

PENTYWYN/PENDINE   *SD*
PR prior to 1813 were said in 1831 to have been destroyed by fire
CB 1783-1803, 1813-1977   M 1794-1978 **Carm RO**
BT 1716, 1718, 1721-2, 1724-5, 1727, 1743-74, 1776-1800, 1802-83 **NLW**

PONT-IETS/PONTYATES   *SD*
‹Llangyndeyrn/Llangendeirne & Llanelli
C 1872-1945   M 1858-1970 **Carm RO**

PONTYBEREM (CAPEL IFAN)   *SD*
An ancient chapel in the parish of Llanelli apparently restored by the Methodists for their own use
    in the eighteenth century, repossessed by the Church in the 1830s. The new church was
    consecrated in 1894
PR C 1839-[1921] recorded in 1933 apparently lost
C 1921-48   M 1838-1971   B 1835-1932 **Carm RO**

PORTHTYWYN/BURRY PORT   *SD*
‹Pen-bre/Pembrey
C 1903-79 Pwll 1924-76   M 1902-76 **Carm RO**

PWLL gweler/see PORTHTYWYN/BURRY PORT

RHYDAMAN/AMMANFORD All Saints   *SD*
C 1915-40   M 1915-23, 1935-43, 1953-70 (Banns 1915-73) **Carm RO**

RHYDAMAN/AMMANFORD St. Michael   *SD*
‹Llandybïe & Y Betws 1903
 M 1893-1971 (Banns 1892-1964)   B 1885-1958 **Carm RO**

ST. CLEARS gweler/see SANCLÊR

*ST. ISHMAEL/LLANISMEL   *SD*
C 1560-1890   M 1561-1920 (Banns 1929-71)   B 1560-1900 **Carm RO**   Fac CMB 1561-1761
NLW
BT 1671-2, 1675, 1677-9, 1681-4, 1686-7, 1690, 1693-4, 1696-9, 1701-3, 1707-8, 1710-11, 1713,
1716-58, 1760-1800, 1802-40, 1842-6, 1848-50, 1853-5, 1879 **NLW**
Cop ts PR M 1561-1640, 1678-1753 **Soc Gen**

SANCLÊR/ST. CLEARS   *SD*
C 1681-1928   M 1681-1970 (Banns 1937-76)   B 1681-1951 **Carm RO**   Fac CB 1681-1813
M 1681-1813, 1837-1959 **NLW**
BT 1672-3, 1681-4, 1686-7, 1702, 1705, 1707-8, 1720, 1722, 1726-35, 1737-8, 1740-62, 1764-5,
1769-71, 1774-81, 1783-9, 1797, 1799-1800, 1802-4, 1806, 1808-33, 1835, 1837-8, 1847, 1851, 1854
NLW

TALACHARN/LAUGHARNE   *SD*
C 1651-1974   M 1639-1971 (Banns 1801-47, 1857-1907)   B 1645-1972 **Carm RO**   Fac C
1651-1812   M 1639-1800   B 1645-1812 **NLW & Soc Gen**
BT 1672, 1677-9, 1681-2, 1686, 1704-5, 1711, 1715, 1717, 1721, 1725-1800, 1802-39, 1841, 1854-5,
1857, 1859-61, 1864, 1868-82, 1884-5, 1887-9 **NLW**
Cop ts PR C (extracts) 1646-1749 M 1639-1747 B (extracts) 1646-1749 with index **Soc Gen**

TALIARIS   *SD*
PR prior to 1813 see Llandeilo Fawr PR
CM 1813- incumbent   B 1813-1927 **Carm RO**
BT 1813-15, 1842-60, 1864 **NLW**
Cop ts CB 1802-12 **NLW**

TALYLLYCHAU/TALLEY   *SD*
C 1685-1979   M 1687-1968   B 1686-1976 **Carm RO**
BT 1671, 1675, 1677-8, 1694, 1719, 1732, 1734-9, 1747-9, 1751-3, 1755-1800, 1802-54, 1873-4
NLW
Cop ts C 1685-1846 M 1687-1968 B 1686-1893 **NLW**

TRE-LECH A'R BETWS   *SD*
C 1663-1896   M 1663-1970   B 1663-1886 **Carm RO**   Fac CMB 1663-1796 **NLW**
BT 1678-86, 1690-1, 1693-1703, 1705, 1707-8, 1710-11, 1713, 1715, 1717-18, 1720-2, 1724-62,
1764-72, 1774-8, 1780-1, 1783-90, 1792-7, 1802-8, 1810-14, 1816-77 **NLW**

TYMBL, Y/TUMBLE   *SD*
‹Llan-non
C 1932-69   M 1927-79 **NLW**

*WHITLAND/HENDY-GWYN (EGLWYS FAIR GLYN TAF)   *SD*
Formerly a chapelry to Llanboidy. Ecclesiastical parish ‹Cyffig/Kiffig, Llanboidy, Llan-gan, and
Llanbedr Felffre/Lampeter Velfrey 1910. PR CB 1783-1807 M 1765-1812 recorded in 1831
apparently lost
C 1813-1932   M 1813-1952   B 1813-1913 **Carm RO**
BT see Llanboidy

YSTRAD-FFIN   *SD*
The ancient chapel, Capel Peulin, in the parish of Llanfair-ar-y-bryn, seems to have had no PR
until it became a separate parish ‹Llanfair-ar-y-bryn & Cil-y-cwm 1875. The new church of
St. Barnabas was substituted for it in 1878
CMB 1875- incumbent
BT 1875-80 **NLW**

CAERNARFON
CAERNARFONSHIRE

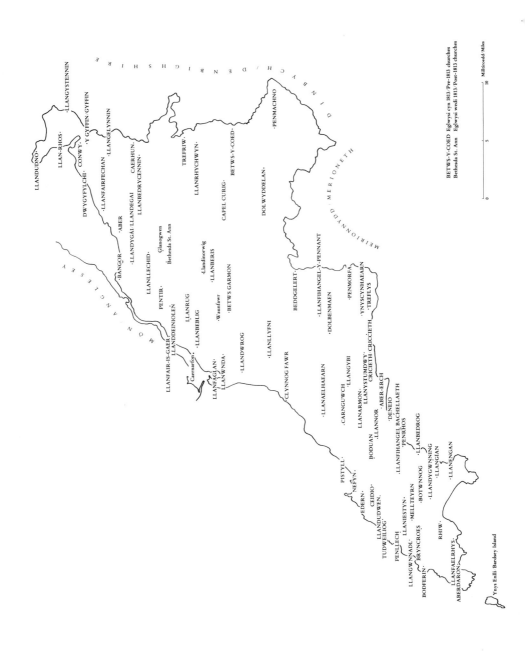

BETWS-Y-COED Eglwysi cyn 1813/Pre-1813 churches
Betbeda St. Ann Eglwysi wedi 1813/Post-1813 churches

Milltiroedd/Miles

DINBYCH/DENBIGHSHIRE

MERIONNYDD/MERIONETH

MÔN/ANGLESEY

LLANDUDNO·
·LLANGYSTENNIN
LLAN-RHOS·
CONWY·
·Y GYFFIN GYFFIN
DWYGYFYLCHI·
·LLANFAIRFECHAN
·LLANGELYNNIN
·LLANDYGÁI LLANDEGAI
CAERHUN·
LLANBEDRYCENNIN·
·ABER
·BANGOR
LLANLLECHID·
Glanogwen
Bethesda St. Ann
PENTIR·
LLANDDEINIOLEN·
LLANFAIR-IS-GAER·
Caernarfon·
·LLANBEBLIG
LLANRUG
·Waunfawr
·Llandinorwig
·LLANBERIS
·BETWS GARMON
LLANFAGLAN·
LLANWNDA·
·LLANDWROG
·LLANLLYFNI
CLYNNOG FAWR·

TREFRIW·
LLANRHYCHWYN·
CAPEL CURIG·
BETWS-Y-COED·
PENMACHNO·
DOLWYDDELAN·

BEDDGELERT·
·LLANFIHANGEL-Y-PENNANT
·PENMORFA
DOLBENMAEN·
·YNYSCYNHAEARN
·TREFLYS
CRICCIETH CRICCIETH·
·ABER-ERCH
·DENEIO

·LLANAELHAEARN
·CARNGUWCH
·LLANGYBI
LLANYSTUMDWY·
LLANARMON·
·LLANNOR
·LLANFIHANGEL BACHELLAETH
·PENRHOS
·LLANBEDROG
BODUAN
·MELLTEYRN
·BOTWNNOG
·LLANDYGWNNING
·LLANGIAN
·LLANENGAN

PISTYLL·
NEFYN·
EDERN·
CEIDIO·
LLANDUDWEN·
TUDWEILIOG·
PENLLECH·
LLANESTYN·
LLANGWNNADL·
BRYNCROES·
RHIW·
BODFERIN·
LLANFAELRHYS·
ABERDARON·

Ynys Enlli/Bardsey Island

ABER (ABERGWYNGREGYN)   *B*
C 1682-1872   M 1682-1837   B 1682-1888 **NLW**   Fac C 1682-1872   M 1682-1837   B 1682-
1943 **GASC**
BT 1676-82, 1687, 1689-1701, 1703-5, 1707-25, 1727-74, 1777-80, 1782-91, 1793-1854, 1883, 1888-
1900 **NLW**

ABERDARON   *B*
PR CMB 1700-29 recorded in 1776 apparently lost
C 1753-1804, 1813-1909   M 1753-1805, 1813-37   B 1753-1804, 1813-93 **NLW**   Fac M 1837-
1930   B 1894-1930 **GASC**
BT 1678-80, 1682-3, 1685-6, 1688-90, 1700-1, 1704-6, 1709-11, 1714-16, 1719-40, 1742-6, 1748-66,
1768-80, 1782-1855, 1857-8, 1860, 1862-4, 1890-1 **NLW**

ABER-ERCH   *B*
C 1600-42, 1673-1812   M 1600-42, 1673-1837   B 1600-42, 1673-1868 **GASC**   Fac **NLW**
BT 1677, 1679-81, 1683, 1685-6, 1688, 1690-3, 1695-1723, 1726-40, 1742, 1744-6, 1748-1865,
1867-75 **NLW**
Cop PR (extracts) C 1652-1774 M 1684-1762 B 1664-1725 J. Jones, *Gleanings from God's Acre within
the Hundred of Lleyn and Commot of Eifionydd...* (Pwllheli, 1903)

ABERGWYNGREGYN gweler/see ABER

BANGOR Cathedral   *B*
C 1727-65, 1779-99, 1825-7   M 1727-58   B 1727-67, 1776-99 incumbent   C 1813-1905   M
1754-1932   B 1813-62 **NLW**   Fac C 1727-65, 1779-99, 1825-7   M 1727-58   B 1727-67,
1776-99 **NLW**   C 1813-47   M 1754-1851   B 1813-51 **GASC**
BT 1727-8, 1740-8, 1750-2, 1754, 1756, 1758-9, 1761-2, 1764-6, 1777-91, 1793-1850, 1859-61 **NLW**

BANGOR St. Mary   *B*
Marriages prior to 1914 were celebrated at the cathedral
C 1864-1918   M 1914-26 **GASC**

*BARDSEY ISLAND/YNYS ENLLI   *B*
Formerly an extra-parochial place. Entries relating to the island appear in PR for Aberdaron

BEDDGELERT   *B*
Included township of Nanmor, co. Merioneth
C 1734-1847   M 1734-1837   B 1734-1857 **NLW**
BT 1676-80, 1683-6, 1688-90, 1692, 1695-1700, 1702-5, 1708-13, 1715-17, 1720-5, 1727-8, 1730-8,
1740, 1742-3, 1745-50, 1752, 1754-1866, 1882-97 **NLW**

BETHESDA Glanogwen gweler/see GLANOGWEN

BETHESDA St. Ann   *B*
ʿLlandygái/Llandegai 1845
C 1813-1909   B 1848-1917 **GASC**
BT 1813, 1817-19, 1822-8, 1874-83 **NLW**

BETWS GARMON   *B*
PR going back 'about forty five years' recorded in 1776 apparently lost
C 1778-1877   M 1813-37   B 1778-1947 **GASC**   Fac B 1862-1947 **NLW**
BT 1676-9, 1681-3, 1686-7, 1689-92, 1704-12, 1714, 1716-18, 1720-4, 1726-7 1729-53, 1755-80, 1782-91, 1793-1867, 1872-3, 1880-9, 1896-7 **NLW**

BETWS-Y-COED   *B*
C 1731-1907   M 1731-1836   B 1731-1885 **GASC**   Mf CB 1731-1812   M 1731-53 **NLW**
BT 1679, 1689-1701, 1703, 1705, 1707-38, 1740-80, 1782-91, 1793-1858 **NLW**

BODFERIN   *B*
The church for this parish fell into decay after the Reformation, and no records survive. It was returned in 1776 as extra-parochial appurtenant to Llaniestyn. The inhabitants attended Llangwnnadl church, but entries relating to Bodferin are also to be found in PR for Aberdaron

BODUAN (BODFEAN, BODFUAN)   *B*
C 1678-1812   M 1678-1837 (Banns 1824-53)   B 1678-1812, 1814-1915 **GASC**
BT 1677-83, 1685-6, 1688-92, 1695, 1697-1709, 1711-22, 1724-40, 1742-3, 1745-6, 1748-64, 1766-1865, 1867-85, 1887 **NLW**

BOTWNNOG   *B*
C 1741-99, 1801-12   M 1741-1811, 1815-37   B 1741-92, 1794-9, 1801-12 **NLW**   Fac C 1813-1982   M 1837-1933   B 1813-1976 **GASC**
BT 1679-81, 1686-9, 1693, 1695-7, 1699-1702, 1704-12, 1714-19, 1721-6, 1729-46, 1748-74, 1776-80, 1782-1865, 1867-87, 1890-2, 1895-8 **NLW**

BRYNCROES   *B*
C 1731-6, 1759-64, 1778-1868   M 1731-6, 1753, 1759-71, 1778-1837   B 1731-8, 1759-64, 1778-1885 **GASC**
BT 1679, 1682, 1684-6, 1689-90, 1695-7, 1699-1701, 1704-5, 1707-35, 1738-9, 1742-6, 1747 or 1748, 1749-61, 1763, 1765-80, 1782-1868, 1905-6 **NLW**

BUAN gweler/see **BODUAN**

CAERHUN   *B*
C 1662-1870   M 1662-1837   B 1662-1876 **GASC**
BT 1676-9, 1681, 1683, 1687, 1689-1701, 1703-23, 1725-43, 1745-74, 1776-91, 1793-1861, 1863-71, 1873-82, 1893-5 **NLW**

CAERNARFON (CAERNARVON) gweler/see **LLANBEBLIG**

CAPEL CURIG   *B*
'Llandygái/Llandegai, Trefriw, Llanrhychwyn, Llanllechid & Llanrwst 1866. PR CMB 1730-1812 recorded in 1831 apparently lost
C 1813- incumbent   M 1754-1837   B 1813-1924 **GASC**
BT 1754-80, 1782-3, 1785-91, 1793-4, 1796-1804, 1806-41, 1843-6 **NLW**

CARNGUWCH   *B*
Entries for M 1754-1812 are in PR for Edern. PR CMB 1772-8 for Pistyll and Carnguwch recorded in 1934 apparently lost
CB 1813- incumbent   M 1754-1861 **GASC**   Fac C 1813-1932   B 1813-1929 **GASC**
BT 1692, 1695-9, 1702-6, 1709, 1711-16, 1718-27, 1729, ?1730, 1731, 1733, 1735-8, 1740-2, 1744-69, 1771-1811, 1813-17, 1819-38, 1840-53, 1855-68, 1878-98, 1901 **NLW**

CEIDIO   *B*
'Boduan
M 1754-1810 **GASC**   Fac M 1901-23 **GASC**
BT 1790, 1813, 1842, 1844-6, 1848-50, 1855-6, 1860-6, 1868-72, 1875-85, 1887-9, 1906 **NLW**

CLYNNOG FAWR   *B*
C 1641-1894   M 1641-1755, 1786-1837 (Banns 1824-55)   B 1641-1891 **GASC**   Fac 1895-1981
   M 1837-1968   B 1891-1981 **GASC**
BT 1689-99, 1701-35, 1737-9, 1742-74, 1776-80, 1782-6, 1788-90, 1792-1865, 1867-85, 1887-95
   NLW

CONWY (CONWAY)   *B*
C 1541-98, 1605-1917   M 1541-98, 1605-1920   B 1541-98, 1605-1927 **NLW**   Fac C 1917-76
   M 1920-73   B 1927-66 **NLW**
BT 1678, ?1690, 1691-3, 1695-1701, 1703-27, 1729-43, 1745-74, 1776-80, 1782-91, 1793-1868,
   1882-3 **NLW**
Cop PR CB 1541-1793 M 1541-1754 Alice Hadley, *Conway Parish Registers...* (London, 1900)

CRICIETH/CRICCIETH   *B*
PR M 1754-1812 recorded in 1831 apparently lost
C 1675, 1688-1751, 1754-1883   M 1695-1751, 1754-72, 1813-37   B 1692-1751, 1754-1906 **NLW**
BT 1677, 1687-92, 1695-7, 1700-2, 1705-38, 1740-6, 1748-85, 1788-1885 **NLW**
Cop PR (extracts) C 1675-1798 M 1715-67 B 1696-1807 J. Jones, *Gleanings from God's Acre...*
   (Pwllheli, 1903)

DENEIO   *B*
The parish included the town of Pwllheli
C 1686-90, 1692-4, 1696-1717, 1749, 1756-1812   M 1686-90, 1692-4, 1696-1717   B 1686-90,
   1692-4, 1696-1717, 1756-1812 **NLW**
BT 1677-82, 1685-6, 1689, 1691-2, 1695, 1697-8, 1700, 1702-22, 1725-35, 1738, 1742-3, 1745,
   1749-52, 1755-9, 1761-76, 1778-1862, 1882, 1885 **NLW**
Cop PR (extracts) C 1749-88 B 1765-1837 J. Jones, *Gleanings from God's Acre...* (Pwllheli, 1903)

DOLBENMAEN   *B*
Entries for CB 1672-1773 and M 1672-1753 are in PR for Penmorfa
C 1672-1773, 1793-4, 1798-1803, 1807, 1809-1910   M 1672-1753, 1786-1837   B 1672-1773,
   1793-4, 1798-1803, 1807, 1809-1907 **NLW**   Fac CB 1798-1912   M 1786-1812 **GASC**
BT 1679-83, 1686, 1688-93, 1695-7, 1699-1703, 1705-18, 1720-40, 1742-3, 1745-6, 1748-82, 1784-
   1886, 1901 **NLW**

DOLWYDDELAN   *B*
C 1718-1896   M 1701-14, 1721-8, 1737-1837   B 1701-14, 1721-9, 1737-1896 **GASC**
BT 1680, 1684, 1686, 1689-93, 1695-9, 1701, 1703-5, 1708-11, 1713-80, 1782-91, 1793-1839, 1841-82
   NLW

DWYGYFYLCHI   *B*
PR CMB 1634- recorded in 1776 and PR C 1757-1811 B 1757-1810 recorded in 1831 apparently lost
C 1813-67   M 1813-37   B 1813-67 **GASC**   M Penmaen-mawr 1883- incumbent
BT 1678-81, 1683, 1686, 1690-5, 1697-1701, 1703-5, 1707-10, 1712-13, 1715-35, 1737, 1740-8,
   1750-7, 1759-61, 1763-80, 1782-91, 1793-7, 1799-1854, 1856-7, 1859-61, 1863-71, 1882-4, 1910
   NLW

EDERN (LLANEDERN)   *B*
C 1700-1868   M 1700-1837   B 1700-1931 **GASC**   Fac C 1868-1930   M 1837-1921 **GASC**
BT 1680-2, 1684-6, 1688-93, 1695, 1697, 1699-1723, 1725-46, 1748-66, 1768-1865, 1867-8, 1877-98,
    1901 **NLW**

EGLWYS-RHOS gweler/see LLAN-RHOS

ENLLI, YNYS gweler/see YNYS ENLLI

GLANOGWEN   *B*
‹Llanllechid 1858
C 1853-1913   B 1856-1928 **GASC**   M 1856- incumbent
BT 1882 **NLW**

GROESLON, Y gweler/see LLANDWROG

GYFFIN, Y/GYFFIN   *B*
C 1707-1901   M 1707-1837   B 1707-1887   Fac M 1837-1970 **NLW**
BT 1677-9, 1683, 1691-5, 1697-1701, 1703-43, 1745-80, 1782-91, 1793-1864 **NLW**

LLANAELHAEARN   *B*
C 1725-34, 1749-64, 1783-1926   M 1725-34, 1751-1834   B 1725-34, 1751-64, 1783-1925 **NLW**
BT 1676, 1679-80, 1683, 1688-9, 1692-1701, 1704-5, 1707-21, 1723-6, 1728-35, 1738-43, 1745-91,
    1793-1842, 1845-69 **NLW**

LLANARMON   *B*
C 1705-1812   M 1706-52, 1791-1837   B 1705-1916 **NLW**
BT 1677-9, 1681-3, 1685-6, 1688-92, 1695, 1697-1740, 1742-6, 1748-80, 1782-1884 **NLW**
Cop PR (extracts) C 1706-1810 M 1707-40 B 1707-1807 J. Jones, *Gleanings from God's Acre...*
    (Pwllheli, 1903)

LLANBEBLIG   *B*
The parish included the borough of Caernarfon
C 1699-1731, 1738-1887 St. Mary 1814-75   M 1699-1731, 1738-1898 (Banns 1823-33, 1839-66)
    B 1699-1915 **GASC**   Fac M Christ Church 1864-1930 **GASC**
BT 1678-9, 1683, 1689-1701, 1703-5, 1707-1886 **NLW**   See also Waunfawr

LLANBEDROG   *B*
C 1691-1921   M 1691-1837   B 1691-1877 **GASC**   Fac **NLW**
BT 1680, 1697-1724, 1726-37, 1739-40, 1742-6, 1748-1865, 1867-85, 1887-90, 1893-9 **NLW**
Cop PR (extracts) C 1691-1812 M 1691-1801 B 1692-1868 J. Jones, *Gleanings from God's Acre...*
    (Pwllheli, 1903)

LLANBEDRYCENNIN   *B*
C 1663-1799   M 1663-1837   B 1663-1799, 1813-1905 **GASC**   Fac C 1813-1940   M 1837-
    1970 **GASC**   Mf CMB 1663-1725 **NLW**
BT 1676-7, ?1680, 1681, 1687, 1689-1713, 1715-43, 1745-80, 1782-91, 1793-1849, 1851-4, 1856-86,
    1913 **NLW**

LLANBERIS   *B*
C 1726-1884   M 1726-1837   B 1726-1915 **GASC**
BT 1677-8, 1681-3, 1689-93, 1695-1701, 1703-91, 1793-1840, 1842-51, 1854-60, 1862-7, 1889-90,
    1892, 1894-7 **NLW**

LLANDDEINIOLEN **B**
PR CMB 1575-1643 defective
C 1575-92, 1633-46, 1660-1712, 1768-1810, 1813-32   M 1575-92, 1633-46, 1660-1712, 1761-97,
   1810-57 (Banns 1837-1902)   B 1575-92, 1633-46, 1660-1712, 1768-1810, 1813-1920 **GASC**
BT 1676-83, 1687, 1689-1701, 1703-17, 1719-43, 1745-74, 1776-80, 1782-91, 1793-1883 **NLW**

*LLANDEGAI/LLANDYGÁI   **B**
C 1674-1731, 1736-1887   M 1674-1731, 1736-1864 (Banns 1836-89)   B 1674-1731, 1736-1908
   NLW
BT 1677-80, 1682-4, 1689-1701, 1703, 1705, 1708-15, 1717-40, 1743-7, 1749-91, 1793-1889, 1891-2,
   1901-15 **NLW**

LLANDINORWIG   **B**
‹Llanddeiniolen 1858
C 1857-   M 1858-   B 1857- incumbent   Fac C 1857-1931   M 1858-1931 **GASC**
BT 1872-3, 1882, 1892-5 **NLW**

LLANDUDNO   **B**
C 1750-1917   M 1754-1881 (Banns 1853-1912) St. George 1881-1923   B 1750-1920 **GASC**
BT 1677, 1680-1, 1689-1701, 1703-8, 1711-20, 1722-7, 1729-61, 1763-75, 1777-91, 1793-1901 **NLW**

LLANDUDWEN   **B**
‹Rhiw. Entries for M 1754-1810 are in PR for Ceidio
C 1815-   B 1825- incumbent   M 1754-1810, 1837-95 **GASC**   Fac C 1815-1928   B 1825-
   1914 **GASC**
BT 1875-7, 1879-81, 1883-7, 1889, 1906 **NLW**   See also Rhiw

LLANDWROG St. Twrog   **B**
C 1593-1862   M 1593-1837   B 1593-1887 **GASC**   Fac C 1863-1932   M 1837-1935   B
   1887-1932 **GASC**
BT 1676-7, 1681, 1683-4, 1687, 1689-1701, 1703-43, ?1745, 1746-65, 1767-80, 1782-91, 1793-1855,
   1860-72, 1874, 1882 **NLW**

LLANDWROG St. Thomas, Y Groeslon   **B**
‹Llandwrog 1858
C 1856-   M 1857- incumbent   B 1856-93 **GASC**
BT 1856-75 **NLW**

LLANDYGÁI/LLANDEGAI   **B**
C 1674-1731, 1736-1887   M 1674-1731, 1736-1864 (Banns 1836-89)   B 1674-1731, 1736-1908
   NLW
BT 1677-80, 1682-4, 1689-1701, 1703, 1705, 1708-15, 1717-40, 1743-7, 1749-91, 1793-1889, 1891-2,
   1901-15 **NLW**

LLANDYGWNNING   **B**
PR CMB 1723- recorded in 1776 apparently lost
C 1761, 1765-6, 1777, 1780-1812   M 1779-1812, 1826   B 1780-1812 **NLW**   Fac C 1813-1979
   M 1837-1969   B 1813-1913 **GASC**
BT 1676-8, 1680-1, 1686, 1688, 1696-9, 1701, 1704-19, 1721-3, 1725-38, 1740, 1742-6, 1748-1865,
   1867 **NLW**

LLANENGAN *B*
C 1679-91, 1700-14, 1730-1903   M 1679-91, 1700-14, 1730-1967   B 1679-91, 1700-14, 1730-1937
NLW
BT 1677-80, 1682-3, 1687, 1689-91, 1695-1735, 1737-46, 1748-80, 1782-1885, 1887-92, 1894-6 **NLW**

LLANFAELRHYS *B*
Entries for CMB before 1812 are in PR for Aberdaron. PR CB 1751- recorded in 1776 apparently
lost
C 1811 only   M 1813-1920 **GASC**   Fac C 1813-1927   B 1813-1931 **GASC**
BT ?1677, 1678, 1680, ?1681, 1683, 1689, 1695, 1700, 1704-5, 1712, 1716, 1718, ?1721-2, 1724-6,
    1728-37, 1739-40, 1743-4, 1748-66, 1768-80, 1782-7, 1789-1865, 1867-70, 1872-4 **NLW**

LLANFAGLAN *B*
PR M 1761-1812 recorded in 1831 and M 1813-37 recorded in 1934 apparently lost
C 1602-52, 1662-1812   M 1602-52, 1662-1764   B 1602-52, 1662-1812 **NLW**   Fac **GASC**
BT ?1676, 1677-9, 1681-3, 1687, 1689-1701, 1703-5, 1708-14, 1716-50, 1752, 1754-7, 1759-74,
    1776-80, 1782-91, 1793-1878, 1881-1913 **NLW**

LLANFAIRFECHAN *B*
C 1634-1706, 1709-1908   M 1634-1706, 1709-1837   B 1634-1706, 1709-1900 **GASC**
BT 1676-80, 1682-4, 1686-7, 1689-1701, 1703-11, 1713-17, 1719-34, 1736-57, 1759-87, 1789-91,
    1793-1898 **NLW**
Cop ms PR C 1660-1810 M 1635-1812 B 1635-1812 **Soc Gen**

LLANFAIR-IS-GAER *B*
Entries for C 1813-69 are in PR for Betws Garmon
C 1675-1785 with gaps, 1785-1813, 1869-1907   M 1675-1754 with gaps   B 1675-1785 with gaps,
    1785-1813, 1864-92 **NLW**   Fac C 1785-1813, 1869-1907   B 1785-1813, 1864-92 **GASC**
BT 1677-83, 1686, 1689-92, 1696-1701, 1704-18, 1720-6, 1729-52, 1754-80, 1782-8, 1790-1, 1793-
    1803, 1805-88 **NLW**

LLANFIHANGEL BACHELLAETH *B*
C 1692-1751, 1753-1812   M 1692-1751, 1753, 1756-1836   B 1692-1749, 1751, 1753-79, 1781-
    1812 **GASC**   Fac CB 1692-1751, 1753-1802   M 1692-1751, 1753, 1756-1802 **NLW**
BT 1693-1721, 1723-34, 1736-40, 1742-3, 1745-6, 1748, 1750-80, 1782-1836, 1838-85, 1887-90,
    1897-8 **NLW**
Cop PR (extracts) C 1693-1804 M 1723-97 B 1698-1803 J. Jones, *Gleanings from God's Acre...*
    (Pwllheli, 1903)

LLANFIHANGEL-Y-PENNANT *B*
PR M 1755-1802 was copied by the incumbent in 1893 into the blank part of PR M 1813-37 not
    from the original (now lost), but from a copy made by Robert Evans, antiquary, of Beddgelert
C 1698-1951   M 1698-1754, 1813-37   B 1698-1959 **NLW**
BT 1676, 1678-80, 1683, 1688-92, 1695-7, 1699-1705, 1707-35, 1737-46, 1748-65, 1767-1885,
    1888-96, 1901, 1905-6 **NLW**
Cop ms PR M 1755-1802 **NLW**

LLANGELYNNIN *B*
C 1733-1811   M 1733-1837   B 1733-1811, 1813-1907 **GASC**
BT 1681, 1683, 1687, 1689-1701, 1703-18, 1720-80, 1782-91, 1793-1860, 1862-4, 1866 **NLW**

LLANGÏAN   *B*
PR CB 1768-99 recorded in 1934 apparently lost
C 1679-1767, 1800-1968   M 1692-1970   B 1692-1767, 1800-69 **NLW**
BT 1679, 1681-2, 1685-6, 1690-2, 1695-1732, 1734-5, 1737-40, 1743, 1745-6, 1748-73, 1775-80, 1782-1873, 1875-83, 1885-9, 1897-1901 **NLW**
Cop PR (extracts) C 1709-57 M 1710-50 B 1709-1864 J. Jones, *Gleanings from God's Acre...* (Pwllheli, 1903)

LLANGWNNADL   *B*
C 1755, 1782-92, 1814, 1820   M 1782-1837   B 1782-92, 1821 **GASC**   Fac B 1813-1969 **GASC**
BT 1677-8, 1680-2, 1689-90, 1692-3, 1695-1705, 1707-35, 1738, 1745, 1749-60, 1763-71, 1773-6, 1778-88, 1790-1868, 1873-4 **NLW**

LLANGYBI   *B*
C 1695-1751, 1754-1813, 1822, 1828   M 1695-1751, 1754-1837   B 1695-1751, 1754-1881 **NLW**
BT 1678, 1682-3, 1685-6, 1688-90, 1692, 1697-1706, 1708-34, 1737-46, 1748-80, 1782, 1784-1865, 1867-81 **NLW**
Cop PR (extracts) C 1701-1812 M 1708-49 B 1703-1874 J. Jones, *Gleanings from God's Acre...* (Pwllheli, 1903)

LLANGYSTENNIN   *SA*
C 1608-41, 1661-1934   M 1608-41, 1661-1970   B 1608-41, 1661-1958 **NLW**
BT 1674-5, 1677-81, 1684-96, 1698-1708, 1710-12, 1717, 1722-7, 1729-31, 1733-1843, 1850 **NLW**
Mf **CROH & CROR**

LLANIESTYN   *B*
CB 1765-1812 **NLW**   C 1813-50   M 1754-1837   B 1813-63 **GASC**   Fac M 1837-1970 (Banns 1824-5, 1903, 1919-81) **GASC**
BT 1676-7, 1679-83, 1685-6, 1695-8, 1700-25, 1727-31, 1734-5, 1737-43, 1745-6, 1748-59, 1761-1864, 1866-70 **NLW**

LLANLLECHID   *B*
C 1690-1737, 1741-72, 1782-1856   M 1690-1737, 1739-1868   B 1690-1772, 1782-1907 **NLW**
Fac **GASC**
BT 1677, 1682, 1690-1701, 1703-23, 1725-80, 1782-7, 1789-91, 1793-1855, 1864-5, 1885-8 **NLW**

LLANLLYFNI   *B*
PR CMB 1696-1738 recorded in 1934 apparently lost
C 1744-83, 1813-1915   M 1744-52, 1754-1882   B 1744-83, 1813-1924 **NLW**   Fac **GASC**
BT 1679, 1681-3, 1687, 1689-1701, 1703-5, 1707-38, 1740-3, 1746-74, 1776-80, 1782-91, 1793-1859, 1863-4, 1882, 1887-8 **NLW**

LLANNOR   *B*
PR at NLW is a draft of originals in GASC, with some variation in entries
C 1724-1802   B 1755-1801 **NLW**   Fac **GASC**   C 1756-1812   M 1755-1837   B 1756-1812 **GASC**   Fac CB 1756-1812 **NLW**
BT 1677-8, 1680-3, 1685-6, 1692, 1695-6, 1698, 1700-26, ?1727, 1729, 1731-3, 1735, 1737-40, 1742-3, 1745, 1750, 1755-73, 1775-80, 1782-1862, 1883-5 **NLW**
Cop PR (extracts) C 1757-1811 B 1760-1803 J. Jones, *Gleanings from God's Acre...* (Pwllheli, 1903)

LLAN-RHOS (EGLWYS-RHOS)   *SA*
C 1758-1898   M 1754-1920 (Banns 1901-33)   B 1758-1916 **GASC**
BT 1668, 1673-4, 1676, 1678, 1681-2, 1687-95, 1698-1716, 1718-1847 **NLW**   Mf **CROH &**
   CROR

LLANRHYCHWYN   *B*
Entries for CMB 1594-1812 are in PR for Trefriw
C 1594-1666, 1767-1812   M 1594-1666, 1754-1837   B 1594-1666, 1767-1812 **GASC**   Fac
   CMB 1594-1627 **NLW**   Fac B 1813-1948 **GASC**
BT 1667, 1676, 1679-80, 1682-3, 1687, 1689, 1693-6, ?1704, 1705-10, 1712-24, 1727-80, 1782-91,
   1793-1858 **NLW**

LLANRUG   *B*
C 1674-96, 1737-1882   M 1674-96, 1737-1922 (Banns 1849-1935)   B 1674-96, 1737-1923 **GASC**
BT 1678-81, 1684, 1687, 1689-1701, 1704-5, 1707-8, 1711-39, 1741-2, 1744-74, 1776-80, 1782-7,
   1789-91, 1793-1867, 1869-74, 1883-1900 **NLW**

LLANWNDA   *B*
C 1600-4, 1606-8, 1615-53, 1662-90, 1753-9, 1770-1902   M 1602, 1605, 1610, 1615-52, 1659-60,
   1676-90, 1753-1809, 1813-37   B 1623-4, 1627-43, 1662-90, 1753-9, 1770-1873 **NLW**   Fac
   GASC   Fac M 1837-1970 **GASC & NLW**
BT 1676-8, 1681, 1683, 1687, 1689-92, 1694-9, 1701, 1703-5, 1708-27, 1729-80, 1783-91, 1793-1809,
   1811-78, 1881-1913 **NLW**

LLANYSTUMDWY   *B*
C 1596-1603, 1606-41, 1647-51, 1653-6, 1658-73, 1675-1724, 1726-35, 1738-66, 1783-97, 1799, 1804,
   1813-91   M 1596-1603, 1607-41, 1648-51, 1663-73, 1675-1724, 1726-30, 1733, 1735, 1738-47,
   1754-1837   B 1596-1603, 1606-41, 1648-53, 1656, 1659, 1662-73, 1675-1724, 1726-35, 1738-68,
   1783-97, 1799, 1803, 1813-1920 **NLW**   Fac (with gaps to 1813) C 1763-1891   M 1763-1837
   B 1763-1920 **GASC**
BT 1676-8, 1680-3, 1685-6, 1688-91, 1693, 1696-8, 1700, 1702, 1704-22, 1725-33, 1735, 1737-46,
   1748-73, 1775-80, 1782-1864, 1867, 1872-85 **NLW**
Cop PR (extracts) C 1658-1845 M 1664-1793 B 1662-1902 J. Jones, *Gleanings from God's Acre...*
   (Pwllheli, 1903)

LLYSFAEN gweler/see Sir Ddinbych/Denbighshire

MELLTEYRN   *B*
C 1741-2, 1744-52, 1763-1812   M 1741-2, 1744-52, 1763-1836   B 1742, 1744-52, 1763-1812
   NLW   Fac C 1813-1976   M 1837-1969   B 1813-1981 **GASC**
BT 1677, 1679, 1681, 1688-91, 1693, 1695-6, 1699-1704, 1706-12, 1714-16, 1718-19, 1721-46,
   1748-73, 1775, 1777-1865, 1867-82, 1884-7, 1890-2, 1895-7 **NLW**

NEFYN (NEVIN)   *B*
C 1692, 1694-1707, 1709, 1712-1813   M 1694-1707, 1712-1812   B 1694-1707, 1712-1813 **NLW**
   C 1813-97   M 1812-1927   B 1813-96 **GASC**   Fac C 1876-1929 **GASC**
BT 1678-83, 1685-6, 1688-92, 1695-8, 1700-27, 1729-38, 1741-3, 1745-6, 1748-61, 1763-75, 1777,
   1779, 1781-1865, 1867, 1889-90, 1894-5 **NLW**

NEFYN St. Mary, Morfa Nefyn   *B*
C 1876- incumbent   M 1873-1915   B 1873-1922 **GASC**   Fac C 1876-1929 **GASC**

PENLLECH *B*
C 1785-1930   M 1786-1922   B 1785-1813 **GASC**
BT 1676-9, 1681-2, 1689-93, 1695-1705, 1707-21, 1723-30, 1732-8, 1740, 1742-6, 1748-65, 1767-1865, 1867-84 **NLW**

PENMACHNO *B*
PR CMB 1598- recorded in 1776 apparently lost
C 1710-1867   M 1714-1838   B 1785-1898 **GASC**
BT 1692-3, 1695-7, 1701, 1703, 1705, 1714-21, 1723-43, 1745-80, 1782-3, 1785-91, 1793-1861, 1872, 1875-82, 1888-98 **NLW**

PENMAEN-MAWR gweler/see DWYGYFYLCHI

PENMORFA *B*
C 1672-1812   M 1672-1812, 1836-7   B 1672-1904 **NLW**   Fac C 1672-1970   M 1672-1812, 1836-65, 1972-81   B 1672-1971 **GASC**
BT 1676-7, 1679-81, 1683, 1686-92, 1695, 1697, 1701-35, 1737-40, 1742-3, 1745-6, 1748-82, 1784-1803, 1805-86, 1901 **NLW**

PENRHOS *B*
‹Aber-erch 1876. Entries for CMB before 1812 are in PR for Aber-erch
CB 1813- incumbent   M 1814-36 **GASC**   Fac C 1813-1944   B 1813-1930 **GASC**   Fac C 1813-1944   M 1814-36   B 1813-1930 **NLW**
BT 1815, 1818-81, 1883, 1885 **NLW**

PENTIR *B*
‹Bangor. PR CMB 1574- recorded in 1776 apparently lost
C 1619-52, 1666-1708   M 1619-47, 1683-1708   B 1616-44, 1664-1712 with gaps **British Library** Add MS 32644   C 1813-57   B 1813-1910 **GASC**   C 1857-   M 1903-   B 1910- incumbent   Fac C 1619-52, 1666-1708   M 1619-47, 1683-1708   B 1616-44, 1664-1712 with gaps **NLW**   Mf C 1619-52, 1666-1708   M 1619-47, 1683-1708   B 1616-44, 1664-1712 with gaps **GASC**
BT 1804, 1813-28, 1830-45, 1847-54 **NLW**

PISTYLL *B*
Entries for M 1754-1812 are in PR for Edern. PR CMB 1772-8 for Pistyll and Carnguwch recorded in 1934 apparently lost
CB 1813- incumbent   M 1813-37 **GASC**   Fac C 1813-1932   M 1837-1931   B 1813-1929 **GASC**
BT 1680, 1682, 1685-6, 1695-1725, 1727-43, 1745-6, 1748-1822, 1824-65, 1867-9, 1877-98, 1901 **NLW**

PORTHMADOG/PORTMADOC gweler/see YNYSCYNHAEARN

PWLLHELI gweler/see DENEIO

RHIW *B*
C 1782-1812   M 1782-1837   B 1782-1812 **GASC**   Fac C 1813-1930   M 1837-1931   B 1813-1931 **GASC**
BT 1676, 1679, 1681-3, 1685, 1689-90, 1692, 1696, 1699-1703, 1705, 1708-27, 1730-1, 1733-5, 1737-46, 1748-80, 1782-1885 **NLW**

TREFLYS   *B*
PR CMB 1692- recorded in 1776 and PR CMB 1767-1812 recorded in 1831 apparently lost
CB 1813- incumbent   M 1813-37, 1934 **NLW**   Fac C 1813-1963   B 1813-1935 **NLW**
BT 1705, 1707-35, 1737-40, 1742-6, 1749, 1751-7, 1759-80, 1782-7, 1789-90, 1792-3, 1795-1861,
    1863-82, 1884-5 **NLW**

TREFRIW   *B*
PR CMB 1733-67 recorded in 1934 apparently lost
C 1594-1666, 1767-1812   M 1594-1666, 1754-1837   B 1594-1666, 1767-1892 **GASC**   Fac
    CMB 1594-1627 **NLW**   Fac C 1813-1937   M 1837-1969 **GASC**
BT 1679-81, 1683, 1687, 1689-90, 1705-10, 1712-24, 1726-80, 1782-91, 1793-1858 **NLW**

TUDWEILIOG   *B*
C 1780-1812   M 1759-1812, 1815-37   B 1780-1889 **GASC**   Fac C 1813-1931   M 1837-
    1932   B 1891-1931 **GASC**
BT 1690, 1698, 1701, 1704, 1710-13, 1717-19, 1721-5, 1727-36, 1738-9, 1741, 1744-6, 1749-73,
    1775-88, 1790-1885, 1887-94 **NLW**

WAUNFAWR   *B*
‹Llanbeblig 1881
C 1878-   M 1881- incumbent
BT 1878-89, 1896 **NLW**

YNYSCYNHAEARN   *B*
The parish included the town of Porthmadog (Portmadoc), registers for which (C 1872- and M
    1886-) are with the incumbent. PR CMB 1692- recorded in 1776 apparently lost
C 1772-1872   M 1754-1886   B 1772-1875 **NLW**   Fac C 1772-1970   M 1754-1886, 1889-
    1969   B 1772-1955 **GASC**
BT 1692, 1696, 1698, 1702, 1704-46, 1748-52, 1754-1865, 1867-8, 1870, 1885-92 **NLW**

YNYS ENLLI/BARDSEY ISLAND   *B*
Formerly an extra-parochial place. Entries relating to the island appear in PR for Aberdaron

DINBYCH
DENBIGHSHIRE

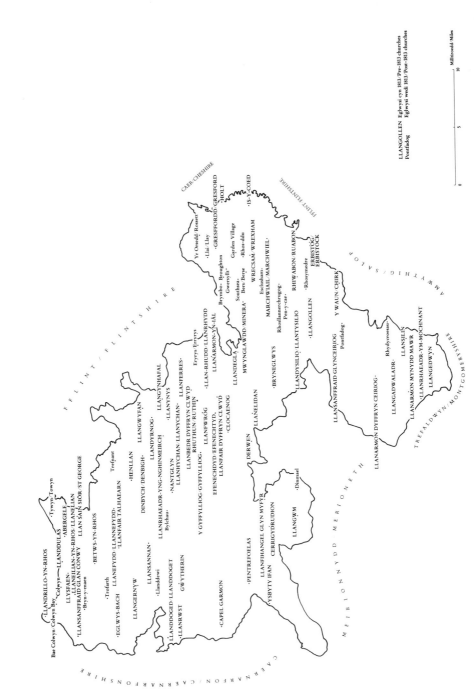

CAER/CHESHIRE

FFLINT/FLINTSHIRE

TREFALDWYN/MONTGOMERYSHIRE

MEIRIONNYDD MERIONETH

CAERNARFON/CAERNARFONSHIRE

AMWYTHIG/SALOP

GRESFFORDD/GRESFORD
HOLT
IS-Y-COED
Yr Orsedd/Rossett
Llai/Llay
Brymbo· Broughton
Gwersyllt·   Garden Village
Southsea·   Rhos-ddu
Bers Berse   WRECSAM/WREXHAM
Esclusham·
MARCHWIAIL/MARCHWIEL·
Pen-y-cae·
Rhosllannerchrugog·
Rhiwabon/Ruabon
Rhosymedre·   ERBISTOG/
ERBISTOCK
MWYNGLAWDD/MINERA·
LLANDEGLA·
LLAN-RHUDD/ LLANRHYDD
LLANARMON-YN-IAL
Eryrys/ Eryrys
·LLANGOLLEN
·BRYNEGLWYS
LLANDYSILIO LLANTYSILIO
Y WAUN CHIRK
LLANSANFFRAID GLYNCEIRIOG·
Pontfadog·
LLANARMON DYFFRYN CEIRIOG·
Rhydycroesau·
LLANSILIN·
LLANGADWALADR·
LLANARMON MYNYDD MAWR·
·LLANRHAEADR-YM-MOCHNANT
LLANGEDWYN·

LLANGWYFAN·
LLANGYNHAFAL·
·LLANYNYS
·LLANFERRES·
LLANFWRÓG·
LLANBEDR DYFFRYN CLWYD
RHUTHUN/RUTHIN
·LLANHYCHAN/LLANYCHAN·
·NANTGLYN
LLANFAIR DYFFRYN CLWYD
EFENECHDYD EFENECHTYD,
·CLOCAENOG
Bylchau·
LLANRHAEADR-YNG-NGHINMEIRCH·
LLANDYRNOG·
DINBYCH DENBIGH·
·HENLLAN
LLANGWYFAN·
DERWEN·
·LLANÉLIDAN

·Trefnant
LLANGERNYW
LLANSANNAN·
·Llanddewi
LLANEFYDD LLANNEFYDD·
·LLANFAIR TALHAEARN
LLANDRILLO-YN-RHOS
·Colwyn——LLANDDULAS
LLYSFAEN·   ·ABERGELE
·LLANELIAN-YN-RHOS /LLANELIAN
·LLANSANFFRAID GLAN CONWY LLAN SAIN SIÔR/ST GEORGE
·Bryn-y-maen
·BETWS-YN-RHOS
·Tywyn Towyn
Bae Colwyn/ Colwyn Bay

·Trofarth
EGLWYS-BACH·
·YSBYTY IFAN
·LLANRWST
·LLANDDOGET /LLANDDOGED
GWYTHERIN·
·PENTREFOELAS
LLANFIHANGEL GLYN MYFYR·
CERRIGYDRUDION·
LLANGWM·
·Dinmael
·CAPEL GARMON

DINBYCH/DENBIGHSHIRE

ABERGELE   *SA*
C 1647-1889   M 1659-1928   B 1647-1904 **NLW**   Mf **CROH & CROR**
BT 1665-8, 1670, 1672-5, 1677, 1679-80, 1682, 1684-7, 1689-96, 1698-1701, 1704, 1706-15, 1722-1842, 1844-5, 1848-51 **NLW**   Mf 1783-1851 **CROH & CROR**
Cop ms PR (extracts) CMB 1647-1883 **NLW**

ACRE-FAIR gweler/see RHOSYMEDRE

BAE COLWYN/COLWYN BAY   *SA*
‹Llandrillo-yn-Rhos 1893
C 1893-1955   M 1891-1952 (Banns 1893-1936)   B 1931-64 **CROR**   Mf (excluding Banns) **CROH & NLW**

BERS/BERSE (BERSE DRELINCOURT)   *SA*
‹Wrecsam/Wrexham 1742
C 1860-1957   M 1890-1955 (Banns 1890-1957) **CROR**   Mf (excluding Banns) **CROH & NLW**

BETWS-YN-RHOS (BETWS ABERGELE)   *SA*
C 1705-1852   M 1705-1837   B 1705-1939 **CROR**   Mf **CROH & NLW**
BT 1663-8, 1670, 1672-4, 1676-9, 1681-2, 1684, 1686-94, 1696, 1698-1703, 1705-16, 1718, 1720-1833 **NLW**   Mf **CROH & CROR**

BROUGHTON   *SA*
‹Wrecsam/Wrexham 1909
C 1890-1925   M 1909-54 (Banns 1909-76)   B 1889-1927 **CROR**   Mf (excluding Banns) **CROH & NLW**

BRYMBO   *SA*
‹Wrecsam/Wrexham 1844
C 1838-1945   M 1839-1971 (Banns 1872-1935, 1949-73)   B 1838-1930 **CROR**   Mf (excluding Banns) **CROH & NLW**
BT 1839-44, 1846-55 **NLW**   Mf **CROH & CROR**

BRYNEGLWYS   *SA*
PR CMB 1682-1730 recorded in 1936 apparently lost
C 1730-1867   M 1730-1970   B 1730-1944 **CROR**   Mf **CROH & NLW**
BT 1662-3, 1666, 1670-84, 1686-96, 1699-1701, 1703-7, 1710, 1712, 1714-20, 1722, 1724-6, 1728-42, 1745-1808, 1810, 1812-50 **NLW**   Mf **CROH & CROR**

BRYN-Y-MAEN   *SA*
‹Llandrillo-yn-Rhos (Colwyn & Bae Colwyn/Colwyn Bay), Llaneilian-yn-Rhos/Llanelian & Llansanffraid Glan Conwy 1900
C 1899-   B 1896- incumbent   M 1900-70 **CROR**   Mf M 1900-70 **CROH & NLW**

BYLCHAU   *SA*
‹Henllan & Llansannan 1855
C 1857-   B 1858- incumbent   M 1858-1969 **CROR**   Mf M 1858-1969 **CROH & NLW**

CAPEL GARMON (ST. GERMAIN)   *SA*
‹Llanrwst 1863
C 1702-49, 1754-1910   M 1707-48, 1754-1969   B 1702-49, 1754-1869 **CROR**   Mf **CROH
& NLW**
BT 1696-7, 1790-1853 **NLW**   Mf **CROH & CROR**

CEGIDOG gweler/see LLAN SAIN SIÔR/ST. GEORGE

CERRIGYDRUDION   *SA*
C 1590-1846   M 1591-1970 (Banns 1824-67)   B 1590-1851 **CROR**   Mf (excluding Banns)
CROH & NLW
BT 1665-8, 1670-2, 1674-7, 1679-96, 1698-1702, 1704-16, 1718, 1720-30, 1732-58, 1760-1840 **NLW**
Mf **CROH & CROR**
Cop ms PR C 1813-31 B 1816-31 **NLW**

*CHIRK/Y WAUN   *SA*
C 1678-80, 1705-1956   M 1611-44, 1648-50, 1661, 1678, 1684, 1719-1971   B 1611-43, 1678-81,
1708-1975 **NLW**   Mf C 1678-1845   M 1611-1971   B 1611-1864 **CROH & CROR**
Fac C 1845-1956   M 1837-1971   B 1864-1975 **CROR**
BT 1663, 1666-8, 1670-3, 1679, 1681-2, 1685-6, 1693, 1697-8, 1702, 1704-1852 **NLW**   Mf 1666-
1852 **CROH & CROR**
Cop ms PR (extracts) C 1705-21 B 1708-96 **Soc Gen**

CLOCAENOG   *SA*
C 1672-1961   M 1676-95, 1709-1965   B 1672-1933 **CROR**   Mf **CROH & NLW**
BT 1676-7, 1679-80, 1682-3, 1685-90, 1692-4, 1697-1708, 1711-32, 1736, 1742-63, 1765-72, 1774-
1863 **NLW**   Mf 1813-63 **CROH & CROR**

COLWYN   *SA*
‹Llandrillo-yn-Rhos, Llaneilian-yn-Rhos/Llanelian & Llysfaen 1844
C 1838-1914   M St. Catherine 1840-1970 St. John 1905-71 (Banns 1905-35)   B 1846-1952
CROR   Mf (excluding Banns) **CROH & NLW**

*COLWYN BAY/BAE COLWYN   *SA*
‹Llandrillo-yn-Rhos 1893
C 1893-1955   M 1891-1952 (Banns 1893-1936)   B 1931-64 **CROR**   Mf (excluding Banns)
CROH & NLW

CYFFYLLIOG gweler/see GYFFYLLIOG, Y

DENBIGH gweler/see DINBYCH

DERWEN   *SA*
C 1633-1891   M 1632-1968   B 1633-1916 **CROR**   Mf **CROH & NLW**
BT 1677-80, 1683, 1686-96, 1698-1716, 1727-32, 1736, 1742-72, 1774-1842, 1844-51 **NLW**   Mf
1813-51 **CROH & CROR**

DINBYCH/DENBIGH   *SA*
C 1683-1983   M 1686-1876 (Banns 1850-1974) St. Mary 1876-1981 St. David 1897-1980 St.
Marcella (Eglwys Wen/Whitchurch) 1928-70   B 1683-1946 **CROR** Mf (excluding Banns)
CROH & NLW
BT 1671-4, 1679-87, 1689-96, 1699, 1705-8, 1713, 1722-37, 1739-1842 **NLW**   Mf **CROH &
CROR**

DINMAEL   *SA*
‹Llangwm 1878
M 1879-1969 **CROR**   Mf **CROH & NLW**

EFENECHDYD/EFENECHTYD   *SA*
C 1693-1812   M 1693-1811, 1813-1960 (Banns 1813-17, 1882-9)   B 1694-1812 **CROR**   Mf C
   1813-1983   B 1813-1981 **CROR**   C 1693-1983   M 1693-1960   B 1694-1981 **CROH**
   C 1693-1812   M 1693-1960   B 1694-1812 **NLW**
BT 1680, 1687-9, 1692-4, 1696-1711, 1713-19, 1721-2, 1724-32, 1734, 1736, 1740, 1742-9, 1751,
   1753-64, 1766-72, 1774-1836, 1855-9, 1861-4 **NLW**   Mf **CROH & CROR**
Cop ts PR C 1693-1761 M 1693-1754 B 1694-1789 **Soc Gen**

EGLWYS-BACH   *SA*
Included township of Maenan, co. Caernarfon
C 1601-62, 1695-1872   M 1601-62, 1695-1837 (Banns 1833-1918)   B 1601-1929 **CROR**   Mf
   (excluding Banns) **CROH & NLW**
BT 1666-8, 1670, 1673, 1675-9, 1681, 1683, 1687, 1690, 1693, 1696, 1699-1705, 1707, 1709, 1711-21,
   1723-40, 1742-1844, 1846-50 **NLW**   Mf 1670-1850 **CROH & CROR**

ERBISTOG/ERBISTOCK   *SA*
Partly in Flintshire. PR B 1815-75 draft only
C 1680-1918   M 1679-1837   B 1679-1812, 1815-75 **CROR**   Mf **CROH & NLW**
BT 1663, 1670-4, 1681-4, 1686-96, 1706-8, 1714, 1717-20, 1722-3, 1725-45, 1747-8, 1750-1835 **NLW**
   Mf 1671-1835 **CROH & CROR**
Cop PR (extracts) C 1680-1795 M 1682-1713 B 1680-1778 *Archaeologia Cambrensis* (1888)

ERYRYS/ERRYRYS   *SA*
‹Llanarmon-yn-Iâl 1861
C 1862-   B 1865- incumbent   M 1864-1970 **CROR**   Fac C 1862-1978   B 1865-1977
   CROR   Mf M 1864-1970 **CROH & NLW**

ESCLUSHAM   *SA*
‹Wrecsam/Wrexham 1879
C 1879-1952   M 1880-1971   B 1879-1952 **CROR**   Mf **CROH & NLW**

FOELAS gweler/see PENTREFOELAS

GARDEN VILLAGE
‹Wrecsam/Wrexham 1928
C 1929-75   M 1950-75 (Banns 1950-71) **CROR**   Mf (excluding Banns) **CROH & NLW**

GLAN CONWY gweler/see LLANSANFFRAID GLAN CONWY

GLYNCEIRIOG gweler/see LLANSANFFRAID GLYNCEIRIOG

GLYNTRAEAN gweler/see PONTFADOG

GRESFFORDD/GRESFORD   *SA*
Included townships of Marford & Hoseley, co. Flint
C 1661-1870   M 1672-1884 (Banns 1776-1836, 1848-1911)   B 1661-1887 **CROR**   Mf
   (excluding Banns) **CROH & NLW**
BT 1670-4, 1677-83, 1688-91, 1694, 1718, 1725-32, 1734-1842, ?1843, 1847, 1849-59, 1861-8, 1870-98
   NLW   1843-4 **CROR**   Mf 1670-1897 **CROH & CROR**

GWERSYLLT   *SA*
‹Gresffordd/Gresford & Wrecsam/Wrexham 1851
C 1851-1934   M 1851-1931   B 1851-1924 **CROR**   Mf **CROH & NLW**

GWYTHERIN   *SA*
PR M 1813-37 recorded in 1936 apparently lost
C 1718-48, 1750-3, 1756-83, 1785-1812   M 1718-48, 1750-3, 1756-1813, 1837-1970 (Banns 1814-22)   B 1718-48, 1750-3, 1756-83, 1785-1812 **NLW**   Mf **CROH & CROR**
BT 1667-74, 1676, 1679-91, 1693-5, 1698-1725, 1727-40, 1742-51, 1753-66, 1769-1835 **NLW**   Mf 1671-1835 **CROH & CROR**

GYFFYLLIOG, Y/GYFFYLLIOG (CYFFYLLIOG)   *SA*
C 1617-25, 1636-50, 1658-1851   M 1617-25, 1637-50, 1658-1717, 1721-1967 (Banns 1824-1940)   B 1617-25, 1636-50, 1658-1953 **CROR**   Mf (excluding Banns) **CROH & NLW**
BT 1663, 1676-7, 1682-3, 1686-90, 1692-1708, 1710-19, 1721-3, 1725-32, ?1734, 1736, 1742-72, 1774-1861 **NLW**   Mf **CROH & CROR**

HENLLAN   *SA*
C 1684-1983   M 1684-1961 (Banns 1834-1903)   B 1684-1939 **CROR**   Mf (excluding Banns) **CROH & NLW**
BT 1668, 1674, 1681-2, 1692, 1694, 1696, 1698, 1703-4, 1707-37, 1739-1849 **NLW**   Mf **CROH & CROR**

HOLT   *SA*
C 1661-1966   M 1661-1971   B 1662-1924 **CROR**   Mf **CROH & NLW**
BT 1600, 1616, 1620-1, 1623, 1625-7, 1629-35, 1637-9, 1641, 1663, 1666, 1668-71, 1673-80, 1682, 1698-1700, 1715-24, 1726-45, 1747-53, 1755-1849 **Ches RO**   1850-60, 1862-4, 1866-9 **NLW**   Mf 1850-60, 1862-4, 1866-9 **CROH & CROR**

IS-Y-COED   *SA*
‹Holt 1826
C 1749-1946   M 1750-5, 1798-1970 (Banns 1824-1960)   B 1750-1927 **CROR**   Mf (excluding Banns) **CROH & NLW**
BT 1749, 1813-49 **Ches RO**   1850-60 **NLW**

KEGIDOG gweler/see LLAN SAIN SIÔR/ST. GEORGE

LLAI/LLAY   *SA*
‹Gresffordd/Gresford 1925
C 1925-61   M 1925-71 (Banns 1925-69) **CROR**   Mf (excluding Banns) **CROH & NLW**

LLANARMON DYFFRYN CEIRIOG   *SA*
C 1625-92 with gaps, 1696-1815   M 1624-92 with gaps, 1696-1813, 1824-37   B 1624-92 with gaps, 1696-1813 **CROR**   Mf **CROH & NLW**
BT 1668, 1677, 1679, 1681-1709, 1714-16, 1718, 1720-3, 1725-42, 1744, 1746-53, 1755-1835 **NLW**   Mf **CROH & CROR**

LLANARMON MYNYDD MAWR   *SA*
C 1695-1700, 1720-1812   M 1699, 1720-1836, 1839-1923   B 1695-1700, 1720-1812 **CROR**   Mf **CROH & NLW**
BT 1672-3, 1681-3, 1690, 1704-5, 1708-9, 1714, 1716-17, 1719, 1721, 1723-35, 1737-45, 1747-67, 1769-80, 1782-1800, 1802-50 **NLW**   Mf **CROH & CROR**
Cop ms/ts PR C 1695-1836 M 1699-1836 B 1695-1812 **CROR**

LLANARMON-YN-IÂL   *SA*
Included township of Bodidris, co. Flint
C 1683-1943   M 1676-8, 1692-1969   B 1677-1937 **CROR**   Mf **CROH & NLW**
BT 1666-7, 1670-3, 1675-7, 1679, 1683-96, 1698-1708, 1710-12, 1714-16, 1719-23, 1725-1836, 1851
    NLW   Mf 1667-1836 **CROH & CROR**

LLANBEDR DYFFRYN CLWYD   *SA*
C 1650-1894   M 1683-1968   B 1650-1888 **CROR**   Mf **CROH & NLW**
BT 1676, 1683, 1687-90, 1692-1702, 1704-19, 1722-3, 1726-32, 1736, 1742-72, 1774-1816, 1818-60
    NLW   Mf 1813-60 **CROH & CROR**
Cop ts PR C 1656-1891 M 1690-1868 B 1652-1883 **Soc Gen**

LLANDDEWI   *SA*
‹Llangernyw 1867
C 1867-   B 1873- incumbent   M 1871-1955 **NLW**   Mf M 1871-1955 **CROH & CROR**

LLANDDOGED/LLANDDOGET   *SA*
Pages from first PR with entries for 1637-9 have been re-used to supply BT for 1702-3
C 1600-37, 1641-1933   M 1600-32, 1660-1752, 1754-1812, 1814-1967   B 1602-37, 1642-1812
    CROR   Mf **CROH & NLW**
BT 1673, 1675-6, 1682-96, 1698, 1702-3, 1707-9, 1712, 1718-1856 **NLW**   Mf **CROH & CROR**

LLANDDULAS   *SA*
C 1761-1947   M 1755-1971 (Banns 1824-1940)   B 1761-1941 **CROR**   Mf (excluding Banns)
    CROH & NLW
BT 1665, 1673, 1677, 1679-83, 1685-90, 1692-3, 1695-6, 1707, 1710-16, 1718-19, 1722-1839 **NLW**
    Mf 1682-1839 **CROH & CROR**

LLANDEGLA   *SA*
C 1710-1896   M 1710-52, 1754-1812, 1814-1970 (Banns 1824-1913)   B 1710-1810, 1813-81
    CROR   Mf (excluding Banns) **CROH & NLW**
BT 1663, 1668, 1670-3, 1676-96, 1698-1758, 1760-3, 1765, 1767-1851 **NLW**   Mf **CROH &
    CROR**

LLANDRILLO-YN-RHOS   *SA*
Included township of Eirias, co. Caernarfon
C 1693-1859   M 1693-1921 (Banns 1902-29)   B 1693-1910 **CROR**   Mf (excluding Banns)
    CROH & NLW
BT 1663, 1672-4, 1680-1, 1691, 1700, 1704-5, 1707, 1712-16, 1718, 1720-6, 1728-1835, 1837-8 **NLW**
    Mf 1702-1838 **CROH & CROR**
Cop ts PR CMB 1693-1713 **NLW**

LLANDYRNOG   *SA*
C 1664-1753 with gaps, 1755-1866   M 1664-1732 with gaps, 1734-1905, 1907-70 (Banns 1823-
    1959)   B 1664-1753 with gaps, 1755-1969 **CROR**   Mf (excluding Banns) **CROH & NLW**
BT 1676, 1678, 1687, 1695-8, 1700-5, 1709-10, 1714-16, 1727-31, 1736, 1742-72, 1774-1838, 1840-5,
    1856 **NLW**   Mf **CROH & CROR**

LLANDYSILIO/LLANTYSILIO   *SA*
C 1677-1717, 1721-55, 1759-1861   M 1677-1717, 1721-82, 1784-1970   B 1678-1717, 1721-55,
    1759-1969 **CROR**   Mf **CROH & NLW**
BT 1671-2, 1674-7, 1680-7, 1691-6, 1698-1701, 1703-98, 1802-3, 1805-36 **NLW**   Mf 1675-1836
    CROH & CROR

LLANEFYDD/LLANNEFYDD   *SA*
PR CMB 1721-1812 recorded in 1936 apparently lost
C 1813-60   M 1754-1964   B 1813-61 **CROR**   Mf **CROH & NLW**
BT 1665-7, 1672-3, 1676-95, 1698-1700, 1702, 1704-14, 1716, 1718, 1720-9, 1731-9, 1741-1818,
    1820-36 **NLW**   Mf **CROH & CROR**

LLANEILIAN-YN-RHOS/LLANELIAN   *SA*
C 1589-1623, 1627-33, 1637-1715, 1719-1935   M 1589-1619, 1627-1811, 1813-1971   B 1589-98,
    1627-1948 **CROR**   Mf **CROH & NLW**
BT 1666, 1671-2, 1674, 1677-8, 1680, 1682-91, 1693, 1701, 1703, 1706, 1708-11, 1714-16, 1718-19,
    1721-1840 **NLW**   1841-3 **CROR**   Mf 1672-1840 **CROH & CROR**

LLANELIDAN   *SA*
C 1686-1846   M 1697-1970   B 1695-1862 **CROR**   Mf **CROH & NLW**
BT 1676-7, 1682, 1686-90, 1692-9, 1701-32, 1736, 1742-1836, 1850-68, 1870-1 **NLW**   Mf **CROH
    & CROR**
Cop ts PR (extracts) C 1686-1770 M 1703-42 B 1694-1766 **Soc Gen**

LLANFAIR DYFFRYN CLWYD   *SA*
C 1680-3, 1691-1979   M 1691-1971 (Banns 1871-1966)   B 1680-3, 1691-1940 **CROR**   Mf
    (excluding Banns) **CROH & NLW**
BT 1683, 1689-1700, 1702-13, 1715-17, 1719-32, 1736, 1742-72, 1774-6, 1778-1864 **NLW**   Mf
    1813-64 **CROH & CROR**

LLANFAIR TALHAEARN   *SA*
C 1669-1854   M 1671-1716, 1718-1961 (Banns 1824-1907)   B 1669-1868 **CROR**   Mf
    (excluding Banns) **CROH & NLW**
BT 1668, 1670-3, 1675, 1677-82, 1684, 1687-90, 1692-6, 1699-1715, 1720-95, 1797-1852 **NLW**
    Mf 1668-1851 **CROH & CROR**

LLANFERRES   *SA*
C 1586-1810, 1813-46   M 1588-1837   B 1587-1810, 1813-59 **CROR**   Mf **CROH & NLW**
BT 1666, 1673-7, 1680-8, 1690-3, 1695-6, 1699-1700, 1703-10, 1712, 1714, 1718-31, 1733-42,
    1744-77, 1779-1837 **NLW**   1841-2 **CROR**   Mf **CROH & CROR**
Cop ts PR C 1611-1845 M 1612-1834 B 1611-1897 **Soc Gen**

LLANFIHANGEL GLYN MYFYR   *SA*
Included township of Cefn-post, co. Merioneth
C 1662-78, 1689-1812   M 1663-77, 1692-1717, 1729-1960 (Banns 1823-1963)   B 1662-1812
    CROR   Mf (excluding Banns) **CROH & NLW**   Fac C 1689-1728   M 1692-1717   B
    1678-1729 **NLW**
BT 1663, 1667-8, 1670, 1672-6, 1678-9, 1681-8, 1690-2, 1694-5, 1698-1702, 1704-15, 1718-1837,
    1842-3 **NLW**   Mf **CROH & CROR**

LLANFWROG   *SA*
C 1638-1936   M 1638-1945 (Banns 1848-1949)   B 1638-1934 **CROR**   Mf (excluding Banns)
    CROH & NLW
BT 1676-8, 1682-3, 1686-90, 1692-6, 1698-1700, 1702-32, 1734, 1736, 1742, 1744, 1746-51, 1753-6,
    1758-72, 1774-1860 **NLW**   Mf 1813-60 **CROH & CROR**
Cop ts PR CB 1638-1755 M 1638-1750 **Soc Gen**

LLANGADWALADR *SA*
C 1736-69, 1776-1813   M 1739-1967   B 1736-70, 1776-1947 **CROR**   Mf **CROH & NLW**
BT 1666-7, 1670-1, 1673, 1679, 1681-7, 1689-90, 1692-1708, 1710-11, 1713-15, 1717, 1719-37, 1739-1835, 1837-41, 1843-54 **NLW**   Mf **CROH & CROR**
Cop ms PR CB 1736-70, 1776-1813 M 1739-1836 **NLW**   ms/ts PR CB 1736-1911 M 1739-1915 **CROR**

LLANGEDWYN *SA*
C 1672-1738, 1745-97, 1813-1931   M 1697-1738, 1745-1837   B 1675-1738, 1745-97, 1813-1937 **NLW**   Mf **CROH & CROR**
BT 1667-70, 1674, 1676-9, 1681-2, 1684-6, 1688, 1690, 1693-6, 1698-1722, 1724-49, 1751-1817, 1819-39 **NLW**   Mf **CROH & CROR**
Cop ms BT CMB 1797-1812 **NLW**   ts C 1672-1847 M 1697-1844 B 1676-1868 (PR 1672-1868 & BT 1797-1812) **CROR**

LLANGERNYW *SA*
C 1570-1617, 1627-38 (misc. entries 1642-71), 1682-1734, 1779-1812, 1825-34, 1858-76   M 1570-1617, 1627-38, 1682-97, 1704-22, 1731-4, 1754-1812   B 1570-1617, 1627-38, 1684-1725, 1731-4, 1779-1812, 1825-34, 1858-79 **NLW**   Mf **CROH & CROR**   CMB 1730-79, 1813- incumbent
BT 1667, 1672-5, 1677, 1682-6, 1689-96, 1698-1701, 1703-6, 1708-16, 1718, 1720-69, 1771-1842 **NLW**   Mf 1672-1842 **CROH & CROR**
Cop PR CMB 1682-1747 (extracts) *Denbighshire Historical Society Transactions*, 18 (1969)

LLANGOLLEN *SA*
C 1623-60, 1670-96, 1699-1706, 1708-1909   M 1587-1625, 1674-92, 1699-1705, 1708-1919 (Banns 1823-1942)   B 1597-1634, 1655-64, 1670-94, 1699-1706, 1708-1971 **CROR**   Mf (excluding Banns) **CROH & NLW**
BT 1662, 1671-7, 1679-80, 1682-5, 1689-90, 1699, 1701-1806, 1808-35 **NLW**   1836-46 **CROR** Mf 1662-1835 **CROH & CROR**
Cop ts PR C 1670-1780 M 1699-1786 B 1670-1790 **Soc Gen**

LLANGWM *SA*
C 1738-1812   M 1738-1965 (Banns 1831-1940)   B 1738-1883 **CROR**   Mf (excluding Banns) **CROH & NLW**   Fac C 1813-1973 **CROR**
BT 1665, 1667-70, 1672-3, 1675-8, 1680-96, 1698-1704, 1706-7, 1710-13, 1716-18, 1720-59, 1761-74, 1776-1801, 1803-19, 1821-41 **NLW**   Mf 1669-1841 **CROH & CROR**

LLANGWYFAN *SA*
C 1723-1812   M 1729-1968   B 1728-1812 **CROR**   Mf **CROH & NLW**
BT 1676, 1682-3, 1687, 1689, 1692-4, 1696-1713, 1715-17, 1721-2, ?1724, 1727-32, 1734, 1736, 1742-72, 1774-1856 **NLW**   Mf **CROH & CROR**

LLANGYNHAFAL *SA*
C 1704-1938   M 1704-1836 (Banns 1784-1952)   B 1704-1940 **CROR**   Mf (excluding Banns) **CROH & NLW**
BT 1676-8, 1682-3, 1687-9, 1692-4, 1696-1732, 1734, 1736, 1742-56, 1758-72, 1774, 1777-1873 **NLW**   Mf **CROH & CROR**
Cop ts PR CB 1706-79 M 1706-47 **Soc Gen**

LLANHYCHAN/LLANYCHAN *SA*
C 1696-1812   M 1696-1812, 1814-33, 1838-1970   B 1696-1812 **CROR**   Mf **CROH & NLW**
BT 1676-7, 1680, 1682, 1692-9, 1701-13, 1715-16, 1727-32, 1734-6, 1743-72, 1774-87, 1790-1843, 1855, 1857-8, 1862 **NLW**   Mf **CROH & CROR**
Cop ts BT CM 1677-96 B 1676-96 & PR CB 1696-1837 M 1696-1833 **NLW & Soc Gen** ts PR (extracts) C 1750-1874 M 1751-1805 B 1750-1832 **Soc Gen**

*LLANNEFYDD/LLANEFYDD *SA*
PR CMB 1721-1812 recorded in 1936 apparently lost
C 1813-60   M 1754-1964   B 1813-61 **CROR**   Mf **CROH & NLW**
BT 1665-7, 1672-3, 1676-95, 1698-1700, 1702, 1704-14, 1716, 1718, 1720-9, 1731-9, 1741-1818, 1820-36 **NLW**   Mf **CROH & CROR**

LLANRHAEADR-YM-MOCHNANT *SA*
Included seven townships in Montgomeryshire
C 1678-92, 1695-1847   M 1682-91, 1697-1919 (Banns 1845-85)   B 1678-92, 1695-1930 **CROR** Mf (excluding Banns) **CROH & NLW**
BT 1663, 1670, 1674-7, 1679, 1681-3, 1691, 1694-6, 1709-13, 1716-1835, 1837-44 **NLW**   Mf **CROH & CROR**
Cop ts PR C 1679-1812 (extracts) 1813-46 M 1675-1839 B 1679-1858 (extracts) **CROR**

LLANRHAEADR-YNG-NGHINMEIRCH *SA*
C 1683-1908   M 1683-1971   B 1683-1863 **CROR**   Mf **CROH & NLW**
BT 1676, 1679, 1688, 1693-4, 1696-8, 1700-32, 1734, 1736, 1742-3, 1745-72, 1774-6, 1778-1842, 1844-6, 1848-52, 1854-6, 1858, 1863 **NLW**   Mf **CROH & CROR**

LLAN-RHUDD/LLANRHYDD *SA*
C 1608-1954   M 1610-1970 (Banns 1852-1958)   B 1610-1877 **CROR**   Mf (excluding Banns) **CROH & NLW**
BT 1676-8, 1680, 1682-3, 1687-90, 1692-9, 1701-7, 1709-19, 1721-32, 1734, 1736, 1742-55, 1757-72, 1774-1861 **NLW**   Mf 1813-61 **CROH & CROR**

LLANRWST *SA*
Included township of Gwedir/Gwydir (or Trewydir), co. Caernarfon
C 1613-16, 1627-8, 1632-1947 St. Mary 1891-1956   M 1615, 1626-8, 1632-90, 1692-1715, 1717-1973 (Banns 1812-1970) St. Mary 1884-1955   B 1615, 1627-9, 1632-1879 St. Mary 1891-1942 **CROR**   Mf (excluding Banns) **CROH & NLW**
BT 1665, 1670, 1672-3, 1675, 1678-9, 1683-4, 1691, 1694, 1696, 1698-1700, 1702, 1705-6, 1708-9, 1711, 1713-18, 1720-31, 1733-5, 1737-1855, 1867-77 **NLW**   Mf **CROH & CROR**

LLAN SAIN SIÔR/ST. GEORGE (CEGIDOG) *SA*
C 1694-1941   M 1696-1971 (Banns 1830-1940)   B 1694-1927 **CROR**   Mf (excluding Banns) **CROH & NLW**
BT 1663, 1665-6, 1668, 1680-1, 1684-6, 1703-4, 1706-8, 1711, 1714-23, 1726-34, 1736-46, 1748-1846 **NLW**   Mf **CROH & CROR**
Cop PR CB 1694-1751 M 1696-1750 with index F.A. Crisp, *The Parish Registers of Kegidog alias St. George...* (1890)   ms PR (extracts) CMB 1694-1874 **NLW**

LLANSANFFRAID GLAN CONWY *SA*
PR 1729-40 was destroyed by fire with the rectory in 1740. CMB 1741-4 are loose copies
C 1660-1730, 1741-1913   M 1695-1729, 1741-1837   B 1662-1729, 1741-1901 **CROR**   Mf **CROH & NLW**
BT 1662, 1664-8, 1671-8, 1681, 1683-6, 1688-93, 1695, 1698-1705, 1708, 1710, 1713-16, 1718-25, 1727-30, 1733-4, 1736-1835, 1838-40 **NLW**   Mf **CROH & CROR**

LLANSANFFRAID GLYNCEIRIOG *SA*
C 1768-1898 M 1754-1970 (Banns 1824-1954) B 1768-1891 **CROR** Mf (excluding Banns)
CROH & NLW
BT 1661-4, 1667-8, 1670-1, 1673-4, 1677, 1679, 1681-2, 1684-6, 1689, 1691-2, 1694-1702, 1704-5, 1715-19, 1724, 1726, 1729-30, 1734, 1736-50, 1753-9, 1761-3, 1765-1837, 1841-7, 1849-51 **NLW**
Mf 1662-1847 **CROH & CROR**
Cop ms PR CB 1768-1805 **NLW**

LLANSANNAN *SA*
C 1727-1888 M 1727-1967 B 1727-1888 **CROR** Mf **CROH & NLW**
BT 1666-8, 1670-1, 1673, 1679, 1681, 1683-5, 1688, 1690-1, 1693-5, 1699-1700, 1702, 1704-7, 1709-14, 1720, 1722-5, 1727-1832 **NLW** Mf 1667-1832 **CROH & CROR**
Cop CMB 1666-1812 (BT 1666-1726 & PR 1727-1812) R. Ellis, *The Registers of the Parish of Llansannan* (Liverpool, 1904)

LLANSILIN *SA*
Included township of Sychdyn, co. Salop
C 1668, 1706-43, 1751-4, 1759-1856 M 1668, 1706-1837 B 1668, 1706-1932 **NLW** Mf
CROH & CROR M (Draft banns) 1896-1913 **CROR**
BT 1666-8, 1670-4, 1676-7, 1679-87, 1689-91, 1698-1708, 1710-45, 1747-59, 1761-1846 **NLW** Mf
CROH & CROR
Cop ms PR C 1668-1838 M 1668-1837 B 1668-1876 **NLW** ms/ts CMB 1666-1913 (PR 1668-1913 & BT 1666-1759) **CROR**

*LLANTYSILIO/LLANDYSILIO *SA*
C 1677-1717, 1721-55, 1759-1861 M 1677-1717, 1721-82, 1784-1970 B 1678-1717, 1721-55, 1759-1969 **CROR** Mf **CROH & NLW**
BT 1671-2, 1674-7, 1680-7, 1691-6, 1698-1701, 1703-98, 1802-3, 1805-36 **NLW** Mf 1675-1836
CROH & CROR

*LLANYCHAN/LLANHYCHAN *SA*
C 1696-1812 M 1696-1812, 1814-33, 1838-1970 B 1696-1812 **CROR** Mf **CROH & NLW**
BT 1676-7, 1680, 1682, 1692-9, 1701-13, 1715-16, 1727-32, 1734-6, 1743-72, 1774-87, 1790-1843, 1855, 1857-8, 1862 **NLW** Mf **CROH & CROR**
Cop ts BT CM 1677-96 B 1676-96 & PR CB 1696-1837 M 1696-1833 **NLW & Soc Gen** ts PR (extracts) C 1750-1874 M 1751-1805 B 1750-1832 **Soc Gen**

LLANYNYS *SA*
C 1626-1727 with gaps, 1739-1891 M 1626-1734 with gaps, 1739-1971 B 1626-1734 with gaps, 1739-1903 **CROR** Mf **CROH & NLW**
BT 1686-9, 1692-4, 1696-1714, 1717-31, 1742-56, 1758-70, 1772, 1774, 1776-1805, 1807-66 **NLW**
Mf 1813-66 **CROH & CROR**
Cop ts PR CMB 1626-1837 **Soc Gen** ts PR/BT CB 1626-1840 M 1626-1837 **NLW**

*LLAY/LLAI *SA*
‹Gresffordd/Gresford 1925
C 1925-61 M 1925-71 (Banns 1925-69) **CROR** Mf (excluding Banns) **CROH & NLW**

LLYSFAEN *SA*
A detached part of Caernarfonshire until 1922. PR CB 1761-1809 recorded in 1831 apparently lost
C 1661-1760, 1809-57 M 1663-1752, 1755-1938 B 1661-1760, 1809-1931 **CROR** Mf
CROH & NLW Fac CB 1661-1760 M 1663-1752 **NLW**
BT 1662-8, 1670-5, 1679-83, 1685-91, 1694-6, 1698-1708, 1710-15, 1718, 1720-1844 **NLW** Mf
CROH & NLW

MARCHWIAIL/MARCHWIEL   *SA*
C 1653-1942   M 1666-1812, 1814-1970   B 1662-1908 **CROR**   Mf **CROH & NLW**
BT 1661-3, 1667-8, 1670, 1672-3, 1677-82, 1684, 1690, 1692-3, 1698, 1700-1, 1703-15, 1718, 1720-1,
    1723-83, 1785-1830, 1832-71 **NLW**   Mf 1667-1871 **CROH & CROR**

MWYNGLAWDD/MINERA   *SA*
‹Wrecsam/Wrexham 1844
C 1786-1894   M 1845-1927 (Banns 1845-91, 1894-1939)   B 1847-1915 **CROR**   Mf (exclud-
    ing Banns) **CROH & NLW**
BT 1772-1816, 1842-4, 1850-9 **NLW**
Cop ms PR C 1786-95 **CROR**

NANTGLYN   *SA*
PR M 1775-92 recorded in 1831 as 'in the possession of one Owen Morris, late parish clerk, from
    whom it cannot be obtained'
C 1719-94, 1813-45   M 1720-53, 1755-73, 1792-1967 (Banns 1871-1958)   B 1719-94, 1813-1958
    CROR   Mf **CROH & NLW**
BT 1663-8, 1670, 1673-4, 1676-7, 1680-94, 1696, 1698-1707, 1711, 1721-3, 1725-6, 1729-35, 1737-68,
    1770-1854 **NLW**   Mf **CROH & CROR**
Cop ms PR CB 1719-94 M 1720-53 **CROR**   ts PR CB 1720-79 M 1720-45 **Soc Gen**

ORSEDD, YR/ROSSETT   *SA*
‹Gresffordd/Gresford (Trefalun/Allington, Burton, Marford & Hoseley) 1840
C 1840-1944   M 1841-1939   B 1841-1916 **CROR**   Mf **CROH & NLW**
BT 1847, 1849-57 **NLW**   Mf **CROH & CROR**

PENTREFOELAS (FOELAS)   *SA*
‹Llanefydd/Llannefydd & Ysbyty Ifan 1772
C 1782-1928   M 1772-1966   B 1773-1881 **CROR**   Mf **CROH & NLW**
BT 1773-99, 1813-56 **NLW**   Mf **CROH & CROR**

PEN-Y-CAE   *SA*
‹Rhiwabon/Ruabon, Rhosllannerchrugog & Rhosymedre 1879
C 1880-1919   M 1880-1971   B 1881-1952 **CROR**   Mf **CROH & NLW**

PONTFADOG (GLYNTRAEAN)   *SA*
‹Llangollen 1848
C 1847-1951   M 1848-1970 (Banns 1906-13) **CROR**   B 1849- incumbent   Mf C 1847-1951
    M 1848-1970 **CROH & NLW**
BT 1847-52 **NLW**   Mf **CROH & CROR**

RHIWABON/RUABON   *SA*
C 1559-1945   M 1599-1964 (Banns 1838-1917, 1932-72)   B 1559, 1599-1963 **NLW**   Mf C
    1559-1828   M 1599-1827   B 1559-1832 **CROH & CROR**   Fac C 1828-1945   M 1827-
    1964   B 1832-1963 **CROR**
BT 1663-8, 1670-2, 1674, 1676, 1679-85, 1690-2, 1694-5, 1698-9, 1701, 1704-9, 1716, 1718-1861,
    1863-7 **NLW**   Mf 1663-1861 **CROH & CROR**

RHOS-DDU   *SA*
‹Wrecsam/Wrexham, Gresffordd/Gresford & Gwersyllt 1886
C 1886-1954   M (Banns 1937-42) **CROR**   M 1887- incumbent   Mf C 1886-1954 **CROH &
    NLW**

RHOSLLANNERCHRUGOG *SA*
‹Rhiwabon/Ruabon 1844
C 1853-1906   M 1854-1930 (Banns 1854-1943, 1948-52)   B 1853-1920 **CROR**   Mf (excluding Banns) **CROH & NLW**

RHOSYMEDRE *SA*
‹Rhiwabon/Ruabon 1844
C 1837-1913   M 1844-1971 (Banns 1880-7, 1892-1932, 1954-61) Acre-fair 1964-70 **CROR**   B 1839- incumbent   Mf C 1837-1913   M 1844-1971 **CROH & NLW**
BT 1851 **NLW**

RHUTHUN/RUTHIN *SA*
C 1592-1964   M 1594-1970 (Banns 1857-1959)   B 1592-1812 **CROR**   Mf (excluding Banns) **CROH & NLW**
BT 1680, 1682-3, 1687, 1689-1719, 1722-30, 1734, 1736, 1742-72, 1774, 1776-1860 **NLW**   Mf 1813-60 **CROH & CROR**
Cop ms PR CB 1828-34 **CROR**   ts PR C 1609-85 M 1608-47 B 1614-1720 **Soc Gen**

RHYDYCROESAU *L*
‹Llansilin, co. Denbigh, & Llanyblodwel, Croesoswallt/Oswestry & Selatyn, co. Salop 1844
C 1838-   M 1845-   B 1839- incumbent

*ROSSETT/YR ORSEDD *SA*
‹Gresffordd/Gresford (Trefalun/Allington, Burton, Marford & Hoseley) 1840
C 1840-1944   M 1841-1939   B 1841-1916 **CROR**   Mf **CROH & NLW**
BT 1847, 1849-57 **NLW**   Mf **CROH & CROR**

*RUABON/RHIWABON *SA*
C 1559-1945   M 1599-1964 (Banns 1838-1917, 1932-72)   B 1559, 1599-1963 **NLW**   Mf C 1559-1828   M 1599-1827   B 1559-1832 **CROH & CROR**   Fac C 1828-1945   M 1827-1964   B 1832-1963 **CROR**
BT 1663-8, 1670-2, 1674, 1676, 1679-85, 1690-2, 1694-5, 1698-9, 1701, 1704-9, 1716, 1718-1861, 1863-7 **NLW**   Mf 1663-1861 **CROH & CROR**

*RUTHIN/RHUTHUN *SA*
C 1592-1964   M 1594-1970 (Banns 1857-1959)   B 1592-1812 **CROR**   Mf (excluding Banns) **CROH & NLW**
BT 1680, 1682-3, 1687, 1689-1719, 1722-30, 1734, 1736, 1742-72, 1774, 1776-1860 **NLW**   Mf 1813-60 **CROH & CROR**
Cop ms PR CB 1828-34 **CROR**   ts PR C 1609-85 M 1608-47 B 1614-1720 **Soc Gen**

*ST. GEORGE/LLAN SAIN SIÔR (CEGIDOG) *SA*
C 1694-1941   M 1696-1971 (Banns 1830-1940)   B 1694-1927 **CROR**   Mf (excluding Banns) **CROH & NLW**
BT 1663, 1665-6, 1668, 1680-1, 1684-6, 1703-4, 1706-8, 1711, 1714-23, 1726-34, 1736-46, 1748-1846 **NLW**   Mf **CROH & CROR**
Cop PR CB 1694-1751 M 1696-1750 with index F.A. Crisp, *The Parish Registers of Kegidog alias St. George...* (1890)   ms PR (extracts) CMB 1694-1874 **NLW**

ST. GERMAIN gweler/see CAPEL GARMON

SOUTHSEA   *SA*
‹Wrecsam/Wrexham 1884
C 1914-51   M 1922-31 (Banns 1922-48) **CROR**   B 1909- incumbent   Mf C 1914-51   M
    1922-31 **CROH & NLW**

*TOWYN/TYWYN   *SA*
‹Abergele 1873
C 1873-1965   M 1877-1966 (Banns 1877-1969) **CROR**   B 1875- incumbent   Mf C 1873-1965
    M 1877-1966 **CROH & NLW**

TREFNANT   *SA*
‹Henllan 1855
C 1855-1920   M 1855-1975 (Banns 1855-1969) **CROR**   B 1857- incumbent   Mf C 1855-1920
    M 1855-1975 **CROH & NLW**

TROFARTH   *SA*
‹Betws-yn-Rhos, Llansanffraid Glan Conwy & Llangernyw 1873
M 1874-1963 **CROR**   CB 1873- incumbent   Mf 1874-1963 **CROH & NLW**

TYWYN/TOWYN   *SA*
‹Abergele 1873
C 1873-1965   M 1877-1966 (Banns 1877-1969) **CROR**   B 1875- incumbent   Mf C 1873-
    1965   M 1877-1966 **CROH & NLW**

WAUN, Y/CHIRK   *SA*
C 1678-80, 1705-1956   M 1611-44, 1648-50, 1661, 1678, 1684, 1719-1971   B 1611-43, 1678-81,
    1708-1975 **NLW**   Mf C 1678-1845   M 1611-1971   B 1611-1864 **CROH & CROR**   Fac
    C 1845-1956   M 1837-1971   B 1864-1975 **CROR**
BT 1663, 1666-8, 1670-3, 1679, 1681-2, 1685-6, 1693, 1697-8, 1702, 1704-1852 **NLW**   Mf 1666-
    1852 **CROH & CROR**
Cop ms PR (extracts) C 1705-21 B 1708-96 **Soc Gen**

WRECSAM/WREXHAM   *SA*
Included township of Abenburyfechan, co. Flint
C1618-45, 1662-1971 St. Mark 1870-1933   M 1632-44, 1662-6, 1668-1972 (Banns 1826-1968)   B
    1620-45, 1650, 1654, 1662-1972 **CROR**   Mf (excluding Banns) **CROH & NLW**
BT 1662-74, 1676-80, 1682, 1684-5, 1687-8, 1703-11, 1718-1858 **NLW**   1858-70 **CROR**   Mf
    1711-1823 **CROR**
Cop PR (extracts) C 1618-1818 M 1637-1823 B 1621-1824 A.N. Palmer, *History of the Town
    of Wrexham* (Wrexham, 1893)   ts PR C 1620-1746 M 1638-1737 B 1625-1775 **Soc Gen**

YSBYTY IFAN   *SA*
Included township of Eidda, co. Caernarfon. PR CMB 1732-1812 recorded in 1936 apparently lost
C 1813-55   M 1813-1968   B 1813-1958 **CROR**   Mf **CROH & NLW**   Fac C 1813-55
    M 1813-42   B 1813-1958 **GASC**
BT 1677, 1679-86, 1688-91, 1695-6, 1698-1700, 1703, 1714, 1725-6, 1729-30, 1732-7, 1739-43, 1745,
    1747-1804, 1806-51 **NLW**   Mf **CROH & CROR**

FFLINT
FLINTSHIRE

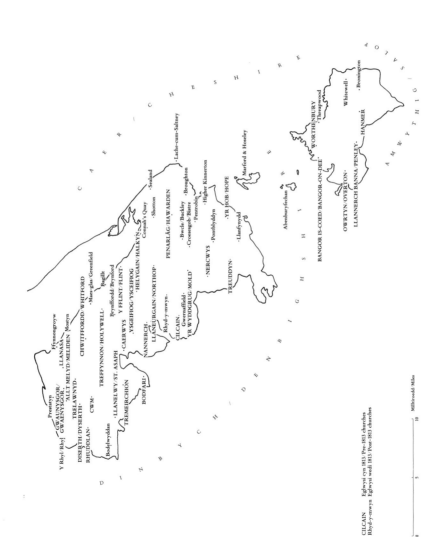

CILCAIN   Eglwysi cyn 1813/ Pre-1813 churches
Rhyd-y-mwyn Eglwysi wedi 1813/ Post-1813 churches

Milltiroedd/ Miles

ALLT MELYD/MELIDEN *SA*
C 1602-26, 1685-7, 1690-1734, 1741-1848   M 1603-26, 1687, 1692-1734, 1742-1837 (Banns 1824-91, 1893-1963)   B 1602-26, 1686-7, 1690-1734, 1741-1908 **CROH**   Mf (excluding Banns) **CROR & NLW**
BT 1668, 1672-3, 1677, 1679, 1681, 1683, 1686, 1692, 1698-1700, 1703-39, 1741-1834, 1851 **NLW** Mf 1673-1851 **CROH & CROR**
Cop PR CB 1602-19 M 1603-17 *Northern Flintshire,* 1 (1913)   ts PR/BT CB 1602-1718 M 1603-1718 **NLW**

BAGILLT *SA*
‹Treffynnon/Holywell 1844
C 1839-1954   M 1841-1943 (Banns 1915-47)   B 1839-1944 **CROH**   Mf (excluding Banns) **CROR & NLW**
BT 1839-57 **NLW**   Mf **CROH & CROR**

BANGOR IS-COED/BANGOR-ON-DEE (BANGOR MONACHORUM) *SA*
Included townships of Eutun/Eyton, Royton, Pickhill and Seswick, co. Denbigh
C 1675-1939   M 1675-1900   B 1675-1887 **CROH**   Mf **CROR & NLW**
BT 1614, 1622-30, 1632-3, 1635-6, 1664, 1666-8, 1670-1, 1673, 1675-7, 1679-85, 1690-1, 1694-1700, 1703-11, 1713-32, 1734-8, 1740-2, 1744-1848 **Ches RO**   1849 **NLW**

*****BISTRE/CROESESGOB** *SA*
‹Yr Wyddgrug/Mold 1844
C 1842-80, 1882-1964   M 1842-1974 (Banns 1898-1974)   B 1843-1950 **CROH**   Mf (excluding Banns) **CROR & NLW**

BODELWYDDAN *SA*
‹Llanelwy/St. Asaph 1860
C 1860-   B 1861- incumbent   M 1860-1959 (Banns 1936-52) **CROH**   Mf M 1860-1959 **CROR & NLW**

BODFARI *SA*
Included township of Aberchwiler/Aberwheeler, co. Denbigh
C 1571-1858   M 1571-1970 (Banns 1823-1972)   B 1572-1915 **CROH**   Mf (excluding Banns) **CROR & NLW**
BT 1662-3, 1665, 1668, 1672-3, 1676-7, 1681-6, 1707-12, 1715, 1717-20, 1722-33, 1735-1836 **NLW** Mf 1665-1836 **CROH & CROR**

BRONINGTON (NEW FENS CHAPEL) *SA*
‹Hanmer 1836
C 1837-1972   M 1852-1970 (Banns 1857-1968)   B 1837-1921 **CROH**   Mf (excluding Banns) **CROR & NLW**

BROUGHTON *SA*
‹Penarlâg/Hawarden 1824
C 1824-1940   M 1841-1950   B 1824-1962 **CROH**   Mf **CROR & NLW**
BT 1824-39, 1871-2 **CROH**

BRYNFFORDD/BRYNFORD *SA*
‹Treffynnon/Holywell & Ysgeifiog/Ysceifiog 1853
C 1877-   M 1855- incumbent   B 1877-1917 **CROH**   Mf B 1877-1917 **CROR & NLW**

BWCLE/BUCKLEY *SA*
‹Penarlâg/Hawarden 1822
C 1822-1921   M 1841-1951 (Banns 1841-1956)   B 1822-1958 **CROH**   Mf (excluding Banns) **CROR & NLW**
BT 1867-72 **CROH**

CAERWYS   *SA*
C 1673-1957   M 1674-1970   B 1674-1936 **CROH**   Mf **CROR & NLW**   Fac C 1673-1790
   M 1674-1754   B 1674-1790 **NLW**
BT 1666-8, 1672-4, 1676-8, 1680-95, 1699-1702, 1704, 1707-9, 1713-38, 1740-1842 **NLW**   Mf
   1667-1842 **CROH & CROR**

CHWITFFORDD/WHITFORD   *SA*
C 1643-1938   M 1656-1926 (Banns 1823-67)   B 1664-1882 **CROH**   Mf (excluding Banns)
   CROR & NLW   Fac CMB 1742-78 **NLW**
BT 1664-5, 1673, 1675, 1677, 1681-3, 1687, 1691-2, 1695-6, 1698-1702, 1704-17, 1719-20, 1722,
   1724-1837 **NLW**   Mf 1734-1837 **CROH & CROR**

CILCAIN   *SA*
C 1577-1875   M 1576-1970   B 1584-1875 **CROH**   Mf **CROR & NLW**
BT 1662-3, 1665-8, 1672-4, 1676-91, 1693-6, 1698-1700, 1702-53, 1755-1842 **NLW**   Mf **CROH
   & CROR**

CONNAH'S QUAY   *SA*
‹Llaneurgain/Northop 1844
C 1837-1927   M 1839-1924 (Banns 1924-36, 1947-51)   B 1837-1933 **CROH**   Mf (excluding
   Banns) **CROR & NLW**

CROESESGOB/BISTRE   *SA*
‹Yr Wyddgrug/Mold 1844
C 1842-80, 1882-1964   M 1842-1974 (Banns 1898-1974)   B 1843-1950 **CROH**   Mf (exclud-
   ing Banns) **CROR & NLW**

CWM   *SA*
C 1727-63, 1765-1939   M 1727-1971   B 1727-63, 1765-1913 **CROH**   Mf **CROR & NLW**
BT 1666-8, 1670-5, 1677-83, 1685-90, 1692, 1694-6, 1698-1700, 1702-13, 1718-23, 1726, 1728-43,
   1745-1838 **NLW**   1841, 1845-50 **CROH**   Mf 1666-1837 **CROH & CROR**
Cop ms PR CB 1727-84 M 1727-54 **NLW**

DISERTH/DYSERTH   *SA*
C 1602-26, 1636-7, 1678-1702, 1705-1811, 1813-1974   M 1603-26, 1635-6, 1678-1702, 1706-54,
   1756-1970 (Banns 1851-1974)   B 1602-25, 1636-7, 1678-1702, 1705-1811, 1813-1935 **CROH**
   Mf (excluding Banns) **CROR & NLW**
BT 1671-2, 1681, 1683, 1687-90, 1692-4, 1696, 1698-1700, 1702-12, 1716-54, 1756, 1758-1815,
   1817-24, 1828-30 **NLW**   Mf **CROH & CROR**

FENS CHAPEL gweler/see BRONINGTON

FFLINT, Y/FLINT   *SA*
See also entries relating to Flint in early PR for Llaneurgain/Northop
C 1598-1685, 1707-1929   M 1598-1685, 1707-20, 1727-1955 (Banns 1823-1968)   B 1598-1720,
   1727-1900 **CROH**   Mf (excluding Banns) **CROR & NLW**
BT 1662-3, 1670-1, 1673-4, 1676, 1678-96, 1698-1702, 1704-32, 1734-9, 1741-5, 1747-53, 1755-60,
   1762-3, 1766-77, 1779-1837 **NLW**   Mf 1663-1837 **CROH & CROR**
Cop PR (extracts) C 1599-1684 M 1607-79 B 1612-85 Henry Taylor, *Historic Notices...of
   Flint* (London, 1883)

FFYNNONGROYW   *SA*
‹Llanasa 1883
C 1884-1968   M 1884-1967 **CROH**   Mf **CROR & NLW**

FLINT gweler/see FFLINT, Y

*GREENFIELD/MAES-GLAS   *SA*
‹Treffynnon/Holywell 1871
M 1913-71 (Banns 1913-74) **CROH**   Mf M 1913-71 **CROR & NLW**

GWAUNYSGOR/GWAENYSGOR   *SA*
C 1538-1760, 1768-1983   M 1538-1970   B 1538-1757, 1768-1812 **CROH**   Mf **CROR & NLW**
BT 1664-7, 1670, 1672-7, 1680-3, 1687, 1689-92, 1694-6, 1703-4, 1706, 1708, 1712-17, 1719-38, 1740-3, 1745-9, 1751-4, 1757-97, 1799-1810, 1812-21, 1823-4, 1827-40, 1850 **NLW**   Mf 1672-1850 **CROH & CROR**
Cop ts PR C 1714-60 M 1715-54 B 1713-57 **CROH & NLW**

GWERNAFFIELD (WAUN)   *SA*
‹Yr Wyddgrug/Mold 1844
C 1838-1935   M 1839-1970 (Banns 1880-1950) **CROH**   B 1839- incumbent   Mf C 1838-1935   M 1839-1970 **CROR & NLW**
BT 1838-43, 1850-1 **NLW**   Mf **CROH & CROR**

*HALKYN/HELYGAIN   *SA*
C 1594-1648, 1651, 1654, 1657, 1661-1706, 1720-1851   M 1595-1641, 1667-1706, 1720-1970   B 1594-1643, 1666-1706, 1720-1911 **CROH**   Mf **CROR & NLW**
BT 1667, 1670-1, 1673-9, 1681-90, 1693-4, 1698-1700, 1702-14, 1719-43, 1747-54, 1756-1850 **NLW**   Mf 1670-1850 **CROH & CROR**

HANMER   *SA*
One of two missing registers was lost when the church was destroyed by fire in 1889
C 1563-1642, 1646-9, 1653-1960   M 1563-1642, 1646-9, 1653-1787, 1813-37 (Banns 1824-81, 1889-1934)   B 1563-1642, 1646-9, 1653-1856, 1884-1935 **CROH**   Mf (excluding Banns) **CROR & NLW**
BT 1586, 1593, 1599, 1601, 1604-5, 1611, 1613-15, 1622-3, 1626-31, 1633-6, 1639-41, 1662, 1666, 1668-9, 1671-7, 1679-84, 1688-91, 1695-1735, 1737-43, 1745-6, 1748-71, 1773-1838 **Ches RO** 1850 **NLW**
Cop ts PR (extracts) CB 1563-1850 M 1563-1749, 1813-50   ts PR M 1749-87 **Soc Gen**

*HAWARDEN/PENARLÂG   *SA*
C 1586-1941   M 1586-1917 (Banns 1823-47)   B 1586-1938 **CROH**   Mf (excluding Banns) **CROR & NLW**
BT 1755-76, 1778, 1784, 1788, 1794-1812, 1824-36, 1838-9, 1870-2 **CROH**
Cop ms PR C 1586-1763 M 1586-1754 B 1586-1766 **CROH**

HELYGAIN/HALKYN   *SA*
C 1594-1648, 1651, 1654, 1657, 1661-1706, 1720-1851   M 1595-1641, 1667-1706, 1720-1970   B 1594-1643, 1666-1706, 1720-1911 **CROH**   Mf **CROR & NLW**
BT 1667, 1670-1, 1673-9, 1681-90, 1693-4, 1698-1700, 1702-14, 1719-43, 1747-54, 1756-1850 **NLW**   Mf 1670-1850 **CROH & CROR**

HIGHER KINNERTON   *C*
‹Dodleston, co. Chester. PR 1570-1903 and BT 1584-1872 with gaps for Dodleston are in Ches RO
C 1868-1966   M 1894-1947 **Ches RO**   B 1894- incumbent

HOB, YR/HOPE   *SA*
C 1668-1904   M 1668-1907 (Banns 1825-93)   B 1668-1943 **CROH**   Mf **CROR & NLW**
BT 1662-6, 1671-4, 1677-83, 1685, 1687, 1690, 1695-6, 1698-9, 1704-11, 1713, 1715-21, 1723-1847,
    1851 **NLW**   Mf **CROH & CROR**

*HOLYWELL/TREFFYNNON   *SA*
C 1677-1968   M 1677-1978 (Banns 1823-1967)   B 1677-1978 **CROH**   Mf (excluding Banns)
    CROR & NLW
BT 1667, 1671-80, 1682, 1685-8, 1690, 1694-6, 1698-1700, 1702-5, 1721-5, 1728-66, 1770-1866
    NLW   Mf **CROH & CROR**
Cop ts PR C 1728-37 B 1718-23 **Soc Gen**

HOPE gweler/see HOB, YR

IS-COED/ISCOYD Whitewell church   *C*
‹Malpas, co. Chester, 1880. BT 1584-1893 with gaps, and Mf of PR 1561-1949 for Malpas are in
    Ches RO
CB 1885-   M 1886- incumbent

KINNERTON, HIGHER gweler/see HIGHER KINNERTON

LACHE-CUM-SALTNEY   *C*
‹Chester St. Mary, co. Chester, & Penarlâg/Hawarden, co. Flint, 1855
C 1853-1964   M 1857-1972 Saltney Ferry 1925-55 **Ches RO**

LLANASA   *SA*
C 1629-1863   M 1629-1882 (Banns 1823-1904)   B 1629-1890 **CROH**   Mf (excluding Banns)
    CROR & NLW
BT 1663-5, 1667-8, 1670-3, 1675, 1677, 1679-1700, 1702-5, 1707-31, 1733-45, 1747-1837 **NLW**
Mf 1670-1837 **CROH & CROR**

LLANELWY/ST. ASAPH   *SA*
Included townships of Meiriadog/Meriadog & Wicwer/Wigfair, co. Denbigh, which became the
    parish of Cefn 1865
C 1593-1668, 1677-1907   M 1603-68, 1671-1873   B 1594-1668, 1671-1883 **CROH**   Mf
    CROR & NLW   Fac C 1593-1668   M 1603-68   B 1594-1868 **NLW**
BT 1667-8, 1672-7, 1680, 1682, 1686, 1690, 1696, 1704-18, 1722-9, 1731-1836 **NLW**   Mf **CROH
    & CROR**

LLANEURGAIN/NORTHOP   *SA*
C 1590-1980   M 1590-1656, 1659-1982 (Banns 1823-1977)   B 1590-1957 **CROH**   Mf (exclud-
    ing Banns) **CROR & NLW**
BT 1662-4, 1666-7, 1670-3, 1675-92, 1696, 1698-1706, 1708-23, 1725-6, 1728-1809, 1811-52 **NLW**
Mf 1791-1852 **CROH & CROR**

LLANFYNYDD   *SA*
‹Yr Hob/Hope 1845. PR MB 1843-92 destroyed in church fire 1892
C 1843-1914   M 1893-1970 **CROH**   B 1893- incumbent   Mf C 1843-1914   M 1893-1970
    CROR & NLW

LLANNERCH BANNA/PENLEY   *SA*
‹Ellesmere, co. Salop, 1869. PR C 1813-73 recorded in 1936 apparently lost. PR for Ellesmere C
    1654-1891 M 1654-1940 B 1654-1898 are in SRO, and BT 1630-1880 with gaps in Lichfield JRO
C 1752-1812, 1873-1968   M 1753, 1867-1970   B 1753-1923 **CROH**   Mf **CROR & NLW**
BT 1663, 1752-1896 **Lichfield JRO**   Fac C 1813-64 **CROH**
Cop ts PR C 1752-1812 M 1753 B 1753-1812 & BT C 1813-64 with index **CROH & SRO**

MAES-GLAS/GREENFIELD *SA*
‹Treffynnon/Holywell 1871
M 1913-71 (Banns 1913-74) **CROH**   Mf M 1913-71 **CROR & NLW**

MARFORD & HOSELEY
Flintshire townships in Gresffordd/Gresford, co. Denbigh. From 1840 in parish of Yr Orsedd/
Rossett, co. Denbigh

*MELIDEN/ALLT MELYD   *SA*
   C 1602-26, 1685-7, 1690-1734, 1741-1848   M 1603-26, 1687, 1692-1734, 1742-1837 (Banns
      1824-91, 1893-1963)   B 1602-26, 1686-7, 1690-1734, 1741-1908 **CROH**   Mf (excluding
      Banns) **CROR & NLW**
   BT 1668, 1672-3, 1677, 1679, 1681, 1683, 1686, 1692, 1698-1700, 1703-39, 1741-1834, 1851 **NLW**
      Mf 1673-1851 **CROH & CROR**
   Cop PR CB 1602-19 M 1603-17 *Northern Flintshire*, 1 (1913)   ts PR/BT CB 1602-1718 M 1603-
      1718 **NLW**

*MOLD/YR WYDDGRUG   *SA*
   C 1612-47, 1653-1875   M 1604-5, 1614-47, 1651-1875 (Banns 1843-74, 1935-51, 1964-73) St. John
      1886-1946   B 1612-47, 1653-1934 **CROH**   Mf (excluding Banns) **CROR & NLW**
   BT 1664-9, 1672-82, 1684-7, 1689-90, 1693-6, 1698-1701, 1703-26, 1728-49, 1751-4, 1756-1856
      NLW   Mf 1678-1856 **CROH & CROR**

MOSTYN   *SA*
‹Chwitffordd/Whitford 1844
C 1846-1916   M 1845-1948   B 1845-1907 **CROH**   Mf **CROR & NLW**

NANNERCH   *SA*
Included township of Penbedw, co. Denbigh
C 1664-1892   M 1664-1846   B 1664-1889 **NLW**   Mf/Fac **CROH**   Mf CB 1664-1770
   M 1664-1755 **CROR**
BT 1667-8, 1670-3, 1679-87, 1699, 1707-8, 1710-15, 1717-59, 1761, 1763, 1765-1851 **NLW**   Mf
   1672-1851 **CROH & CROR**

NERCWYS (NERQUIS)   *SA*
‹Yr Wyddgrug/Mold
C 1665-1724, 1732-1862   M 1669-1724, 1732-1836   B 1669-1724, 1732-1856 **CROH**   Mf
   CROR & NLW
BT 1670-3, 1676-84, 1687-9, 1691-3, 1695, 1697-8, 1700-8, 1710-92, 1794-1846, 1848-51 **NLW**
   Mf **CROH & CROR**

NEWMARKET gweler/see TRELAWNYD

*NORTHOP/LLANEURGAIN   *SA*
   C 1590-1980   M 1590-1656, 1659-1982 (Banns 1823-1977)   B 1590-1957 **CROH**   Mf (ex-
      cluding Banns) **CROR & NLW**
   BT 1662-4, 1666-7, 1670-3, 1675-92, 1696, 1698-1706, 1708-23, 1725-6, 1728-1809, 1811-52 **NLW**
      Mf 1791-1852 **CROH & CROR**

OWRTYN/OVERTON   *SA*
‹Bangor 1868
C 1602-39, 1654-1723, 1727-1859   M 1602-44, 1654-1724, 1727-1837   B 1602-51, 1654-1864
   CROH   Mf **CROR & NLW**
BT 1604, 1615, 1617, 1620, 1624-9, 1633, 1635, 1639, 1666-9, 1671, 1674-7, 1680-5, 1688-91, 1694-
   1700, 1702-3, 1705, 1707-23, 1725-37, 1739-1838 **Ches RO**
Cop ms PR (extracts) CM 1721-80 B 1681-1780 **NLW**

PENARLÂG/HAWARDEN   *SA*
C 1586-1941   M 1586-1917 (Banns 1823-47)   B 1586-1938 **CROH**   Mf (excluding Banns)
CROR & NLW
BT 1755-76, 1778, 1784, 1788, 1794-1812, 1824-36, 1838-9, 1870-2 **CROH**
Cop ms PR C 1586-1763 M 1586-1754 B 1586-1766 **CROH**

*PENLEY/LLANNERCH BANNA   *SA*
‹Ellesmere, co. Salop, 1869. PR C 1813-73 recorded in 1936 apparently lost. PR for Ellesmere
    C 1654-1891 M 1654-1940 B 1654-1898 are in SRO, and BT 1630-1880 with gaps in Lichfield
    JRO
C 1752-1812, 1873-1968   M 1753, 1867-1970   B 1753-1923 **CROH**   Mf **CROR & NLW**
BT 1663, 1752-1896 **Lichfield JRO**   Fac C 1813-64 **CROH**
Cop ts PR C 1752-1812 M 1753 B 1753-1812 & BT C 1813-64 with index **CROH & SRO**

PENTROBIN (PENYMYNYDD)   *SA*
‹Penarlâg/Hawarden 1843
C 1843-1902   M 1881-1975 **CROH**   B 1843- incumbent   Mf B 1843-1983 **CROH**   C 1843-
    1902   M 1881-1975   B 1843-1983 **CROR & NLW**
BT 1849, 1859, 1870-2 **CROH**

PONTBLYDDYN   *SA*
‹Yr Wyddgrug/Mold 1836
C 1836-1965   M 1839-1948   B 1836-1946 **CROH**   Mf **CROR & NLW**
BT 1836-8, 1840-3, 1851 **NLW**   Mf 1836-43 **CROH & CROR**

PRESTATYN   *SA*
‹Allt Melyd/Meliden & Llanasa 1860
C 1861-1949   M 1863-1971 (Banns 1863-1971)   B 1864-1950 **CROH**   Mf (excluding Banns)
CROR & NLW

RHUDDLAN   *SA*
C 1681-1748, 1759-1918   M 1682-1748, 1754-1940 (Banns 1824-1954)   B 1681-1748, 1759-1934
CROH   Mf (excluding Banns) **CROR & NLW**
BT 1681-2, 1684, 1686-7, 1689-92, 1694-6, 1698-1718, 1720-6, 1728-56, 1759-1834 **NLW**   Mf
CROH & CROR
Cop ts PR (extracts) C 1681-1717 M 1686-1712 B 1681-1742 **Soc Gen**

RHYD-Y-MWYN   *SA*
‹Cilcain, Helygain/Halkyn, Yr Wyddgrug/Mold & Llaneurgain/Northop 1865
C 1864-1978   M 1866-1970   B 1863-1977 **CROH**   Mf **CROR & NLW**

RHYL, Y/RHYL   *SA*
‹Rhuddlan 1835
C 1841-1921   M Holy Trinity 1844-1963 St. Thomas 1889-1924 (Banns 1899-1926, 1950-65) St.
    Ann 1909-27 (Banns 1928-69)   B 1859-1965 **CROH**   Mf (excluding Banns) **CROR &
    NLW**

*ST. ASAPH/LLANELWY   *SA*
Included townships of Meiriadog/Meriadog & Wicwer/Wigfair, co. Denbigh, which became the
    parish of Cefn 1865
C 1593-1668, 1677-1907   M 1603-68, 1671-1873   B 1594-1668, 1671-1883 **CROH**   Mf
    CROR & NLW   Fac C 1593-1668   M 1603-68   B 1594-1868 **NLW**
BT 1667-8, 1672-7, 1680, 1682, 1686, 1690, 1696, 1704-18, 1722-9, 1731-1836 **NLW**   Mf **CROH**
    & CROR

SALTNEY gweler/see LACHE-CUM-SALTNEY

SEALAND **SA**
‹Penarlâg/Hawarden 1867
CM 1867- incumbent
BT 1872 **CROH**

SHOTTON **SA**
‹Penarlâg/Hawarden 1902
C 1902-53 M 1902-55 **CROH** Mf **CROR & NLW**

THREAPWOOD **C**
‹Worthenbury, co. Flint, & Malpas, co. Chester, 1817. Formerly an extra-parochial place. The
 Flintshire part of the parish was transferred to Cheshire in 1896
C 1817-1944 **Ches RO** M 1837- B 1829- incumbent
BT 1817-40 **Ches RO**

TREFFYNNON/HOLYWELL **SA**
C 1677-1968 M 1677-1978 (Banns 1823-1967) B 1677-1978 **CROH** Mf (excluding Banns)
 CROR & NLW
BT 1667, 1671-80, 1682, 1685-8, 1690, 1694-6, 1698-1700, 1702-5, 1721-5, 1728-66, 1770-1866
 NLW Mf **CROH & CROR**
Cop ts PR C 1728-37 B 1718-23 **Soc Gen**

TRELAWNYD (NEWMARKET) **SA**
C 1696-1719, 1752-1909 M 1699-1719, 1752-1970 (Banns 1824-1934) B 1696-1719, 1752-1904
 CROH Mf (excluding Banns) **CROR & NLW**
BT 1663, 1670, 1672-5, 1677-84, 1687, 1694, 1696, 1698-1703, 1707-8, 1710, 1712-18, 1720-43,
 1745-62, 1764-1812, 1814-24, 1827-40, 1858 **NLW** Mf **CROH & CROR**
Cop PR C 1696-1713 M 1699-1713 B 1696-1714 *Northern Flintshire,* 1 (1913) cop ms PR C
 1752-1909 M 1752-1910 B 1752-1912 **NLW**

TREMEIRCHION **SA**
C 1599-1862 M 1599-1952 (Banns 1824-1929) B 1599-1966 **CROH** Mf (excluding Banns)
 CROR & NLW Fac CB 1599-1810 M 1599-1753 **NLW**
BT 1665-8, 1670-4, 1677-84, 1686-91, 1693, 1695-6, 1698-1713, 1715-17, 1719-1839 **NLW** Mf
 1665-1835 **CROH & CROR**
Cop ts PR C 1604-1758 M 1604-1753 B 1604-1760 **Soc Gen**

TREUDDYN **SA**
‹Yr Wyddgrug/Mold
C 1611-92, 1695-1728, 1732-1923 M 1618-92, 1696-1727, 1732-1908 (Banns 1824-99) B
 1613-92, 1695-1728, 1732-1857 **CROH** Mf (excluding Banns) **CROR & NLW**
BT 1667, 1670-4, 1676-89, 1691, 1693-6, 1699, 1701-8, 1710-19, 1721-1834, 1838-50 **NLW** Mf
 1672-1834 **CROH & CROR**

WAUN gweler/see GWERNAFFIELD

WHITEWELL gweler/see IS-COED/ISCOYD

*WHITFORD/CHWITFFORDD **SA**
C 1643-1938 M 1656-1926 (Banns 1823-67) B 1664-1882 **CROH** Mf (excluding Banns)
 CROR & NLW Fac CMB 1742-78 **NLW**
BT 1664-5, 1673, 1675, 1677, 1681-3, 1687, 1691-2, 1695-6, 1698-1702, 1704-17, 1719-20, 1722,
 1724-1837 **NLW** Mf 1734-1837 **CROH & CROR**

WORTHENBURY   *SA*
‹Bangor 1689
C 1597-1749, 1755-1936   M 1598-1749, 1754-1970   B 1597-1749, 1755-1939 **CROH**   Mf
  CROR & NLW
BT 1599, ?1600, 1601, 1603-5, 1611, 1613-15, 1618-19, 1622-9, 1631, 1633-5, 1639, 1662, 1664,
  1666-72, 1674, 1676-7, 1679-85, 1688-91, 1695-1700, 1702-14, 1718-35, 1737-46, 1754, 1756-69,
  1771-94, 1796-1815, 1817-42, 1844-8 **Ches RO**   1850-9, 1861-70, 1873-4, 1876 **NLW**   Mf
  1850-9, 1861-70, 1873-4, 1876 **CROH & CROR**

WYDDGRUG, YR/MOLD   *SA*
C 1612-47, 1653-1875   M 1604-5, 1614-47, 1651-1875 (Banns 1843-74, 1933-51, 1964-73) St. John
  1886-1946   B 1612-47, 1653-1934 **CROH**   Mf (excluding Banns) **CROR & NLW**
BT 1664-9, 1672-82, 1684-7, 1689-90, 1693-6, 1698-1701, 1703-26, 1728-49, 1751-4, 1756-1856
  NLW   Mf 1678-1856 **CROH & CROR**

YSGEIFIOG/YSCEIFIOG   *SA*
C 1662-1867   M 1662-1838 (Banns 1823-1905, 1914-17)   B 1662-1910 **CROH**   Mf (exclud-
  ing Banns) **CROR & NLW**
BT 1666-8, 1670-9, 1681-92, 1694-6, 1699-1712, 1714-15, 1717-18, 1720-36, 1739-1841 **NLW**

MAESYFED
RADNORSHIRE

TREFALDWYN / MONTGOMERYSHIRE

A M W Y T H I G / S A L O P

ABERTEIFI / CARDIGANSHIRE

BUGEILDY·

LLANBADARN FYNYDD·

LLANDDEWI-YN-HEIOB/HEYOPE·

LLANANNO·
LLANBISTER·

SAINT HARMON·   TREFYCLAWDD/KNIGHTON·
ABATY CWM-HIR/ABBEY CWM-HIR·   LLANGYNLLO·

LLANDDEWI YSTRADENNI·   BLEDDFA   PYLLALAI/PILLETH
RHAEADR GWY/RHAYADER,   LLANFIHANGEL RHYDIEITHON· LLANDDEWI-YN-HWYTYN/WHITTON ·NORTON
LLANSANFFRAID CWMTEUDDWR· LLANFIHANGEL RHYDITHON· CASGOB/CASCOB
NANTMEL·   DISGOED/DISCOED
LLANFIHANGEL HELYGEN·   LLANBADARN FAWR·   LLANANDRAS/PRESTEIGNE
                                        Evancoyd·
LLANLLŶR/LLANYRE·   LLANDEGLAU/LLANDEGLEY   MAESYFED/NEW RADNOR·
LLANDRINDOD·   ·CEFN-LLYS
                              PENCRAIG/OLD RADNOR·
·DISERTH   LLANFIHANGEL NANT MELAN·
BETWS DISERTH·   LLANFAIR LLYTHYFNWG/
LLANSANFFRAID-YN-ELFAEL·   GLADESTRY·
                    GLASGWM   COLFA/COLVA
                CREGRINA   LLANFIHANGEL DYFFRYN ARWY/
LLANELWEDD   MICHAELCHURCH-ON-ARROW
        LLANFAREDD   YR EGLWYS NEWYDD/NEWCHURCH
    RHIWLEN/RHULEN   ·BRYN-GWYN
        ·LLANBADARN GARREG   BETWS CLEIRWY/
        LLANBADARN-Y-GARREG   ·BETWS CLYRO
·ABEREDW   LLANBEDR CASTELL-PAEN/
        ·LLANBEDR PAINSCASTLE·
        ·LLANDDEWI FACH
LLANDEILO GRABAN   ·CLEIRWY/CLYRO
LLANSTEFFAN/
LLANSTEPHAN·   LLOWES·
            Y CLAS-AR-WY/GLASBURY
        ·BOCHRWD/BOUGHROOD

BRYCHEINIOG - BRECKNOCKSHIRE

HEFFORDD / HEREFORDSHIRE

NANTMEL Eglwysi cyn 1813/Pre-1813 churches
Evancoyd Eglwysi wedi 1813/Post-1813 churches

Milltiroedd/Miles
0   5   10

MAESYFED/RADNORSHIRE

ABATY CWM-HIR/ABBEY CWMHIR *SB*
An ancient chapel of ease with CMB before 1831 entered in PR Llanbister
C 1831-1981   M 1831-1971 (Banns 1833-1960)   B 1831-1978 **NLW**
BT 1831-7, 1841-3, 1864-7 **NLW**

ABEREDW *SB*
PR C 1690-1719 M 1700-19 B 1695-1719 recorded in 1831 apparently lost
CB 1740-   M 1740-53, 1785-1812 incumbent   M 1754-83, 1813-1971 **NLW**
BT 1687, 1706-7, 1710, 1713-35, 1737-9, 1742-7, 1749, 1751-4, 1756-8, 1760-95, 1797-1810, 1813-34,
    1836-43 **NLW**
Cop ms PR C 1740-1900 M 1740-1968 B 1740-1901   ms BT CMB 1687, 1701-8, 1713-21 **Soc Gen**

BEGUILDY gweler/see BUGEILDY *SB*

BETWS CLEIRWY/BETWS CLYRO *SB*
An ancient chapelry with CMB entered in PR Cleirwy/Clyro

BETWS DISERTH *SB*
PR M 1763-1812 recorded in 1900 terrier and inventory apparently lost
C 1731-1980   M 1731-52, 1813-39 (Banns 1824-1956)   B 1731-1958 **NLW**
BT 1687, 1707, 1714-18, 1720-47, 1749-84, 1786-95, 1797-1809, 1813-38, 1840-4, 1846, 1865-7
    NLW

BLEDDFA *SB*
CMB 1608- incumbent
BT 1701, 1707, 1710, 1714-23, 1726-95, 1797-1809, 1813-14, 1816-41, 1843, 1864-7 **NLW**

BOCHRWD/BOUGHROOD *SB*
C 1689-1709, 1711-1979   M 1695-1708, 1711-1970 (Banns 1824-70)   B 1689-1709, 1711-19,
    1729-1973 **NLW**
BT 1687, 1701, 1713-20, 1723, 1725-95, 1797-1809, 1813-35, 1838-40, 1845-7 **NLW**

BRYN-GWYN *SB*
PR M 1798-1812 recorded in 1900 inventory apparently lost
CB 1614-29, 1632-4, 1664-73, 1687-92, 1715-19, 1721-2, 1725-76, 1782-1981   M 1614-29, 1632-4,
    1664-73, 1687-92, 1715-19, 1721-2, 1725-98, 1813-1971 (Banns 1824-1981) **NLW**
BT 1687, 1707, 1713-17, 1719-95, 1797-1809, 1813-46, 1849-52 **NLW**

BUGEILDY/BEGUILDY *SB*
C 1703-1893   M 1703-1837 (Banns 1850-1934)   B 1703-1959 **NLW**
BT 1701, 1706-7, 1710, 1713-34, 1736-95, 1797-1809, 1813-39, 1841-4 **NLW**

CASGOB/CASCOB *SB*
CMB ?1624- incumbent
BT 1701, 1707-10, 1713-21, 1723-51, 1753-78, 1780-94, 1796-1809, 1813-53 **NLW**

CEFN-LLYS *SB*
C 1671-1901   M 1671-1842   B 1671-1947 **NLW**
BT 1701, 1708, 1713-25, 1727-77, 1779-1809, 1813-39, 1842-3, 1864-7, 1869 **NLW**

CLAS-AR-WY, Y/GLASBURY All Saints   *SB*
‹Y Clas-ar-Wy/Glasbury St. Peter 1882 (see under Brycheiniog/Brecknockshire). It has no
  separate register of burials
C 1882-   M 1883- incumbent

CLEIRWY/CLYRO   *SB*
C 1688-1880   M 1688-1971   B 1688-1853 **NLW**
BT 1714-18, 1720-1, 1724-6, 1728-36, 1738-47, 1749-95, 1797-1809, 1813-65, 1867-72 **NLW**

COLFA/COLVA   *SB*
PR CB 1797-1812 recorded in 1831 apparently lost
CB 1663-1794   M 1663-1971 **NLW**
BT 1687, 1690, 1705, 1707, 1713-63, 1765-83, 1785-1806, 1808-9, 1813-38, 1840-50 **NLW**

CREGRINA (CRAIG FURUNA)   *SB*
Diocesan records suggest that *c.* 1790 this parish had registers going back to 1647
CB 1685-1729, 1754-1812   M 1685-1729, 1754-1836, 1841-1967 **NLW**
BT 1713-14, 1716-45, 1748-58, 1760-6, 1768-70, 1772-95, 1797-1809, 1813-48 **NLW**

CWMTEUDDWR gweler/see LLANSANFFRAID CWMTEUDDWR

DISERTH   *SB*
PR 1734-1812 recorded in 1935 apparently lost. Pre-1734 registers destroyed by fire (1831 survey)
C 1813-64   M 1757-1839 (Banns 1757-1886)   B 1813-1915   Fac CB 1734-1812   M 1734-56
  NLW
BT 1687, 1701, 1715-26, 1728-1809, 1813-38, 1840-4, 1846, 1865-7 **NLW**
Cop ts PR CB 1734-1812 M 1734-56 **NLW & Soc Gen**

DISGOED/DISCOED   *H*
A chapelry in the parish of Llanandras/Presteigne. CB 1805-12 entered in PR Llanandras/Presteigne
  according to the 1831 survey
C 1680-1805   M 1680-1933 (Banns 1755-1811, 1822-1951)   B 1680-1805 **HRO**

EGLWYS NEWYDD, YR/NEWCHURCH   *SB*
PR M 1814-35 recorded in 1900 inventory apparently lost
CB 1708-1981   M 1708-48, 1755-1811, 1837-1971 (Banns 1825-1981) **NLW**
BT 1701, 1708, 1712-26, 1728-63, 1765-83, 1785-97, 1799-1806, 1808-9, 1813-16, 1818-53 **NLW**

EVANCOYD   *SB*
‹Pencraig/Old Radnor 1866
C incumbent   M 1872-1971 **NLW**

*GLADESTRY/LLANFAIR LLYTHYFNWG   *SB*
C 1683-1946   M 1683-1971   B 1683-1929 **NLW**
BT 1687, 1713-57, 1759-95, 1797-1809, 1813, 1815, 1822-32, 1834-9, 1841-7, 1849-52 **NLW**

*GLASBURY/Y CLAS-AR-WY All Saints   *SB*
‹Y Clas-ar-Wy/Glasbury St. Peter 1882 (see under Brycheiniog/Brecknockshire). It has no
  separate register of burials
C 1882-   M 1883- incumbent

GLASGWM (GLASCOMBE)   *SB*
CB 1679-1797   M 1679-1837   Fac C 1813-1980   M 1837-1971   B 1813-1979 **NLW**
BT 1687, 1690, 1704-7, 1709, 1713-21, 1723-76, 1778-83, 1785-8, 1790-5, 1797-1806, 1808-9, 1813-45
  NLW

*HEYOPE/LLANDDEWI-YN-HEIOB   *SB*
PR CMB 1711-33 recorded in 1831 apparently lost
CB 1679-1711, 1733-97, 1805-11   M 1679-1711, 1733-69, 1781-1835, 1838-1959, 1962-70   Fac B
1813-1980 **NLW**
BT 1687, 1701, 1708, 1710, 1714-19, 1721-95, 1797-1809, 1813-36, 1839-40, 1842-6, 1848-53 **NLW**

*KNIGHTON/TREFYCLAWDD   *SB*
C 1599-1964   M 1599-1754, 1775-1971 (Banns 1946-78)   B 1599-1959 **NLW**   M 1754-75
incumbent
BT 1662-1833, 1836, 1838-46 **HRO**

LLANANDRAS/PRESTEIGNE   *H*
Included several townships in co. Hereford
C 1561-1912   M 1561-1922 (Banns 1754-1812, 1824-1948)   B 1561-1904 **HRO**
BT 1659-99, 1701-43, 1745-1833, 1836-56, 1880-1 **HRO**

LLANANNO   *SB*
CB 1721-1812   M 1721-1837 (Banns 1824-1941) **NLW**
BT 1687, 1701, 1705-8, 1710, 1713-29, 1731-65, 1767-83, 1785-9, 1791-1809, 1813-14, 1817-47
NLW

LLANBADARN FAWR   *SB*
C 1696-1778, 1781-1911   M 1696-1894   B 1696-1778, 1781-1919 **NLW**
BT 1701, 1705-8, 1713, 1715-71, 1773-95, 1797-1809, 1813-18, 1823-49, 1864-5 **NLW**

LLANBADARN FYNYDD   *SB*
C 1678-1709, 1721-1892   M 1678-1709, 1721-1837 (Banns 1831-1939)   B 1678-1709, 1721-1958
NLW
BT 1687, 1707-8, 1710-11, 1713, 1715-65, 1767-95, 1797-1809, 1813-14, 1816-47 **NLW**

LLANBADARN GARREG/LLANBADARN-Y-GARREG   *SB*
PR CMB 1789-1812 recorded in 1831 apparently lost
CB 1813- incumbent   M 1814-1971 **NLW**
BT 1704, 1713-19, 1721-55, 1757-66, 1769, 1773, 1775, 1777-1809, 1813-38, 1840-8 **NLW**

LLANBEDR CASTELL-PAEN/LLANBEDR PAINSCASTLE   *SB*
C 1726-1981   M 1726-1971 (Banns 1836-1980)   B 1726-1980 **NLW**
BT 1687, 1707, 1709-10, ?1713, 1714-18, 1721-33, 1736-44, 1746-95, 1797-1809, 1813-50 **NLW**

LLANBISTER   *SB*
PR CMB 1682-1704 recorded in 1831 apparently lost
CB 1705-1812   M 1705-1837 (Banns 1854-1901) **NLW**
BT 1705-8, 1710, 1713-95, 1797-1809, 1813-37, 1840 **NLW**   Mf BT CMB 1785-1840 **Soc Gen**

LLANDDEWI FACH   *SB*
C 1775-1981   M 1754-1971 (Banns 1829-1900, 1980)   B 1775-1960 **NLW**
BT 1687, 1713-21, 1724-33, 1735-63, 1765-95, 1797-1809, 1813-17, 1819-35, 1837-41 **NLW**

LLANDDEWI-YN-HEIOB/HEYOPE   *SB*
PR CMB 1711-33 recorded in 1831 apparently lost
CB 1679-1711, 1733-97, 1805-11   M 1679-1711, 1733-69, 1781-1835, 1838-1959, 1962-70   Fac B
1813-1980 **NLW**
BT 1687, 1701, 1708, 1710, 1714-19, 1721-95, 1797-1809, 1813-36, 1839-40, 1842-6, 1848-53 **NLW**

LLANDDEWI-YN-HWYTYN/WHITTON   *SB*
CMB 1600- incumbent
BT 1687, 1690, 1706-8, 1715-33, 1735-70, 1772-95, 1797-1809, 1813-14, 1816-18, 1820-41 **NLW**

LLANDDEWI YSTRADENNI   *SB*
C 1732-51, 1758-1946   M 1732-51, 1754-1971 (Banns 1826-1957)   B 1732-51, 1758-1981 **NLW**
BT 1690-1, 1705-8, 1713-27, 1729-54, 1756-95, 1797-1805, 1807-9, 1813-37, 1839-51, 1855-9 **NLW**

LLANDEGLAU/LLANDEGLEY   *SB*
Diocesan records suggest that *c.* 1790 this parish had registers going back to 1672
C 1727-1914   M 1727-1838   B 1727-1812 **NLW**
BT 1706, 1713-16, 1718, 1720-32, 1734-62, 1765-1805, 1807-9, 1813-59, 1868 **NLW**

LLANDEILO GRABAN   *SB*
CB 1660-   M 1660-1837 incumbent   M 1837-1971 **NLW**
BT 1687, 1706, 1708, 1714-19, 1721-8, 1730-95, 1797-1805, 1807-9, 1813-42, 1844, 1846-53 **NLW**

LLANDRINDOD   *SB*
C 1734-1901   M 1734-1844   B 1734-1947 **NLW**
BT 1701, 1707, 1714-18, 1720-3, 1725-6, 1728-30, 1732, 1734-43, 1745-95, 1797-1809, 1813-38, 1840-1, 1843, 1864-7, 1869-70 **NLW**

LLANELWEDD   *SB*
C 1773-1981   M 1796-1971   B 1773-1982 **NLW**
BT 1714, 1717-25, 1727-9, 1731-62, 1764-7, 1769-95, 1797-1805, 1807-9, 1813-16, 1818, 1820-3, 1825-7, 1829-55, 1867-71 **NLW**

LLANFAIR LLYTHYFNWG/GLADESTRY   *SB*
C 1683-1946   M 1683-1971   B 1683-1929 **NLW**
BT 1687, 1713-57, 1759-95, 1797-1809, 1813, 1815, 1822-32, 1834-9, 1841-7, 1849-52 **NLW**

LLANFAREDD   *SB*
C 1698-1713, 1730-1984   M 1698-1713, 1730-1960   B 1698-1713, 1730-1979 **NLW**
BT 1706-8, 1713-15, 1717-18, 1720-54, 1756-8, 1760-95, 1797-1809, 1813-36, 1838-43 **NLW**

LLANFIHANGEL DYFFRYN ARWY/MICHAELCHURCH-ON-ARROW   *H*
CMB 1741- incumbent
BT 1662-7, 1669-1743, 1745-1833, 1836, 1838-41, 1849-50, 1852 **HRO**

LLANFIHANGEL HELYGEN   *SB*
A note in BT Llanllŷr/Llanyre 1713 says that 'there was no register ever kept at Llanvyhangell it being no burial place but what there happens is inserted in the registers of Nantmell and Llanyre'
C 1732-78 with gaps, 1781-99, 1806-12   M 1755-96, 1805-10, 1814-34   B 1811, 1828 **NLW**
BT 1736, 1784-8, 1790, 1792-8, 1801-8, 1814-15, 1817, 1821, 1823-37, 1839-45 **NLW**

LLANFIHANGEL NANT MELAN   *SB*
C 1700-1929   M 1700-1809, 1813-1967   B 1700-1812 **NLW**
BT 1705-7, 1709, 1713-18, 1720-70, 1772-95, 1797-1809, 1813-19, 1821-3, 1825-33, 1836, 1838-41, 1843-64, 1866-7, 1871-2 **NLW**

LLANFIHANGEL RHYDIEITHON/LLANFIHANGEL RHYDITHON   *SB*
C 1725, 1732-47, 1749-55, 1758-1944   M 1732-47, 1749-1837   B 1732-47, 1749-55, 1758-1812 **NLW**
BT 1687, 1704-8, 1710, 1714-95, 1797-1809, 1813-55 **NLW**

LLANGYNLLO *SB*
CMB 1744- incumbent
BT 1687, 1690, 1702, 1705-11, 1713-68, 1770-1809, 1813-54 **NLW**

LLANLLŶR (-YN-RHOS)/LLANYRE *SB*
PR CB 1735-59 M 1735-59, 1772-94 recorded in 1831 apparently lost
C 1760-1903   M 1759-72, 1783, 1795-1837   B 1760-1963 **NLW**
BT 1705, 1713-16, 1718-25, 1727-55, 1757, 1759-77, 1779-95, 1797-1809, 1813-18, 1823-36, 1839-43, 1864-7 **NLW**

LLANSAINTFFRAID-IN-ELWELL gweler/see LLANSANFFRAID-YN-ELFAEL

LLANSANFFRAID CWMTEUDDWR *SB*
PR CMB 1682-[1736] recorded in 1831 apparently lost
C 1737-1811, 1813-97   M 1737-1837, 1972-8 Nant-gwyllt 1875-1971   B 1737-1811, 1813-1936 **NLW**
BT 1687, 1690, 1701, 1706-8, 1710, 1713-17, 1719-24, 1726-64, 1766-95, 1797-1809, 1813-36, 1838, 1864-73 **NLW**

LLANSANFFRAID-YN-ELFAEL/LLANSAINTFFRAID-IN-ELWELL *SB*
Diocesan records suggest that *c.* 1790 this parish had registers going back to 1603
C 1767-1930   M 1813-1957   B 1767-1980 **NLW**
BT 1701, 1707, 1713-14, 1716-95, 1797-1809, 1813-15, 1818-55, 1864 **NLW**

LLANSTEFFAN/LLANSTEPHAN *SB*
PR CB 1666-1812 M 1666-1756 recorded in 1831 and 'dilapidated' PR CB 1696-1813 recorded in 1900 inventory apparently lost
C 1813-1981   M 1754-1971 (Banns 1884-1962)   B 1813-1980 **NLW**
BT 1690, 1707, 1713, 1715-29, 1731-63, 1765-95, 1797-1809, 1813-42, 1844, 1865-7, 1869 **NLW**

*LLANYRE/LLANLLŶR (-YN-RHOS) *SB*
PR CB 1735-59 M 1735-59, 1772-94 recorded in 1831 apparently lost
C 1760-1903   M 1759-72, 1783, 1795-1837   B 1760-1963 **NLW**
BT 1705, 1713-16, 1718-25, 1727-55, 1757, 1759-77, 1779-95, 1797-1809, 1813-18, 1823-36, 1839-43, 1864-7 **NLW**

LLOWES *SB*
PR CMB 1661-94 recorded in 1831 apparently lost
C 1701-1954   M 1701-53, 1760-1969 (Banns 1823-67)   B 1701-1955 **NLW**
BT 1714-15, 1719-1809, 1813-17, 1819-41 **NLW**

MAESYFED/NEW RADNOR *SB*
PR M 1755-1812 recorded in 1935 apparently lost
C 1644-1878   M 1644-1754, 1801-1970 (Banns 1823-1942)   B 1644-1918 **NLW**
BT 1660, 1662-6, 1668, 1688, 1690-6, 1698, 1700-4, 1706-46, 1748-1833, 1836-7, 1843-6 **HRO**
Cop ts PR CMB 1644-1708 with index **NLW & Soc Gen**

*MICHAELCHURCH-ON-ARROW/LLANFIHANGEL DYFFRYN ARWY *H*
CMB 1741- incumbent
BT 1662-7, 1669-1743, 1745-1833, 1836, 1838-41, 1849-50, 1852 **HRO**

NANT-GWYLLT gweler/see LLANSANFFRAID CWMTEUDDWR

NANTMEL   *SB*
C 1742-1937   M 1742-1980 (Banns 1823-1939)   B 1742-1882 **NLW**
BT 1705, 1709, 1713, 1715-19, 1721-4, 1726-40, 1743-95, 1797-1809, 1813-37, 1839-43, 1864-73
   NLW

*NEWCHURCH/YR EGLWYS NEWYDD   *SB*
PR M 1814-35 recorded in 1900 inventory apparently lost
CB 1708-1981   M 1708-48, 1755-1811, 1837-1971 (Banns 1825-1981) **NLW**
BT 1701, 1708, 1712-26, 1728-63, 1765-83, 1785-97, 1799-1806, 1808-9, 1813-16, 1818-53 **NLW**

*NEW RADNOR/MAESYFED   *SB*
PR M 1755-1812 recorded in 1935 apparently lost
C 1644-1878   M 1644-1754, 1801-1970 (Banns 1823-1942)   B 1644-1918 **NLW**
BT 1660, 1662-6, 1668, 1688, 1690-6, 1698, 1700-4, 1706-46, 1748-1833, 1836-7, 1843-6 **HRO**
Cop ts PR CMB 1644-1708 with index **NLW & Soc Gen**

NORTON (NORTYN)   *SB*
C 1704-1922   M 1704-1970 (Banns 1824-1982)   B 1704-1984 **NLW**
BT 1631, 1660-2, 1664-6, 1669-1717, 1719-47, 1749-78, 1780-1834, 1836-41, 1843-67, 1871-3 **HRO**

PENCRAIG/OLD RADNOR   *SB*
Included the township of Lower Harpton, co. Hereford
CB 1682-1735, 1806-12   M 1682-1735, 1761-1803 **NLW**   C 1736-1805, 1813-64   M 1736-54,
   1804-1961 (Banns 1824-1937)   B 1736-1805, 1813-1945 **HRO**
BT 1660-4, 1666-90, 1692-4, 1696-1735, 1737-44, 1754-1833, 1836-51, 1853, 1855-6, 1862-70 **HRO**

PILLETH gweler/see PYLLALAI

*PRESTEIGNE/LLANANDRAS   *H*
Included several townships in co. Hereford
C 1561-1912   M 1561-1922 (Banns 1824-1948)   B 1561-1904 **HRO**
BT 1659-99, 1701-43, 1745-1833, 1836-56, 1880-1 **HRO**

PYLLALAI/PILLETH   *SB*
Earliest registers destroyed by fire 1772
CMB 1771- incumbent
BT 1687, 1690, 1698, 1706-8, 1710, 1714-26, 1728, 1731-51, 1753-61, 1763-95, 1797-1809, 1813-17,
   1819-55 **NLW**

RHAEADR GWY/RHAYADER   *SB*
PR CMB 1737-59 recorded in 1935 apparently lost
C 1759-1925   M 1761-1980 (Banns 1828-1968)   B 1759-1903 **NLW**
BT 1779-1809, 1813-38, 1864-9, 1871-2 **NLW**

RHIWLEN/RHULEN   *SB*
PR C 1783-1812 B 1786-1812 recorded in 1831 apparently lost
CB 1813- incumbent   M 1773-1807, 1813-36, 1842-1971   Fac CB 1813-1981 **NLW**
BT 1687, 1699, 1707, 1713-43, 1745-50, 1752-3, 1755-61, 1764-6, 1768-76, 1779-80, 1782-95, 1799-
   1806, 1808-9, 1813-17, 1819, 1821, 1823, 1825-9, 1833-6, 1838-45, 1847-50 **NLW**

SAINT HARMON   *SB*
PR CB 1794-1812 recorded in 1831 apparently lost. Diocesan records suggest that *c.* 1790 this parish
   had registers going back to 1696
C 1751-4, 1757-79, 1821-65   M 1751-3, 1758-1971   B 1751-4, 1757-79, 1813-89 **NLW**
BT 1687, 1701, 1704-5, 1710, 1713-15, 1717-95, 1797-1809, 1813-41, 1865 **NLW**

TREFYCLAWDD/KNIGHTON   *SB*
C 1599-1964   M 1599-1754, 1775-1971 (Banns 1946-78)   B 1599-1959 **NLW**   M 1754-75
   incumbent
BT 1662-1833, 1836, 1838-46 **HRO**

*WHITTON/LLANDDEWI-YN-HWYTYN   *SB*
CMB 1600- incumbent
BT 1687, 1690, 1706-8, 1715-33, 1735-70, 1772-95, 1797-1809, 1813-14, 1816-18, 1820-41 **NLW**

MEIRIONNYDD
MERIONETH

CAERNARFON / CAERNARFONSHIRE

DINBYCH / DENBIGH

Blaenau Ffestiniog·

GWYDDELWERN

BETWS GWERFUL GOCH

Llawrybetws·

·CORWEN

·FFESTINIOG

LLANGAR   LLANSANFFRAID GLYNDYFRDWY

LLANFROTHEN

·MAENTWROG

Fron-goch·

·Penrhyndeudraeth

LLANFOR   LLANDDERFEL

·LLANDRILLO-YN-EDEIRNION

·LLANDECWYN

Y Bala/Bala·

·TRAWSFYNYDD

LLANYCIL·

·Rhosygwaliau

LLANFIHANGEL-Y-TRAETHAU

LLANGYWER/LLANGOWER·

·Harlech

LLANUWCHLLYN·

·LLANFAIR
·LLANDANWG
·LLANBEDR

·LLANENDDWYN
·LLANDDWYWE

·LLANFACHRETH

LLANELLTUD/LLANELLTYD

·Bryncoedifor

LLANYMAWDDWY

·Bont-ddu   DOLGELLAU

·LLANABER

MALLWYD·

TAL-Y-LLYN

LLANFIHANGEL-Y-PENNANT·

Corris·

·LLANGELYNNIN

·LLANEGRYN

TYWYN/TOWYN   PENNAL·

Aberdyfi/Aberdovey·

ABERTEIFI/CARDIGANSHIRE

TREFALDWYN/MONTGOMERYSHIRE

TAL-Y-LLYN   Eglwysi cyn 1813/Pre-1813 churches
Corris   Eglwysi wedi 1813/Post-1813 churches

Milltiroedd/Miles
0   5   10

MEIRIONNYDD/MERIONETH

ABERDYFI/ABERDOVEY *B*
‹Tywyn/Towyn 1844
C 1848-   B 1846- incumbent   M 1846-1933 **GASD**   Fac C 1848-1929   B 1846-1939 **GASD**
   Fac M 1846-1933 **NLW**
BT 1846-57, 1876, 1883 **NLW**

BALA, Y Christ Church   *SA*
‹Llanycil 1855
Fac M 1880-1933 **GASD**

BETWS GWERFUL GOCH   *SA*
C 1685-1769, 1813-1981   M 1695-1960   B 1685-1769, 1782-1969 **GASD**   Mf **CROH &**
   CROR   Fac C 1685-1846   M 1695-1837   B 1685-1870 **NLW**
BT 1670-3, 1676-8, 1681-4, 1686-91, 1693-6, 1698-1701, 1703-4, 1706-8, 1710-21, 1723-1836 **NLW**
   Mf 1802-36 **CROH & CROR**

BLAENAU FFESTINIOG   *B*
‹Ffestiniog 1844
CM 1844- incumbent   B 1844-95 **GASD**
BT 1893 **NLW**

BONT-DDU, Y   *B*
‹Llanaber 1887
C 1860-   M 1888-   B 1887- incumbent
BT 1887-8, 1890-1, 1893, 1901 **NLW**

BRYNCOEDIFOR   *B*
‹Dolgellau 1853
CB 1852-   M 1858- incumbent
BT 1852-7, 1876-1905 **NLW**

CORRIS   *B*
‹Tal-y-llyn, co. Merioneth, & Llanwrin, co. Montgomery 1861
CM 1862-   B 1861- incumbent   Fac C 1862-1928   M 1862-1930 (Banns 1894-1929)   B
   1861-1929 **GASD**
BT 1888-9, 1907-8 **NLW**

CORWEN   *SA*
C 1719-1889   M 1722-1837   B 1719-1904 **GASD**   Fac M 1837-1935   B 1889-1935 **GASD**
   Mf C 1719-1889   M 1722-54, 1813-37   B 1719-1904 **CROH & CROR**
BT 1667-8, 1670-9, 1681-7, 1690-2, 1694-6, 1699-1716, 1718-23, 1725-30, 1732-7, 1739-1834 **NLW**
   Mf **CROH & CROR**

DOLGELLAU   *B*
C 1640-1812   M 1640-52, 1655-67, 1670, 1674-1753   B 1640-50, 1653, 1656-8, 1660-7, 1669-71,
   1673-1812 **NLW**   C 1813-1944   M 1765-1887   B 1813-88 **GASD**   Fac CB 1640-1812
   M 1640-1753 **GASD**
BT 1677-8, 1683-5, 1687-91, 1693-8, 1700-19, 1721-4, 1727, 1729-33, 1735, 1742-5, 1747-88, 1790-
   1870, 1884-94 **NLW**

FFESTINIOG   *B*
C 1695-1811, 1813-1909   M 1695-1913   B 1695-1811, 1813-1908 **GASD**   Fac CMB 1695-
1791 **NLW**
BT 1676-80, 1683-4, 1687, 1689-92, 1696, 1698-9, 1701-3, 1705-11, 1713-24, 1726-7, 1729-34,
1737-8, 1740, 1742-1851 **NLW**

FRON-GOCH   *SA*
‹Llanfor, Llandderfel & Llanycil 1859
C 1859-1969   M (Banns) 1866-1961   B 1865-1979 **GASD**   M 1862- incumbent

GLYNDYFRDWY gweler/see LLANSANFFRAID GLYNDYFRDWY

GWYDDELWERN   *SA*
C 1691-1704, 1720-1936   M 1696-1705, 1720-1837   B 1695-1706, 1720-1812 **NLW**   Mf
CROH & CROR
BT 1662-3, 1665-8, 1670-1, 1673, 1675-83, 1685, 1695-6, 1698, 1701-3, 1706, 1709-10, 1716-17,
1720-1837 **NLW**   Mf **CROH & CROR**

HARLECH gweler/see LLANDANWG

LLANABER   *B*
PR CMB 1726- recorded in 1776 apparently lost
C 1750-1897   M 1755-1886   B 1750-1915 **GASD**   Fac C 1813-97   M 1755-1812, 1837-86
B 1813-1915 **NLW**
BT 1676-9, 1681, 1683-4, 1694, 1696-8, 1700, 1706, 1708, 1714-16, 1719, 1729-34, 1738, 1740,
1742-75, 1777-1844, 1887-91 **NLW**

LLANBEDR   *B*
CB 1627-1812   M 1627-1754, 1813-38 **GASD**   M 1754-1811 **NLW**   Fac C 1627-1812   M
1627-1754, 1813-38   B 1627-1812 **NLW**
BT 1676-80, ?1681, 1684-92, 1694-7, 1699-1700, 1702-8, 1710-24, 1726-7, 1729-34, 1738, 1740,
1742-90, 1792-1808, 1810-53, 1870-95, 1909-10, 1912-13 **NLW**

LLANDANWG   *B*
The parish included the town of Harlech. PR CMB 1695-1812 recorded in 1934 apparently lost
M 1811-34   B 1813-1902 **GASD**   C 1813-   M 1834-   B 1902- incumbent   Mf CB
1695-1812   M 1695-1754 **GASD**   Fac CB 1695-1812   M 1695-1754 **NLW**
BT 1676-8, 1680-1, 1684-5, 1687-91, 1694-8, 1700-3, 1705-7, 1709-24, 1726-34, 1738, 1740, 1742-56,
1758-1852, 1869-70, 1872-97 **NLW**
Cop ms PR (extracts) M 1754-1808 **NLW**

LLANDDERFEL   *SA*
C 1598-1613, 1615-1888   M 1598-1613, 1615-1912   B 1598-1613, 1615-1866 **GASD**   Mf C
1785-1888   B 1781-1866 **CROH & CROR**
BT 1662-6, 1668, 1670-87, 1689-96, 1698-1702, 1704-17, 1719, 1721-4, 1726-1811, 1813-35, 1837-9
NLW   Mf **CROH & CROR**
Cop ts PR (extracts) CMB 1602-1721, 1757 **Soc Gen**

LLANDDWYWE   *B*
C 1674-82, 1684-1711, 1743-1812   M 1674-82, 1684-1711, 1743-88, 1813-37   B 1674-82, 1684-
1711, 1743-1812 **NLW**
BT 1677-8, 1680, 1683-5, 1687-96, 1698-1715, 1717-24, 1726-7, 1729-34, 1738, 1742-3, 1745-50,
1752-6, 1758-1836, 1905-6, 1910, 1913-14 **NLW**

LLANDECWYN *B*
PR CMB 1668-1802 damaged and defective
C 1668-94, 1728-66, 1768-1813   M 1668-94, 1728-1837   B 1668-94, 1728-66, 1768-1813 **GASD**
Fac C 1813-1952   M 1837-1966   B 1813-1950 **GASD**
BT 1676-8, 1680-1, 1683-91, 1693-1700, 1702-17, 1719-23, 1725-7, 1729-34, 1737-8, 1740, 1742-56, 1758-1886 **NLW**
Cop PR (extracts) CMB 1678-1735 *Merioneth Historical and Record Society Journal,* 4 (1962)

LLANDRILLO-YN-EDEIRNION *SA*
C 1686-1716, 1720-1921   M 1686-1716, 1731-1971   B 1686-1716, 1720-1868 **GASD**   Fac B
1868-1935 **GASD**   Mf C 1686-1921   M 1686-1837   B 1686-1868 **CROH & CROR**
BT 1662-3, 1665-8, 1670-93, 1695-6, 1698-1709, 1713-16, 1719-21, 1723-1822, 1824-33, 1851 **NLW**
Mf **CROH & CROR**

LLANEGRYN *B*
C 1723-65, 1773-1878   M 1723-1837   B 1723-65, 1773-1868 **GASD**
BT 1676, 1678-9, 1681, ?1683, 1684, 1687-90, 1692-8, 1700-1, 1703-4, ?1706-7, 1708-24, 1727, 1729, 1731-2, 1734, 1740, 1742-9, 1751-1865 **NLW**

LLANELLTUD/LLANELLTYD *B*
C 1681-1718, 1730-1812   M 1681-1718, 1730-1837   B 1681-1718, 1730-1914 **GASD**   Fac C
1813-77   M (Banns) 1824-1928 **GASD**
BT 1676-8, 1680-1, 1683-91, 1693-1703, 1705-19, 1721-4, 1726-7, 1729-31, 1733-4, 1738, 1740, 1744, 1746, 1748-1836, 1874-92, 1894-6, 1899-1900 **NLW**

LLANENDDWYN *B*
C 1694-1700, 1702-9, 1718-1901   M 1694-1700, 1702-9, 1718-1837   B 1694-1700, 1702-9, 1718-1913 **NLW**   Fac **GASD**
BT 1677-81, 1683-91, 1693-9, 1701-15, 1717-24, 1727, 1729, 1731-4, 1738, 1740-1836, 1905-8, 1910, 1913 **NLW**

LLANFACHRETH *B*
C 1635-90, 1720-1927   M 1635-90, 1720-1837   B 1635-90, 1720-1855 **GASD**   Fac **NLW**
BT 1676, 1678, 1680-1, 1683-1703, 1705-7, 1709-24, 1726, 1729-34, 1738, 1740, 1742, 1744, 1746, 1748, 1750-3, 1756-1833, 1835-6, 1888-92, 1905 **NLW**

LLANFAIR (LLANFAIR JUXTA HARLECH) *B*
PR CB 1695-1812 M 1695-[1774] recorded in 1934 apparently lost
CB 1746-56   M 1746-53 **NLW**   M 1775-1812 **GASD**   Mf CB 1695-1812   M 1695-1753
GASD   Fac CB 1695-1812   M 1695-1753 **NLW**
BT 1676-9, 1683-91, 1694-5, 1698-1711, 1713-14, 1716-24, 1726, 1729-34, 1738, 1740, 1742-1838, 1894-5, 1900-10 **NLW**

LLANFIHANGEL-Y-PENNANT *B*
C 1770-1812   M 1754-1812   B 1770-1964 **GASD**
BT 1676, 1678-80, 1683-4, 1686-9, 1691, 1693-6, 1703-12, 1714-16, 1720-4, 1727-34, 1737-8, 1740, 1742-5, 1747-57, 1759-63, 1765-70, 1772-9, 1781-1865 **NLW**

LLANFIHANGEL-Y-TRAETHAU *B*
PR CB 1690-1813 M 1690-1754 damaged and defective
C 1690-1928   M 1690-1837 (Banns 1831-1934)   B 1690-1918 **GASD**   Fac M 1837-1970
GASD
BT 1676, 1678-81, 1683-97, 1699-1704, 1706-17, 1719-20, 1722-4, 1726-7, 1729-34, 1737-8, 1740, 1742-56, 1758-1858, 1872 **NLW**
Cop PR (extracts) CMB 1692-1712 *Merioneth Historical and Record Society Journal,* 4 (1962)

LLANFOR   *SA*
C 1722-1812   M 1722-1954   B 1722-1858   Fac C 1813-1977   B 1858-1966 **GASD**   Fac C
    1722-1812   M 1722-1835   B 1722-1858 **NLW**
BT 1666-8, 1670, 1672-4, 1676-95, 1698-1833, 1835 **NLW**

LLANFROTHEN   *B*
C 1677-1812   M 1677-1837   B 1677-1915 **GASD**   Fac CB 1772-1812 **NLW**
BT 1677-8, 1681, 1689-90, 1693-5, 1703, 1705, 1707-23, 1727, 1729-34, 1737-8, 1740, 1742-50, 1752,
    1754-1848 **NLW**

LLANGAR   *SA*
C 1614-1710, 1721-1848   M 1614-1710, 1721-1837   B 1614-1710, 1721-1919 **GASD**   Mf
    CROH & CROR   Fac **NLW**   Fac M 1837-1933 **GASD**
BT 1664, 1666-8, 1671, 1673-6, 1678-86, 1688-96, 1698, 1700-2, 1705-16, 1718-1831 **NLW**   Mf
    CROH & CROR
Cop ts PR CB 1614-1806 M 1615-1708, 1724-1811 **Soc Gen**

LLANGELYNNIN   *B*
C 1618-92, 1702-20, 1722-1861   M 1618-65, 1678-92, 1702-20, 1722-76, 1778-1865   B 1618-92,
    1702-20, 1722-1919 **NLW**
BT 1676, 1678-9, 1684, 1686-7, 1689, 1692, 1694-7, 1700-2, 1704, 1706-24, 1726-7, 1729-34, 1738,
    1740, 1742-50, 1752-76, 1778-1847 **NLW**

LLANGELYNNIN   *B*
Society of Friends burial ground, Llwyn-du
BT 1876-8, 1880, 1883-4 **NLW**

LLANGYWER/LLANGOWER   *SA*
C 1603-50, 1654, 1662-79, 1727-1812   M 1627-38, 1665, 1676-7, 1727-1815   B 1626, 1628-46,
    1672-7, 1727-1812 **NLW**   C 1813-1978   M 1816-1964 **GASD**
BT 1668, 1671-9, 1681, 1684-6, 1688, 1690-6, 1699-1702, 1704-41, 1743-1837, 1850, 1852 **NLW**

LLANSANFFRAID GLYNDYFRDWY   *SA*
C 1767-1898   M 1770-1816, 1818-37   B 1767-1905 **GASD**   Mf **CROH & CROR**   Fac M
    1837-1930 **GASD**   Fac C 1767-87, 1813-98   M 1767-87, 1818-37   B 1767-87, 1813-1905
    NLW
BT 1682, 1685-6, 1785-96, 1798, 1811-39 **NLW**   Mf 1685-1839 **CROH & CROR**

LLANSANFFRAID GLYNDYFRDWY St. Thomas   *SA*
'Corwen 1863
C 1859-   M 1860-   B 1862- incumbent   Fac M 1860-1930 **GASD**

LLANUWCHLLYN   *SA*
C 1697-1763, 1770-1812   M ?1697-1751, 1785-1837   B 1697-1763, 1770-1845 **NLW**   Fac C
    1697-1763, 1770-1932   M ?1697-1751, 1785-1806, 1813-1930   B 1697-1763, 1770-1932 **GASD**
BT 1668, 1671-8, 1681-2, 1684, 1686, 1695-6, 1698, 1700-4, 1706-1825, 1827-37, 1850, 1852 **NLW**
    Mf **CROH & CROR**

LLANYCIL   *SA*
C 1615-1890   M 1615-1837 (Banns 1890-1951)   B 1615-1966 **GASD**   Fac M 1837-1932
    GASD
BT 1663, 1666-77, 1680-1, 1685-92, 1695-6, 1699-1702, 1704-18, 1720-1833 **NLW**   Mf **CROH &**
    CROR

LLANYMAWDDWY   *B*
CB 1627-87 with gaps, 1735-55, 1770-1811   M 1627-87 with gaps, 1735-1811, 1813-1970 **NLW**
BT 1666-7, 1672-4, 1684-8, 1700-7, 1709, 1711-13, 1715, 1717-21, 1725-1830, 1832-42, 1881-5 **NLW**

LLAWRYBETWS   *SA*
‹Llanfor, Llandderfel & Gwyddelwern 1864
C 1864-   M 1865-   B 1864- incumbent   Fac M 1865-1930 **GASD**

MAENTWROG   *B*
C 1695-1926   M 1695-1837   B 1695-1879 **GASD**   Fac CMB 1695-1800 **NLW**
BT 1676-80, 1683, ?1686, 1687, 1691-3, 1696, 1698-1709, 1711, 1713-25, 1729-34, ?1737, 1738, 1740,
    1742-55, 1757-64, 1766-1851, 1893 **NLW**

MALLWYD   *B*
C 1568-78, 1580-6, 1600-24, 1630-4, 1658-67, 1669-1894   M 1568-78, 1580-6, 1600-24, 1630-4,
    1658-67, 1669-1967   B 1568-78, 1580-6, 1600-24, 1630-4, 1658-67, 1669-1876 **NLW**
BT 1667-8, 1672-5, 1678, 1680-2, 1684, 1688-96, 1700-8, 1710-11, 1714, 1716-20, 1722-3, 1725-49,
    1750-63, 1765-1814, 1816-32, 1834-8, 1882-5 **NLW**
Cop PR CMB 1568-1610 *Montgomeryshire Collections,* 30 & 32 (1898-1902)

PENNAL   *B*
C 1721-1812   M 1721-1843 (Banns 1830-43)   B 1721-1862 **GASD**   Fac **NLW**   Fac C
    1813-1929   B 1862-1928 **GASD**
BT 1676-81, 1683-4, 1686-1701, 1703-7, 1709, 1713-16, 1718, 1720-5, 1727, 1729-34, 1737-8, 1740,
    1742-87, 1790-1837, 1839-40, 1882 **NLW**

PENRHYNDEUDRAETH   *B*
‹Llanfihangel-y-traethau, Llandecwyn & Llanfrothen 1858
CMB 1858- incumbent
BT 1895-6, 1905-6, 1908, 1910 **NLW**

RHOSYGWALIAU   *SA*
‹Llanfor 1856
C 1838-   M 1839-   B 1842- incumbent   Fac B 1842-1966 **GASD**

TAL-Y-LLYN   *B*
C 1683-1820   M 1683-1837   B 1683-1901 **GASD**   Fac C 1813-1934   B 1903-31 **GASD**
    Fac C 1811-20   M 1811-37   B 1811-1901 **NLW**
BT 1676-8, 1680-1, 1684, 1687-98, 1700-24, 1726-7, 1729-34, 1737-8, 1740, 1742-1883 **NLW**

TOWYN gweler/see **TYWYN**

TRAWSFYNYDD   *B*
C 1685-1835   M 1685-1850   B 1685-1845 **GASD**   Fac M 1754-1850 **NLW**
BT 1680-1, 1687-91, 1693-4, 1696-7, 1699-1700, 1702, 1705-8, 1710-13, 1717-24, 1726-7, 1729-34,
    1737-8, 1740, 1742-1839, 1887-90 **NLW**

TYWYN/TOWYN   *B*
C 1663-1715, 1721-1848   M 1663-1715, 1721-1918   B 1663-1715, 1721-1903 **GASD**
BT 1678-9, 1687-92, ?1693, 1695-1713, 1715-19, 1721, 1723-4, 1726, 1729-34, 1737-8, 1740, 1742-
    1837, 1839 **NLW**

MÔN
ANGLESEY

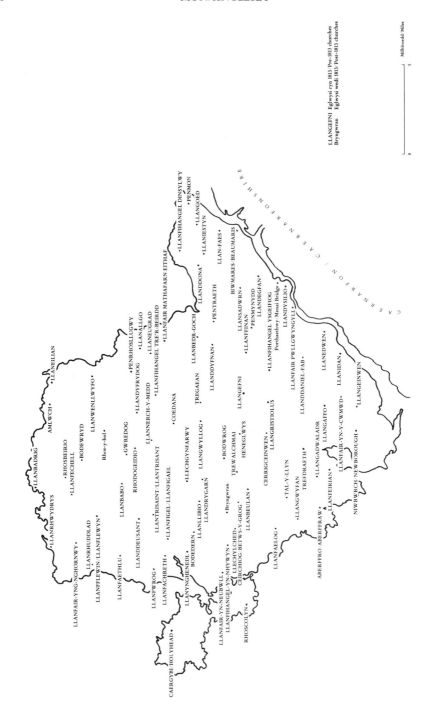

LLANGEFNI Eglwysi cyn 1813/Pre-1813 churches
Bryngwran   Eglwysi wedi 1813/Post-1813 churches

Milltiroedd/Miles

0   5

MÔN/ANGLESEY

ABERFFRO/ABERFFRAW *B*
C 1719-1914   M 1719-1970 (Banns 1850-1951)   B 1719-1941 **GASL**   Fac **NLW**
BT 1675-9, 1682-6, 1689, 1692-3, 1695-1703, 1705-9, 1712-27, 1729-35, 1737-63, 1765-6, 1768-91,
    1793, 1795-1839, 1845-7, 1849-71 **NLW**

AMLWCH *B*
PR CMB 1630-1705 damaged
CMB 1630, 1634, 1636, 1638-41, 1643, 1645, 1664, 1666-7, 1692-1729   C 1732-1801, 1805-1925
    M 1732-1869 (Banns 1823-60)   B 1732-1801, 1805-52 **NLW**   Fac C 1692-1925   M 1692-
    1869   B 1692-1851 **GASL**
BT 1675, 1678, 1682-6, 1689, 1692-9, 1701-4, 1706-31, 1733-5, 1737-51, 1753-66, 1768-70, 1772-93,
    1795-1858 **NLW**

BEAUMARIS gweler/see BIWMARES

BETWS-Y-GROG gweler/see CEIRCHIOG

BIWMARES/BEAUMARIS *B*
C 1649-59, 1668-1739, 1741-1894, 1900-48   M 1653-6, 1668-70, 1675, 1677-1971   B 1653, 1655,
    1668-71, 1676-1739, 1741-1956 **NLW**   Fac C 1655-1947   M 1655-1971   B 1655-1957
    GASL
BT 1699, 1703, 1713-25, 1727-9, 1731, 1734, 1737, 1741-2, 1745-72, 1774-5, 1777-91, 1793-4, 1796-
    1848 **NLW**
Cop ts PR C 1723-81 M 1724-53 B 1724-81 **Soc Gen**

BODEDERN *B*
PR CB 1695-1812 M 1695-1748 recorded in 1934 apparently lost
C 1813-53   M 1754-1837   B 1813-1913 **NLW**   Mf CMB 1695-1712, 1722-33, 1739-48 **NLW**
    Fac C Caergeiliog 1946-55 **GASL**
BT 1678-80, 1682-3, 1686, 1689-90, 1693-1700, 1702, 1706-11, 1713-31, 1733-5, 1737-66, 1768-91,
    1793-1836, 1838-62, 1871, 1881-3, 1885-1900 **NLW**

BODEWRYD *B*
‹Llaneilian
C 1776-1812   M 1755-6, 1773-1831   B 1776-1812 **GASL**   Fac C 1813-1972 **GASL**   Fac C
    1776-1812   M 1755-6, 1773-1831 **NLW**
BT 1817-21, 1823, 1834-85, 1887, 1904, 1906 **NLW**

BODWROG *B*
PR CMB 1617-84 recorded in 1934 apparently lost
CB 1758-77   M 1754-1837 **GASL**   Fac **NLW**
BT 1682-5, 1689-90, 1692-1713, 1715-24, 1728-31, 1733, 1735, 1737-53, 1755-66, 1768-91, 1793-
    1862, 1864-7, 1870-5 **NLW**

BRYNGWRAN *B*
‹Llechylched
BT 1843 **NLW**

CAERGEILIOG gweler/see BODEDERN

CAERGYBI/HOLYHEAD   *B*
C 1737-1903   M 1737-1915   B 1737-1893 **NLW**   Fac C 1813-1902   M 1755-1915
   B 1813-54 **GASL**
BT 1682, 1689-90, 1693-1706, 1708-9, 1711-16, 1718-22, 1724, 1726-30, 1733-4, 1737-91, 1793, 1795,
   1797-1836, 1845-6, 1859 **NLW**
Cop ts CMB 1682-1840 with index (BT 1682-1735 & PR 1737-1840) **NLW & Soc Gen**

CEIDIO gweler/see RHODOGEIDIO

CEIRCHIOG/BETWS-Y-GROG (HOLYROOD CHURCH)   *B*
‹Llanbeulan. Church closed *c.* 1843 and PR CB 1813- were subsequently used to record baptisms
   (from 1895) and burials (from 1891) at Llechylched. PR M 1754-1811 recorded in 1831
   apparently lost
C 1813-43 incumbent   M 1813-42 **GASL**   B 1813-91 incumbent   Fac M 1813-42 **NLW**
BT 1676-8, 1686, 1690, 1692-4, 1697-1702, 1704, 1707-9, 1711-12, 1714-19, 1722, 1724, 1726-7,
   1729-31, 1733-5, 1737-8, 1740-51, 1753-63, 1765-6, 1768-91, 1793-7, 1799, 1802-46, 1891 **NLW**

CERRIGCEINWEN   *B*
C 1721-1942   M 1721-1837   B 1721-1812 **GASL**   Fac CB 1721-1812   M 1721-1837 **NLW**
BT 1676, 1678-80, 1683-5, 1689-90, 1692, 1694-7, 1699-1701, 1706-31, 1733-5, 1737, 1739-55,
   1757-66, 1768-80, 1782-91, 1793-1843, 1845-8, 1851-4, 1866-7, 1882-91 **NLW**

COEDANA   *B*
PR C 1783-1812 M 1783-1811 B 1786-1812 recorded in 1831 apparently lost
M 1813-36 **GASL**   C 1813-   M 1837-   B 1814- incumbent   Fac M 1813-36 **NLW**
BT 1685-6, 1689, 1693, 1695-1702, 1704-11, 1713-16, 1718-26, 1728, 1731, 1733-42, 1744-5, 1747-56,
   1758-9, 1762-6, 1768-73, 1775-7, 1779-83, 1785-91, 1793-1882, 1884-93, 1906 **NLW**

EGLWYS AIL gweler/see LLANGADWALADR

GWREDOG   *B*
An ancient chapelry of Llantrisaint without pre-1813 registers
M 1839-63 **GASL**   Fac **NLW**
BT see Rhodogeidio

HENEGLWYS   *B*
C 1693-1763, 1777-1825   M 1693-1837   B 1693-1763, 1777-1900 **GASL**   Fac C 1693-1763,
   1777-1825   M 1693-1763, 1777-90, 1793-1812   B 1693-1763, 1777-1900 **NLW**
BT 1677-80, 1682-4, 1686-7, 1692-8, 1700-7, 1712-31, 1733-5, 1737-59, 1761-6, 1768-73, 1775-80,
   1782-91, 1793-1896 **NLW**

*****HOLYHEAD/CAERGYBI**   *B*
C 1737-1903   M 1737-1915   B 1737-1893 **NLW**   Fac C 1813-1902   M 1755-1915   B
   1813-54 **GASL**
BT 1682, 1689-90, 1693-1706, 1708-9, 1711-16, 1718-22, 1724, 1726-30, 1733-4, 1737-91, 1793, 1795,
   1797-1836, 1845-6, 1859 **NLW**
Cop ts CMB 1682-1840 with index (BT 1682-1735 & PR 1737-1840) **NLW & Soc Gen**

LLANALLGO   *B*
Entries for CMB 1725-63 are in PR for Llaneugrad
C 1725-63, 1813-1903   M 1725-89, 1833-6   B 1725-63, 1825-1918 **GASL**   Fac M 1754-89
   with index, 1833-6   B 1825-1918 **NLW**   Fac M 1837-1970 **GASL**
BT 1682-6, 1689-90, 1692, 1694-5, 1697-8, 1701-11, 1714-27, 1729-31, 1733, 1735, 1737-52, 1754-73,
   1775-7, 1779-91, 1793-1835 **NLW**

LLANBABO   *B*
Early PR (CB 1740-1814 & M 1754-73) are in poor condition
C 1740-1814   M 1754-73 with gaps, 1773-1812, 1814-37   B 1740-1812 **GASL**   Fac CB 1777-1810   M 1814-37 **NLW**
BT 1683, 1685-6, 1689-90, 1692-6, 1698-1702, 1705-12, 1715-20, 1722, 1724-6, 1728-31, 1733-5, 1737-66, 1768-91, 1793-1863, 1865-70 **NLW**
Cop ms PR CB 1777-1810 **GASL**

LLANBADRIG   *B*
C 1731-1813   M 1731-1837   B 1731-1861 **GASL**   Fac **NLW**
BT 1680, 1682-6, 1689-90, 1693-5, 1700-11, 1713-15, 1717-31, 1733-5, 1737-66, 1768-70, 1772-1837, 1840, 1842-54, 1869-79, 1882-4, 1889-97, 1899-1904, 1909-11 **NLW**   nd [19th c.] **GASL**
Fac 1812-35 **GASL**

LLANBEDR-GOCH   *B*
C 1754-1812   M 1754-81, 1784-1836   B 1754-1812 **GASL**   Fac C 1767-1921   M 1754-81, 1784-1836   B 1767-1921 **NLW**
BT 1680, 1682-6, 1689-90, 1692-4, 1696-1720, 1722-31, 1733-5, 1737-51, 1753-66, 1768-87, 1789-91, 1793-1833, 1836-41, 1844-53, 1866 **NLW**

LLANBEULAN   *B*
PR CMB 1748- recorded in 1776 apparently lost
C 1775-1959   M 1754-1889, 1893-1952   B 1775-1812 **NLW**
BT 1676-9, 1682-6, 1689-90, 1692-1704, 1706-16, ?1717, 1719-31, 1734-5, 1737-45, 1747-63, 1765-6, 1768-91, 1793-1852, 1855-9, 1864-77, 1879-91, 1894-5, 1898, 1900 **NLW**

LLANDDANIEL-FAB   *B*
‹Llanidan
C 1746-1812   M 1746-1838   B 1748-1812 **GASL**   Fac C 1746-1812   M 1746-56, 1813-38   B 1748-1812 **NLW**
BT 1677-80, 1682-6, 1689-90, 1692-1714, 1716-27, 1730-1, 1733-5, 1737, 1742-3, 1745-57, 1759-91, 1794-1802, 1804-60, 1865-6, 1877-80, 1882 **NLW**

LLANDDEUSANT   *B*
CB 1754-74   M 1761-97 **NLW**   CB 1791-1806   M 1813-37 **GASL**   Fac CB 1791-1806 **NLW**
BT 1683, 1686, 1689, 1694-1709, 1711-13, 1715-22, 1724-31, 1733-5, 1737-66, 1768-77, 1779-91, 1793-1843, 1845, 1849-70 **NLW**

LLANDDONA   *B*
PR M 1754-1812 recorded in 1831 apparently lost
C 1762-1899   M 1813-37   B 1762-1813 **GASL**   Fac C 1813-98   M 1813-37 **NLW**
BT 1675, ?1677, 1683-5, 1690-1706, 1708-16, 1719-24, 1726-7, 1729-31, 1733-5, 1737-46, 1748-9, 1751-66, 1768-77, 1779-82, 1785, 1787-91, 1793-4, 1796-1864 **NLW**

LLANDDYFNAN   *B*
C 1661-1715, 1723-1899   M 1663-1714, 1723-1837   B 1668-87, 1723-1907 **GASL**   Fac C 1661-1899   M 1663-1837   B 1668-1907 **NLW**   M 1837-1966 **GASL**
BT 1675, 1678, 1689-90, 1695-1731, 1733, 1735, 1737-66, 1768-91, 1793-1882, 1888-90, 1895 **NLW**
Cop ts PR & BT C 1665-1750 M 1663-1749 B 1663-1750 **GASL**

LLANDEGFAN   *B*
CB 1547-53, 1557-63, 1571-3, 1575-6, 1594-1640, 1642-4, 1646-9, 1651-3, 1657-8, 1660-6, 1668,
   1672, 1733-41, 1751-2, 1755-87, 1789-1976   M 1547-53, 1557-63, 1571-3, 1575-6, 1594-1640,
   1642-4, 1646-9, 1651-3, 1657-8, 1660-6, 1668, 1672, 1733-41, 1751-2, 1754-1971 **NLW**
BT 1686, 1692-6, 1698-1701, 1703-27, 1730-1, 1733-4, 1738, 1740-3, 1745, 1747-52, 1755, 1757-66,
   1769-75, 1778-91, 1793-1829, 1831-60 **NLW**
Cop ms PR CMB 1547-1672 **NLW**

LLANDRYGARN   *B*
C 1739-1934   M 1739-1837   B 1739-1812 **GASL**   Fac CB 1739-1812   M 1739-1837 **NLW**
BT 1679, 1683, 1685-6, 1689-90, 1692-1724, 1727-31, 1733-5, 1738-62, 1764-6, 1768-80, 1782-91,
   1793-1862, 1864-5, 1867, 1869-75, 1877-83 **NLW**

LLANDYFRYDOG   *B*
PR CMB 1589-1633 recorded in 1934 apparently lost
C 1690-1709, 1725-1811, 1813-1943   M 1690-1709, 1727-1837 (Banns 1824-39, 1877, 1939-62)
   B 1690-1709, 1727-1811, 1813-1914 **NLW**
BT 1678, 1683-6, 1690, 1692-5, 1697-1720, 1722-3, 1725-31, 1733-5, 1737-58, 1760-6, 1768-89, 1791,
   1793-1899 **NLW**

LLANDYSILIO   *B*
The parish included the town of Porthaethwy/Menai Bridge
C 1755-94, 1803-97   M 1755-94, 1803-37   B 1755-94, 1803-1925 **GASL**   Fac **NLW**
BT 1679, 1684, 1689-90, 1692-5, 1697, 1699-1726, 1728-31, 1733-4, 1738, 1743, 1747, 1749-51,
   1753-60, 1761-3, 1765-6, 1768-9, 1771-2, 1774, 1776-80, 1782-91, 1793-1833, 1850, 1853, 1865-6,
   1896-7 **NLW**

LLANEDWEN   *B*
‹Llanidan
C 1747-1812   M 1747-1837   B 1747-1812 **GASL**   Fac **NLW**
BT 1672, 1677-8, 1680, 1685-6, 1689-90, 1692-6, 1698, 1701-31, 1733, 1745, 1748-66, 1768-91, 1793-
   1854, 1856-62, 1877-80 **NLW**

LLANEILIAN   *B*
C 1733-1841   M 1733-53, 1758-1837   B 1733-57, 1767-78, 1781-1888 **NLW**
BT 1675-80, 1682-6, 1689, 1692-1707, 1709-31, 1733-5, 1737-65, 1768-73, 1775-81, 1783-91, 1793-
   1836, 1838-41, 1844-7, 1873-1906, 1909-11 **NLW**

LLANERCH-Y-MEDD gweler/see **LLANNERCH-Y-MEDD**

LLANEUGRAD   *B*
C 1725-1812   M 1725-1805, 1813-37   B 1725-1812 **GASL**   Fac **NLW**   Fac M 1837-1966
   GASL
BT 1680, 1682, 1684-5, 1689-90, 1693-4, 1705-11, 1713-22, 1724-7, 1729-31, 1733-5, 1738-66,
   1768-83, 1785-9, 1791, 1793-4, 1796-1823, 1825, 1827-8, 1830-5, 1852-64, 1866-70, 1885, 1889-90
   NLW

LLANFACHRETH   *B*
C 1682-1812   M 1702-1837   B 1682-1812 **GASL**   Fac **NLW**
BT 1675-6, 1678, 1680, 1683-6, 1689-90, 1692-1731, 1733-5, 1737-45, 1747-66, 1768-91, 1793-1836,
   1838-48, 1852-82, 1886-92, 1894-6, 1901 **NLW**

LLANFAELOG *B*
PR CMB 1689-1812 recorded in 1831 apparently lost
C 1813-1959   M 1754-94, 1796-1971   B 1813-1941 **NLW**
BT 1677-80, 1682-6, 1689-90, 1692-1704, 1706-8, 1710-17, 1719-25, 1727, 1730-1, 1733-5, 1737-8,
   1741-5, 1747-66, 1768-80, 1782-91, 1793-1827, 1829-52, 1864-1900 **NLW**

LLAN-FAES *B*
PR CMB 1727-67 recorded in 1934 apparently lost
C 1770-1975   M 1754-1970   B 1770-1962 **NLW**
BT 1689-90, 1695-9, 1701-7, 1709-13, 1715, 1717-31, 1733-5, 1739, 1742-64, 1766, 1769, 1771-2,
   1775, 1777-81, 1783-91, 1793-5, 1797-1835, 1838-40, 1844-66, 1889 **NLW**

LLANFAETHLU *B*
PR CMB 1683- recorded in 1776 apparently lost
C 1743-1812   M 1743-1837   B 1743-1812 **GASL**   Fac CB 1743-1812   M 1743-1837
   NLW   C 1813-1974   B 1813-1950 **GASL**
BT ?1672-3, 1678-9, 1684, 1689-90, 1693, 1695-1726, 1728-31, 1733-5, 1737-42, 1744-66, 1768-81,
   1783-91, 1793-1866, 1868-85, 1891, 1902 **NLW**
Cop ts PR/BT CMB 1678-1840 with index **NLW & Soc Gen**

LLANFAIR MATHAFARN EITHAF *B*
C 1753-1803, 1805-73   M 1753-1812   B 1753-1803, 1805-88 **GASL**   Fac **NLW**
BT 1678, 1684, 1686, 1690, 1692, 1694-1705, 1708-11, 1713-35, 1737-49, 1751, 1753-66, 1768-91,
   1793-1837, 1839-59, 1865-82, 1888-92 **NLW**

LLANFAIR PWLLGWYNGYLL *B*
C 1754-63, 1783-5, 1787-1812   M 1757-86, 1795-1810   B 1754-63, 1783-5, 1787-1812 **NLW**
BT 1678-9, 1682-5, 1689, 1691-9, 1702-4, 1706, 1708-31, 1733-4, 1738-9, 1741-2, 1746-66, 1768-74,
   1776-80, 1782-91, 1793-1833, 1850-66, 1896-7 **NLW**
Cop ms PR C 1831-2 **NLW**

LLANFAIR-YNG-NGHORNWY *B*
C 1732-1812   M 1732-1837   B 1732-1812 **GASL**   Fac CB 1732-1812   M 1732-1837 **NLW**
   C 1813-1974   B 1813-1938 **GASL**
BT 1669, 1673, 1675-8, 1680, 1683, 1685-6, 1689-90, 1705, 1708, 1711, 1713, 1715-16, 1718-24,
   1728-31, 1733-5, 1737-9, 1741-66, 1768-90, 1792-1836, 1838-69, 1894-8, 1900-13 **NLW**

LLANFAIR-YN-NEUBWLL *B*
‹Rhoscolyn. PR going 'one hundred & fifty years back' recorded in 1776, PR 1768-1812 recorded in
   1831 and PR M 1774-1812 recorded in 1934 apparently lost
CB 1813- incumbent   M 1813-37 **NLW**
BT nd, 1677, 1683-6, 1689-90, 1695-1702, 1706-9, 1711, 1713-17, 1719-31, 1733-5, 1737-58, 1760,
   1763, 1765-6, 1768-71, 1773-1862, 1876, 1878-84 **NLW**
Cop ts PR/BT CB 1677-1841 (BT 1677-1812) M 1677-1837 (BT 1677-1773) with index **Soc**
   Gen   ts PR/BT CMB 1677-1812 with index **NLW**

LLANFAIR-YN-Y-CWMWD *B*
An ancient chapelry of Llanidan, without registers before 1885. 'This small parish contains 150 acres
   of cultivated land. The church has been for years in a state of such dilapidation as to preclude the
   performance of divine service, but is at present being rebuilt' (Angharad Llwyd, *History of the*
   Island of Mona (Ruthin, 1833), p. 259)

LLANFECHELL B

C 1691-1801, 1806-67 M 1691-1837 B 1691-1801, 1806-89 **GASL**   Fac C 1691-1757,
   1806-67 M 1691-1837 B 1691-1757, 1806-89 **NLW**
BT 1680, 1682, 1689-90, 1693-5, 1697-1731, 1733-5, 1737-66, 1768-1850, 1852-4, 1858, 1864-6
   NLW

LLANFEIRIAN

This church was in ruins at visitation in 1776. For PR entries see Llangadwaladr

LLANFFINAN B

PR CMB 1690-1807 has been damaged and is defective
C 1690-1807 M 1690-1837 B 1690-1807 **GASL**   Fac M 1754-1837 **NLW**
BT 1675, 1677-8, 1680, 1690, 1693-5, 1698-1708, 1710, 1712-27, 1729-31, 1733, 1735, 1737-41,
   1743-6, 1748-51, 1753-66, 1768-80, 1782-91, 1793-1833, 1837-45, 1847-62 **NLW**

LLANFFLEWIN/LLANFLEWYN B

PR CMB 1755-64 recorded in 1831 apparently lost
C 1794-1818 M 1784-1809, 1813-37 B 1794-1818 **GASL**   Fac M 1813-37 **NLW**
BT 1689-90, 1693, 1695, 1697-9, 1701-2, 1705, 1709-14, 1716-17, 1719, 1722-7, 1730-1, 1733-4,
   1737-55, 1757-66, 1768-77, 1779-91, 1793-1872, 1888-96, 1898-1907, 1909, 1912, 1914 **NLW**

LLANFIGEL/LLANFIGAEL B

Early entries are in PR for Llanfachreth
CMB 1682-1805 **GASL**
BT 1682, 1684-6, 1689, 1692-3, 1695-1701, 1703-31, 1733-5, 1737-44, ?1746, 1747-8, 1750-66,
   1768-91, 1793-1806, 1808-14, 1844-5, 1847-50, 1852-3, 1855-7, 1859-80, 1882, 1886, 1888-91, 1893
   NLW

LLANFIHANGEL DINSYLWY B

C 1762-1815 M 1814-37 B 1762-1815 **GASL**
BT ?1686, 1692-3, 1695-6, 1698, 1700-7, 1709-12, 1715, 1717-21, 1723-5, 1727-31, 1734-5, ?1737,
   1738-43, 1745-6, 1750-2, 1754-9, 1761-6, 1771-9, 1781-4, 1786-91, 1793-5, 1797-1811, 1813-41,
   1844-54, 1856, 1858, 1908, 1911-15 **NLW**

LLANFIHANGEL TRE'R-BEIRDD B

C 1695-1811 M 1695-1811, 1814-37 B 1695-1811, 1813-1920 **GASL**   Fac M 1838-1968
   GASL   Fac C 1695-1811 M 1695-1754 B 1695-1811, 1813-1920 **NLW**
BT 1678, ?1683-5, 1686, 1690, 1692-1700, 1702-31, 1733-5, 1737-66, 1768-70, 1772-90, 1793-1899
   NLW

LLANFIHANGEL-YN-NHYWYN B

'Rhoscolyn. PR going 'one hundred & fifty years back' recorded in 1776 and PR 1788-1812
   recorded in 1831 apparently lost
CB 1813- M 1837- incumbent Fac C 1813-1967 **GASL**
BT ?1679, ?1683, 1685, 1689-90, 1692-7, 1700-6, 1708, 1710-11, 1713-28, 1731, 1733-5, ?1737,
   1739-53, 1755-66, 1768-91, 1793-1838, 1840-9, 1851-60, 1878-83 **NLW**

LLANFIHANGEL YSGEIFIOG B

C 1703-1854 M 1703-1837 B 1703-1866 **GASL**   Fac C 1813-54 M 1813-37 B 1813-66
   NLW
BT 1675, 1677-8, 1682-5, 1689, 1694-5, 1697-1706, 1708-26, 1729-31, 1733-5, 1737-8, 1740-66,
   1768-72, 1774-82, 1784-91, 1793-1835, 1837-45, 1847-54, 1864-5 **NLW**

*LLANFLEWYN/LLANFFLEWIN **B**
PR CMB 1755-64 recorded in 1831 apparently lost
C 1794-1818   M 1784-1809, 1813-37   B 1794-1818 **GASL**   Fac M 1813-37 **NLW**
BT 1689-90, 1693, 1695, 1697-9, 1701-2, 1705, 1709-14, 1716-17, 1719, 1722-7, 1730-1, 1733-4,
   1737-55, 1757-66, 1768-77, 1779-91, 1793-1872, 1888-96, 1898-1907, 1909, 1912, 1914 **NLW**

LLANFWROG   **B**
PR CMB 1638- recorded in 1776 apparently lost
C 1760-1805   M 1754-1836   B 1760-1805 **GASL**   Fac CB 1760-1805   M 1754-1836 **NLW**
   C 1813-1977   B 1813-1980 **GASL**
BT 1672-3, 1677-9, 1685-6, 1689-99, ?1701, 1702-10, 1712-31, 1733-5, 1737-47, 1749-66, 1768-77,
   1779-80, 1782-91, 1793-1863, 1865-9, 1873, 1875-85, 1891-1902 **NLW**
Cop ts PR/BT CB 1672-1840 M 1677-1839 **Soc Gen**

LLANGADWALADR (EGLWYS AIL) & LLANFEIRIAN   **B**
C 1610-1812   M 1610-1812   B 1610-1913 **GASL**   Fac C 1610-1812   M 1610-1754   B
   1610-1913 **NLW**
BT 1676-80, 1682-3, 1685-6, 1689, 1691-4, 1696-1708, 1710-19, 1721-31, 1733-5, 1737-66, 1768-77,
   1779-80, 1782-91, 1793-9, 1801-84, 1886-95 **NLW**

LLANGAFFO   **B**
PR CMB 1659-1812 recorded in 1934 apparently lost
C 1813- incumbent   M 1755-1837   B 1814-1918 **GASL**   Fac M 1755-1837   B 1814-1918
   NLW
BT 1679, 1682-6, 1690, 1692-1701, 1703-29, 1731, 1733-5, 1737-60, 1762-6, 1768-87, 1789-91, 1793-
   1810, 1813-83 **NLW**

LLANGEFNI   **B**
C 1709-1871   M 1709-1837   B 1709-1918 **GASL**   Fac **NLW**
BT 1669, 1676, 1678, 1680, 1683-5, 1689-90, 1693, 1695-1707, 1710-17, 1721-31, 1733-5, 1738-43,
   1745-9, 1751-9, 1761-6, 1768-89, 1791, 1793-1882 **NLW**

LLANGEINWEN   **B**
PR CB 1790-1811 recorded in 1934 apparently lost
C 1688-1787, 1813-80   M 1688-1787, 1790-1837 (Banns 1823-57)   B 1688-1812 **GASL**   Fac
   C 1688-1787, 1813-80   M 1688-1787, 1790-1837   B 1688-1812 **NLW**
BT 1675, 1678-9, 1682-6, 1689-90, 1692-1719, 1721-31, 1733-5, 1737-66, 1768-91, 1793-1883 **NLW**

LLANGOED   **B**
PR CMB going 'as far back as the reign of Edward the Sixth' recorded in 1776 apparently lost
C 1763-1905   M 1754-1837   B 1763-1908 **GASL**   Fac C 1763-1888   M 1754-1837   B
   1763-1908 **NLW**
BT 1682-3, 1685-6, 1689, 1692-5, 1697, 1699-1725, 1728-31, 1733-4, 1737-40, 1742-6, 1748-58,
   1760-6, 1769-91, 1793-1849, 1851-6, 1908-14, 1917 **NLW**

LLANGRISTIOLUS   **B**
Entries for CB 1757-80 and C 1916-42 are in PR for Cerrigceinwen
C 1757-1942   M 1754-1837 (Banns 1824-49)   B 1757-1918 **GASL**   Fac C 1781-1916   M
   1754-1837   B 1781-1918 **NLW**
BT 1675, 1678-80, 1683-4, 1689, 1693-8, 1700, 1703-5, 1709-10, 1712-13, 1716-31, 1733-5, 1737-66,
   1768-77, 1779-91, 1793-1849, 1851-4, 1864-92 **NLW**

LLANGWYFAN *B*
‹Trefdraeth. PR CB 1759- recorded in 1776 apparently lost. PR CB 1775-1811 has been damaged
C 1775-1811   M 1754-1836, 1838-1971   B 1775-1811, 1813-1976 **GASL**   Fac **NLW**
BT 1718-20, 1728, 1730-1, 1734-5, 1737-48, 1750-63, 1765-76, 1778-83, 1785-91, 1793-1837,
    1839-42, 1844-51, 1853-61, 1902-13, 1915-16 **NLW**

LLANGWYLLOG   *B*
PR CMB 1618- recorded in 1776 apparently lost
C 1777-1811   M 1800-9   B 1777-1811 **GASL**   Fac **NLW**
BT 1677-9, 1683-6, 1689-90, 1692-1727, 1729-31, 1733-5, 1737-66, 1768-91, 1793-1882, 1884-93,
    1906 **NLW**

LLANGYNFARWY gweler/see **LLECHGYNFARWY**

LLANIDAN   *B*
CMB 1666-1734 **NLW**   C 1746-85, 1787-1848   M 1746-1837   B 1746-85, 1787-1902 **GASL**
    Fac C 1746-85, 1787-1848   M 1746-1837   B 1746-85, 1787-1902 **NLW**
BT 1676, 1678, 1680, ?1689, 1690, 1697-8, 1701-11, 1713-27, 1729-31, 1733-5, 1743, 1745-6, 1748-66,
    1768-91, 1794-1861, 1865-7, 1869, 1881-3, 1886, 1895-7 **NLW**

LLANIESTYN   *B*
PR CMB 1755-1812 recorded in 1831 apparently lost
CB 1813- incumbent   M 1813-34 **GASL**   Fac M 1813-34 **NLW**
BT 1682-3, 1685-6, 1692-5, 1697-1719, 1721-4, ?1726, 1727-31, 1735, 1737-66, 1768-91, 1793-1849,
    1852-7, 1908-15 **NLW**

LLANLLIBIO   *B*
The church for this parish was described at visitation in 1776 as 'in ruins time immemorial'; it was
    formerly a chapelry of Llantrisaint. No records survive. The inhabitants attended the churches of
    Bodedern and Llantrisaint

LLANNERCH-Y-MEDD   *B*
‹Amlwch, Gwredog, Llechgynfarwy & Rhodogeidio 1854. Formerly a chapelry of Amlwch
C 1761-1878   M 1754-1833, 1835-6   B 1761-1905 **GASL**   Fac **NLW**
BT 1851, 1875-85 **NLW**

LLANRHUDDLAD   *B*
PR CMB 1737-1812 recorded in 1831 apparently lost
C 1813-92   M 1813-1918 (Banns 1847-72) **GASL**   B 1813- incumbent   Fac C 1813-92   M
    1813-1918 **NLW**
BT 1676, 1679-80, 1683, 1686, 1689-94, 1697-1700, 1702, 1704-7, 1709-11, 1713-16, 1719-25,
    1727-31, 1733-4, 1737-66, 1768-91, 1793-1801, 1803-72, 1888-1914, 1916 **NLW**

LLANRHWYDRYS   *B*
PR CB 1792-1818 has been damaged
C 1747-1818   M 1747-1834   B 1747-1818   Fac C 1813-1971 **GASL**
BT ?1680, 1683, 1685-6, 1690, 1692-3, 1695, 1697, 1699-1702, 1704-31, 1733-5, 1737-9, 1741-60,
    1762-6, 1768-91, 1793-1855, 1857-68, 1870-3, 1894-5, 1898, 1900-1, 1906-13 **NLW**

LLANSADWRN   *B*
C 1584-1725, 1731-1812   M 1584-1837   B 1584-1725, 1731-1812 **GASL**   Fac CB 1584-1725
    M 1584-1725, 1754-1837 **NLW**
BT 1692, 1694, 1696-1702, 1704-11, 1713-31, 1733-5, 1737-40, 1742-3, 1747-61, 1763-6, 1768-75,
    1777, 1779-87, 1789-91, 1793-1871, 1876-82, 1884-90 **NLW**

LLANTRISAINT/LLANTRISANT   *B*

PR M 1813-37 recorded in 1934 apparently lost

C 1745-1812   M 1745-1812, 1837-1918   B 1745-1812 **GASL**

BT 1683, 1685, 1689-90, 1692-7, 1699-1719, 1723, 1725, 1729, 1731, 1738-41, 1743-66, 1768-91,
  1793-1846, 1848-85, 1887-96, 1900-9 **NLW**

LLANWENLLWYFO   *B*

PR CB 1792-8 recorded in 1934 apparently lost

C 1763-91, 1813-1931   M 1762-1969   B 1763-91, 1813-83 **NLW**

BT 1690, 1693-9, 1701-3, 1706-9, 1713-31, 1733-4, ?1735, 1737-53, 1755-61, 1763-6, 1768-80,
  1782-91, 1793-1915 **NLW**

LLANYNGHENEDL   *B*

C 1713-1813, 1817-18   M 1713-96, 1800-37   B 1713-1813 **GASL**   Fac **NLW**

BT 1675-6, 1679-80, 1683-6, 1689-90, 1692-7, 1699-1731, 1733-5, 1737-58, 1760-6, 1768-91, 1793-
  1853, 1855-82, 1886-91, 1893-6, 1901 **NLW**

LLECHGYNFARWY (LLANGYNFARWY)   *B*

C 1743-1812   M 1743-92, 1794-1837   B 1743-1812 **GASL**   Fac **NLW**

BT nd, 1682-6, 1689-90, 1692-8, 1700-5, 1707-15, 1717-22, 1728, 1734, 1737-9, 1741-6, 1749-66,
  1768-91, 1793-1851, 1857, 1869, 1872-4, 1877-9 **NLW**

LLECHYLCHED   *B*

Entries for C 1896- and B 1891- are in PR for Ceirchiog

C 1803-95   M 1813-36 (Banns 1847-72)   B 1803-90 **NLW**   Fac M (Banns) 1847-72 **GASL**

BT 1676-8, 1682-6, 1689-90, 1692-1701, 1703-31, 1733-5, 1737-9, 1741, 1743, 1745, 1747-63, 1765-6,
  1768-75, 1777-91, 1793-1852, 1855-9, 1864-86, 1888-9, 1891-3 **NLW**

MENAI BRIDGE gweler/see LLANDYSILIO

NIWBWRCH/NEWBOROUGH   *B*

'Some remains of a register as far backward as 1581 but very imperfect' recorded in 1776

C 1721-1908   M 1721-1837, 1925-7 (Banns 1924-7)   B 1721-1863 **GASL**   Fac C 1721-1908
  M 1721-54, 1813-37   B 1721-1863 **NLW**

BT 1676, 1678, 1680, 1682-5, 1690, 1692-3, 1695-1704, 1706-8, 1710-31, 1733-5, 1737-66, 1768-1837,
  1839-53, 1913-14 **NLW**

PENMON   *B*

C 1693-1812   M 1693-1812, 1814-37   B 1693-1812 **GASL**   Fac **NLW**

BT ?1679, 1686, 1690, 1695, 1699-1707, ?1709, 1710-31, 1733-5, 1737, 1739, 1741-65, 1769, ?1771,
  1772-9, 1781-91, 1793-1806, 1808-36, 1838-40, 1844-66, 1889 **NLW**

PENMYNYDD   *B*

PR CB 1741-62 M 1741-53 recorded in 1831 apparently lost

C 1759-1812   M 1754-1837   B 1759-1925 **GASL**   Fac **NLW**

BT 1675, 1677-9, 1685-6, 1689-90, 1692-3, 1695-1706, 1708-31, 1733-4, 1738-44, 1746-66, 1768-78,
  1780, 1782-3, 1785-91, 1793-1831, 1833-5, 1839-42, 1844-53, 1855-60, 1864-6, 1891 **NLW**

PENRHOSLLUGWY   *B*

C 1578-1766   M 1578-1803, 1811-37   B 1578-1766, 1813-1908 **GASL**   C 1813-   M 1837- incumbent   Fac M 1837-1967 **GASL**   Fac C 1578-1766   M 1578-1766, 1811-37   B 1578-
  1766, 1813-1908 **NLW**

BT 1675, 1677-8, 1680, 1682-6, 1689-90, 1692, 1696-8, 1700-1, 1703-11, 1713- 21, 1723-31, 1733-5,
  1737-66, 1768-91, 1793-1802, 1804-41, 1848-60, 1862-73 **NLW**

PENTRAETH   *B*
C 1740-1915   M 1740-65, 1767-1837   B 1740-63, 1768-79, 1781-1981 **GASL**   Fac C 1740-69,
    1781-1915   M 1740-64, 1781-1837   B 1740-69, 1781-1859 **NLW**   M 1837-1970 **GASL**
BT 1664-5, 1679, 1682-6, 1689, 1692-3, 1695-7, 1700-5, 1707-14, 1716-19, 1721-31, 1733-5, 1737-66,
    1768-79, 1781-91, 1793-1853, 1896 **NLW**

PORTHAETHWY gweler/see LLANDYSILIO

RHODOGEIDIO (CEIDIO)   *B*
‹Llantrisaint. It was claimed in 1776 that ‘almost all the parish christen at Llannerchymedd being
    nearer for most of the inhabitants’. Earlier PR recorded in 1831 as ‘accidentally destroyed by fire’
C 1783-1812   M 1754-1836   B 1783-1812 **GASL**   Fac **NLW**
BT 1694-6, 1698, 1700, 1702, 1704, 1706-10, 1712-30, 1737-42, 1744-6, 1748-66, 1768-73, 1775-91,
    1793-1851, 1857, 1872-82 **NLW**

RHOSBEIRIO   *B*
‹Llaneilian
C 1813-1923   M 1852-1912   B 1813-1962 **GASL**   Fac **NLW**
BT 1813, 1865, 1867-8, 1870, 1873-6, 1880-1, 1883, 1885, 1887, 1906 **NLW**

RHOSCOLYN   *B*
C 1732-59, 1765, 1767, 1769-1892, 1901-2   M 1732-54, 1772-1837   B 1732-59, 1763, 1770-1810,
    1813-81 **NLW**
BT 1678, 1683-6, 1689-90, 1692, 1695-6, 1700-1, 1703, 1705-9, 1711-17, 1719-27, 1729, 1731, 1733-5,
    1737-58, 1760-6, 1768-77, 1779-91, 1793-1867, 1876, 1878-84 **NLW**
Cop ts PR/BT CMB 1678-1841 **NLW**

RHOS-Y-BOL   *B*
‹Amlwch 1876
C 1875-   M 1878-   B 1877- incumbent
BT 1875-85 **NLW**

TAL-Y-LLYN   *B*
‹Llanbeulan. In 1776 the church was said to have ‘received a thorough rep[ai]r about four years
    ago, but [it] has not been served these twelve years’
C 1845-1970 **NLW**

TREFDRAETH   *B*
PR CMB 1709-29 is damaged and defective
C 1551-1707, 1709-29, 1760-99, 1801-67   M 1552-1707, 1709-29, 1756-1838   B 1551-1707,
    1709-29, 1760-99, 1801-70 **GASL**   Fac C 1551-1707, 1709-29, 1760-99, 1801-67   M 1552-
    1707, 1709-29, 1756-76, 1813-38   B 1551-1707, 1709-29, 1760-99, 1801-70 **NLW**
BT 1682-5, 1689-90, 1692-6, 1698-1706, 1708, 1712-15, 1717-27, 1729-31, 1733-5, 1737-47, 1750,
    1753-5, 1757-63, 1765-6, 1768-81, 1783-91, 1793-1861, 1902-16 **NLW**
Cop PR C 1551-1633 M 1552-1633 B 1551-1634 *Anglesey Antiquarian Society Transactions* (1924)

TREGAEAN   *B*
C 1708-1812   M 1708-1836   B 1708-1812 **GASL**   Fac **NLW**
BT 1678-80, 1682-4, 1686, 1689-90, 1692-5, 1697-1718, 1721-9, 1733-5, 1739-51, 1753-9, 1761-6,
    1768-9, 1771-7, 1779-91, 1793-1859, 1861-5, 1868-75 **NLW**

TREWALCHMAI   *B*
C 1727-1880   M 1727-1837   B 1727-1906 **GASL**   Fac C 1727-1880   M 1727-54, 1813-37
    B 1727-1906 **NLW**
BT 1675-6, 1680, 1682, 1692-1731, 1733-5, 1737-9, 1741-58, 1760-6, 1768-91, 1793-1896, 1901-3,
    1906 **NLW**

MORGANNWG
GLAMORGAN

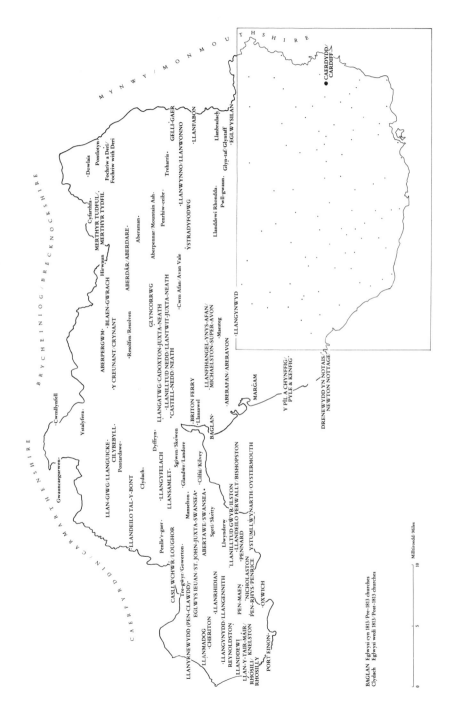

CAERDYDD/
CARDIFF

Y N O T H S H I R E

M Y N W Y / M O N M O U

B R Y C H E I N I O G / B R E C K N O C K S H I R E

·Dowlais
·Pontlotyn
Cyfarthfa·   Fochriw a Deri/
MERTHYR TUDFUL/   Fochriw with Deri
MERTHYR TYDFIL

GELLI-GAER·
·LLANFABON

Treharris·
Penrhiw-ceibr·   Llanbradach·
Aberpennar/Mountain Ash·   ·EGLWYSILAN
Aberaman·   ·LLANWYNNO/LLANWONNO
·LLANWYNNO/LLANWONNO

Glyn-taf/Glyntaff·
Hirwaun   ABERDÂR/ABERDARE·   Poll-gwaun.
·BLAEN-GWRACH   Llanddewi Rhondda·
ABERPERGWM·
·Y CREUNANT/CRYNANT   GLYNCORRWG

Ystalyfera·   ·Resolfen/Resolven   ·YSTRADYFODWG

·Cwnllynfell
Gwauncaegurwen·

Dyffryn·   LLANGATWG/CADOXTON-JUXTA-NEATH
CILYBEBYLL·   ·LLANLLTUD NEDD/LLANTWIT-JUXTA-NEATH
Pontardawe·   ·CASTELL-NEDD/NEATH
LLAN-GIWG/LLANGUICKE·   ·Cwm Afan/Avan Vale   ·LLANGYNWYD
·LLANDEILO TAL-Y-BONT

Clydach·   LLANFIHANGEL-YNYS-AFAN/
·LLANGYFELACH   MICHAELSTON-SUPER-AVON
Penlle'r-gaer·   LLANSAMLET·   ·Maesteg
Manselton·   ·Glandwr/Landore
·BRITON FERRY
Tre-gŵyr/ Gowerton·   Sgiwen/Skewen·   ·Llansawel
·Clâs/ Kilvey   BAGLAN·
CASLLWCHWR/ LOUGHOR   Sgeti/Sketty·   ·ABERAFAN/ABERAVON
EGLWYS IEUAN/ ST. JOHN-JUXTA-SWANSEA·
LLANYRNEWYDD (PEN-CLAWDD)·   ABERTAWE/ SWANSEA·   MARGAM
·CHERITON   Y PÎL A CHYNFFIG/
LLANMADOG   ·LLANRHIDIAN   Llwynderw·   PYLE & KENFIG·
·LLANGYNYDD/ LLANGENNITH   ·LLANILLTUD GŴYR/ILSTON
REYNOLDSTON·   ·PENNARD   ·LLANDEILO FERWALLT/ BISHOPSTON
·LLANDDEWI   YSTUMLLWYNARTH/ OYSTERMOUTH   DRENEWYDD YN NOTAIS/
PEN-MAEN·   ·NICHOLASTON   NEWTON NOTTAGE
LLAN-Y-TAIR-MAIR/
RHOSILI/   KNELSTON·
RHOSSILY   ·PEN-RHYS/ PENRICE
·OXWICH

·PORT EINON·

Milltiroedd/ Miles

0   5   10

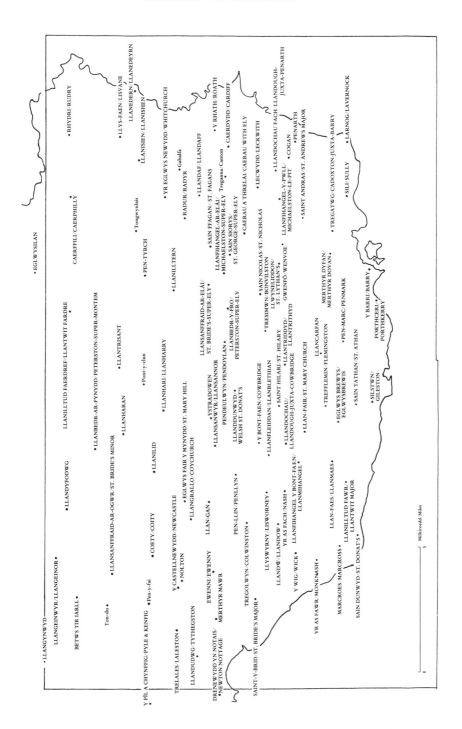

ABERAFAN/ABERAVON *LL*
PR CB 1597-1734 recorded in 1831 but not in *A digest of the parish registers within the diocese of Llandaff* ... (Cardiff, 1905) apparently lost
C 1748-1904   M 1747-1911   B 1747-1927 **Glam RO**   Fac CMB 1748-1812 **NLW**
BT 1696, 1721-1861, 1863-9 **NLW**

ABERAMAN *LL*
‹Aberdâr/Aberdare 1888
C 1889-   M 1887- incumbent
BT 1900 **NLW**

ABERAVON gweler/see **ABERAFAN**

ABERDÂR/ABERDARE *LL*
C St. John 1734-1897   M St. John 1734-53, 1756-7, 1769-1937 St. Elvan 1855-1918   B St. John
   1734-1916 **Glam RO**   C 1815-50, 1898-   M 1813-   B 1815-44, 1853-8, 1916- incumbent
   Fac M 1812-37 **Glam RO**
BT 1717, 1724-1863, 1900-4 **NLW**
Cop ms PR CB 1734-1821 M 1734-57, 1769-1836 **NLW**

ABERPENNAR/MOUNTAIN ASH *LL*
‹Aberdâr/Aberdare & Llanwynno/Llanwonno 1863
C 1859-   M 1865- incumbent
BT 1859-74 **NLW**

ABERPERGWM *LL*
An ancient chapelry of Llangatwg/Cadoxton-juxta-Neath. Separate parish from 1861
M 1837-1944 (Banns 1945-68) **Glam RO**   CB 1849- incumbent
BT 1849-50 **NLW**

ABERTAWE/SWANSEA Christ Church *SB*
‹St. Mary 1874
C 1872-1927   M 1872-1919 (Banns 1889-1900) **Glam RO**
BT 1872-80 **NLW**

ABERTAWE/SWANSEA Eglwys Ieuan/St. John *SB*
Dedication transferred in 1880 from old church in High Street (now St. Matthew) to newly-built
   church at Hafod. Diocesan records suggest that *c.* 1790 the registers went back to 1760
C 1797-1800, 1813-1923   M 1813-1918 (Banns 1843-1958)   B 1797-1800, 1813-85 **Glam RO**
BT 1785, 1787-9, 1791-8, 1800, 1802-3, 1805-73 **NLW**

ABERTAWE/SWANSEA Holy Trinity *SB*
‹St. Mary 1843
C 1856-1939   M 1877-1941   B 1901-16 **Glam RO**
BT 1856-82, 1885-6 **NLW**

ABERTAWE/SWANSEA St. Barnabas *SB*
‹St. Mary 1914
C 1915-58   M 1929-52 **Glam RO**

ABERTAWE/SWANSEA St. Gabriel   *SB*
‹St. Mary 1889
C 1889-1914   M 1890-1922 **Glam RO**
BT 1889-91 **NLW**

ABERTAWE/SWANSEA St. James   *SB*
‹St. Mary 1867
C 1867-1924   M 1867-1926 (Banns 1899-1921) **Glam RO**
BT 1867-82 **NLW**

ABERTAWE/SWANSEA St. Jude   *SB*
‹St. Mary 1921
C 1896-1921   M 1896-1928 (Banns 1896-1928) **Glam RO**

ABERTAWE/SWANSEA St. Luke, Cwmbwrla   *SB*
‹Y Cocyd/Cockett 1911
C 1886-1914   M 1890-1949 (Banns 1905-27) **Glam RO**

ABERTAWE/SWANSEA St. Mark   *SB*
‹St. Mary 1888
C 1888-1918   M 1888-1931 (Banns 1888-1903) **Glam RO**
BT 1894-5 **NLW**

ABERTAWE/SWANSEA St. Mary   *SB*
C 1631-1706, 1712-1928   M 1631-1706, 1712-1924 (Banns 1823-37, 1872-3, 1894-1924)   B 1631-
    1706, 1712-1937 & cremated remains 1957-79 **Glam RO**   Fac PR CMB 1631-1706 **NLW**
BT 1676-8, 1681, 1683-4, 1686, 1690, 1693, 1695-7, 1700-2, 1704, 1713, 1717, 1725-36, 1738,
    1740-59, 1761-86, 1788-92, 1794-1800, 1802-3, 1805-82, 1885, 1887-95, 1898-1905 **NLW**

ABERTAWE/SWANSEA St. Matthew   *SB*
‹St. Mary & St. John 1886
M 1886-1927 **Glam RO**

ABERTAWE/SWANSEA St. Nicholas   *SB*
‹St. Mary 1886. Closed 1920
C 1886-1920   M 1886-1920 (Banns 1886-1901, 1908-19) **Glam RO**

ABERTAWE/SWANSEA St. Nicholas-on-the-Hill   *SB*
‹St. Jude 1933
C 1924-42 Good Shepherd Mission 1927-46   M 1937-50 **Glam RO**

ABERTAWE/SWANSEA St. Peter, Y Cocyd/Cockett   *SB*
‹St. Mary 1878
C 1856-1943   M 1857-1919 (Banns 1908-39)   B 1856-1923 **Glam RO**
BT 1856-9, 1861-75 **NLW**
Cop ms PR M 1859-69 **NLW**

ABERTAWE/SWANSEA St. Thomas   *SB*
‹St. Mary 1888
C 1888-1924   M 1888-1927 **Glam RO**
BT 1888-9 **NLW**

AS FACH, YR/NASH   *LL*

Extra-parochial. A private chapel at one time. The manor was the only house in the parish, which comprises only 200 acres. Population since 1800 averaged about 10, until recent housing developments

AS FAWR, YR/MONKNASH   *LL*

At visitation in 1781 there was 'an old register book of paper here, but sadly abused before I had care of it; and but few leaves remain of it; it goes, in some part of it, as far back as 1677.' PR CMB 1746-1812 recorded in 1831 apparently lost by 1940

M 1754-1837 **Glam RO**   CB 1813- incumbent

BT 1721, 1723-7, 1730-7, 1739-40, 1743, 1745, 1747-8, 1750-1820, 1822-45, 1848-62, 1865, 1869-74 **NLW**

*AVAN VALE/ CWM AFAN (ABERGWYNFI)   *LL*

‹Glyncorrwg & Llangynwyd 1906

C 1907-16   M 1907-14 **Glam RO**

BAGLAN   *LL*

PR CMB 1626-1768 recorded in 1831 but not in *A digest* ... (Cardiff, 1905) apparently lost

C 1769-1874   M 1769-1923 (Banns 1824-1930)   B 1769-1904 **Glam RO**

BT 1721, 1723-1817, 1819, 1821-67 **NLW**

BARRI, Y/BARRY   *LL*

C 1724-1921   M 1725-1808, 1816-1925   B 1724-1958 **Glam RO**

BT 1724-45, 1747-50, 1752-70, 1772-1813, 1815-87, 1889, 1891, 1894 **NLW**

Cop ts PR C 1724-1812 M 1724-1808 B 1724-1811 **Glam RO**

BARRI, Y/BARRY St. Paul   *LL*

‹Merthyr Dyfan/Merthyr Dovan

M 1901-27 (Banns 1947-63, 1969-77) **NLW**

BETWS TIR IARLL   *LL*

C 1725-45, 1760-1817   M 1722-5   B 1723-46, 1760-1819 **NLW**

BT 1721, 1723-45, 1747-1821, 1823-66, 1868, 1870-6 **NLW**

*BISHOPSTON/LLANDEILO FERWALLT   *SB*

C 1716-1807, 1810-1965   M 1716-1941   B 1716-1807, 1810-1900 **NLW**

BT 1671, 1675, 1677-8, 1681-2, 1686-7, 1690, 1693, 1696-8, 1700-2, 1704, 1707-8, 1710, 1712-13, 1716, 1727-31, 1733-76, 1778-1800, 1802-3, 1805, 1807-82, 1885, 1887-90 **NLW**

Cop ms PR CMB 1716-1812 **NLW**

BLAEN-GWRACH   *LL*

An ancient chapelry with pre-1812 entries of CMB included in PR Glyncorrwg (1831 survey). D. Rhys Phillips noted here PR C 1813- M 1834- B 1781- in *The History of the Vale of Neath* (Swansea, 1925), 127

CB 1895-   M 1837- incumbent   (Banns 1896-1950) **Glam RO**

BT 1846-60 **NLW**

BONT-FAEN, Y/COWBRIDGE   *LL*

C 1718-24, 1735-7, 1744-5, 1750-1, 1753-1972   M 1753-1971 (Banns 1894-1975)   B 1735-7, 1750-1, 1753-1928 **Glam RO**

BT 1721, 1724-31, 1733-7, 1739-46, 1748-1881 **NLW**

*BONVILSTON (BOULSTON)/TRESIMWN   *LL*
PR M 1813-37 apparently lost. Hearsay evidence recorded in 1940 reply to NLW questionnaire
    that 'some old registers were seen burning at Bonvilston House after the death of a Mr. Bassett'
CB 1761-1983   M 1758-1812, 1837-1970 (Banns 1824-1977)   B 1761-1982 **Glam RO**
BT 1696, 1724-1817, 1819-24, 1826-42, 1845-55, 1857-81 **NLW**

BRITON FERRY St. Clement   *LL*
Built 1866, and replaced St. Mary as the parish church. For St. Mary see Llansawel
C 1668-1731, 1739-1969 St. Thomas 1936-65   M 1668-1731, 1739-1944 (Banns 1867-1954)
   B 1686-1731, 1744-1924 **Glam RO**
BT 1696, 1721, 1723-1818, 1820-67 **NLW**

*CADOXTON-JUXTA-BARRY/TREGATWG   *LL*
Earlier PR possibly mutilated : some entries C 1644-5, 1662-3 on dorse of BT 1735 & 1738
C 1753-72, 1781-90, 1806-9, 1813-89, 1925-51   M 1754-83, 1813-37   B 1752-73, 1781-95, 1803-8
   Barry Dock St. Mary (Banns 1956-63) **Glam RO**
BT 1724-43, 1745-1867, 1869 **NLW**

*CADOXTON-JUXTA-NEATH/LLANGATWG   *LL*
There was a tradition here that some of the church registers were thrown 'gleefully' into the
    vicarage fire by 'the demented wife of a former incumbent', D. Rhys Phillips, *The History of the*
    Vale of Neath (Swansea, 1925), 74
Lay register CMB 1638-47, 1653-79 **Glam RO**
C 1738-1965   M 1738-1935 (Banns 1823-44)   B 1738-1919 **Glam RO**
BT 1721, 1723-33, 1735-6, 1738-1842, 1848-56, 1858-65, 1867-8, 1870-2 **NLW**

CAERAU A THRELÁI/CAERAU WITH ELY   *LL*
PR M 1754-1812 supposed in 1831 to be with the executors of the Rev. William Davies now
    apparently lost
C 1742-56, 1761-1952, 1961-73   M 1741-55, 1813-36, 1843-1972   B 1742-56, 1761-1812, 1815-
    1974 **Glam RO**   Mf C 1742-56, 1761-74   M 1741-55   B 1742-56, 1761-72 **NLW**
BT 1724-40, 1742-3, 1745-7, 1751-2, 1754-1824, 1826-67, 1869-70, 1878-82 **NLW**

CAERDYDD/CARDIFF All Saints   *LL*
‹St. Mary 1867
CMB 1867- incumbent
BT 1867-8 **NLW**

CAERDYDD/CARDIFF St. Andrew   *LL*
‹St. John 1884
CM 1863-   B 1884-1911 incumbent
BT 1863-4, 1869-73, 1875-84 **NLW**

CAERDYDD/CARDIFF St. Dyfrig   *LL*
‹St. Mary 1895
C 1885-94 (Banns 1930-43)   B 1895-1927 **Glam RO**

CAERDYDD/CARDIFF St. John   *LL*
C 1669-1869   M 1669-1871   B 1669-1868 **Glam RO**   Mf CMB 1669-96 **NLW**
BT 1717, 1724-1914, 1916 **NLW**
Cop ts PR CM 1813-40 (Adult C 1841-68) B 1813-41 with index **Soc Gen**   C 1813-40 **Glam RO**

CAERDYDD/CARDIFF St. Mary   *LL*
Attached to St. John 1607-1847
C 1843-1932   M 1847-1923 (Banns 1902-10) **Glam RO**
BT 1843-77 **NLW**

CAERDYDD/CARDIFF St. Samson   *LL*
‹St. Mary & St. Paul, Grangetown 1924
C 1904-18 (Banns 1930-40) **Glam RO**

CAERDYDD/CARDIFF St. Stephen   *LL*
‹St. Mary 1887
C 1878-1927   M 1912-25 (Banns 1912-48) **Glam RO**

CAERFFILI/CAERPHILLY St. Martin   *LL*
‹Bedwas & Eglwysilan 1850. PR M 1754-1812 recorded in 1831 as being in a separate volume at
   Eglwysilan now apparently lost
C 1834-1924 Pwll-y-pant 1899-1902   M 1813-20, 1850-1925 (Banns 1868-1915)   B 1822-1923
   Glam RO   Fac C 1834-1904   B 1822-89 **NLW**
BT 1816-24, 1826-41, 1847-8, 1850-5, 1857-76 **NLW**

*CANTON/TREGANNA   *LL*
‹Llandaf/Llandaff 1858
C 1858-1924   M 1858-1927 (Banns 1914-55, 1961-8) **Glam RO**
BT 1858-69, 1880-90 **NLW**

*CARDIFF/CAERDYDD All Saints   *LL*
St. Mary 1867
CMB 1867- incumbent
BT 1867-8 **NLW**

*CARDIFF/CAERDYDD St. Andrew   *LL*
‹St. John 1884
CM 1863-   B 1884-1911 incumbent
BT 1863-4, 1869-73, 1875-84 **NLW**

*CARDIFF/CAERDYDD St. Dyfrig   *LL*
‹St. Mary 1895
C 1885-94 (Banns 1930-43)   B 1895-1927 **Glam RO**

*CARDIFF/CAERDYDD St. John   *LL*
C 1669-1869   M 1669-1871   B 1669-1868 **Glam RO**   Mf CMB 1669-96 **NLW**
BT 1717, 1724-1914, 1916 **NLW**
Cop ts PR CM 1813-40 (Adult C 1841-68) B 1813-41 with index **Soc Gen**   C 1813-40 **Glam RO**

*CARDIFF/CAERDYDD St. Mary   *LL*
Attached to St. John 1607-1847
C 1843-1932   M 1847-1923 (Banns 1902-10) **Glam RO**
BT 1843-77 **NLW**

*CARDIFF/CAERDYDD St. Samson   *LL*
‹St. Mary & St. Paul, Grangetown 1924
C 1904-18 (Banns 1930-40) **Glam RO**

*CARDIFF/CAERDYDD St. Stephen   *LL*
‹St. Mary 1877
C 1878-1927   M 1912-25 (Banns 1912-48) **Glam RO**

CASLLWCHWR/LOUGHOR   *SB*
C 1717-1921   M 1717-1924   B 1717-1912 **Glam RO**   Mf C 1813-50   M 1754-1812 **NLW**
BT 1678-9, 1681-2, 1684, 1686-7, 1694-6, 1700-2, 1704, 1707-8, 1713, 1718, 1725-7, 1730-4, 1736-7,
   1740-2, 1745-7, 1750-1, 1753-7, 1759-96, 1798-1800, 1802-3, 1805-83, 1885, 1887-92 **NLW**
Cop ts PR M 1754-1837 with index **NLW & Soc Gen**

CASTELL-NEDD/NEATH   *LL*
Lay register CMB 1638-47, 1653-79 **Glam RO**
C 1692-1785, 1787-1833   M 1694-1837   B 1692-1784, 1786-1847 **Glam RO**
BT 1721, 1723-1861, 1866-8

CASTELLNEWYDD, Y/NEWCASTLE   *LL*
C 1745-1943   M 1745-1900 (Banns 1823-81)   B 1745-1897 **NLW**
BT 1721, 1723-63, 1765-1824, 1826-62, 1865-76 **NLW**

CHERITON   *SB*
PR CB 1783-1812 recorded in 1831 apparently lost (Glam RO survey 1951). Terrier & inventory
   1900 states that an old register was 'supposed to have perished from damp, having been kept in a
   wooden box in the church'
M 1757-1810, 1813-37 **NLW**
BT 1671-2, 1684, 1700-1, 1704, 1708, 1712-13, 1725, 1727, 1729-39, 1741, 1743-50, 1752-7, 1759-61,
   1764-7, 1770-1, 1774, 1778, 1781-3, 1785-1800, 1802-3, 1805, 1807-22, 1824-40, 1843-4, 1848-82,
   1885, 1887-96, 1898-1905, 1907 **NLW**
Cop ms PR & BT CMB 1672-1841 **Glam RO**

CILFÁI/KILVEY   *SB*
‹Llansamlet & Abertawe/Swansea St. Mary 1881
C 1845-1932   M 1857-1936 (Banns 1857-1927) **Glam RO**

CILYBEBYLL   *LL*
PR CMB 1736-67 M 1755-1812 recorded in *A digest ...* (Cardiff, 1905) apparently lost (Glam RO
   survey 1951). At visitation in 1781 the PR were said to go 'as far down as 1704'
Lay register CMB 1638-47, 1653-79 **Glam RO**
C 1773-1931   M 1813-1929   B 1768, 1774-1812 **Glam RO**
BT 1721, 1723-92, 1794-1821, 1824-68 **NLW**

CLUN, Y gweler/see LLWYNDERW

CLYDACH St. John   *SB*
‹Llangyfelach & Llangatwg/Cadoxton-juxta-Neath 1847
C 1847-94 St. Mary 1905-22   M 1847-87 St. Mary 1905-31 Trebannws/Trebanos 1912-35
   B 1847-1927 **Glam RO**
BT 1847-53, 1855-7, 1859-67 **NLW**

CLYNE gweler/see LLWYNDERW

COCYD, Y/COCKETT gweler/see ABERTAWE/SWANSEA St. Peter

COETY/COITY   *LL*
C 1694, 1702, 1713, 1720-1918   M 1738-57, 1759-1950   B 1720-1916 **Glam RO**   Mf 1694,
   1702, 1713, 1720-1844 **NLW**
BT 1721, 1723-30, 1732-56, 1758-1857, 1873-5 **NLW**

COGAN   *LL*
C 1784-1830, 1857, 1932-48   M 1935-45   B 1784-1812 **NLW**   M 1786-1808, 1813-21 **Glam RO**
BT 1724-52, 1754, 1756-1826, 1828-30 **NLW**
Cop ts PR C 1830-80 **NLW & Glam RO**

COITY gweler/see COETY

*COLWINSTON/TREGOLWYN   *LL*
At visitation in 1781 PR was said to go 'so far back as February 1694/5'
C 1766-1951   M 1771-1806, 1813-1949   B 1766-1812 **NLW**
BT 1696, 1721, 1723-51, 1753-1862 **NLW**   Mf **Glam RO**

*COWBRIDGE/Y BONT-FAEN   *LL*
C 1718-24, 1735-7, 1744-5, 1750-1, 1753-1972   M 1753-1971 (Banns 1894-1975)   B 1735-7, 1750-1, 1753-1928 **Glam RO**
BT 1721, 1724-31, 1733-7, 1739-46, 1748-1881 **NLW**

*COYCHURCH/LLANGRALLO   *LL*
C 1736-94, 1797-1959   M 1736-1808, 1813-1953 (Banns 1899-1969)   B 1736-1867, 1882-1935 **Glam RO**
BT 1721, 1723-4, 1726-87, 1789-90, 1792-4, 1797-1862 **NLW**

CREUNANT, Y/CRYNANT   *LL*
An ancient chapelry of Llangatwg/Cadoxton-juxta-Neath with earlier CMB entered in the registers of the mother church
C 1878- incumbent   M 1838-1942   B 1879-1938 **Glam RO**

CWM AFAN (ABERGWYNFI)/AFAN VALE   *LL*
‹Glyncorrwg & Llangynwyd 1906
C 1907-16   M 1907-14 **Glam RO**

CWMAFAN/CWMAVON gweler/see LLANFIHANGEL-YNYS-AFAN/MICHAELSTON-SUPER-AVON

CWMBWRLA gweler/see ABERTAWE/SWANSEA St. Luke

CWMLLYNFELL   *SD*
‹Brynaman
M 1905-76 (Banns 1924-74) **Carm RO**

CYFARTHFA   *LL*
‹Merthyr Tudful/Merthyr Tydfil 1857
C 1857-1916   M 1857-1928 (Banns 1857-1916) **NLW**

CYNCOED gweler/see LLANEDERN/LLANEDEYRN

CYNFFIG gweler/see PÎL A CHYNFFIG, Y/PYLE & KENFIG

DOWLAIS   *LL*
‹Merthyr Tudful/Merthyr Tydfil 1837
C 1839-1908 Eglwys Gymraeg 1927-8   M 1838-1929 (Banns 1895-1907, 1910-40)   B 1839-55, 1881-1920 **Glam RO**
BT 1839-53, 1862-3 **NLW**

DRENEWYDD YN NOTAIS/NEWTON NOTTAGE *LL*
At visitation in 1781 the earliest PR was said to include entries of CMB 1687-8, 1691-1703, 1708-14
  but these had apparently been lost by 1831. PR CB 1782-1812 has had leaves cut out
C 1715-1941　　M 1715-1957 (Banns 1875-1911)　　B 1715-1952 **NLW**
BT 1722-1805, 1807-23, 1825-38, 1847-61 **NLW**

DYFFRYN　　*LL*
Llangatwg/Cadoxton-juxta-Neath & Sgiwen/Skewen 1873
CMB 1871- incumbent
BT 1909-10 **NLW**

EGLWYS BREWYS/EGLWYSBREWIS　　*LL*
PR CB 1813- post 1951 M 1781-1808 recorded in 1951 apparently lost (Glam RO survey)
C 1750-1811　　M 1752, 1820-1923, 1935-70　　B 1752-1807 **Glam RO**
BT 1721, 1724-6, 1728, 1731, 1743, 1745, 1747-98, 1800-17, 1834-5 **NLW**

EGLWYS FAIR Y MYNYDD/ST. MARY HILL　　*LL*
PR CMB 1738-87 recorded in 1951 apparently lost (Glam RO survey)
C 1787-1812　　M 1837-1970　　B 1787-1811 **Glam RO**　　M 1755-1838 **NLW**
BT 1696, 1721, 1723-7, 1729-46, 1748-9, 1751-1860 **NLW**

EGLWYSILAN　　*LL*
C 1679-1930 Senghennydd 1898-1917 Senghennydd Welsh Church 1909-47　　M 1695-1847, 1853-
  1922 (Banns 1823-34, 1844-1901)　　B 1694-1929 **Glam RO**　　Mf C 1679-1748, 1769-1812
  　M 1695-1748　　B 1694-1748, 1769-1812 **NLW**
BT 1696-7, 1717, 1724-1875, 1877, 1880, 1890-1 **NLW**
Cop ts PR C 1679-1747 **NLW**

EGLWYS NEWYDD, YR/WHITCHURCH　　*LL*
PR CB 1766-76 M 1754-1812 recorded in 1831 but not in *A digest ...* (Cardiff, 1905) apparently lost
C 1732-66, 1778-1938　　M 1732-58, 1813-1929　　B 1732-66, 1777-1932 **Glam RO**
BT 1717, 1724, 1732, 1734-48, 1750-1, 1754-1875 **NLW**

ELY gweler/see CAERAU A THRELÁI/CAERAU WITH ELY

EWENNI/EWENNY　　*LL*
C 1738, 1754, 1757, 1767-1812　　M 1755-1923　　B 1714-61, 1769-1942 **Glam RO**
BT 1721, 1723-1817, 1819-67, 1870-98 **NLW**

FFYNNON TAF A NANTGARW gweler/see TONGWYNLAIS

*FLEMINGSTON (FLIMSTON)/TREFFLEMIN　　*LL*
CMB 1576-1725 **NLW**　　CB 1726-1812　　M 1726-48, 1757-1968　　Fac CMB 1576-1725 **Glam
RO**
BT 1721, 1724-39, 1741-51, 1753-9, 1761-1814, 1816-17, 1819-29, 1831-54, 1856, 1858-63, 1865-70
  NLW

FOCHRIW A DERI/FOCHRIW WITH DERI　　*LL*
‹Pontlotyn & Bargod/Bargoed 1921
C 1917-　　M 1911-　　B 1924- incumbent　　(Banns 1911-49) **Glam RO**

GABALFA　　*LL*
‹Llandaf/Llandaff 1876
C 1876-1927　　M 1877-1926 **Glam RO**
BT 1876-85, 1887-1913 **NLW**

GELLI-GAER   *LL*
PR CB 1707-1800 M 1707-53 recorded in 1940 apparently lost
C 1813-1933 Gilfach 1907-23   M 1755-1929 (partly indexed)   B 1812-1922 (partly indexed)
   Glam RO   Mf C 1813-36   M 1802-37 **NLW**   CB 1707-1800   M 1707-53 **Glam RO &
   NLW**
BT 1696, 1717-18, 1724-1800, 1802-9, 1811-12, 1814-15, 1817-70 **NLW**
Cop ts PR (extracts) C 1759-1800 B 1708-93 **Glam RO**

*GILESTON/SILSTWN   *LL*
PR M 1783-1810 recorded in 1951 apparently lost (Glam RO survey)
C 1701-1812   M 1701-79   B 1702-1811 **Glam RO**
BT 1721-2, 1724-32, 1734-8, 1740-2, 1744-9, 1751-5, 1757-8, 1760-8, 1771-1818, 1820-80 **NLW**

GILFACH gweler/see GELLI-GAER

GLAIS, Y gweler/see LLANSAMLET

GLANDŴR/LANDORE   *SB*
‹Llangyfelach 1906
C 1906-33   M 1891-1926 (Banns 1891-1931) **Glam RO**

GLYNCORRWG   *LL*
CMB 1702-1813 **NLW**   C 1750-3, 1813-1905   M 1750-3, 1813-1914 (Banns 1824-1923)   B
   1750-3, 1813-1908 **Glam RO**
BT 1721, 1723-8, 1730-61, 1763-1813, 1815-19, 1821-2, 1824-36, 1839-60 **NLW**
Cop ts PR CMB 1750-3 **NLW**

GLYN-TAF/GLYNTAFF   *LL*
‹Eglwysilan, Llanilltud Faerdref/Llantwit Fardre, Llanwynno/Llanwonno 1848
CM 1848-   B 1849- incumbent   St. Luke, Rhydyfelin (Banns 1964-76) **Glam RO**
BT 1848-77 **NLW**

*GOWERTON/TRE-GŴYR   *SB*
‹Casllwchwr/Loughor *c.* 1920. PR C 1881- M 1883- recorded in 1935 apparently lost
C 1906-56 (Banns 1882-1959) **Glam RO**

GWAUNCAEGURWEN (LLANFAIR CWM-GORS)   *SD*
‹Llan-giwg/Llanguicke
C 1936-76   M 1892-1971 (Banns 1925-74) **Carm RO**

GWENFÔ/WENVOE   *LL*
C 1585-1971   M 1585-1970 (Banns 1824-1973)   B 1585-1983 **Glam RO**   Fac/Mf CMB 1585-
   1739 **NLW**
BT 1724-1866 **NLW**
Cop ts C 1740-1971 M 1741-1971 B 1740-1973 **Glam RO**

HIRWAUN   *LL*
‹Aberdâr/Aberdare, co. Glamorgan & Penderyn, co. Brecknock 1886
C 1858-1944   M 1884-1941 (Banns 1899-1960) **Glam RO**

*ILSTON/LLANILLTUD GŴYR   *SB*
CB 1653-99, 1730-1812   M 1653-99, 1730-57   Fac M 1754-1811 **NLW**
BT 1672, 1678-9, 1681-3, 1686-7, 1693, 1697, 1700-2, 1704, 1711-13, 1716, 1727-56, 1758-98, 1800,
   1802-3, 1805-41, 1843-4, 1846-82, 1885, 1887-8, 1890 **NLW**
Cop ts BT 1672-1837 **Glam RO**

KENFIG gweler/see PÎL A CHYNFFIG, Y/PYLE & KENFIG

*KILVEY/CILFÁI   *SB*
‹Llansamlet & Abertawe/Swansea St. Mary 1881
C 1845-1932   M 1857-1936 (Banns 1857-1927) **Glam RO**

*KNELSTON/LLAN-Y-TAIR-MAIR   *SB*
Ancient ruined church without records. See Llanddewi
BT 1784, 1790-4, 1872-4, 1876-83 **NLW**

*LALESTON/TRELALES   *LL*
C 1742-1937   M 1742-1839   B 1742-1936 **NLW**
BT 1721, 1723-1869, 1871-5 **NLW**

*LANDORE/GLANDŴR   *SB*
‹Llangyfelach 1906
C 1906-33   M 1891-1926 (Banns 1891-1931) **Glam RO**

LARNOG/LAVERNOCK   *LL*
PR CMB 1733-1812 recorded in 1831 as being in one volume apparently lost in part
C 1769-1956   M 1769-1812, 1815-36, 1842-1902 (Banns 1883-1943)   B 1778-1812, 1821-1964
   Glam RO
BT 1724-7, 1729-1830, 1832-73, 1875-6, 1878-9, 1881, 1883 **NLW**

LECWYDD/LECKWITH   *LL*
C 1781-1966   M 1781-1810, 1813-1963 (Banns 1823-1959)   B 1781-1812 **NLW**
BT 1724-52, 1754-69, 1771-1876, 1878 **NLW**
Cop ts PR CMB 1830-80 **NLW & Glam RO**

*LISVANE/LLYS-FAEN   *LL*
C 1760-1810, 1813-22, 1862-1980   M 1755-1861   B 1760-1812 **Glam RO**
BT 1724-5, 1777-1821, 1823-7, 1829-30, 1832-80, 1883-4, 1886 **NLW**

*LISWORNEY/LLYSWYRNY   *LL*
C 1684-1735, 1737-9, 1747-1812   M 1588-1634, 1687, 1696-1737, 1753   B 1602-38, 1657-9,
   1663-1715, 1719-34, 1747-84 **NLW**   M 1754-1811, 1813-34, 1837-1970 (Banns 1823-1981)
   B 1785-1812 **Glam RO**
BT 1721, 1723-72, 1774-1867 **NLW**

LLANBEDR-AR-FYNYDD/PETERSTON-SUPER-MONTEM   *LL*
C 1745-1811, 1813-1970   M 1745-1970   B 1745-1812 **Glam RO**
BT 1721, 1732-5, 1737-48, 1750-3, 1755-95, 1797-1848, 1850-60 **NLW**

LLANBEDR-Y-FRO/PETERSTON-SUPER-ELY   *LL*
C 1749-78, 1780-1966   M 1754-1931   B 1749-78, 1780-7, 1790-1932 **Glam RO**
BT 1724-59, 1761-1815, 1817-21, 1824-31, 1833-67 **NLW**
Cop printed PR CB 1749-1812 M 1754-1812 (ed. A.F.C. Chichester-Langley, 1888)

*LLANBLETHIAN/LLANFLEIDDAN   *LL*
C 1661-94, 1734-7, 1748-50, 1757-61, 1766-1893   M 1664-89, 1734-7, 1748, 1754-5, 1767-70, 1776-
   1971 (Banns 1823-1919)   B 1661-5, 1674-9, 1685-96, 1734-7, 1748-50, 1758-1893 **Glam RO**
   Fac CMB 1661-96 **NLW**
BT 1696, 1721, 1723-31, 1733-45, 1747-1879, 1881 **NLW**
Cop ts PR CMB 1661-96 **NLW**

LLANBRADACH   *LL*
‹Caerffili/Caerphilly & Ystradmynach 1904
C 1899-   M 1904- incumbent
BT 1909-14 **NLW**

LLANCARFAN   *LL*
C 1618-40, 1724-63, 1775-1810, 1813-1901   M 1618-40, 1724-63, 1788-1970 (Banns 1828-1920)
   B 1618-40, 1724-63, 1775-1810, 1813-1976 **Glam RO**
BT 1696, 1724-6, 1728-35, 1737-1867, 1870-2 **NLW**

LLANDAF/LLANDAFF   *LL*
CM 1724-1874   B 1724-1968 **Glam RO**   (Banns 1867-1905) **NLW**
BT 1717, 1725-51, 1753-1890, 1894-6, 1899-1910 **NLW**

LLANDDEWI   *SB*
CMB 1719-1812 recorded in 1952 apparently lost (Glam RO survey)
C 1813-1978   M 1813-1970   B 1813-1976 **Glam RO**
BT 1678, 1684, 1686, 1697, 1702, 1704, 1707, 1710, 1712, 1717, 1725, 1727-31, 1733-6, 1738-9, 1741-
    1800, 1802-3, 1805-6, 1808-31, 1833-48, 1850-62, 1864-83 **NLW**
Cop ms PR CMB 1718-1812 **NLW**

LLANDDEWI RHONDDA   *LL*
‹Llanwynno/Llanwonno 1914. Church erected 1851
C 1897-1916   M 1854-1924 **Glam RO**   B 1894- incumbent

LLANDDUNWYD/WELSH ST. DONAT'S   *LL*
C 1726-36, 1758-1981   M 1726-47, 1757-1970 (Banns 1824-1979)   B 1726-1982 **Glam RO**
BT 1724-51, 1753, 1755-69, 1771-89, 1791-1802, 1804-68, 1870-3, 1875-6, 1878, 1881 **NLW**

LLANDEILO FERWALLT/BISHOPSTON   *SB*
C 1716-1807, 1810-1965   M 1716-1941   B 1716-1807, 1810-1900 **NLW**
BT 1671, 1675, 1677-8, 1681-2, 1686-7, 1690, 1693, 1696-8, 1700-2, 1704, 1707-8, 1710, 1712-13,
    1716, 1727-31, 1733-76, 1778-1800, 1802-3, 1805, 1807-82, 1885, 1887-90 **NLW**
Cop ms PR CMB 1716-1812 **NLW**

LLANDEILO TAL-Y-BONT   *SB*
C 1662-1757, 1782-1950   M 1662-1928 (Banns 1883-1918)   B 1662-1757, 1782-1960 **NLW**
BT 1672, 1679, 1681-2, 1684, 1693, 1696-8, 1700-1, 1703-4, 1710, 1712-13, 1718, 1725, 1727, 1729,
    1731-4, 1736-46, 1749-1800, 1802-3, 1805-59, 1861-5, 1868, 1872-3 **NLW**

LLANDOCHAU FACH/LLANDOUGH-JUXTA-PENARTH   *LL*
At visitation in 1781 PR CB was said 'to go back as far as the year 1754'
C 1784-1938   M 1755-1973 (Banns 1929-70)   B 1784-1928 **NLW**
BT 1724-52, 1754-64, 1766-1876, 1878 **NLW**
Cop ts PR CB 1813-80 M 1830-84 **NLW & Glam RO**

LLANDOCHAU/LLANDOUGH-JUXTA-COWBRIDGE   *LL*
C 1583-1812   M 1585-1744, 1756-1812, 1814-39   B 1583-1812 **Glam RO**   Fac CB 1583-1812
   M 1583-1744 **NLW**
BT 1721, 1724-90, 1792-1863 **NLW**

LLANDOW gweler/see **LLANDŴ**

LLANDUDWG/TYTHEGSTON   *LL*
C 1758-1812, 1830-1   M 1757-1837   B 1766-1812 **NLW**
BT 1721, 1723-1835, 1837-60, 1862-9, 1871-5 **NLW**

LLANDŴ/LLANDOW   *LL*
CB 1688-1812   M 1745-1836 **NLW**
BT 1723-4, 1727-1860, 1865 **NLW**

LLANDYFODWG   *LL*
PR earliest date given as 1748 in 1831 survey
C 1770-1897   M 1755-1812   B 1770-1905 **NLW**   Mf CB 1770-1812   M 1755-1812
   Glam RO
BT 1696, 1721, 1723-79, 1781-1864 **NLW**   Mf 1696, 1721, 1723-55 **Glam RO**

LLANEDERN/LLANEDEYRN   *M*
C 1701-9, 1713-1978 Cyncoed 1926-78   M 1701-9, 1715-1982 (Banns 1824-1971) Cyncoed
   1930-79 (Banns 1972-7)   B 1701-9, 1714-1929 **Glam RO**
BT 1717, 1724-1811, 1813-43, 1845-9, 1853-8, 1864-9 **NLW**
Cop ts PR CMB 1700-1837 with index **NLW & Soc Gen**

LLANENEWYR gweler/see LLANYRNEWYDD

LLANFABON   *LL*
PR CB 1694-1768 M 1694-1753 recorded in 1831 but not in *A digest* ... (Cardiff, 1905) apparently
   lost
C 1769-1916   M 1754-1916 (Banns 1857-1929) Nelson 1904-16   B 1769-1922 **NLW**
BT 1717, 1724-1870 **NLW**

LLAN-FAES/LLANMAES   *LL*
CMB 1583-1812 **NLW**   Fac **Glam RO**
BT 1721, 1723-30, 1732-52, 1754-76, 1778-1869, 1871 **NLW**

LLAN-FAIR/ST. MARY CHURCH   *LL*
C 1584-1812   M 1577-1759, 1761-1839   B 1602-1812 **Glam RO**   Fac C 1577-1812   M
   1577-1818   B 1602-1812 **NLW**
BT 1721, 1724-7, 1729-1854, 1856-63 **NLW**

LLANFIHANGEL-AR-ELÁI/MICHAELSTON-SUPER-ELY   *LL*
CB 1761-1814   M 1754-1835 **NLW**
BT 1721, 1724-6, 1728-79, 1781-1820, 1823-6, 1828-38, 1840-69 **NLW**

LLANFIHANGEL Y BONT-FAEN/LLANMIHANGEL   *LL*
PR 1755-1812 recorded in 1951 apparently lost (Glam RO survey). At visitation in 1781 PR was
   said to go back to 1731 and there was a separate PR M in use
CMB 1813- incumbent
BT 1813-16, 1820-1, 1836-50, 1852-81 **NLW**

LLANFIHANGEL-YNYS-AFAN/MICHAELSTON-SUPER-AVON   *LL*
Diocesan records suggest that in 1805 this parish had PR going back to 1769
C 1785-1890   M 1786-1930 (Banns 1827-30, 1835-43, 1845-90)   B 1785-1862, 1868-90 **Glam
   RO**
BT 1696, 1723-8, 1730-1819, 1821-70 **NLW**

LLANFIHANGEL-Y-PWLL/MICHAELSTON-LE-PIT   *LL*
At visitation in 1771 the rector admitted that 'the last curate's register book I could never find it'
C 1783-1980   M 1783, 1786-7, 1813-1968   B 1784-1980 **Glam RO**
BT 1724-5, 1729-36, 1738-53, 1755-62, 1764-1876, 1878, 1882-1913 **NLW**

LLANFLEIDDAN/LLANBLETHIAN   *LL*
C 1661-94, 1734-7, 1748-50, 1757-61, 1766-1893   M 1664-89, 1734-7, 1748, 1754-5, 1767-70, 1776-
     1971 (Banns 1823-1919)   B 1661-5, 1674-9, 1685-96, 1734-7, 1748-50, 1758-1893 **Glam RO**
     Fac CMB 1661-96 **NLW**
BT 1696, 1721, 1723-31, 1733-45, 1747-1879, 1881 **NLW**
Cop ts PR CMB 1661-96 **NLW**

LLANFRYNACH gweler/see PEN-LLIN/PENLLYN

LLAN-GAN   *LL*
At visitation in 1781 this parish had no PR for recording marriages
C 1688-1978   M 1725-47, 1763, 1792-1970 (Banns 1824-1977)   B 1708, 1716, 1724-1812 **Glam
     RO**   Mf C 1688-1812   M 1725-47, 1763   B 1708, 1716, 1724-1812 **NLW**
BT 1721, 1723-45, 1747-1810, 1812-50, 1855-60 **NLW**

LLANGATWG/CADOXTON-JUXTA-NEATH   *LL*
There was a tradition here that some of the church registers were thrown 'gleefully' into the
     vicarage fire by 'the demented wife of a former incumbent', D. Rhys Phillips, *The History of the
     Vale of Neath* (Swansea, 1925), 74
Lay register CMB 1638-47, 1653-79 **Glam RO**
C 1738-1965   M 1738-1935 (Banns 1823-44)   B 1738-1919 **Glam RO**
BT 1721, 1723-33, 1735-6, 1738-1842, 1848-56, 1858-65, 1867-8, 1870-2 **NLW**

LLANGEINWYR/LLANGEINOR   *LL*
At visitation in 1771 this parish was said to have a PR going 'about thirty years back'
C 1782-1892   M 1755-1898   B 1782-1882 **NLW**
BT 1723-1865 **NLW**

*LLANGENNITH/LLANGYNYDD   *SB*
C 1726-1812   M 1754-1807, 1813-37   B 1742-1812 **Glam RO**
BT 1671, 1673, 1677-9, 1682-3, 1686-9, 1691, 1693-4, 1696-7, 1700-1, 1704, 1707-8, 1710-11, 1713,
     1725, 1727-37, 1739, 1741, 1743-95, 1797-1800, 1802-3, 1809-31, 1833-46, 1848-51, 1853, 1855-82,
     1885, 1887-96, 1898-9 **NLW**

LLAN-GIWG/LLANGUICKE   *SB*
PR CB 1767-1812 recorded in 1831 apparently lost
C 1703-67, 1813-92   M 1704-1859 (Banns 1823-61)   B 1703-67, 1813-81 **Glam RO**
BT 1672, 1677, 1682-3, 1685-6, 1690, 1693, 1696-7, 1701-2, 1704, 1707-8, 1711-13, 1725, 1727-8,
     1730-4, 1736-52, 1754-79, 1782-95, 1797-1800, 1802-3, 1805-35, 1839-42, 1844, 1846-7, 1851-6,
     1858, 1863, 1866 **NLW**

LLANGRALLO/COYCHURCH   *LL*
C 1736-94, 1797-1959   M 1736-1808, 1813-1953 (Banns 1899-1969)   B 1736-1867, 1882-1935
     Glam RO
BT 1721, 1723-4, 1726-87, 1789-90, 1792-4, 1797-1862 **NLW**

LLANGUICKE gweler/see LLAN-GIWG

LLANGYFELACH   *SB*
PR B 1813-1915 recorded in 1966 apparently lost
C 1693-1798, 1802-1905   M 1693-1931 (Banns 1847-1925)   B 1693-1797, 1802-12 **Glam RO**
   Fac CMB 1693-1750 **NLW**
BT 1682-3, 1686-7, 1693, 1697, 1700-1, 1707, 1710, 1712-13, 1716, 1727-80, 1782-90, 1792-1800,
   1802-3, 1805-7, 1809-53 **NLW**   Mf CMB 1682-1794 **Soc Gen**

LLANGYNWYD   *LL*
C 1662-1769, 1849-76   M 1662-1753, 1851-69   B 1662-1769, 1856-75 **Glam RO**   C 1769-
   1849   M 1754-1851 (Banns 1847-63)   B 1769-1856   Mf CB 1662-1769   M 1662-1753
   NLW
BT 1721, 1723-1882 **NLW**

LLANGYNYDD/LLANGENNITH   *SB*
C 1726-1812   M 1754-1807, 1813-37   B 1742-1812 **Glam RO**
BT 1671, 1673, 1677-9, 1682-3, 1686-9, 1691, 1693-4, 1696-7, 1700-1, 1704, 1707-8, 1710-11, 1713,
   1725, 1727-37, 1739, 1741, 1743-95, 1797-1800, 1802-3, 1809-31, 1833-46, 1848-51, 1853, 1855-82,
   1885, 1887-96, 1898-9 **NLW**

LLANHARAN   *LL*
C 1615-58, 1720-1984   M 1754-1967   B 1641-69, 1719-1812, 1814-1943 **Glam RO**
BT 1721, 1723-9, 1741, 1743-1820, 1822-4, 1826-33, 1846-9, 1851-64, 1868, 1876 **NLW**   1821,
   1877-8 **Glam RO**

LLANHARI/LLANHARRY   *LL*
PR 1750-1812 recorded in 1831 but not in *A digest ...* (Cardiff, 1905) apparently lost
C 1813-1983   M 1814-1983   B 1813-1982 **Glam RO**
BT 1725-44, 1747, 1751-1820, 1823-36, 1838-91 **NLW**

LLANILID   *LL*
C 1706-1809   M 1729-52, 1754-1834   B 1729-31, 1734-44, 1747-1812 **NLW**
BT 1696, 1721, 1723-1820, 1822-3, 1826-33, 1846, 1848-63, 1868, 1875-6 **NLW**
Cop ms BT 1696, 1721, 1723-8 **Glam RO**

LLANILLTERN   *LL*
PR 1726-1812 recorded in 1831 but not in *A digest ...* (Cardiff, 1905) apparently lost. Formerly a
   chapelry of Sain Ffagan/St. Fagans. At visitation in 1781 the earliest PR was 'very good from the
   year 1695'
CMB 1813- incumbent   M 1756-67 **NLW**
BT 1717, 1724-40, 1742-4, 1747-9, 1752, 1755, 1758-63, 1765-90, 1792-1814, 1816-30, 1832-68
   NLW

LLANILLTUD FACH gweler/see **LLANILLTUD NEDD**

LLANILLTUD FAERDREF/LLANTWIT FARDRE   *LL*
C 1626-1835, 1837-40, 1846-1934   M 1626-1972 (Banns 1947-59)   B 1626-1832, 1834, 1837-43,
   1846-1949 **Glam RO**
BT 1717, 1724-39, 1741-74, 1776-1828, 1831-2, 1837-9, 1846-61, 1864-5, 1868-9, 1873-4 **NLW**

LLANILLTUD FAWR/LLANTWIT MAJOR   *LL*
At visitation in 1771 this parish had PR going back to 1598
C 1721-1948   M 1721-1975   B 1721-1971 **NLW**
BT 1721, 1723-1868, 1870 **NLW**
Cop ts PR CB 1721-1812 M 1724-1812 **Glam RO**

LLANILLTUD GŴYR/ILSTON   *SB*
CB 1653-99, 1730-1812   M 1653-99, 1730-57   Fac M 1754-1811 **NLW**
BT 1672, 1678-9, 1681-3, 1686-7, 1693, 1697, 1700-2, 1704, 1711-13, 1716, 1727-56, 1758-98, 1800,
    1802-3, 1805-41, 1843-4, 1846-82, 1885, 1887-8, 1890 **NLW**
Cop ts BT 1672-1837 **Glam RO**

LLANILLTUD NEDD/LLANTWIT-JUXTA-NEATH   *LL*
Lay register CMB 1638-47, 1653-79 **Glam RO**
C 1695-1780, 1787-1896   M 1696-1837   B 1696-1780, 1786-1847 **Glam RO**
BT 1698-9, 1721, 1723-94, 1796-1861 **NLW**

LLANISIEN/LLANISHEN   *LL*
CB 1752-1914   M 1754-1939 (Banns 1873-1926) **Glam RO**   Mf CB 1752-1812 **NLW**
BT 1717, 1724-57, 1759-99, 1801-27, 1829-30, 1832, 1834-43, 1845-62, 1864-85 **NLW**

LLANMADOG   *SB*
PR M 1757-1812 recorded in terrier & inventory 1900 apparently lost (Glam RO survey 1952)
CB 1724-1812   M 1724-57, 1813-37 **NLW**
BT 1672, 1683, 1690, 1700-1, 1704, 1707-8, 1710, 1712-13, 1725, 1727-43, 1745-76, 1778-97,
    1799-1800, 1802-3, 1805-6, 1808-17, 1819-20, 1822-35, 1839-82, 1885, 1887-96, 1898-1905,
    1908-10 **NLW**
Cop ms PR & BT C 1673-1840 MB 1672-1840 **Glam RO**

*LLANMAES/LLAN-FAES   *LL*
CMB 1583-1812 **NLW**   Fac **Glam RO**
BT 1721, 1723-30, 1732-52, 1754-76, 1778-1869, 1871 **NLW**

*LLANMIHANGEL/LLANFIHANGEL Y BONT-FAEN   *LL*
PR 1755-1812 recorded in 1951 apparently lost (Glam RO survey). At visitation in 1781 PR was
    said to go back to 1731 and there was a separate PR M in use
CMB 1813- incumbent
BT 1813-16, 1820-1, 1836-50, 1852-81 **NLW**

LLANRHIDIAN   *SB*
C 1730-1885   M 1730-1837 (Banns 1754-1930)   B 1730-1908 **NLW**
BT 1671, 1678, 1686-7, 1691, 1697, 1700-2, 1704, 1707-8, 1710, 1718, 1725, 1727-8, 1730-41,
    1743-57, 1759-61, 1764-7, 1770-1, 1774-5, 1778-9, 1781-1800, 1802-3, 1805-38, 1840-8, 1850-8,
    1860-75, 1878-82 **NLW**

LLANSAMLET   *SB*
C 1704-1920 M 1704-88, 1792-1959 (Banns 1899-1943) Y Glais 1884-1970 B 1704-1935 **Glam RO**
BT 1672, 1677-8, 1680-1, 1683-7, 1690, 1693, 1695-7, 1701-2, 1707-8, 1710, 1712-13, 1716-17, 1725,
    1727-1800, 1802-3, 1805-17, 1819-72, 1876-8 **NLW**

LLANSANFFRAID-AR-ELÁI/ST. BRIDE'S-SUPER-ELY   *LL*
At visitation in 1781 the PR was said to go back sixty years
CB 1747-1814   M 1754-1970 **Glam RO**
BT 1717, 1724-51, 1753-60, 1762-1800, 1802, 1804-21, 1823-48, 1851-70 **NLW**

LLANSANFFRAID-AR-OGWR/ST. BRIDE'S MINOR   *LL*
C 1723-1802, 1813-1949   M 1725-30, 1734-1947   B 1723-1807, 1813-1942 **Glam RO**
BT 1696, 1721, 1723-1816, 1819, 1821-62, 1869-73 **NLW**

LLANSANWYR/LLANSANNOR *LL*
CB 1727-1812   M 1727-1971 (Banns 1823-1975) **NLW**
BT 1724-49, 1751-1854, 1856-68, 1880 **NLW**

LLANSAWEL *LL*
Ancient parish church until 1866. Chapel-of-ease to Briton Ferry St. Clement 1866-1913. Rebuilt
    1891-2 and made a separate ecclesiastical parish 1913
C 1913-51   M 1913-40   B 1913-65 **Glam RO**

LLANTRIDDYD/LLANTRITHYD *LL*
C 1597-1979   M 1571-1653, 1663-1752, 1756-1811, 1816-1970   B 1571-1978 **Glam RO**
BT 1724-1874, 1876, 1878 **NLW**
Cop printed PR C 1597-1810 M 1571-1751 B 1571-1810 (ed. H.S.Hughes,1888)

LLANTRISANT *LL*
C 1728-1921   M 1728-1920 (Banns 1857-1927)   B 1728-1908 **NLW**   Fac C 1728-1854   M 1844
    B 1728-1858 **Glam RO**
BT 1717-18, 1724-1881 **NLW**

LLANTRITHYD gweler/see **LLANTRIDDYD**

*****LLANTWIT FARDRE/LLANILLTUD FAERDREF** *LL*
C 1626-1835, 1837-40, 1846-1934   M 1626-1972 (Banns 1947-59)   B 1626-1832, 1834, 1837-43,
    1846-1949 **Glam RO**
BT 1717, 1724-39, 1741-74, 1776-1828, 1831-2, 1837-9, 1846-61, 1864-5, 1868-9, 1873-4 **NLW**

*****LLANTWIT-JUXTA-NEATH/LLANILLTUD NEDD** *LL*
Lay register CMB 1638-47, 1653-79 **Glam RO**
C 1695-1780, 1787-1896   M 1696-1837   B 1696-1780, 1786-1847 **Glam RO**
BT 1698-9, 1721, 1723-94, 1796-1861 **NLW**

*****LLANTWIT MAJOR/LLANILLTUD FAWR** *LL*
At a visitation in 1771 this parish had PR going back to 1598
C 1721-1948   M 1721-1975   B 1721-1971 **NLW**
BT 1721, 1723-1868, 1870 **NLW**
Cop ts PR CB 1721-1812 M 1724-1812 **Glam RO**

LLANWYNNO/LLANWONNO *LL*
C 1717-1897   M 1717-1910   B 1717-1894 **NLW**
BT 1717, 1724-1860, 1907-8 **NLW**

LLANYRNEWYDD (PEN-CLAWDD) *SB*
‹Llanrhidian 1925
C 1841-84   M 1835-1971 (Banns 1854-1959)   B 1841-90 **Glam RO**
BT 1853-4 **NLW**

LLAN-Y-TAIR-MAIR/KNELSTON *SB*
Ancient ruined church without records. See Llanddewi
BT 1784, 1790-4, 1872-4, 1876-83 **NLW**

LLWYNDERW (Y CLUN/CLYNE CHAPEL) *SB*
‹Ystumllwynarth/Oystermouth 1956
M 1908-25 (Banns 1908-39) **Glam RO**

LLWYNELIDDON/ST. LYTHAN'S   *LL*
C 1750-1985   M 1748-1970   B 1749-1983 **Glam RO**
BT 1724-31, 1733-5, 1737-47, 1751-7, 1759-66, 1768-1863 **NLW**

LLYS-FAEN/LISVANE   *LL*
C 1760-1810, 1813-22, 1862-1980   M 1755-1861   B 1760-1812 **Glam RO**
BT 1724-5, 1777-1821, 1823-7, 1829-30, 1832-80, 1883-4, 1886 **NLW**

LLYSWYRNY/LISWORNEY   *LL*
C 1684-1735, 1737-9, 1747-1812   M 1588-1634, 1687, 1696-1737, 1753   B 1602-38, 1657-9,
    1663-1715, 1719-34, 1747-84 **NLW**   M 1754-1811, 1813-34, 1837-1970 (Banns 1823-1981)
    B 1785-1812 **Glam RO**
BT 1721, 1723-72, 1774-1867 **NLW**

*LOUGHOR/CASLLWCHWR   *SB*
C 1717-1921   M 1717-1924   B 1717-1912 **Glam RO**   Mf C 1813-50   M 1754-1812 **NLW**
BT 1678-9, 1681-2, 1684, 1686-7, 1694-6, 1700-2, 1704, 1707-8, 1713, 1718, 1725-7, 1730-4, 1736-7,
    1740-2, 1745-7, 1750-1, 1753-7, 1759-96, 1798-1800, 1802-3, 1805-83, 1885, 1887-92 **NLW**
Cop ts PR M 1754-1837 with index **NLW & Soc Gen**

MAESTEG   *LL*
‹Llangynwyd
C 1845- incumbent
BT 1845-82 **NLW**

MANSELTON   *SB*
‹Abertawe/Swansea St. John *c.* 1919
C 1911-42   M 1906-28 (Banns 1908-28) **Glam RO**

MARCROES/MARCROSS   *LL*
PR CB 1731-1812, described at visitation in 1781 as 'a small register book of parchment carefully
    kept,' and recorded in 1940 apparently lost
M 1756-1811, 1814-36 **Glam RO**
BT 1696, 1722-39, 1741-1870 **NLW**

MARGAM   *LL*
C 1672-1951 Port Talbot 1850-95   M 1675-1837   B 1672-1953 Port Talbot 1850-95 **Glam RO**
    Fac C 1672-1763   M 1672-1755   B 1675-1754 **NLW**
Cop ts PR C 1672-1858 M 1672-1862 B 1672-1840 partly indexed **Soc Gen**

MERTHYR DYFAN/MERTHYR DOVAN   *LL*
At visitation in 1781 this parish had PR CB beginning 1753. Pre-1812 records were said to be
    missing in 1831
C 1813-1928   M 1754-1812, 1814-36, 1839-1925 (Banns 1901-53) **NLW**   B 1813- incumbent
BT 1724-43, 1745-65, 1767-1853, 1855-64, 1867-82, 1884-7 **NLW**

MERTHYR MAWR   *LL*
CB 1749-1812   M 1756-1970 **Glam RO**
BT 1696, 1721, 1723-1874 **NLW**

MERTHYR TUDFUL/MERTHYR TYDFIL   *LL*
C 1704-1910   M 1704-1946 (Banns 1792-1832, 1889-94 St. David 1911-61)   B 1704-1888 **NLW**
BT 1717, 1724-38, 1740-1851, 1855-8 **NLW**

*MICHAELSTON-LE-PIT/LLANFIHANGEL-Y-PWLL   *LL*

At visitation in 1771 the rector admitted that 'the last curate's register book I could never find it'
C 1783-1980   M 1783, 1786-7, 1813-1968   B 1784-1980 **Glam RO**
BT 1724-5, 1729-36, 1738-53, 1755-62, 1764-1876, 1878, 1882-1913 **NLW**

*MICHAELSTON-SUPER-AVON/LLANFIHANGEL-YNYS-AFAN   *LL*

Diocesan records suggest that in 1805 this parish had PR going back to 1769
C 1785-1890   M 1786-1930 (Banns 1827-30, 1835-43, 1845-90)   B 1785-1862, 1868-90 **Glam RO**
BT 1696, 1723-8, 1730-1819, 1821-70 **NLW**

*MICHAELSTON-SUPER-ELY/LLANFIHANGEL-AR-ELÁI   *LL*

CB 1761-1814   M 1754-1835 **NLW**
BT 1721, 1724-6, 1728-79, 1781-1820, 1823-6, 1828-38, 1840-69 **NLW**

*MONKNASH/YR AS FAWR   *LL*

At visitation in 1781 there was 'an old register book of paper here, but sadly abused before I had
    care of it; and but few leaves remain of it; it goes, in some part of it, as far back as 1677'. PR
    CMB 1746-1812 recorded in 1831 apparently partly lost by 1940
M 1754-1837 **Glam RO**   CB 1813- incumbent
BT 1721, 1723-7, 1730-7, 1739-40, 1743, 1745, 1747-8, 1750-1820, 1822-45, 1848-62, 1865, 1869-74
    NLW

*MOUNTAIN ASH/ABERPENNAR   *LL*

‹Aberdâr/Aberdare & Llanwynno/Llanwonno 1863
C 1859-   M 1865- incumbent
BT 1859-74 **NLW**

*NASH/YR AS FACH   *LL*

Extra-parochial. A private chapel at one time. The manor was the only house in the parish, which
    comprises only 200 acres. Population since 1800 averaged about 10, until recent housing
    developments

*NEATH/CASTELL-NEDD   *LL*

Lay register CMB 1638-47, 1653-79 **Glam RO**
C 1692-1785, 1787-1833   M 1694-1837   B 1692-1784, 1786-1847 **Glam RO**
BT 1721, 1723-1861, 1866-8 **NLW**

NELSON gweler/see LLANFABON

*NEWCASTLE/Y CASTELLNEWYDD   *LL*

C 1745-1943   M 1745-1900 (Banns 1823-81)   B 1745-1897 **NLW**
BT 1721, 1723-63, 1765-1824, 1826-62, 1865-76 **NLW**

*NEWTON NOTTAGE/DRENEWYDD YN NOTAIS   *LL*

At visitation in 1781 the earliest PR was said to include entries of CMB 1687-8, 1691-1703, 1708-14
    but these had apparently been lost by 1831. PR CB 1782-1812 has had leaves cut out
C 1715-1941   M 1715-1957 (Banns 1875-1911)   B 1715-1952 **NLW**
BT 1722-1805, 1807-23, 1825-38, 1847-61 **NLW**

NICHOLASTON   *SB*
PR 1766-87 recorded in 1831 but not listed in terrier & inventory 1900 apparently lost (Glam RO survey 1952)
C 1787-1811   M 1797-1969   B 1788-1811 **Glam RO**
BT 1671-2, 1677-9, 1681-4, 1686-7, 1690-1, 1696-7, 1701, 1707-8, 1710, 1713, 1716, 1725, 1727-54, 1756-8, 1760-75, 1777-89, 1791-1800, 1802-3, 1805-46, 1849-70, 1873, 1875-9, 1882, 1885, 1887-93, 1895-6, 1898 **NLW**
Cop ts BT 1671-1837 **Glam RO**

NOLTON   *LL*
An ancient chapelry with earlier entries of CMB included in PR Coety/Coity
C 1840-1946   M 1837-1940 **Glam RO**   B 1841- incumbent
BT 1844, 1847-57, 1873-5 **NLW**

OXWICH   *SB*
PR 1655-1771 recorded in 1831 and 1728-68 recorded in 1940 apparently lost (Glam RO survey 1952). The latter was listed in terrier & inventory 1900 as being 'leaves of parchment simply sewn together' containing entries of C 1728-72 M 1724-61 B1724-72
CB 1772-1812   M 1777-1970 (Banns 1824-1970) **Glam RO**
BT 1671-2, 1677-9, 1681-4, 1686-7, 1690-1, 1696, 1701, 1704, 1707-8, 1710, 1713-16, 1723, 1725, 1727-31, 1733, 1735-67, 1769-71, 1773-93, 1795-6, 1798-1800, 1802-3, 1805-41, 1843-4, 1847-79, 1881-2, 1885, 1887-96, 1898-9 **NLW**
Cop ms PR & BT CB 1672-1837 M 1673-1837 **Glam RO**

*OYSTERMOUTH/YSTUMLLWYNARTH   *SB*
C 1719-1929   M 1719-1922 (Banns 1824-47)   B 1719-1954 **NLW**
BT 1671-2, 1690, 1693, 1695-7, 1700-1, 1716, 1727-61, 1763-5, 1768-86, 1788-93, 1795, 1797-1800, 1802-3, 1805, 1808-71 **NLW**
Cop ts PR C 1715-1840 M 1714-1840 B 1719-1840 with index **NLW & Soc Gen**

PENARTH St. Augustine   *LL*
PR 1768-1812 recorded in 1831 but not in *A digest* ... (Cardiff, 1905) apparently lost. At visitation in 1781 it was recorded that a new PR had been bought 'not above two months ago' for registering M as well as CB: 'The same doth for all uses in our little parish'. Pre-1769 register was reported lost as early as 1771 visitation
C 1813-1938   M 1813-1922 (Banns 1824-90, 1899-1905, 1913-46)   B 1813-1921 **Glam RO**
BT 1724-47, 1749, 1751-1813, 1815-16, 1818-25, 1827-30, 1832-51, 1853-88 **NLW**
Cop ts PR C 1835-63 M 1831-79 B 1832-86 **NLW & Soc Gen & Glam RO**

PENARTH All Saints   *LL*
‹St. Augustine 1895
C 1891-1923   M 1895-1926 (Banns 1915-29) **Glam RO**

PEN-CLAWDD gweler/see LLANYRNEWYDD

PENDEULWYN/PENDOYLAN   *LL*
C 1569-1632, 1634, 1645   M 1569-1629   B 1569-1633, 1669-72 **NLW**   C 1727-1955   M 1727-1975 (Banns 1823-1961)   B 1727-68, 1787-1968   Fac C 1569-1632, 1634, 1645   M 1569-1629   B 1569-1633, 1669-72 **Glam RO**
BT 1717, 1724-33, 1735-9, 1741-3, 1745-52, 1754-80, 1782-1868 **NLW**

PENLLE'R-GAER   *SB*
‹Llangyfelach 1937
C 1865-1932   M 1851-1960   B 1866-1915 **Glam RO**

PEN-LLIN/PENLLYN (LLANFRYNACH)   *LL*
PR 1733-1812 recorded in 1831 apparently lost
CB 1813-1902   M 1813-1970 (Banns 1824-1976) **NLW**
BT 1721, 1723-1851, 1854-6 **NLW**

PEN-MAEN   *SB*
Diocesan records suggest that *c.* 1790 the registers went 'but 50 years back'
C 1765-1813   M 1765-1970   B 1768-1810 **Glam RO**
BT 1686-7, 1690, 1696-7, 1700-1, 1704, 1707-8, 1710, 1712-13, 1716, 1730-3, 1735, 1737-56, 1758-9, 1761-1800, 1802, 1804-70, 1873-5, 1880, 1885, 1887, 1891-1902 **NLW**
Cop ms PR & BT C 1687-1837 M 1686-1836 B 1686-1837 **Glam RO**

PEN-MARC/PENMARK   *LL*
At visitation in 1781 PR said to go back with 'considerable omissions' to 1726
C 1751, 1764-1972   M 1751, 1755-1970 (Banns 1939-80)   B 1751, 1764-1985 **Glam RO**   Fac
    C 1751, 1764-1893   M 1751, 1755-1841   B 1751, 1764-1897 **NLW**
BT 1696, 1724-46, 1748-56, 1758-70, 1772-1861, 1863-6, 1868, 1873-87, 1890 **NLW**

PENNARD   *SB*
Diocesan records suggest that *c.* 1790 the registers went back to 1720
C 1743-1965   M 1743-1971   B 1743-1944 **NLW**
BT 1677-9, 1681-4, 1686, 1690, 1693, 1696-7, 1699-1702, 1704, 1707, 1710, 1713, 1716, 1718, 1725, 1727, 1729-40, 1742-71, 1773-6, 1778-80, 1782-95, 1797-1800, 1802-3, 1805-6, 1808-82, 1885, 1887-91 **NLW**
Cop ms PR CB 1743-67 M 1743-54 **NLW**

PENRHIW-CEIBR   *LL*
‹Aberpennar/Mountain Ash 1897
C 1883-1929   M 1884-1919 (Banns 1884-97, 1904-39)   B 1904-26 **Glam RO**

PEN-RHYS/PENRICE   *SB*
PR M 1776-1811 recorded in 1831 apparently lost (Glam RO survey 1952)
C 1638-52, 1677, 1682-1716, 1728-1812   M [1631]-74/5, 1681, 1724-73   B 1637-56/7, 1681-4, 1707-16, 1724-1812 **Glam RO**
BT 1672, 1677-9, 1683, 1686-7, 1690, 1701, 1708, 1710, 1713, 1716, 1718, 1725, 1727-33, 1735-45, 1747-67, 1769-71, 1774-1800, 1802-3, 1805-7, 1809-36, 1838, 1840-1, 1843-4, 1846-82 **NLW**
Cop ts PR C 1638-1715 M 1631-74 B 1643-1715 & ms PR & BT C 1638-1837 M 1631-1837 B 1640-1837 **Glam RO**

PENTRE gweler/see YSTRADYFODWG

PEN-TYRCH   *LL*
At visitation in 1771 the PR were said to begin in 1664 and to be 'carefully kept and in good preservation'
C 1678-9, 1723-1842, 1846-53, 1858-61, 1864-6, 1868   M 1695-1703, 1724-53, 1813-78, 1882-1946 (Banns 1813-34, 1887-95)   B 1695-1700, 1723-1841, 1846-53 **Glam RO**
BT 1717, 1724-1821, 1823-33, 1837-40, 1846-53, 1859-61, 1864-6, 1868-9, 1871-4 **NLW**

PEN-Y-FAI   *LL*
‹Y Castellnewydd/Newcastle 1903
M 1904-58 (Banns 1904-62) **Glam RO**

*PETERSTON-SUPER-ELY/LLANBEDR-Y-FRO *LL*
C 1749-78, 1780-1966 M 1754-1931 B 1749-78, 1780-7, 1790-1932 **Glam RO**
BT 1724-59, 1761-1815, 1817-21, 1824-31, 1833-67 **NLW**
Cop printed PR CB 1749-1812 M 1754-1812 (ed. A.F.C. Chichester-Langley, 1888)

*PETERSTON-SUPER-MONTEM/LLANBEDR-AR-FYNYDD *LL*
C 1745-1811, 1813-1970 M 1745-1970 B 1745-1812 **Glam RO**
BT 1721, 1732-5, 1737-48, 1750-3, 1755-95, 1797-1848, 1850-60 **NLW**

PÎL A CHYNFFIG, Y/PYLE & KENFIG *LL*
C 1695-1920 M 1695-1837 (Banns 1824-60, 1904-49) B 1695-1925 **Glam RO**
BT 1696, 1721, 1723-4, 1726-47, 1749-1872 **NLW**

PONTARDAWE *SB*
‹Llan-giwg/Llanguicke
C 1862-1915 M 1863-1934 **Glam RO**

PONTLOTYN *LL*
‹Gelli-gaer 1870
C 1870- M 1864- B 1871- incumbent Fac C 1870-1918 M 1864-1928 B 1871-1910
  Glam RO

PONT-Y-CLUN A THAL-Y-GARN/PONTYCLUN WITH TALYGARN *LL*
‹Llantrisant 1924
M 1908-71 Tal-y-garn 1963-77 (Banns 1908-71) B 1903-53 **Glam RO**

PORT EINON *SB*
PR M 1807-12 recorded in 1831 apparently lost (Glam RO survey 1952)
C 1740-81, 1786-1921 M 1741-1806, 1813-1970 (Banns 1807-1912) B 1741-82, 1787-1939
  Glam RO
BT 1672, 1681-2, 1684, 1693, 1696-8, 1708, 1710, 1713, 1716, 1725, 1727-33, 1735-9, 1741-89, 1792-
  1800, 1805-83 **NLW**
Cop ms PR & BT CB 1672-1837 M 1673-1837 with index **Glam RO**

PORTHCERI/PORTHKERRY *LL*
C 1776-1969 M 1754-1811, 1815-36, 1841-1983 (Banns 1824-1908) B 1776-1985 **Glam RO**
  Fac M 1754-1811, 1815-36 **NLW**
BT 1724-49, 1751, 1753-5, 1757-8, 1760-77, 1779-1895 **NLW**
Cop ms PR CB 1776-1900 M 1754-1811, 1815-36, 1841-1900 **Glam RO**

PWLL-GWAUN *LL*
‹Llantrisant
C 1920- B 1931- incumbent M 1920-56 **NLW**

*PYLE & KENFIG/Y PÎL A CHYNFFIG *LL*
C 1695-1920 M 1695-1837 (Banns 1824-60, 1904-49) B 1695-1925 **Glam RO**
BT 1696, 1721, 1723-4, 1726-47, 1749-1872 **NLW**

RADUR/RADYR *LL*
C 1725-1916 M 1725-1971 (Banns 1824-65) Christ Church 1906-57 B 1725-1926 **Glam RO**
BT 1717, 1724-45, 1747-1829, 1832-76 **NLW**

RESOLFEN/RESOLVEN   *LL*
‹Llanilltud Nedd/Llantwit-juxta-Neath 1850. The ancient chapel here was in ruins at visitation in 1763 and none of its records survive
C 1850-1953   M 1850-1919 (Banns 1852-61)   B 1850-1948 **Glam RO**
BT 1850-61 **NLW**

REYNOLDSTON   *SB*
PR M 1787-1812 recorded in terrier & inventory 1900 apparently lost (Glam RO survey 1952)
CB 1713-1812   M 1713-86, 1813-37 **Glam RO**
BT 1682-4, 1686, 1690, 1700, 1707-8, 1710, 1712-13, 1716, 1727-31, 1733-6, 1738-42, 1744-7, 1749-58, 1760-76, 1778-91, 1793-1800, 1802-3, 1805-73 **NLW**

RHATH, Y/ROATH St. German   *LL*
‹St. Margaret 1887
C 1884-1927   M 1887-1918 **Glam RO**

RHATH, Y/ROATH St. Margaret   *LL*
C 1731-1923   M 1732-1926 (Banns 1872-1926)   B 1740-1876 **Glam RO**
BT 1717, 1724, 1726-7, 1731-52, 1754-1807, 1809-15, 1817-38, 1840-55 **NLW**

RHATH, Y/ROATH St. Saviour   *LL*
‹St. German 1893
C 1886-1952 St. Francis 1913-67   M 1893-1972 **NLW**

RHOSILI/RHOSILLY   *SB*
C 1641-2, 1665-1807, 1813-1978   M 1665-6, 1671-1970 (Banns 1823-1937)   B 1642, 1644-5, 1665-1807, 1813-1911 **Glam RO**
BT 1671-2, 1677-9, 1682-3, 1685-8, 1694, 1696-7, 1700-1, 1704, 1707-8, 1710, 1712-13, 1725, 1727, 1729-31, 1733-6, 1738-90, 1794-1800, 1802-3, 1805-69, 1871-82, 1885, 1887-94, 1896, 1898 **NLW**
Cop ts PR C 1642, 1665-1807, 1813-36 M 1665, 1671-1836 B 1644-5, 1665-1807, 1813-36 **Glam RO**

RHYDRI/RUDRY   *M*
C 1626-33, 1639-1758, 1767-1937   M 1640-65, 1696-1970 (Banns 1824-1976)   B 1637?-66, 1695-1757, 1767-1935 **Glam RO**
BT 1717, 1724-90, 1792-1887 **NLW**
Cop ts PR C 1626-1757 M 1640-1757 B 1637-1757 **Glam RO**

RHYDYFELIN gweler/see GLYN-TAF/GLYNTAFF

*ROATH/Y RHATH St. German   *LL*
‹St. Margaret 1887
C 1884-1927   M 1887-1918 **Glam RO**

*ROATH/Y RHATH St. Margaret   *LL*
C 1731-1923   M 1732-1926 (Banns 1872-1926)   B 1740-1876 **Glam RO**
BT 1717, 1724, 1726-7, 1731-52, 1754-1807, 1809-15, 1817-38, 1840-55 **NLW**

*ROATH/Y RHATH St. Saviour   *LL*
‹St. German 1893
C 1886-1952 St. Francis 1913-67   M 1893-1972 **NLW**

*RUDRY/RHYDRI *M*
C 1626-33, 1639-1758, 1767-1937   M 1640-65, 1696-1970 (Banns 1824-1976)   B 1637?-66, 1695-1757, 1767-1935 **Glam RO**
BT 1717, 1724-90, 1792-1887 **NLW**
Cop ts PR C 1626-1757 M 1640-1757 B 1637-1757 **Glam RO**

SAIN DUNWYD/ST. DONAT'S *LL*
C 1572-1658, 1663-1812   M 1570-1655, 1664-1729, 1743, 1747, 1755-1970   B 1571-1658, 1663-1812 **NLW**
BT 1696, 1721, 1723-42, 1745-1830, 1832-4, 1836-69, 1871 **NLW**

SAIN FFAGAN/ST. FAGANS *LL*
C 1689-1882   M 1689-1837   B 1689-1966 **NLW**
BT 1717, 1724-1872 **NLW**

SAIN NICOLAS/ST. NICHOLAS *LL*
C 1762-1915   M 1755-1930 (Banns 1824-1973)   B 1762-1966 **Glam RO**
BT 1724-54, 1756-1881, 1883 **NLW**

SAIN SIORYS/ST. GEORGE-SUPER-ELY *LL*
C 1693-1739, 1753-1983   M 1697-1733, 1758-1970   B 1695-1732, 1757-1812, 1814-1984 **Glam RO**   Mf 1695-1814 **NLW**
BT 1724-1820, 1822-31, 1833-68 **NLW**

SAINT ANDRAS/ST. ANDREWS MAJOR *LL*
C 1744-57, 1771-1931   M 1749-1940 (Banns 1824-1920)   B 1745-56, 1772-1940 **Glam RO**
BT 1696, 1724-1863, 1865-6, 1869-70, 1872-3 **NLW**

SAIN TATHAN/ST. ATHAN *LL*
PR C 1891- *c.* 1973 recorded in 1979 apparently lost
C 1677-95, 1750-1891   M 1683-95, 1720-1964   B 1663-95, 1719-50, 1760-7, 1771-1939 **Glam RO**
BT 1721, 1724-87, 1789-1820, 1822-76 **NLW**
Cop ms PR C 1675-95, 1750-1812 M 1683-95, 1720-54 B 1663-95, 1719-1812 **NLW**

*ST. BRIDE'S MAJOR/SAINT-Y-BRID *LL*
C 1723-1849   M 1723-1807, 1813-37   B 1723-1955 **Glam RO**
BT 1721, 1723-1864 **NLW**

*ST. BRIDE'S MINOR/LLANSANFFRAID-AR-OGWR *LL*
C 1723-1802, 1813-1949   M 1725-30, 1734-1947   B 1723-1807, 1813-1942 **Glam RO**
BT 1696, 1721, 1723-1816, 1819, 1821-62, 1869-73 **NLW**

*ST. BRIDE'S-SUPER-ELY/LLANSANFFRAID-AR-ELÁI *LL*
At visitation in 1781 the PR was said to go back sixty years
CB 1747-1814   M 1754-1970 **Glam RO**
BT 1717, 1724-51, 1753-60, 1762-1800, 1802, 1804-21, 1823-48, 1851-70 **NLW**

*ST. DONAT'S/SAIN DUNWYD *LL*
C 1572-1658, 1663-1812   M 1570-1655, 1664-1729, 1743, 1747, 1755-1970   B 1571-1658, 1663-1812 **NLW**
BT 1696, 1721, 1723-42, 1745-1830, 1832-4, 1836-69, 1871 **NLW**

*ST. FAGANS/SAIN FFAGAN   *LL*
C 1689-1882   M 1689-1837   B 1689-1966 **NLW**
BT 1717, 1724-1872 **NLW**

*ST. GEORGE-SUPER-ELY/SAIN SIORYS   *LL*
C 1693-1739, 1753-1983   M 1697-1733, 1758-1970   B 1695-1732, 1757-1812, 1814-1984 **Glam
    RO   Mf** 1695-1814 **NLW**
BT 1724-1820, 1822-31, 1833-68 **NLW**

SAINT HILARI/ST. HILARY   *LL*
C 1690-1984   M 1690-1970 (Banns 1913-63)   B 1690-1985 **Glam RO**
BT 1721, 1724-52, 1754-1852, 1854-5, 1857-61, 1864, 1866 **NLW**

ST. JOHN-JUXTA-SWANSEA gweler/see ABERTAWE/SWANSEA Eglwys Ieuan/St. John

*ST. LYTHAN'S/LLWYNELIDDON   *LL*
C 1750-1985   M 1748-1970   B 1749-1983 **Glam RO**
BT 1724-31, 1733-5, 1737-47, 1751-7, 1759-66, 1768-1863 **NLW**

*ST. MARY CHURCH/LLAN-FAIR   *LL*
C 1584-1812   M 1577-1759, 1761-1839   B 1602-1812 **Glam RO**   Fac C 1584-1812   M
    1577-1818   B 1602-1812 **NLW**
BT 1721, 1724-7, 1729-1854, 1856-63 **NLW**

*ST. MARY HILL/EGLWYS FAIR Y MYNYDD   *LL*
PR CMB 1738-87 recorded in 1951 apparently lost (Glam RO survey)
C 1787-1812   M 1837-1970   B 1787-1811 **Glam RO**   M 1755-1838 **NLW**
BT 1696, 1721, 1723-7, 1729-46, 1748-9, 1751-1860 **NLW**

*ST. NICHOLAS/SAIN NICOLAS   *LL*
C 1762-1915   M 1755-1930 (Banns 1824-1973)   B 1762-1966 **Glam RO**
BT 1724-54, 1756-1881, 1883 **NLW**

SAINT-Y-BRID/ST. BRIDE'S MAJOR   *LL*
C 1723-1849   M 1723-1807, 1813-37   B 1723-1955 **Glam RO**
BT 1721, 1723-1864 **NLW**

SENGHENNYDD gweler/see EGLWYSILAN

SGETI/SKETTY   *SB*
‹Abertawe/Swansea St. Mary 1851
C 1850-1913   M 1851-1918 (Banns 1850-88, 1909-19)   B 1851-1920 **Glam RO**
BT 1851-63, 1865-9, 1871-8 **NLW**

SGIWEN/SKEWEN   *LL*
‹Llangatwg/Cadoxton-juxta-Neath 1844
C 1850-1936   M 1850-1932 (Banns 1866-1951)   B 1851-1929 **Glam RO**
BT 1850-61, 1864-7, 1873-81 **NLW**

SILI/SULLY   *LL*
C 1759-1928   M 1754-1836 (Banns 1823-1931)   B 1759-1812 **Glam RO**
BT 1724-33, 1735-46, 1748-1827, 1830-4, 1838-61, 1864-6, 1870, 1872, 1874-80, 1884, 1898-1907
    NLW

SILSTWN/GILESTON   *LL*
PR M 1783-1810 recorded in 1951 apparently lost (Glam RO survey)
  C 1701-1812   M 1701-79   B 1702-1811 **Glam RO**
  BT 1721-2, 1724-32, 1734-8, 1740-2, 1744-9, 1751-5, 1757-8, 1760-8, 1771-1818, 1820-80 **NLW**

*SKETTY/SGETI   *SB*
‹Abertawe/Swansea St. Mary 1851
  C 1850-1913   M 1851-1918 (Banns 1850-88, 1909-19)   B 1851-1920 **Glam RO**
  BT 1851-63, 1865-9, 1871-8 **NLW**

*SKEWEN/SGIWEN   *LL*
‹Llangatwg/Cadoxton-juxta-Neath 1844
  C 1850-1936   M 1850-1932 (Banns 1866-1951)   B 1851-1929 **Glam RO**
  BT 1850-61, 1864-7, 1873-81 **NLW**

*SULLY/SILI   *LL*
  C 1759-1928   M 1754-1836 (Banns 1823-1931)   B 1759-1812 **Glam RO**
  BT 1724-33, 1735-46, 1748-1827, 1830-4, 1838-61, 1864-6, 1870, 1872, 1874-80, 1884, 1898-1907
  NLW

*SWANSEA/ABERTAWE Christ Church   *SB*
‹St. Mary 1874
  C 1872-1927   M 1872-1919 (Banns 1889-1900) **Glam RO**
  BT 1872-80 **NLW**

*SWANSEA/ABERTAWE Holy Trinity   *SB*
‹St. Mary 1843
  C 1856-1939   M 1877-1941   B 1901-16 **Glam RO**
  BT 1856-82, 1885-6 **NLW**

*SWANSEA/ABERTAWE St. Barnabas   *SB*
‹St. Mary 1914
  C 1915-58   M 1929-52 **Glam RO**

*SWANSEA/ABERTAWE St. Gabriel   *SB*
‹St. Mary 1889
  C 1889-1914   M 1890-1922 **Glam RO**
  BT 1889-91 **NLW**

*SWANSEA/ABERTAWE St. James   *SB*
‹St. Mary 1867
  C 1867-1924   M 1867-1926 (Banns 1899-1921) **Glam RO**
  BT 1867-82 **NLW**

*SWANSEA/ABERTAWE St. John/Eglwys Ieuan   *SB*
Dedication transferred in 1880 from old church in High Street (now St. Matthew) to newly-built
  church at Hafod. Diocesan records suggest that *c.* 1790 the registers went back to 1760
  C 1797-1800, 1813-1923   M 1813-1918 (Banns 1843-1958)   B 1797-1800, 1813-85 **Glam RO**
  BT 1785, 1787-9, 1791-8, 1800, 1802-3, 1805-73 **NLW**

*SWANSEA/ABERTAWE St. Jude   *SB*
‹St. Mary 1921
  C 1896-1921   M 1896-1928 (Banns 1896-1928) **Glam RO**

*SWANSEA/ABERTAWE St. Luke, Cwmbwrla   *SB*
‹St. Peter 1911
C 1886-1914   M 1890-1949 (Banns 1905-27) **Glam RO**

*SWANSEA/ABERTAWE St. Mark   *SB*
‹St. Mary 1888
C 1888-1918   M 1888-1931 (Banns 1888-1903) **Glam RO**
BT 1894-5 **NLW**

*SWANSEA/ABERTAWE St. Mary   *SB*
C 1631-1706, 1712-1928   M 1631-1706, 1712-1924 (Banns 1823-37, 1872-3, 1894-1924)   B 1631-
   1706, 1712-1937 & cremated remains 1957-79 **Glam RO**   Fac PR CMB 1631-1706 **NLW**
BT 1676-8, 1681, 1683-4, 1686, 1690, 1693, 1695-7, 1700-2, 1704, 1713, 1717, 1725-36, 1738,
   1740-59, 1761-86, 1788-92, 1794-1800, 1802-3, 1805-82, 1885, 1887-95, 1898-1905 **NLW**

*SWANSEA/ABERTAWE St. Matthew   *SB*
‹St. Mary & St. John 1886
M 1886-1927 **Glam RO**

*SWANSEA/ABERTAWE St. Nicholas   *SB*
‹St. Mary 1886. Closed 1920
C 1886-1920   M 1886-1920 (Banns 1886-1901, 1908-19) **Glam RO**

*SWANSEA/ABERTAWE St. Nicholas-on-the-Hill   *SB*
‹St. Jude 1933
C 1924-42   Good Shepherd Mission 1927-46   M 1937-50 **Glam RO**

*SWANSEA/ABERTAWE St. Peter, Y Cocyd/Cockett   *SB*
‹St. Mary 1878
C 1856-1943   M 1857-1919 (Banns 1908-39)   B 1856-1923 **Glam RO**
BT 1856-9, 1861-75 **NLW**
Cop ms PR M 1859-69 **NLW**

*SWANSEA/ABERTAWE St. Thomas   *SB*
‹St. Mary 1888
C 1888-1924   M 1888-1927 **Glam RO**
BT 1888-9 **NLW**

TAFFS WELL & NANTGARW gweler/see TONGWYNLAIS

TON-DU   *LL*
‹Y Castellnewydd/Newcastle 1923
C 1868-1915   M 1869-1971   B 1868-1933 **Glam RO**
BT see Y Castellnewydd/Newcastle

TONGWYNLAIS   *LL*
‹Yr Eglwys Newydd/Whitchurch
C 1879-1968   Ffynnon Taf/Taffs Well & Nantgarw 1897-1933 **Glam RO**

TONPENTRE gweler/see YSTRADYFODWG

TREBANNWS/TREBANOS gweler/see CLYDACH

TREFFLEMIN/FLEMINGSTON [FLIMSTON] *LL*
CMB 1576-1725 **NLW**   CB 1726-1812   M 1726-48, 1757-1968   Fac CMB 1576-1725 **Glam RO**
BT 1721, 1724-39, 1741-51, 1753-9, 1761-1814, 1816-17, 1819-29, 1831-54, 1856, 1858-63, 1865-70
   NLW

TREGANNA/CANTON St. John   *LL*
‹Llandaf/Llandaff 1858
C 1858-1924   M 1858-1927 (Banns 1914-55, 1961-8) **Glam RO**
BT 1858-69, 1880-90 **NLW**

TREGATWG/CADOXTON-JUXTA-BARRY   *LL*
Earlier PR possibly mutilated : some entries C 1644-5, 1662-3 on dorse of BT 1735 & 1738
C 1753-72, 1781-90, 1806-9, 1813-89, 1925-51   M 1754-83, 1813-37   B 1752-73, 1781-95, 1803-8
   Barry Dock St. Mary (Banns 1956-63) **Glam RO**
BT 1724-43, 1745-1867, 1869 **NLW**

TREGOLWYN/COLWINSTON   *LL*
At visitation in 1781 PR was said to go 'so far back as February 1694/5'
C 1766-1951   M 1771-1806, 1813-1949   B 1766-1812 **NLW**
BT 1696, 1721, 1723-51, 1753-1862 **NLW**   Mf **Glam RO**

TRE-GŴYR/GOWERTON   *SB*
‹Casllwchwr/Loughor *c.* 1920. PR C 1881- M 1883- recorded in 1935 apparently lost
C 1906-56 (Banns 1882-1959) **Glam RO**

TREHARRIS   *LL*
‹Llanfabon, Merthyr Tudful/Merthyr Tydfil, Gelli-gaer 1900
St. Cynon M 1863-1971   B 1907-51 St. Matthias C 1896-1944   M 1900-45 (Banns 1912-60)
   Glam RO

TRELÁI gweler/see CAERAU A THRELÁI/CAERAU WITH ELY

TRELALES/LALESTON   *LL*
C 1742-1937   M 1742-1839   B 1742-1936 **NLW**
BT 1721, 1723-1869, 1871-5 **NLW**

TRESIMWN/BONVILSTON (BOULSTON)   *LL*
PR M 1813-37 apparently lost. Hearsay evidence recorded in 1940 reply to NLW questionnaire
   that 'some old registers were seen burning at Bonvilston House after the death of a Mr. Bassett'
C 1761-1983   M 1758-1812, 1837-1970 (Banns 1824-1977)   B 1761-1982 **Glam RO**
BT 1696, 1724-1817, 1819-24, 1826-42, 1845-55, 1857-81 **NLW**

*TYTHEGSTON/LLANDUDWG   *LL*
C 1758-1812, 1830-1   M 1757-1837   B 1766-1812 **NLW**
BT 1721, 1723-1835, 1837-60, 1862-9, 1871-5 **NLW**

*WELSH ST. DONAT'S/LLANDDUNWYD   *LL*
C 1726-36, 1758-1981   M 1726-47, 1757-1970 (Banns 1824-1979)   B 1726-1982 **Glam RO**
BT 1724-51, 1753, 1755-69, 1771-89, 1791-1802, 1804-68, 1870-3, 1875-6, 1878, 1881 **NLW**

*WENVOE/GWENFÔ *LL*
C 1585-1971 M 1585-1970 (Banns 1824-1973) B 1585-1983 **Glam RO** Fac/Mf CMB
1585-1739 **NLW**
BT 1724-1866 **NLW**
Cop ts C 1740-1971 M 1741-1971 B 1740-1973 **Glam RO**

*WHITCHURCH/YR EGLWYS NEWYDD *LL*
PR CB 1766-76 M 1754-1812 recorded in 1831 but not in *A digest* . . . (Cardiff, 1905) apparently
lost
C 1732-66, 1778-1938 M 1732-58, 1813-1929 B 1732-66, 1777-1932 **Glam RO**
BT 1717, 1724, 1732, 1734-48, 1750-1, 1754-1875 **NLW**

WIG, Y/WICK *LL*
PR CB pre-1802 recorded in 1831 as being lost. At visitation in 1781 the earliest PR was said to go
back 'as far as the year 1570'
C 1802-1915 M 1754-1837 (Banns 1825-1923) B 1802-12 **Glam RO**
BT 1721, 1723-91, 1793-1864 **NLW**

YSTALYFERA *SB*
‹Llan-giwg/Llanguicke. The newer church of St. David was made parish church on formation of
separate parish 1903
Holy Trinity C 1874-1917 M (Banns 1893-1934) B 1868-1934 St. David C 1890-1922
M 1903-1926 **Glam RO**

YSTRADOWEN *LL*
C 1761-1973 M 1754-1971 B 1761-1974 **NLW**
BT 1696, 1725-41, 1743, 1745-1886 **NLW**

YSTRADYFODWG *LL*
C 1719-1944 M 1719-61, 1779-1973 Pentre 1891-1971 Tonpentre 1920-58 (Banns 1864-1977
Pentre 1891-1973 Tonpentre 1920-65) B 1719-1968 **Glam RO** Mf CB 1719-34 M 1719-
1742 **NLW**
BT 1717, 1724-34, 1736-1819, 1821-39, 1841-3, 1850, 1858, 1861-7 **NLW**
Cop ts PR CB 1719-1812 M 1719-61 **NLW**

YSTUMLLWYNARTH/OYSTERMOUTH *SB*
C 1719-1929 M 1719-1922 (Banns 1824-47) B 1719-1954 **NLW**
BT 1671-2, 1690, 1693, 1695-7, 1700-1, 1716, 1727-61, 1763-5, 1768-86, 1788-93, 1795, 1797-1800,
1802-3, 1805, 1808-71 **NLW**
Cop ts PR C 1715-1840 M 1714-1840 B 1719-1840 with index **NLW & Soc Gen**

MYNWY
MONMOUTHSHIRE

MYNWY/MONMOUTHSHIRE

ABERBARGOD/ABERBARGOED gweler/see BEDWELLTE/BEDWELLTY

ABER-BIG/ABERBEEG gweler/see LLANHILEDD/LLANHILLETH

ABER-CARN   *M*
‹Mynyddislwyn 1921
C 1904-24   M 1917-71 (Banns 1917-68) **Gwent RO**

*ABERGAVENNY/Y FENNI Holy Trinity   *M*
‹St. Mary 1895
C 1888-1976   M 1895-1971 (Banns 1923-50)   B 1895-1958 **Gwent RO**

*ABERGAVENNY/Y FENNI St. Mary   *M*
C 1653-89, 1692-1707, 1719-1872   M 1653-8, 1663-88, 1695-1706, 1719-1895 (Banns 1763-8, 1776-
   1853, 1905-26, 1941-60)   B 1653-89, 1691-1707, 1710-1917 **Gwent RO**
BT 1696, 1725-1835, 1863-86 **NLW**

ABERSYCHAN   *M*
‹Trefddyn/Trevethin 1844
C 1835-1901   M 1844-1915 (Banns 1889-1902, 1920-31 Garndiffaith 1922-63)   B 1835-95
   Gwent RO
BT see Trefddyn/Trevethin

ABERTYLERI/ABERTILLERY   *M*
‹Aberystruth 1854
C 1855-1934   M 1854-1970 (Banns 1854-1967) **Gwent RO**

ABERYSTRUTH   *M*
At visitation in 1771 the register was said to go back 'about ninety six years'
C 1736-1838   M 1736-1836   B 1736-1829 **NLW**
BT 1696, 1725-99, 1801-59 (see also Cendl/Beaufort & Nant-y-glo) **NLW**
Cop ms PR/BT (extracts) CMB 1736-1847 **NLW**

ALLTEURYN/GOLDCLIFF   *M*
C 1728-1924   M 1728-1900, 1903-55   B 1728-1981 **Gwent RO**
BT 1725-50, 1753-6, 1758-98, 1800-19, 1824-48, 1850, 1852-7, 1859-68, 1870, 1872-80, 1882-92
   NLW

BASALEG/BASSALEG   *M*
C 1742-62, 1768-1908   M 1743-1922 (Banns 1933-50)   B 1742-62, 1768-1922 **Gwent RO**
BT 1725-31, 1735-75, 1777-1876 **NLW**

*BEAUFORT/CENDL   *M*
‹Llangatwg/Llangattock & Llangynidr, co. Brecknock, Aberystruth & Bedwellte/Bedwellty 1846.
   New church of St. David replaced St. John as parish church 1890
C 1843-1958   M 1891-1975 St. John 1873-1946 (Banns 1891-1971)   B 1896-1961 St. John
   1843-1915 **Gwent RO**

BEDWAS   *M*
C 1635-1767, 1769-1936   M 1653-1811, 1813-1971 (Banns 1930-54, 1956-61)   B 1653-1753,
   1769-1942 **Gwent RO**   Fac CMB 1653-98 **NLW**
BT 1717, 1725-64, 1766-75, 1777-1811, 1813-88 **NLW**
Cop ms PR C 1641-1767 M 1653-1754 B 1653-1753 **Gwent RO**   C 1635-1715 M 1715-39
   B 1724-81 with index **Soc Gen**

BEDWELLTE/BEDWELLTY   *M*
C 1624-1812, 1815-1954, 1957-75 Aberbargod/Aberbargoed 1905-79   M 1634-1974 (Banns
    1755-1825, 1829-62, 1960-82)   B 1634-1812, 1815-1903 **Gwent RO**   Fac C 1624-1812
    M 1634-1754   B 1634-1812 **NLW**
BT 1696, 1717, 1724-75, 1777-97, 1799-1811, 1813-79 (see also Tredegar) **NLW**
Cop ms PR CMB 1624-1812 **NLW**   M 1815-17 **Soc Gen**

BETWS, Y/BETTWS   *M*
PR CB 1785-1810 M 1756-1812 recorded in 1831 apparently lost
C 1696-1757, 1813-1969   M 1696-1752, 1834-1971 (Banns 1826-1977)   B 1696-1759, 1823-1977
    Gwent RO
BT 1725-75, 1777-1834, 1836, 1838-40, 1844, 1847, 1849-50, 1852, 1856-7, 1860-4, 1867-9, 1871-2
    NLW

BETWS NEWYDD   *M*
C 1734-1974   M 1734-73, 1796-1836   B 1734-1973 **NLW**
BT 1696, 1726, 1728-1821, 1823-4, 1826, 1832-76 (see also Llan-arth) **NLW**

*BISHTON/TREFESGOB   *M*
PR stolen from the church in 1821 (1831 survey). Visitation returns give conflicting evidence with
    regard to earlier PR, there being no PR CB in 1781 where there had been one ten years earlier
C 1793-1813   M 1800-1967 **Gwent RO**
BT 1696, 1725-56, 1758-96, 1798-1819, 1823, 1826-43, 1845-57, 1859-68, 1870-1, 1873-7 **NLW**

BLAENAFON/BLAENAVON   *M*
‹Llanofer/Llanover, Llan-ffwyst/Llanfoist, Llanwenarth & Abersychan 1860
C 1804-1950   M 1805-1971 (Banns 1805-40)   B 1805-74, 1885-1936 **Gwent RO**
BT 1806-42, 1847-51 **NLW**

BRYNBUGA/USK   *M*
At visitation in 1771 the incumbent claimed that 'the most antient date I can find in the parish is
    from 1701'
C 1742-1963   M 1742-1957 (Banns 1824-1965)   B 1742-1953 **Gwent RO**
BT 1696, 1725-1858, 1865-1900 **NLW**
Cop ms PR/BT (extracts) CMB 1696-1785 **NLW**

BRYNGWYN   *M*
C 1660-1934   M 1665-1738, 1751-2, 1755-1811, 1813-1970   B 1666-1740, 1744-70, 1772-1925
    Gwent RO
BT 1696, 1725-1823, 1826-72, 1874-92 **NLW**
Cop ms PR (extracts) CMB 1664-1802 **NLW**

CAERLLION/CAERLEON gweler/see LLANGADOG/LLANGATTOCK-JUXTA-CAERLEON

CAER-WENT   *M*
C 1704-13, 1752-1944   M 1706-13, 1753-1834, 1839-1970   B 1568-1713, 1752-1811, 1813-1915
    Gwent RO   Fac C 1704-13   M 1706-13   B 1568-1713 **NLW**
BT 1725-50, 1752-1881 **NLW**
Cop printed PR C 1704-12 & extracts 1752-1812 M 1706-13, 1753-1812 B 1568-1605, 1630-60 with
    gaps, 1661-1711 & extracts 1753-1811 (ed. J.A. Bradney 1920)

CALDICOT   *M*
C 1716-1888   M 1719-1837 (Banns 1754-1812, 1900-35)   B 1716-1812 **Gwent RO**
BT 1725-39, 1741-61, 1763-1870, 1872-4, 1879-80 **NLW**

CAS-GWENT/CHEPSTOW   *M*
CB 1595-1757, 1761-1924   M 1595-1611, 1695-1925 (Banns 1779-1813, 1912-26, 1953-66) **Gwent
 RO**
BT 1725-30, 1732-63, 1765-1812, 1875-96 **NLW**
Cop printed PR (extracts) C 1595-1743 M 1595-1819 B 1595-1924 (ed. I. Waters)

CASNEWYDD/NEWPORT All Saints   *M*
‹St. Woolos 1899
C 1898-1952   M 1899-1978 (Banns 1899-1908, 1913-62) **Gwent RO**

CASNEWYDD/NEWPORT Holy Trinity   *M*
‹St. Woolos 1864. Closed 1975
C 1852-7, 1864-1975   M 1862-1975 (Banns 1887-1956, 1960-7) **Gwent RO**
BT 1864-84 **NLW**

CASNEWYDD/NEWPORT St. John Evangelist & St. Mary   *M*
‹Eglwys y Drindod/Christchurch 1860. St. Mary acted as parish church 1949-52 owing to fire
 damage at St. John
C 1866-1975 St. Mary 1899-1952   M 1861-1977 St. Mary 1949-52 **Gwent RO**

CASNEWYDD/NEWPORT St. Mark   *M*
‹St. Woolos 1875
C 1875-1968   M 1875-1971 (Banns 1932-46) **Gwent RO**

CASNEWYDD/NEWPORT St. Matthew   *M*
‹St. John Evangelist 1911
C 1896-1938   M 1911-71 (Banns 1911-74) **Gwent RO**

CASNEWYDD/NEWPORT St. Paul   *M*
‹St. Woolos 1839
C 1837-1927   M 1840-1930 **Gwent RO**

CASNEWYDD/NEWPORT St. Stephen   *M*
‹Holy Trinity 1921. Joined with Holy Trinity 1970
C 1884-95 **Gwent RO**

CASNEWYDD/NEWPORT St. Woolos   *M*
C 1702-42, 1769-1931   M 1702-49, 1754-1930 (Banns 1795-1807)   B 1702-43, 1769-1882 **Gwent
 RO**
BT 1725-75, 1777-1837, 1843-50, 1852-87 **NLW**
Cop ms PR (extracts) CMB 1702-1835 **NLW**

CEMAIS/KEMEYS INFERIOR   *M*
At visitation in 1781 it was claimed that the register went back to 1662
C 1701-1951   M 1701-1906, 1910-47 (Banns 1823-1924)   B 1701-1812 **NLW**
BT 1725-1819, 1821, 1823-9, 1831-67, 1869-79, 1881, 1886-8 **NLW**
Cop ts C 1701-1840 M 1701-1837 B 1701-1838 **NLW & Soc Gen**

CEMAIS COMAWNDWR/KEMEYS COMMANDER   *M*

At visitation in 1771 a PR 'bear[ing] date 1740' was recorded, but by 1781 it was said that 'this affair has been greatly neglected by former ministers, nor is there any register found prior to the year 1780 of births and burials. At present [1781] there is one duly kept'. Neither of these registers nor that of marriages said to be then in use seems to have survived

C 1813-1973   M 1813-1970 **NLW**   B 1813- incumbent   Fac B 1813-1976 **NLW**

BT 1696, 1726-57, 1759-60, 1762-1811, 1813-65, 1867-75, 1877-8 **NLW**

CENDL/BEAUFORT   *M*

‹Llangatwg/Llangattock & Llangynidr, co. Brecknock, Aberystruth & Bedwellte/Bedwellty 1846. New church of St. David replaced St. John as parish church 1890

C 1843-1958   M 1891-1975 St. John 1873-1946 (Banns 1891-1971)   B 1896-1961 St. John 1843-1915 **Gwent RO**

CHAPEL HILL (ABATY TYNDYRN/TINTERN ABBEY)   *M*

C 1695-1957   M 1695-1970   B 1695-1812 **Gwent RO**

BT 1725-1828, 1830-69 **NLW**

*CHEPSTOW/CAS-GWENT   *M*

CB 1595-1757, 1761-1924   M 1595-1611, 1695-1925 (Banns 1779-1813, 1912-26, 1953-66) **Gwent RO**

BT 1725-30, 1732-63, 1765-1812, 1875-96 **NLW**

Cop printed PR (extracts) C 1595-1743 M 1595-1819 B 1595-1924 (ed. I. Waters)

*CHRISTCHURCH/EGLWYS Y DRINDOD   *M*

PR CMB 1695-1736 B 1767-77 C 1778-85 CB 1794-1812 M 1926-34 irredeemably damaged by fire in 1949

C 1695-1736, 1743-58, 1778-85, 1794-1931   M 1695-1736, 1743-1934 (Banns 1824-73)   B 1695-1736, 1743-58, 1767-77, 1794-1974 **NLW**

BT 1725-54, 1757-1888 **NLW**

Cop ms PR 1695-1736, 1743-89 **NLW**

CHWILGRUG/WILCRICK   *M*

PR C 1786-1812 M 1755-85, 1804 B 1781-4 recorded in 1831 as being 'chiefly on loose paper' now apparently lost

C 1814-1967   M 1814-1961   B 1824-1974 **Gwent RO**

BT 1725-41, 1743-54, 1756-75, 1777, 1779-95, 1797-1800, 1802-17, 1819-31, 1833-68, 1870-6 **NLW**

CILGWRRWG/KILGWRRWG   *M*

At visitation in 1771 this chapel, apparently annexed to Llan-gwm, was said to have no PR of its own. 'The Ecclesiastical Court takes no notice of this chapel...' claimed the incumbent

C 1806-12   M 1816-1958   B 1774-1812 **Gwent RO**

BT 1814, 1817-19, 1821-53, 1857-60 **NLW**

COEDCERNYW/COEDKERNEW   *M*

CMB 1654-1732 with gaps   CB 1733-1812   M 1733-1969 **NLW**

BT 1696, 1725-55, 1757-75, 1777-8, 1780-1837, 1839-42, 1844, 1847-8, 1852-5, 1857, 1860-73 **NLW**

COED-Y-MYNACH/MONKSWOOD   *M*

At visitation in 1771 the curate wrote, 'We have no register books. The parishioners expect the impropriator to furnish them with those books which he refuses to do. I always keep a book of my own and return yearly copies of it to the registrar's office'. Neither his book nor his returns seem to have survived

C 1783-1802, 1807-1961   M 1783-1837, 1839-1924, 1926-57 (Banns 1866, 1871)   B 1783-1804, 1807-1962 **Gwent RO**

BT 1813-19, 1821-63, 1865-9, 1874-1900 **NLW**

CRYMLYN/CRUMLIN   *M*

‹Pen-maen, Llanhiledd/Llanhilleth, Trefddyn/Trevethin, & Mynyddislwyn 1921

C 1845-1940   M 1904-40 **Gwent RO**

CWMBRÂN gweler/see LLANFRECHFA

CWMCARFAN/CWMCARVAN   *M*

C 1660-5, 1668-73, 1681-90, 1693-1705, 1741-1976   M 1660-3, 1681-90, 1693-1705, 1741-1969   B 1662-3, 1668-73, 1681-1705, 1741-1976 **NLW**

BT 1696, 1726-43, 1745-1868, 1874-85 **NLW**

CWM-CARN   *M*

‹Mynyddislwyn, Rhisga/Risca 1922

C 1919-49   M 1923-71 (Banns 1923-66) **Gwent RO**

CWM-IOU/CWMYOY   *M*

C 1708-92, 1798-1801, 1805-1950   M 1708-1971 (Banns 1809-12, 1823-1958)   B 1708-91, 1805-1976 **Gwent RO**

BT 1843-67, 1873, 1875-6 **NLW**

DDEFAWDON, Y/DEVAUDEN   *M*

‹Yr Eglwys Newydd ar y Cefn/Newchurch

C 1839-1955   M 1958-70 **Gwent RO**

BT 1839-48, 1851-73 **NLW**

*DINGESTOW/LLANDDINGAD   *M*

C 1742-1965   M 1742-1811, 1814-37   B 1742-1983   Mf 1742-1837 **NLW**   (Banns 1824-1973) **Gwent RO**

BT 1696, 1725-30, 1733-46, 1750-1818, 1820-64, 1874-90 **NLW**

DIXTON   *H*

C 1661-1870   M 1661-1837   B 1661-1852 **HRO**

BT 1661-9, 1671-94, 1696-1833, 1836 **HRO**   1843-62, 1864-71, 1873-7, 1879-81 **NLW**

Cop ts PR C 1813-69 M 1813-37 B 1813-52 with index **NLW & Soc Gen & Gwent RO** ts PR/BT M 1754-1812 **Gwent RO & NLW**

DRENEWYDD GELLI-FARCH/SHIRENEWTON   *M*

C 1730-69, 1771-1971   M 1733-1971 (Banns 1803-7, 1848-1928)   B 1730-1955 **Gwent RO**

BT 1725, 1729-38, 1740-1867, 1881-7 **NLW**

*EBBW VALE/GLYNEBWY Christ Church   *M*

‹Tredegar, Aberystruth, Cendl/Beaufort 1870

C 1858-1967 St. John 1902-54   M 1870-1976 (Banns 1954-64) St. John 1910-70   B 1900-29 **Gwent RO**

EGLWYS NEWYDD AR Y CEFN, YR/NEWCHURCH   *M*
C 1710-78, 1780-1942   M 1710-1970   B 1711-78, 1780-1897 **Gwent RO**
BT 1725-1868 **NLW**

EGLWYS Y DRINDOD/CHRISTCHURCH   *M*
PR CMB 1695-1736 B 1767-77 C 1778-85 CB 1794-1812 M 1926-34 irredeemably damaged by fire
     in 1949
C 1695-1736, 1743-58, 1778-85, 1794-1931   M 1695-1736, 1743-1934 (Banns 1824-73)   B 1695-
     1736, 1743-58, 1767-77, 1794-1974 **NLW**
BT 1725-54, 1757-1888 **NLW**
Cop ms PR 1695-1736, 1743-89 **NLW**

FENNI, Y/ABERGAVENNY Holy Trinity   *M*
‹St. Mary 1895
C 1888-1976   M 1895-1971 (Banns 1923-50)   B 1895-1958 **Gwent RO**

FENNI, Y/ABERGAVENNY St. Mary   *M*
C 1653-89, 1692-1707, 1719-1872   M 1653-8, 1663-88, 1695-1706, 1719-1895 (Banns 1763-8,
     1776-1853, 1905-26, 1941-60)   B 1653-89, 1691-1707, 1710-1917 **Gwent RO**
BT 1696, 1725-1835, 1863-86 **NLW**

*FLEUR-DE-LIS/TRE-LYN   *M*
‹Mynyddislwyn, Bedwellte/Bedwellty, Bedwas & Gelli-gaer 1896
C 1897-1961   M 1897-1978 (Banns 1897-1938, 1943-50)   B 1904-67 **Gwent RO**

GARNDIFFAITH gweler/see ABERSYCHAN

GLYNEBWY/EBBW VALE Christ Church   *M*
‹Tredegar, Aberystruth, Cendl/Beaufort 1870
C 1858-1967 St. John 1902-54   M 1870-1976 (Banns 1954-64) St. John 1910-70   B 1900-29
     Gwent RO

GOETRE   *M*
C 1695-1728, 1732-1960   M 1695-1728, 1732-1971   B 1695-1728, 1732-1957 **Gwent RO**
BT 1696, 1725-1865, 1899 **NLW**
Cop ms PR CB 1695-1776 M 1695-1768 **NLW**   ms PR CMB 1695-1865 **Soc Gen**

*GOLDCLIFF/ALLTEURYN   *M*
C 1728-1924   M 1728-1900, 1903-55   B 1728-1981 **Gwent RO**
BT 1725-50, 1753-6, 1758-98, 1800-19, 1824-48, 1850, 1852-7, 1859-68, 1870, 1872-80, 1882-92
     NLW

GRIFFITHSTOWN   *M*
‹Llanfrechfa & Pant-teg/Panteg 1898
C 1888-1961   M 1888-1971 (Banns 1888-1949) **Gwent RO**

GRYSMWNT, Y/GROSMONT   *M*
C 1589-1638, 1662-72, 1678-1860   M 1589-1638, 1662-72, 1678-1913   B 1589-1638, 1662-72,
     1678-1954 **NLW**
BT 1698-9, 1725-31, 1734-46, 1749-1835, 1837-43, 1845, 1848, 1855-61, 1863-4, 1868-73 **NLW**
Cop printed PR CMB 1589-1812 (ed. J.A. Bradney 1921)

GWERNESNI/GWERNESNEY   *M*
PR CB 1758-82 M 1757-82 recorded in 1831 apparently lost. At visitation in 1771 the register was
    said to go back to 1728
CB 1783-1812   M 1783-1840 **NLW**
BT 1725-55, 1757-1817, 1819-21, 1824-5, 1827, 1829-68, 1874 **NLW**

GWNDY/UNDY   *M*
C 1760-1891   M 1754-1971   B 1760-1800, 1813-1924 **Gwent RO**
BT 1696, 1725-1869, 1871-90, 1892-5 **NLW**

HENGASTELL/OLDCASTLE   *M*
C 1784-1976   M 1773-1804, 1815-35, 1837-1960   B 1784-1812, 1816-1974 **Gwent RO**
BT 1702-4, 1707-11, 1714-17, 1723-1809, 1813, 1815-17, 1821-38, 1845-78, 1880, 1882-3 **NLW**

HENLLYS   *M*
PR CB 1765-1812 M 1754-1812 recorded in 1831 apparently lost. M 1813-37 missing in 1935
C 1813-1974   M 1838-1971 (Banns 1825-1974)   B 1813-1976 **Gwent RO**
BT 1696, 1725-75, 1777-1865, 1871-2, 1874-5 **NLW**

IFFTWN/IFTON   *M*
There are no visible remains of this church, and the parish has long been associated with Roggiet.
    No separate records survive

*ITTON/LLANDDINOL   *M*
At visitation in 1781 the registers were said to begin in 1702
CB 1773-1812   M 1775-1836 **Gwent RO**
BT 1725-1820, 1822-32, 1834, 1836-62, 1864-8 **NLW**

*KEMEYS COMMANDER/CEMAIS COMAWNDWR   *M*
At visitation in 1771 a PR 'bear[ing] date 1740' was recorded, but by 1781 it was said that 'this
    affair has been greatly neglected by former ministers, nor is there any register found prior to
    the year 1780 of births and burials. At present [1781] there is one duly kept'. Neither of these
    registers nor that of marriages said to be then in use seems to have survived
C 1813-1973   M 1813-1970 **NLW**   B 1813- incumbent   Fac B 1813-1976 **NLW**
BT 1696, 1726-57, 1759-60, 1762-1811, 1813-65, 1867-75, 1877-8 **NLW**

*KEMEYS INFERIOR/CEMAIS   *M*
At visitation in 1781 it was claimed that the register went back to 1662
C 1701-1951   M 1701-1906, 1910-47 (Banns 1823-1924)   B 1701-1812 **NLW**
BT 1725-1819, 1821, 1823-9, 1831-67, 1869-79, 1881, 1886-8 **NLW**
Cop ts C 1701-1840 M 1701-1837 B 1701-1838 **NLW & Soc Gen**

*KILGWRRWG/CILGWRRWG   *M*
At visitation in 1771 this chapel, apparently annexed to Llan-gwm, was said to have no PR of its
    own. 'The Ecclesiastical Court takes no notice of this chapel...' claimed the incumbent
C 1806-12   M 1816-1958   B 1774-1812 **Gwent RO**
BT 1814, 1817-19, 1821-53, 1857-60 **NLW**

LANGSTONE   *M*
At visitation in 1781 there was here 'an ancient register book', but no starting date was given
C 1758-1979   M 1755-1971 (Banns 1824-1972)   B 1755, 1763-97, 1802, 1805-11, 1813-1979
    Gwent RO
BT 1696, 1725-51, 1753-1877, 1879-80 **NLW**
Cop ms PR CB 1763-1812 M 1755-1812 **NLW**

*LISWERRY/LLYSWYRY   *M*
‹Eglwys y Drindod/Christchurch & Casnewydd/Newport St. John Evangelist 1922
C 1899-1944   M 1923-41 **Gwent RO**

LLAN-ARTH   *M*
C 1598-1729, 1734-79, 1789-1896   M 1598-1729, 1734-1837 (Banns 1824-1914)   B 1598-1729,
  1734-79, 1789-1895 **Gwent RO**
BT 1696, 1725-1876, 1878-82, 1896-1907 **NLW**

LLANBADOG   *M*
CB 1582-1709   M 1592-1708 **University College Cardiff**   C 1710-1893   M 1710-1969
  B 1710-1905 **NLW**
BT 1696, 1725-1870, 1876 **NLW**
Cop printed PR 1582-1709 (ed. J.A. Bradney 1919)   ms PR 1582-1709 **Cardiff Central Library**
  ms PR CB 1710-1812 M 1711-54 **NLW**

LLANBEDR GWYNLLŴG/PETERSTONE WENTLLOOG   *M*
PR 1707-84, 1800-12 recorded in 1831 apparently lost
CB 1813- incumbent   M 1754-1812, 1845-1954 **NLW**
BT 1725-75, 1777-92, 1794-1865 **NLW**

LLANDDEWI FACH   *M*
C 1741-98   M 1741-54, 1813-36, 1838-1966 (Banns 1826-1956)   B 1741-1812 **Gwent RO**
BT 1725-6, 1728-1868, 1870-6 **NLW**
Cop ms/ts PR C 1741-1861 M 1741-1836 B 1741-1845 **NLW**   ts PR C 1813-61 B 1813-45
  Soc Gen

LLANDDEWI NANT HODNI/LLANTHONY   *M*
‹Cwm-iou/Cwmyoy
C 1769-98, 1813-1976   M 1832-7, 1866-1969   B 1769-94, 1813-1973 **Gwent RO**
BT 1835, 1843, 1845-53, 1855-66, 1873, 1875-6 **NLW**

LLANDDEWI RHYDDERCH   *M*
C 1670-1732, 1735-1923   M 1695-1730, 1736-1810, 1813-1970   B 1670-1732, 1735-1978 **Gwent
  RO**
BT 1725-32, 1735-1817, 1819-58, 1864-74, 1876-7 **NLW**
Cop printed PR CB 1670-1732 M 1695-1730, 1754-83 (ed. J.A. Bradney 1919)

LLANDDEWI YSGYRYD/LLANDDEWI SKIRRID   *M*
PR M 1754-1806 the only volume to be found in 1831 now apparently lost
C 1550-1729 with gaps, 1813-1978   M 1551-1729 with gaps, 1813-1971   B 1549-1729 with gaps,
  1813-1982 **NLW**
BT 1725-33, 1735-1847, 1852-6, 1858-78 **NLW**

LLANDDINGAD/DINGESTOW   *M*
C 1742-1965   M 1742-1811, 1814-37   B 1742-1983   Mf 1742-1837 **NLW**   (Banns 1824-
  1973) **Gwent RO**
BT 1696, 1725-30, 1733-46, 1750-1818, 1820-64, 1874-90 **NLW**

LLANDDINOL/ITTON   *M*
At visitation in 1781 the registers were said to begin in 1702
CB 1773-1812   M 1775-1836 **Gwent RO**
BT 1725-1820, 1822-32, 1834, 1836-62, 1864-8 **NLW**

LLANDEGFEDD   *M*

At visitation in 1771 the register was said to go back 'as far as the year 1652 but imperfect'

C 1746-1812   M 1747-95, 1815-16, 1838-1966   B 1747-1812 **Gwent RO**

BT 1725-1813, 1815-73 **NLW**

Cop ms/ts PR C 1746-1855 M 1746-1832 B 1746-1850 **NLW**   ts PR C 1813-50 **Soc Gen**

LLANDEILO BERTHOLAU/LLANTILIO PERTHOLEY   *M*

CMB 1591- incumbent (Gwent RO survey 1966)

BT 1725-1811, 1813-75 **NLW**

LLANDEILO GRESYNNI/LLANTILIO CROSSENNY   *M*

PR 1609-44 transcribed by Walter Powell (1582-1656) is now lost

C 1719-1967   M 1719-1971 (Banns 1754-1812)   B 1719-1876 **Gwent RO**

BT 1696, 1725-84, 1787-1836, 1838-40, 1842-50, 1852-5, 1857, 1859, 1861-2, 1865, 1867, 1869, 1871, 1887-8 **NLW**

Cop printed PR C 1629-44 B 1609-28 (ed. J.A. Bradney, 1916 from Powell's ms copy at the Bodleian Library, Oxford)

LLANDENNI/LLANDENNY   *M*

C 1710-15, 1722-42, 1764-1813   M 1711-15, 1723-49, 1754-1839   B 1710-15, 1722-49, 1764-1812 **Gwent RO**

BT 1725-1815, 1817-30, 1832-7, 1839-68, 1871-2 **NLW**

Cop ms PR CB 1710-49, 1764-1812 M 1710-49 **NLW**

LLANDEVAUD   *M*

At visitation in 1771 this was described as 'a chapel of ease belonging to Langwm. We have no register book. We never have any marriages here.' By 1809 only the chancel remained standing (LL/VC/38). PR begin with the opening of the new church built on the old foundations in 1843

C 1843-   M 1849-   B 1846- incumbent (Gwent RO survey 1965)

BT 1848-67, 1869-70, 1872-81 **NLW**

LLANDOGO   *M*

C 1694-1942   M 1698-1748, 1750-2, 1755-1971 (Banns 1835-1974)   B 1694-1811, 1813-87 **Gwent RO**

BT 1725-9, 1731-1872 **NLW**

LLANEIRWG/ST. MELLONS   *M*

CMB 1717-20 in PR Llanedern/Llanedeyrn (Morgannwg/Glamorgan)

C 1722-1900   M 1722-1844   B 1722-1904   Fac C 1900-58   M 1837-1961   B 1904-63 **NLW** St. Dyfrig, Llanrhymni/Llanrumney M 1970-9 **Glam RO**

BT 1725-75, 1777-1844, 1846-61, 1864-9 **NLW**

Cop ts PR CMB 1717-20 **NLW**

LLANELEN   *M*

C 1766-1959   M 1754-1971 (Banns 1825-1976)   B 1766-1922 **NLW**

BT 1696, 1725-31, 1733-45, 1747-1860, 1862-70 **NLW**

Cop ts PR C 1766-1959 M 1754-1971 B 1766-1812 **NLW**

LLANFABLE/LLANVAPLEY   *M*

C 1699-1977   M 1699-1752, 1754-1812, 1815-37, 1840-1965 (Banns 1824-1976)   B 1699-1973 **Gwent RO**

BT 1725-1810, 1813-53, 1855, 1859, 1864-70, 1879-83, 1898-1912 **NLW**

LLANFACHES/LLANVACHES   *M*
PR CMB in current use at visitation in 1771 & 1781 apparently lost
C 1796-1973   M 1796-1971 (Banns 1826-1973)   B 1796-1812 **Gwent RO**
BT 1725-44, 1746-8, 1750-3, 1755-1865, 1867-70, 1872-85 **NLW**

LLANFAIR CILGEDIN/LLANFAIR KILGEDDIN   *M*
C 1733-1977   M 1733-53, 1757-1811, 1813-1971   B 1733-1812 **Gwent RO**   Fac C 1813-1977
    M 1777-1811 **NLW**
BT 1696, 1725-42, 1744-1870, 1872 **NLW**

LLANFAIR ISGOED/LLANFAIR DISGOED   *M*
CB 1681-   M 1680- incumbent (Gwent RO survey 1970)
BT 1725-1878, 1880-1 **NLW**
Cop printed PR C 1681-1796, 1803-12 M 1680-1726, 1758-95 B 1680-1803 (ed. J. A. Bradney 1920)

LLANFARTHIN/LLANMARTIN   *M*
PR CB 1778-1812 recorded in 1831 apparently lost. M 1755-1837 badly damaged by damp (Gwent
    RO survey 1979). At visitation in 1805 PR went back to 1736
CB 1813-1979   M 1839-1970 **Gwent RO**
BT 1725-44, 1746-1801, 1803-17, 1819-76 **NLW**

LLAN-FFWYST/LLANFOIST   *M*
C 1736-1975   M 1736-1971 (Banns 1824-47, 1890-1933)   B 1736-1945 **NLW**
BT 1725-32, 1734-51, 1753-4, 1756-75, 1777-1806, 1808-10, 1813, 1815-16, 1820-37, 1841-58, 1862-
    1865, 1869, 1880 (see also Blaenafon/Blaenavon) **NLW**
Cop ms BT/PR 1725-1810 **NLW**

LLANFIHANGEL (NEAR ROGGIET)   *M*
At visitation in 1805 the registers were said to go back to 1739
C 1754-1812, 1814-1975   M 1757-1810 (Banns 1863-?4) **Gwent RO**   B 1813- incumbent
BT 1725-1808, 1810, 1812-67, 1869 **NLW**

LLANFIHANGEL CRUCORNAU/LLANFIHANGEL CRUCORNEY   *M*
C 1727-1900   M 1728-48, 1755-1971 (Banns 1755-88, 1790-1958)   B 1629-40, 1678-1921 **Gwent
    RO**
BT 1696, 1725-1872 **NLW**
Cop ts PR/BT C 1727-1802 M 1727-49 B 1629-40, 1678-1802 incumbent & **Gwent RO**

*LLANFIHANGEL GOBION/LLANFIHANGEL-Y-GOFION   *M*
C 1752-1977   M 1755-1811, 1813-36, 1844-1968   B 1751-1975 **Gwent RO**
BT 1696, 1725-32, 1734-47, 1749-54, 1756-1827, 1829-39, 1841-59, 1863-4, 1866-71 **NLW**
Cop ms PR/BT (extracts) CMB 1696-1812 **NLW**

LLANFIHANGEL LLANTARNAM   *M*
C 1727-1883, 1894-1927   M 1727-1971 (Banns 1824-90, 1894-1915, 1961-74)   B 1727-1889,
    1897-1945 **Gwent RO**
BT 1725-7, 1729-1855 **NLW**
Cop ms PR (extracts) CMB 1727-1809 **NLW**

LLANFIHANGEL NIGH USK gweler/see LLANFIHANGEL-Y-GOFION/LLANFIHANGEL
    GOBION

LLANFIHANGEL PONT-Y-MOEL   *M*
C 1739-1976   M 1754-1970   B 1754-1806, 1813-1944, 1950-64 **Gwent RO**
BT see Mamheilad/Mamhilad
Cop ms PR CMB 1739-1869 **Soc Gen**

LLANFIHANGEL ROGGIET gweler/see LLANFIHANGEL(NEAR ROGGIET)

LLANFIHANGEL TORYMYNYDD   *M*
C 1594-1806 with gaps   M 1699-1747 with gaps, 1754-1812 (Banns 1916-38)   B 1594-1773 with
   gaps, 1785-1803 **NLW**
BT 1725-1819, 1821-2, 1824-5, 1827-62 **NLW**
Cop ms PR CMB 1602-1773 **NLW**

LLANFIHANGEL TRODDI/MITCHEL TROY   *M*
C 1590-1717, 1728-1889   M 1590-1717, 1728-1970   B 1590-1717, 1728-1923 **Gwent RO**
BT 1725-1865, 1879-83 **NLW**
Cop ms PR CB (extracts) 1732-1812 M 1736-54 **NLW**

LLANFIHANGEL-Y-FEDW/MICHAELSTON-Y-VEDW   *M*
C 1660-1713, 1742-1926   M 1660-1715, 1743-1983 (Banns 1754-1812, 1821-3)   B 1658-1714,
   1734, 1742-1967 **Glam RO**   Fac **Gwent RO**   Fac (Banns 1823-51) **Glam RO**
BT 1696, 1725-75, 1777-1886, 1889-91 **NLW**

LLANFIHANGEL-Y-GOFION/LLANFIHANGEL GOBION   *M*
C 1752-1977   M 1755-1811, 1813-36, 1844-1968   B 1751-1975 **Gwent RO**
BT 1696, 1725-32, 1734-47, 1749-54, 1756-1827, 1829-39, 1841-59, 1863-4, 1866-71 **NLW**
Cop ms PR/BT (extracts) CMB 1696-1812 **NLW**

LLANFIHANGEL YSTUM LLYWERN/LLANFIHANGEL YSTERN LLEWERN   *M*
C 1695-1739, 1754-1812   M 1696-1736, 1755-1811, 1813-34, 1842-1969   B 1695-1739, 1755-
   1975 **Gwent RO**
BT 1725-41, 1743-6, 1748-1818, 1820-81 **NLW**
Cop printed PR 1695-1812 (ed. J.A. Bradney 1920)   ms PR CB 1695-1812 M 1695-1772 **NLW**

LLANFOCHA/ST. MAUGHAN'S   *M*
CB 1733-1812   M 1733-1841 **NLW**
BT 1696, 1725-1847, 1850-73 **NLW**

*LLANFOIST/LLAN-FFWYST   *M*
C 1736-1975   M 1736-1971 (Banns 1824-47, 1890-1933)   B 1736-1945 **NLW**
BT 1725-32, 1734-51, 1753-4, 1756-75, 1777-1806, 1808-10, 1813, 1815-16, 1820-37, 1841-58, 1862-
   1865, 1869, 1880 (see also Blaenafon/Blaenavon) **NLW**
Cop ms BT/PR 1725-1810 **NLW**

LLANFRECHFA   *M*
C 1727-1971   M 1727-1963 (Banns 1763-1804, 1839-1965)   B 1727-68, 1777-1958 **Gwent RO**
BT 1725-41, 1743-1852, 1854-68, 1870-4 including Cwmbrân from 1860 **NLW**
Cop ms PR CB (extracts) 1727-1812 M 1754-1812 **NLW**

LLANGADOG/LLANGATTOCK-JUXTA-CAERLEON   *M*
C 1695-1838   M 1695-1837   B 1695-1858 **NLW**
BT 1696, 1725-1905 **NLW**

LLANGATWG DYFFRYN WYSG/LLANGATTOCK NIGH USK   *M*
C 1598-1716, 1727-1977   M 1598-1707, 1727-1812, 1814-1970 (Banns 1905-69)   B 1598-1716,
   1727-1978 **Gwent RO**
BT 1696, 1725-36, 1738-1829, 1833-5, 1848-55, 1864-74 **NLW**

LLANGATWG FEIBION AFEL/LLANGATTOCK VIBON AVEL   *M*
C 1683-1877   M 1683-1836   B 1683-1812 **NLW**
BT 1696, 1725-9, 1731-1847, 1850-69 **NLW**

LLANGATWG LINGOED/LLANGATTOCK LINGOED   *M*
C 1696-1980   M 1696-1970 (Banns 1819-37)   B 1696-1982 **NLW**
BT 1696, 1725-1868, 1870-80 **NLW**
Cop ms PR CB 1696-1810 M 1696-1812 **NLW**

*LLANGEVIEW/LLANGYFIW   *M*
   C 1709-31, 1755-1812, 1814   M 1713-1841   B 1711-1812 **NLW**
BT 1725-1858, 1860-7 **NLW**

*LLANGIBBY/LLANGYBI   *M*
   CB 1679-1812   M 1679-1839 **NLW**
BT 1696, 1725-1868 **NLW**
Cop ms/ts PR CMB 1680-1838 with index **NLW & Soc Gen**

LLANGIWA/LLANGUA   *H*
C 1714-53, 1768-1810   M 1714-63, 1817-43   B 1714-63, 1768-1810 **HRO**
BT 1696, 1725-32, 1734-56, 1758-1805, 1807-9, 1811-15, 1817-44, 1850, 1855 **NLW**

LLANGOFEN/LLANGOVAN   *M*
CB 1689-1715, 1720-3, 1727-8, 1733-1982   M 1689-1715, 1720-3, 1727-8, 1733-49, 1755-1968
   (Banns 1826-1982) **NLW**
BT 1725-1875 **NLW**

LLANGUA gweler/see LLANGIWA

LLAN-GWM UCHAF   *M*
CB 1663-1812   M 1663-1840 **NLW**
BT 1696, 1725-1861 **NLW**
Cop ms/ts PR 1663-1812 **NLW**   ts PR 1663-1733 **Cardiff Central Library**

LLANGYBI/LLANGIBBY   *M*
CB 1679-1812   M 1679-1839 **NLW**
BT 1696, 1725-1868 **NLW**
Cop ms/ts PR CMB 1680-1838 with index **NLW & Soc Gen**

LLANGYFIW/LLANGEVIEW   *M*
C 1709-31, 1755-1812, 1814   M 1713-1841   B 1711-1812 **NLW**
BT 1725-1858, 1860-7 **NLW**

LLANHENWG/LLANHENNOCK   *M*
PR C 1696-1812 MB 1697-1812 recorded in 1935 apparently lost (Gwent RO survey)
CMB 1813- incumbent
BT 1725-49, 1751-73, 1775-1874 **NLW**
Cop ms PR CB 1695-1738, 1753-1810 M 1695-1738, 1753-60 **NLW**

LLANHILEDD/LLANHILLETH   *M*
CB 1733-1813 M 1733-90 recorded in 1935 apparently lost
C 1813-1913   M 1813-1911   B 1813-1930 Aber-big/Aberbeeg C 1909-25   M 1911-41
   B 1911-34 **Gwent RO**
BT 1725-1861 **NLW**
Cop ms PR (extracts) CMB 1733-1838 **NLW**

LLANISIEN/LLANISHEN *M*
C 1597-1731, 1738-1951   M 1663-1725, 1738-1812, 1815-1971 (Banns 1824-1914)   B 1596-1731,
    1738-1812 **Gwent RO**
BT 1696, 1725-1819, 1821-76 **NLW**

LLANLLYWEL/LLANLLOWELL   *M*
CB 1664-1811   M 1664-1775, 1815-35, 1839-1968 **NLW**
BT 1696, 1725-33, 1735, 1737-8, 1740-1, 1743-1829, 1832-67, 1874 **NLW**
Cop ms PR C 1676-1811 M 1695-1753 B 1677-1811 **NLW**

*LLANMARTIN/LLANFARTHIN   *M*
PR CB 1778-1812 recorded in 1831 apparently lost. M 1755-1837 badly damaged by damp (Gwent
    RO survey 1979). At visitation in 1805 PR went back to 1736
CB 1813-1979   M 1839-1970 **Gwent RO**
BT 1725-44, 1746-1801, 1803-17, 1819-76 **NLW**

LLANOFER/LLANOVER   *M*
PR 1661-1706 recorded in 1935 apparently lost
C 1708-1973   M 1708-1837 (Banns 1823-94)   B 1708-1930 **NLW**
BT 1696-7, 1725-34, 1737-8, 1741-1865, 1869-70, 1906 (see also Blaenafon/Blaenavon) **NLW**

LLANRHYMNI/LLANRUMNEY gweler/see LLANEIRWG/ST. MELLONS

LLANSANFFRAID/LLANSANTFRAED   *M*
At visitation in 1781 the rector noted that, on taking up the incumbency in 1770, he had 'establish'd
    a proper register here'. Being unable to 'find any prior to that time', he surmised that 'the
    parish being so very small, and of so few inhabitants, I suppose very little attention was paid to
    this article by my predecessors'
C 1753-1807   M 1772-1805, 1815-37, 1846-1965   B 1753-1811 **Gwent RO**
BT 1772-3, 1775-99, 1801-16, 1819, 1822-7, 1829-46, 1849-57, 1864-6 **NLW**

LLANSANFFRAID GWYNLLŴG/ST. BRIDE'S WENTLLOOG   *M*
C 1713-25, 1732-1812   M 1695-1971   B 1695-1714, 1729-1812 **NLW**
BT 1725-66, 1768-75, 1777-1821, 1823-8, 1830-7, 1840, 1844, 1847, 1852-5, 1857, 1860-73 **NLW**

LLANSANTFRAED gweler/see LLANSANFFRAID

LLAN-SOE/LLANSOY   *M*
C 1592-1652, 1654, 1659-60, 1663-1710, 1747-54, 1760, 1764-1812   M 1592-1647, 1664-9, 1697-
    1705, 1749, 1752-3, 1755-1812   B 1593-1650, 1653, 1663-8, 1671, 1674, 1679, 1688-9, 1695-1730,
    1747, 1750, 1752-3, 1765-1812 **NLW**
BT 1697, 1725-1868, 1870-9, 1881-4 **NLW**
Cop ms PR CB 1594-1812 M 1594-1754 **NLW**

LLANTARNAM gweler/see LLANFIHANGEL LLANTARNAM

*LLANTHONY/LLANDDEWI NANT HODNI   *M*
'Cwm-iou/Cwmyoy
C 1769-98, 1813-1976   M 1832-7, 1866-1969   B 1769-94, 1813-1973 **Gwent RO**
BT 1835, 1843, 1845-53, 1855-66, 1873, 1875-6 **NLW**

*LLANTILIO CROSSENNY/LLANDEILO GRESYNNI   *M*
PR 1609-44 transcribed by Walter Powell (1582-1656) is now lost
C 1719-1967   M 1719-1971 (Banns 1754-1812)   B 1719-1876 **Gwent RO**
BT 1696, 1725-84, 1787-1836, 1838-40, 1842-50, 1852-5, 1857, 1859, 1861-2, 1865, 1867, 1869, 1871, 1887-8 **NLW**
Cop printed PR C 1629-44 B 1609-28 (ed. J.A. Bradney, 1916 from Powell's ms copy at the Bodleian Library, Oxford)

*LLANTILIO PERTHOLEY/LLANDEILO BERTHOLAU   *M*
CMB 1591- incumbent (Gwent RO survey 1966)
BT 1725-1811, 1813-75 **NLW**

LLANTRISAINT FAWR/LLANTRISSENT   *M*
At visitation in 1781 it was claimed that the register went back to 1702
C 1744-   M 1744-8, 1783-   B 1743- incumbent (Gwent RO survey 1959)
BT 1725-9, 1731-49, 1751-1864, 1866-8 **NLW**
Cop ts PR C 1813-43 B 1813-40 with index **NLW & Soc Gen**

*LLANVACHES/LLANFACHES   *M*
PR CMB in current use at visitation in 1771 & 1781 apparently lost
C 1796-1973   M 1796-1971 (Banns 1826-1973)   B 1796-1812 **Gwent RO**
BT 1725-44, 1746-8, 1750-3, 1755-1865, 1867-70, 1872-85 **NLW**

*LLANVAPLEY/LLANFABLE   *M*
C 1699-1977   M 1699-1752, 1754-1812, 1815-37, 1840-1965 (Banns 1824-1976)   B 1699-1973 **Gwent RO**
BT 1725-1810, 1813-53, 1855, 1859, 1864-70, 1879-83, 1898-1912 **NLW**

*LLANVETHERINE/LLANWYTHERIN   *M*
PR CMB 1693-1812 in one volume recorded in 1831 now apparently lost
C 1745-52, 1813-1980   M 1754-1810, 1813-1970   B 1813-1981 **NLW**
BT 1696-7, 1725-1875 **NLW**

LLANWARW/WONASTOW   *M*
C 1674-1752, 1759-62, 1765-1812   M 1718-52   B 1674-1747, 1759-62, 1765-1812 **NLW**
BT 1725-50, 1752-5, 1758-1861 **NLW**

LLANWENARTH CITRA   *M*
C 1725-1811, 1813-66   M 1725-1901, 1903-53 (Banns 1823-82)   B 1725-1891 **Gwent RO**
BT 1725-1870 (see also Blaenafon/Blaenavon) **NLW**
Cop ms PR (extracts) CMB 1726-1808 **NLW**

LLANWENARTH ULTRA (GOFILON/GOVILON)   *M*
‹Llanwenarth Citra 1865
C 1860-1961   M 1866-1980 (Banns 1887-1971)   B 1860-1936 **Gwent RO**

LLAN-WERN   *M*
PR 1750-1813 recorded in 1935 at Trefesgob/Bishton apparently lost
C 1814-   M 1820-   B 1815- incumbent (Gwent RO survey 1965)
BT 1725-31, 1759, 1762-1816, 1818-21, 1834-67, 1869, 1871 **NLW**

LLANWYNELL/WOLVESNEWTON   *M*
At visitation in 1771 it was claimed that the register went back to 1680
CB 1716-1812   M 1716-1970 **Gwent RO**
BT 1725-52, 1755-97, 1799-1807, 1809-16, 1818-27, 1829-30, 1832, 1834-62 **NLW**

LLANWYTHERIN/LLANVETHERINE *M*
PR CMB 1693-1812 in one volume recorded in 1831 now apparently lost
C 1745-52, 1813-1980   M 1754-1810, 1813-1970   B 1813-1981 **NLW**
BT 1696-7, 1725-1875 **NLW**

LLYSWYRY/LISWERRY *M*
‹Eglwys y Drindod/Christchurch & Casnewydd/Newport St. John Evangelist 1922
C 1899-1944   M 1923-41 **Gwent RO**

MACHEN *M*
C 1670-1850   M 1670-1837   B 1670-1849 **NLW**
BT 1696, 1725-68, 1770-5, 1777-1828, 1830-77 **NLW**

MAENDY gweler/see CASNEWYDD/NEWPORT St. John Evangelist

MAERUN/MARSHFIELD *M*
C 1653-1713, 1715-27, 1732-5, 1742-1938   M 1653-1713, 1715-27, 1732-5, 1742-1913 (Banns 1824-
   1952)   B 1653-1713, 1715-27, 1732-5, 1742-1812 **NLW**
BT 1725-1867 **NLW**

MAGWYR/MAGOR *M*
At visitation in 1771 it was recorded that ‘the new book’ went ‘about twenty years back’. Neither
   that register nor the implied older one seem to have survived
C 1799-1813   M 1754-1812, 1814-1974   B 1799-1914 **Gwent RO**
BT 1725-9, 1733-40, 1742-1880 **NLW**
Cop ms PR (extracts) CB 1799-1835 M 1754-1813 **NLW**

MAINDEE gweler/see CASNEWYDD/NEWPORT St. John Evangelist

MALPAS *M*
PR 1733-1812 recorded in 1831 apparently lost
C 1813-1930   M 1759-1932 (Banns 1761-6, 1834-1924)   B 1813-1925 **Gwent RO**
BT 1725-75, 1777-90, 1792-1809, 1811-15, 1817-26, 1828-34, 1836-42, 1844-8, 1851-2, 1854 **NLW**

MAMHEILAD/MAMHILAD *M*
C 1686-1954   M 1699-1811, 1813-1963, 1966-9   B 1686-1936 **Gwent RO**
BT 1725-71, 1773-4, 1776-1861 **NLW**
Cop ms PR CMB 1682-1837 **Soc Gen**

*****MARSHFIELD/MAERUN** *M*
C 1653-1713, 1715-27, 1732-5, 1742-1938   M 1653-1713, 1715-27, 1732-5, 1742-1913 (Banns 1824-
   1952)   B 1653-1713, 1715-27, 1732-5, 1742-1812 **NLW**
BT 1725-1867 **NLW**

MATHARN/MATHERN *M*
PR CB 1792-1812 recorded in 1831 apparently lost
C 1576-1630, 1656, 1661, 1663-4, 1669-1739, 1742-92   M 1565-1632, 1644-7, 1651, 1676, 1680,
   1684-1739, 1754-1835 (Banns 1819-35)   B 1565-1645, 1664-7, 1676, 1679-80, 1684-1739,
   1742-92 **NLW**
BT 1696, 1725-34, 1736-43, 1745-9, 1751-2, 1754-1826, 1828-76 **NLW**
Cop ms PR/BT CB 1565-1792 M 1565-1812 **NLW**

*MICHAELSTON-Y-VEDW/LLANFIHANGEL-Y-FEDW   *M*
    C 1660-1713, 1742-1926   M 1660-1715, 1743-1983 (Banns 1754-1812, 1821-3)   B 1658-1714,
        1734, 1742-1967 **Glam RO**   Fac **Gwent RO**   Fac (Banns 1823-51) **Glam RO**
    BT 1696, 1725-75, 1777-1886, 1889-91 **NLW**

*MITCHEL TROY/LLANFIHANGEL TRODDI   *M*
    C 1590-1717, 1728-1889   M 1590-1717, 1728-1970   B 1590-1717, 1728-1923 **Gwent RO**
    BT 1725-1865, 1879-83 **NLW**
    Cop ms PR CB (extracts) 1732-1812 M 1736-54 **NLW**

*MONKSWOOD/COED-Y-MYNACH   *M*
    At visitation in 1771 the curate wrote, 'We have no register books. The parishioners expect the
        impropriator to furnish them with those books which he refuses to do. I always keep a book of
        my own and return yearly copies of it to the registrar's office.' Neither his book nor his returns
        seem to have survived
    C 1783-1802, 1807-1961   M 1783-1837, 1839-1924, 1926-57 (Banns 1866, 1871)   B 1783-1804,
        1807-1962 **Gwent RO**
    BT 1813-19, 1821-63, 1865-9, 1874-1900 **NLW**

*MONMOUTH/TREFYNWY St. Mary   *M*
    CMB 1598-1754 with gaps **NLW**   C 1755-1908   M 1754-1918 (Banns 1823-47, 1915-64)   B
        1755-1918 **Gwent RO**
    BT 1660-88, 1690-4, 1696-1833, 1836-42 **HRO**   1843-59, 1862-9 **NLW**

*MONMOUTH/TREFYNWY St. Thomas Overmonnow   *M*
    ‹St. Mary 1831
    C 1846-1910   M 1846-1942 (Banns 1846-1939)   B 1850-4 **Gwent RO**
    BT 1846-60, 1862, 1865, 1867 **NLW**

MOUNTON   *M*
    At visitation in 1805 it was stated that no register was kept at this chapel before the appointment
        of Edward Lewis to the curacy in 1789
    C 1790-   M 1845-   B 1790- incumbent
    BT 1813-16, 1818, 1820-2, 1824-58, 1860-75 **NLW**

MYNYDDISLWYN   *M*
    C 1664-1918   M 1656-84, 1687-1743, 1750-1922 (Banns 1911-51)   B 1664-1743, 1745-1933
        Gwent RO
    BT 1717, 1725-75, 1777-1842 **NLW**

NANT-Y-GLO   *M*
    ‹Aberystruth 1844
    C 1844-   M 1855- incumbent
    BT 1844-55, 1857-63 **NLW**

*NASH/TREFONNEN   *M*
    C 1733-1943   M 1733-1970   B 1733-1984 **Gwent RO**
    BT 1725-50, 1753-5, 1758-1819, 1823, 1827-62, 1864-70 **NLW**

*NEWBRIDGE/TRECELYN   *M*
    ‹Pen-maen 1914
    C 1888-1960   M 1922-77 (Banns 1922-55) **Gwent RO**

*NEWCHURCH/YR EGLWYS NEWYDD AR Y CEFN   *M*
C 1710-78, 1780-1942   M 1710-1970   B 1711-78, 1780-1897 **Gwent RO**
BT 1725-1868 **NLW**

*NEWPORT/CASNEWYDD All Saints   *M*
‹St. Woolos 1899
C 1898-1952   M 1899-1978 (Banns 1899-1908, 1913-62) **Gwent RO**

*NEWPORT/CASNEWYDD Holy Trinity   *M*
‹St. Woolos 1864. Closed 1975
C 1852-7, 1864-1975   M 1862-1975 (Banns 1887-1956, 1960-7) **Gwent RO**
BT 1864-84 **NLW**

*NEWPORT/CASNEWYDD St. John Evangelist & St. Mary   *M*
‹Eglwys y Drindod/Christchurch 1860. St. Mary acted as parish church 1949-52 owing to fire
    damage at St. John
C 1866-1975   St. Mary 1899-1952   M 1861-1977   St. Mary 1949-52 **Gwent RO**

*NEWPORT/CASNEWYDD St. Mark   *M*
‹St. Woolos 1875
C 1875-1968   M 1875-1971 (Banns 1932-46) **Gwent RO**

*NEWPORT/CASNEWYDD St. Matthew   *M*
‹St. John Evangelist 1911
C 1896-1938   M 1911-71 (Banns 1911-74) **Gwent RO**

*NEWPORT/CASNEWYDD St. Paul   *M*
‹St. Woolos 1839
C 1837-1927   M 1840-1930 **Gwent RO**

*NEWPORT/CASNEWYDD St. Stephen   *M*
‹Holy Trinity 1921. Joined with Holy Trinity 1970
C 1884-95 **Gwent RO**

*NEWPORT/CASNEWYDD St. Woolos   *M*
C 1702-42, 1769-1931   M 1702-49, 1754-1930 (Banns 1795-1807)   B 1702-43, 1769-1882 **Gwent
    RO**
BT 1725-75, 1777-1837, 1843-50, 1852-87 **NLW**
Cop ms PR (extracts) CMB 1702-1835 **NLW**

*NEW TREDEGAR/TREDEGAR NEWYDD   *M*
‹Tredegar & Bedwellte/Bedwellty 1900
C 1896-1974   M 1897-1982 (Banns 1961-82) **Gwent RO**

OAKDALE   *M*
‹Pen-maen; parish church of Pen-maen since 1970
M 1956-71 **Gwent RO**

*OLDCASTLE/HENGASTELL   *M*
C 1784-1976   M 1773-1804, 1815-35, 1837-1960   B 1784-1812, 1816-1974 **Gwent RO**
BT 1702-4, 1707-11, 1714-17, 1723-1809, 1813, 1815-17, 1821-38, 1845-78, 1880, 1882-3 **NLW**

PANT-TEG/PANTEG   *M*
C 1598-1969   M 1598-1982   B 1598-1904 **Gwent RO**   Fac CMB 1598-1785 **NLW**
BT 1725-51, 1753-1848, 1850-2, 1854 **NLW**
Cop ts PR C 1768-85 M 1730-55, 1767-85 B 1767-84 **Soc Gen**   ms CMB 1598-1812 **Gwent RO**

PEN-ALLT *M*

At visitation in 1781 there was here 'an imperfect register so far back as 1695'

C 1779-1869   M 1765-1812, 1815-1970   B 1779-1902 **Gwent RO**

BT 1725-91, 1793-1849, 1851-70 **NLW**

PEN-CLAWDD/PEN-Y-CLAWDD   *M*

C 1730-1982   M 1731-1811, 1815-1969 (Banns 1826-1982)   B 1727-1981 **NLW**

BT 1696, 1725-32, 1734-86, 1788-94, 1796-1875 **NLW**

PEN-HW/PENHOW   *M*

C 1725-1961   M 1725-1975   B 1725-1812 **Gwent RO**

BT 1725-1839, 1846-51, 1853-4, 1857, 1860-72, 1875, 1880-5 **NLW**

Cop ms PR CB 1725-1812 M 1725-60 **NLW**

PEN-MAEN   *M*

‹Mynyddislwyn 1845. See also Oakdale

C 1852-1934   M 1858-1969   B 1858-1930 **Gwent RO**

BT 1852-72 **NLW**

PEN-RHOS   *M*

PR 1560-1641 transcribed by Walter Powell (1582-1656) was 'much mouseaten' *c.* 1650 and is
  now entirely lost

C 1721-1816   M 1718-1808, 1814-35   B 1718-53, 1765-1815 **NLW**   C 1813-1915   M 1837-
  1969 **Gwent RO**

BT 1696, 1725-1834, 1836, 1838-87 **NLW**

Cop printed PR C 1560, 1565, 1573-98, 1606-41 M 1573-98, 1611-39 B 1573-98, 1611-40 (ed.
  J. A. Bradney, 1916 from Powell's ms. copy at the Bodleian Library, Oxford)

PENTERI/PENTERRY   *M*

C 1726-1812   M 1721-1805, 1813-34   B 1723-1809 **Gwent RO**

BT 1727, 1729-70, 1772, 1776-1815, 1817-24, 1826-76 **NLW**   1877 **Gwent RO**

*PEN-Y-CLAWDD/PEN-CLAWDD   *M*

C 1730-1982   M 1731-1811, 1815-1969 (Banns 1826-1982)   B 1727-1981 **NLW**

BT 1696, 1725-32, 1734-86, 1788-94, 1796-1875 **NLW**

*PETERSTONE WENTLLOOG/LLANBEDR GWYNLLŴG   *M*

PR 1707-84, 1800-12 recorded in 1831 apparently lost

CB 1813- incumbent   M 1754-1812, 1845-1954 **NLW**

BT 1725-75, 1777-92, 1794-1865 **NLW**

PILLGWENLLI gweler/see CASNEWYDD/NEWPORT Holy Trinity

PONTNEWYDD   *M*

‹Pen-maen 1885

C 1884-1914 **Gwent RO**   M 1860-   B 1888- incumbent

PONTNEWYNYDD   *M*

‹Trefddyn/Trevethin 1845

C 1845-1954   M 1845-1971 (Banns 1936-47, 1957-71) **Gwent RO**

BT 1857-63, 1866, 1868-9, 1871 **NLW**

PORTHSGIWED/PORTSKEWETT   *M*

C 1593-1926   M 1593-1953   B 1593-1771, 1776-1911 **Gwent RO**

BT 1725-57, 1760-90, 1792-1829, 1831-70, 1873, 1875, 1879-82 **NLW**

RAGLAN gweler/see RHAGLAN

REDWICK   *M*
At visitation in 1781 PR CB was said to begin in 1752
C 1699-1721, 1785-1938   M 1719-21, 1754-1811, 1813-1969   B 1785-1813 **Gwent RO**
BT 1725-37, 1739, 1741-9, 1751-1879 **NLW**

RHAGLAN/RAGLAN   *M*
At visitation in 1781 there was 'an old register here that goes as far back as very near the time of
  registers being first established'
C 1722-1863   M 1722-44, 1754-1839   B 1722-1868 **Gwent RO**
BT 1725-42, 1744-1873 **NLW**

RHISGA/RISCA   *M*
PR C 1736-1812 B 1779-1812 recorded in 1831 apparently lost
C 1813-1946   M 1754-1823, 1825-1958 (Banns 1834-1925, 1942-72)   B 1813-1935 **Gwent RO**
BT 1696, 1725-75, 1777-1840, 1842, 1845-52, 1876 **NLW**

RHYMNI/RHYMNEY   *M*
‹Bedwellte/Bedwellty 1843
C 1843-1942   M 1843-1971 (Banns 1947-54)   B 1843-1916 **Gwent RO**
BT 1843-61, 1863-5 **NLW**

RISCA gweler/see RHISGA

ROCKFIELD   *M*
CB 1696-1712, 1737-1812   M 1696-1711, 1737-1839 **NLW**
BT 1696, 1725-61, 1763-75, 1777-89, 1791-1851, 1854-68, 1873-87 **NLW**
Cop ms PR CB 1697-1712, 1737-1812 M 1697-1712, 1737-53 **NLW**

ROGGIET   *M*
C 1752-1960   M 1754-1811, 1814-38 (Banns 1825-78, 1898-1946)   B 1750-1812 **Gwent RO**
BT 1725-1867 **NLW**

*RUMNEY/TREDELERCH   *M*
PR M 1754-1812 recorded in 1831 apparently lost. At visitation in 1781 there was here a register
  going back 'about 120 years but in very bad preservation'
CB 1744-1812   M 1744-86, 1804-37 **NLW**
BT 1696, 1725-75, 1777, 1779-1865 **NLW**

SAIN PŶR/ST. PIERRE   *M*
PR 1686-1812 recorded in 1831 apparently lost. At visitation in 1771 it was said that CMB were
  'register'd in the register book belonging to Portskewett'
CMB 1813- incumbent (Gwent RO survey 1955)
BT 1696, 1725-35, 1737-43, 1745, 1757-8, 1774, 1789, 1794-6, 1800, 1803-6, 1808-70, 1873, 1877-81
  NLW

ST. ARVANS   *M*
PR destroyed by fire *c*. 1708. The entries for years before that date were recorded from memory in
  1708 (see earliest extant PR)
C 1684-1890   M 1683-1917 (Banns 1792-1959)   B 1694-1912 **Gwent RO**
BT 1725-47, 1749-56, 1758-1824, 1826-70 **NLW**

*ST. BRIDE'S NETHERWENT/SAINT-Y-BRID   *M*
At visitation in 1771 the PR was said to go back 'about a hundred years'. PR CB 1771-1812
    recorded in 1831 apparently lost
CB 1813-   M 1754- incumbent (Gwent RO survey 1965)
BT 1725-9, 1731-54, 1756-1822, 1824-79, 1881-90 **NLW**

*ST. BRIDE'S WENTLLOOG/LLANSANFFRAID GWYNLLŴG   *M*
C 1713-25, 1732-1812   M 1695-1971   B 1695-1714, 1729-1812 **NLW**
BT 1725-66, 1768-75, 1777-1821, 1823-8, 1830-7, 1840, 1844, 1847, 1852-5, 1857, 1860-73 **NLW**

*ST. MAUGHAN'S/LLANFOCHA   *M*
CB 1733-1812   M 1733-1841 **NLW**
BT 1696, 1725-1847, 1850-73 **NLW**

*ST. MELLONS/LLANEIRWG   *M*
CMB 1717-20 in PR Llanedern/Llanedeyrn (Morgannwg/Glamorgan)
C 1722-1900   M 1722-1844   B 1722-1904   Fac C 1900-58   M 1837-1961   B 1904-63
    NLW   St. Dyfrig, Llanrhymni/Llanrumney M 1970-9 **Glam RO**
BT 1725-75, 1777-1844, 1846-61, 1864-9 **NLW**
Cop ts PR CMB 1717-20 **NLW**

*ST. PIERRE/SAIN PŶR   *M*
PR 1686-1812 recorded in 1831 apparently lost. At visitation in 1771 it was said that CMB were
    'register'd in the register book belonging to Portskewett'
CMB 1813- incumbent (Gwent RO survey 1955)
BT 1696, 1725-35, 1737-43, 1745, 1757-8, 1774, 1789, 1794-6, 1800, 1803-6, 1808-70, 1873, 1877-81
    NLW

ST. THOMAS OVERMONNOW gweler/see TREFYNWY/MONMOUTH

SAINT-Y-BRID/ST. BRIDE'S NETHERWENT   *M*
At visitation in 1771 the PR was said to go back 'about a hundred years'. PR CB 1771-1812
    recorded in 1831 apparently lost
CB 1813-   M 1754- incumbent (Gwent RO survey 1965)
BT 1725-9, 1731-54, 1756-1822, 1824-79, 1881-90 **NLW**

*SHIRENEWTON/DRENEWYDD GELLI-FARCH   *M*
C 1730-69, 1771-1971   M 1733-1971 (Banns 1803-7, 1848-1928)   B 1730-1955 **Gwent RO**
BT 1725, 1729-38, 1740-1867, 1881-7 **NLW**

*SKENFRITH/YNYSGYNWRAIDD   *M*
C 1639-1745 with gaps, 1751-65, 1767-1925, 1928   M 1639-1731 with gaps, 1755-1837 (Banns
    1824-1947)   B 1639-1745 with gaps, 1751-65, 1767-1917 **NLW**
BT 1726-84, 1786-7, 1789-1860 **NLW**

*TINTERN PARVA/TYNDYRN   *M*
PR 1694-1812 recorded in 1831 apparently lost
C 1813-1922   M 1756-1811, 1814-1970 **Gwent RO**   B 1813- incumbent (Gwent RO survey 1970)
BT 1725-1867 **NLW**

TRECELYN/NEWBRIDGE   *M*
‹Pen-maen 1914
C 1888-1960   M 1922-77 (Banns 1922-55) **Gwent RO**

TREDEGAR St. George   *M*
‹Bedwellte/Bedwellty 1836
C 1838-1969   M 1840-1974 (Banns 1943-77)   B 1851-1937 **Gwent RO**
BT 1838-61 **NLW**

TREDEGAR NEWYDD/ NEW TREDEGAR   *M*
‹Tredegar & Bedwellte/Bedwellty 1900
C 1896-1974   M 1897-1982 (Banns 1961-82) **Gwent RO**

TREDELERCH/RUMNEY   *M*
PR M 1754-1812 recorded in 1831 apparently lost. At visitation in 1781 there was here a register
    going back 'about 120 years but in very bad preservation'
CB 1744-1812   M 1744-86, 1804-37 **NLW**
BT 1696, 1725-75, 1777, 1779-1865 **NLW**

TREDYNOG/TREDUNNOCK   *M*
CMB 1695-1812 **NLW**
BT 1696, 1725-70, 1772-1849, 1851-74, 1876-7, 1879 **NLW**
Cop ms/ts PR C 1695-1847 M 1695-1767, 1813-37 B 1695-1848 **NLW & Soc Gen**

TREFDDYN/TREVETHIN   *M*
C 1665-1709, 1726-1939   M 1655-1709, 1726-1923 (Banns 1823-55, 1891-1903, 1907-46)   B
    1655-1709, 1726-1933 **Gwent RO**   Fac 1690-1709 **NLW**
BT 1696, 1725-1844 (see also Blaenafon/Blaenavon) **NLW**
Cop ms PR CMB 1652-69, 1695-1709 & ts PR CB 1714, 1726-1812 M 1714, 1726-94 with index
    NLW   ts PR CMB 1652-1709, 1714-1812 with extracts to 1837 **Soc Gen**

TREFESGOB/BISHTON   *M*
PR stolen from the church in 1821 (1831 survey). Visitation returns give conflicting evidence with
    regard to earlier PR, there being no PR CB in 1781 where there had been one ten years earlier
C 1793-1813   M 1800-1967 **Gwent RO**
BT 1696, 1725-56, 1758-96, 1798-1819, 1823, 1826-43, 1845-57, 1859-68, 1870-1, 1873-7 **NLW**

TREFONNEN/NASH   *M*
C 1733-1943   M 1733-1970   B 1733-1984 **Gwent RO**
BT 1725-50, 1753-5, 1758-1819, 1823, 1827-62, 1864-70 **NLW**

TREFYNWY/MONMOUTH St. Mary   *M*
CMB 1598-1754 with gaps **NLW**   C 1755-1908   M 1754-1918 (Banns 1823-47, 1915-64)   B
    1755-1918 **Gwent RO**
BT 1660-88, 1690-4, 1696-1833, 1836-42 **HRO**   1843-59, 1862-9 **NLW**

TREFYNWY/MONMOUTH St. Thomas Overmonnow   *M*
‹St. Mary 1831
C 1846-1910   M 1846-1942 (Banns 1846-1939)   B 1850-4 **Gwent RO**
BT 1846-60, 1862, 1865, 1867 **NLW**

*TREGARE/TRE'R-GAER   *M*
There are references to and extracts from the lost sixteenth-century register in *The Diary of Walter
    Powell of Llantilio Crossenny* (ed. J.A. Bradney : Bristol, 1907)
C 1751-1983   M 1751-1837 (Banns 1914-82)   B 1751-1984 **NLW**
BT 1725-36, 1738-1818, 1820-65, 1867-77 **NLW**
Cop ms BT (extracts) CMB 1696-1805 **NLW**

*TRELLECK/TRYLEG   *M*
At visitation in 1781 it was claimed that the register went back to 1602
C 1763-1976   M 1773-1971 (Banns 1824-1963)   B 1763-1966 **NLW**
BT 1696, 1725-1876, 1879-81 **NLW**

TRELLECK GRANGE   *M*
At visitation in 1771 it was claimed that 'there is no register book of births and burials (as for
    burials there are none here); there are no returns made to the registrar's office, nor has the
    Court at any time (as far as I know) taken any notice of this chapel'
C 1770-1811   M 1771-1811, 1813-1946, 1950-63 **Gwent RO**
BT 1813-14, 1816-19, 1821-30, 1832-57, 1859-74 **NLW**

TRE-LYN/FLEUR-DE-LIS   *M*
‹Mynyddislwyn, Bedwellte/Bedwellty, Bedwas & Gelli-gaer 1896
C 1897-1961   M 1897-1978 (Banns 1897-1938, 1943-50)   B 1904-67 **Gwent RO**

TRE'R-GAER/TREGARE   *M*
There are references to and extracts from the lost sixteenth-century register in *The Diary of Walter
    Powell of Llantilio Crossenny* (ed. J.A. Bradney : Bristol, 1907)
C 1751-1983   M 1751-1837 (Banns 1914-82)   B 1751-1984 **NLW**
BT 1725-36, 1738-1818, 1820-65, 1867-77 **NLW**
Cop ms BT (extracts) CMB 1696-1805 **NLW**

*TREVETHIN/TREFDDYN   *M*
C 1655-1709, 1726-1939   M 1655-1709, 1726-1923 (Banns 1823-55, 1891-1903, 1907-46)   B
    1655-1709, 1726-1933 **Gwent RO**   Fac 1690-1709 **NLW**
BT 1696, 1725-1844 (see also Blaenafon/Blaenavon) **NLW**
Cop ms PR CMB 1652-69, 1695-1709 & ts PR CB 1714, 1726-1812 M 1714, 1726-94 with index
    NLW   ts PR CMB 1652-1709, 1714-1812 with extracts to 1837 **Soc Gen**

TROSTRE/TROSTREY   *M*
CB 1723-33, 1758-66, 1779-1801, 1805-1975   M 1732, 1761-1802, 1804-12, 1816-36, 1838-1966
    (Banns 1824-?1979) **NLW**
BT 1725, 1728-34, 1737-1876 **NLW**

TRYLEG/TRELLECK   *M*
At visitation in 1781 it was claimed that the register went back to 1602
C 1763-1976   M 1773-1971 (Banns 1824-1963)   B 1763-1966 **NLW**
BT 1696, 1725-1876, 1879-81 **NLW**

TYNDYRN/TINTERN PARVA   *M*
PR 1694-1812 recorded in 1831 apparently lost
C 1813-1922   M 1756-1811, 1814-1970 **Gwent RO**   B 1813- incumbent (Gwent RO survey
    1970)
BT 1725-1867 **NLW**

*UNDY/GWNDY   *M*
C 1760-1891   M 1754-1971   B 1760-1800, 1813-1924 **Gwent RO**
BT 1696, 1725-1869, 1871-90, 1892-5 **NLW**

*USK/BRYNBUGA *M*

At visitation in 1771 the incumbent claimed that 'the most antient date I can find in the parish is from 1701'

C 1742-1963   M 1742-1957 (Banns 1824-1965)   B 1742-1953 **Gwent RO**

BT 1696, 1725-1858, 1865-1900 **NLW**

Cop ms PR/BT (extracts) CMB 1696-1785 **NLW**

VICTORIA   *M*

‹Glynebwy/Ebbw Vale

C 1908-68   M 1901-68 (Banns 1907-28) **Gwent RO**

WHITSON   *M*

C 1728-1816   M 1728-1970   B 1728-1984 **Gwent RO**

BT 1725-52, 1754, 1758-1825, 1827-68, 1870, 1872, 1875-80, 1882-9, 1891-2 **NLW**

*WILCRICK/CHWILGRUG   *M*

PR C 1786-1812 M 1755-85, 1804 B 1781-4 recorded in 1831 as being 'chiefly on loose paper' now apparently lost

C 1814-1967   M 1814-1961   B 1824-1974 **Gwent RO**

BT 1725-41, 1743-54, 1756-75, 1777, 1779-95, 1797-1800, 1802-17, 1819-31, 1833-68, 1870-6 **NLW**

*WOLVESNEWTON/LLANWYNELL   *M*

At visitation in 1771 it was claimed that the register went back to 1680

CB 1716-1812   M 1716-1970 **Gwent RO**

BT 1725-52, 1755-97, 1799-1807, 1809-16, 1818-27, 1829-30, 1832, 1834-62 **NLW**

*WONASTOW/LLANWARW   *M*

C 1674-1752, 1759-62, 1765-1812   M 1718-52   B 1674-1747, 1759-62, 1765-1812 **NLW**

BT 1725-50, 1752-5, 1758-1861 **NLW**

YNYS-DDU   *M*

‹Mynyddislwyn

C 1916-66   M 1927-71 (Banns 1927-74) **Gwent RO**

YNYSGYNWRAIDD/SKENFRITH   *M*

C 1639-1745 with gaps, 1751-65, 1767-1925, 1928   M 1639-1731 with gaps, 1755-1837 (Banns 1824-1947)   B 1639-1745 with gaps, 1751-65, 1767-1917 **NLW**

BT 1726-84, 1786-7, 1789-1860 **NLW**

PENFRO
PEMBROKESHIRE

PENFRO/PEMBROKESHIRE

ABERDAUGLEDDAU/MILFORD HAVEN   *SD*
'Steynton 1891. Consecrated 1808
C 1808-33, 1860-1960   M 1891-1975   B 1877-1955 **Pemb RO**
BT see Steynton

ABERGWAUN/FISHGUARD   *SD*
Diocesan records suggest that *c.* 1790 this parish had a register going back to 1761
C 1799-1912   M 1785-1837 (Banns 1902-40)   B 1799-1854 **NLW**
BT 1685, 1799-1829, 1831-47, 1863-4 **NLW**
Cop ms PR C 1783-1854 M 1785-1837 B 1799-1854 **NLW**

*AMBLESTON/TREAMLOD   *SD*
CB 1765-1974   M 1776-1968 **NLW**
BT 1685, 1799-1862, 1864 **NLW**

AMROTH   *SD*
PR C -1785 recorded in 1831 as having been destroyed
C 1786-1913   M 1754-1970   B 1786-1874 **Pemb RO**
BT 1799-1835, 1837-51, 1853-89 **NLW**

ANGLE   *SD*
PR ancient volumes reputedly destroyed by fire (1831 survey; cf. Castellmartin/Castlemartin) and
    CMB 1733- recorded in 1933 apparently lost
C 1784-1864   M 1755-1970 (Banns 1856-1962)   B 1784-1902 **NLW**
BT 1685-6, 1799-1807, 1809-99 **NLW**

ARBERTH/NARBERTH   *SD*
C 1676-1703, 1762-1918   M 1676-1703, 1754-1805, 1811-1964 (Banns 1811-42, 1896-1966)   B
    1676-1703, 1762-1898 **Pemb RO**   Fac 1676-1845 **NLW**
BT 1799-1801, 1803, 1805, 1807-67, 1872-3 **NLW**
Cop ts PR (extracts) C 1681-1844, 1854-84 M 1756-1837 **NLW**

BAYVIL gweler/see BEIFIL, Y

BEGELI/BEGELLY   *SD*
C 1759-1934   M 1771-1933   B 1759-1934 **NLW**
BT 1685-6, 1799-1809, 1811-88, 1892, 1896-7 **NLW**

BEIFIL, Y/BAYVIL   *SD*
Diocesan records suggest that *c.* 1790 this parish had registers going back to 1767
C 1813-93   B 1813-1908 **NLW**
BT 1674-6, 1679-82, 1685-6, 1688-9, 1700-1, 1703, 1799-1802, 1804-15, 1821-60, 1862, 1864-5,
    1867-8, 1870-5, 1877, 1879, 1882-3, 1885-8 **NLW**

*BLETHERSTON/TREFELEN   *SD*
CB 1653-1980   M 1653-1971 **NLW**
BT 1772, 1799, 1801-38, 1840-57, 1859-70, 1872-3, 1875-9, 1881-3 **NLW**

BONT-FAEN, Y/PONTVANE   *SD*
Diocesan records suggest that *c.* 1790 this parish had registers going back to 1748
M 1815-1971 **Pemb RO**   CB 1813- incumbent
BT 1676, 1678-9, 1681-4, 1686, 1800-13, 1815-19, 1821-40, 1845-7, 1850, 1853, 1855 **NLW**

BOSHERSTON   *SD*
CB 1670-1783   M 1670-1752 **NLW**
BT 1799-1807, 1809-87 **NLW**

BOULSTON   *SD*
C 1799-1939   M 1754-1928 (Banns 1837-1923)   B 1799-1913 **Pemb RO**   Mf M 1754-1809
NLW
BT 1813-22, 1837, 1839 **NLW**

BREUDETH/BRAWDY   *SD*
PR CB 1783-1812 M 1754-1812 recorded in 1831 apparently lost. M 1813-37 B 1813-82 were
    missing in 1933 and are also apparently lost. Diocesan records suggest that *c.* 1790 the registers
    went back to 1764
C 1813-1915   M 1837-1966 (Banns 1935-60)   B 1882-1915 **Pemb RO**
BT 1799-1800, 1802, 1804-9, 1811-67, 1872-82, 1884-5, 1887-96 **NLW**
Cop ts PR (extracts) C 1813-96 **NLW**

BRIDELL   *SD*
PR CMB 1705-1809 recorded in 1831 apparently lost
C 1810-12   M 1755-9, 1810-36   B 1810-11 **NLW**
BT 1674-5, 1678-81, 1683, 1685-6, 1689, 1700, 1709, 1799-1801, 1806-7, 1809-43, 1846-52, 1854-73,
    1875-80 **NLW**

BURTON   *SD*
C 1689-99, 1716-1922   M 1689-99, 1716-1837 (Banns 1823-1905)   B 1689-99, 1716-1895 **NLW**
BT 1799-1807, 1809-67, 1869-73 **NLW**
Cop ts PR (extracts) C 1689-1804 M 1695-1808 B 1695-1811 **NLW**   ts PR M 1754-1837 **Soc Gen**

CAERIW/CAREW   *SD*
C 1718-1951   M 1718-1971 (Banns 1811-1932)   B 1718-1966 **Pemb RO**
BT 1685-6, 1799-1801, 1803-68, 1870-9, 1884-9, 1896-9, 1901-5 **NLW**

CAMROS/CAMROSE   *SD*
Diocesan records suggest that *c.* 1790 the registers went back to 1749
C 1795-1934   M 1754-1929   B 1795-1860, 1879 **NLW**   Fac **Pemb RO**
BT 1799-1804, 1806, 1809-48, 1852-83, 1888-97 **NLW**
Cop ts PR (extracts) C 1813-1906 M 1838-96 B 1861-1907 **NLW**

CAPEL COLMAN   *SD*
PR CB 1777-1812 recorded in 1831 apparently lost
CB 1813- incumbent   M 1770-1834 **NLW**
BT 1806, 1810-11, 1813-17, 1820, 1823-36, 1838, 1840-56, 1858-67, 1870-1, 1873-8 **NLW**

*CAREW/CAERIW   *SD*
C 1718-1951   M 1718-1971 (Banns 1811-1932)   B 1718-1966 **Pemb RO**
BT 1685-6, 1799-1801, 1803-68, 1870-9, 1884-9, 1896-9, 1901-5 **NLW**

CARNHEDRYN gweler/see LLANHYWEL/LLANHOWEL

CAS-FUWCH/CASTLEBYTHE   *SD*
Civil register 1653-7 (**Cardiff Central Library** MS.4.44) Mf **NLW**
C 1777-1813   M 1752, 1756-72, 1775-1920   B 1777-1813 **NLW**
BT 1677-80, 1685-6, 1799, 1801, 1803, 1805-11, 1813-16, 1819-20, 1825-9, 1831-9, 1841, 1843,
    1845-80, 1885-98 **NLW**
Cop ts PR (extracts) CMB 1781-1883 **NLW**

CAS-LAI/HAYSCASTLE   *SD*
PR C 1800-12 M 1810-37 B 1798-1812 recorded in 1933 and M 1787-1812 recorded in 1831
    apparently lost. Diocesan records suggest that *c.* 1790 the registers went back to 1764
M 1837-1968   B 1813-1941 **Pemb RO**   C 1813- incumbent
BT 1799-1808, 1810-66, 1872-89, 1891-6 **NLW**
Cop ts PR C 1800-12 M 1810 B 1798-1812 **NLW**

CAS-MAEL/PUNCHESTON   *SD*
Civil register 1653-9 (**Cardiff Central Library** MS.4.44) Mf **NLW**. PR M 1813-37 recorded in
    1933 apparently lost
CB 1789-1807   M 1797-1810, 1838-1967 **NLW**
BT 1675-6, 1678-83, 1686, 1688, 1799, 1801-4, 1806-7, 1809-11, 1813-43, 1845-8, 1852-9 **NLW**

CASNEWYDD-BACH/LITTLE NEWCASTLE   *SD*
Civil register 1654-8 (**Cardiff Central Library** MS.4.44) Mf **NLW**
CB 1783-1813   M 1813-1966 **NLW**
BT 1679-80, 1685, 1799, 1801, 1803, 1805-9, 1811-79, 1885 **NLW**

CASTELL GWALCHMAI/WALWYN'S CASTLE   *SD*
CMB 1755-1813 **NLW**
BT 1772, 1801-6, 1809-14, 1818-74 **NLW**

CASTELLHENRI/HENRY'S MOAT   *SD*
M 1755-1837 **NLW**   CB 1813- incumbent
BT 1674-6, 1678-84, 1686, 1689, 1799, 1803-5, 1807-16, 1818-37, 1839-48, 1850, 1853, 1855, 1858-9,
    1861-7, 1871, 1874, 1878-89, 1897-1906 **NLW**

CASTELLMARTIN/CASTLEMARTIN   *SD*
PR CMB pre-1782 destroyed by fire (see note in earliest extant register)
C 1782-1877   M 1782-1971   B 1782-1975 **NLW**
BT 1685-6, 1799-1805, 1807, 1809-57, 1859-60, 1864-90 **NLW**

*CASTLEBYTHE/CAS-FUWCH   *SD*
Civil register 1653-7 (**Cardiff Central Library** MS.4.44)   Mf **NLW**
C 1777-1813   M 1752, 1756-72, 1775-1920   B 1777-1813 **NLW**
BT 1677-80, 1685-6, 1799, 1801, 1803, 1805-11, 1813-16, 1819-20, 1825-9, 1831-9, 1841, 1843,
    1845-80, 1885-98 **NLW**
Cop ts PR (extracts) CMB 1781-1883 **NLW**

CASTLEMARTIN gweler/see CASTELLMARTIN

CAS-WIS/WISTON   *SD*
C 1653-66, 1715-1878   M 1653-66, 1715-1970   B 1653-66, 1715-1921 **NLW**
BT 1799-1806, 1808-82 **NLW**

CILGERRAN   *SD*
C 1708-96, 1806-86   M 1708-1837   B 1708-96, 1806-75 **NLW**
BT 1674-6, 1678-85, 1687, 1689, 1702-3, 1705, 1799-1805, 1807-62, 1871, 1873-80, 1882, 1885-7
    NLW

CILGWYN   *SD*
‹Nyfer/Nevern
CB 1775-1811   M 1759-82 **NLW**
BT see Nyfer/Nevern

CILRHEDYN   *SD*
Closed 1981. Diocesan records suggest that *c.* 1790 this parish had registers going back to 1701
C 1800-1978   M 1754-1837   B 1800-12 **NLW**
BT 1676, 1678-81, 1683, 1685-9, 1702-3, 1705, 1799-1807, 1809-57, 1861, 1864-5, 1868-70, 1872-4
    NLW
Cop ts PR (extracts) CMB 1771-1904 **NLW**

CLARBESTON   *SD*
C 1718-1812   M 1724-1813, 1837-1970 (Banns 1755-1812, 1825-1952)   B 1725-1812 **Pemb RO**
BT 1799-1806, 1809-67, 1878-82 **NLW**

CLUNDERWEN/CLYNDERWEN   *SD*
‹Llanfallteg
M 1956-71 **Pemb RO**

CLYDAU/CLYDEY   *SD*
CB 1701-1812   M 1701-1837 **NLW**
BT 1674, 1676, 1678-80, 1682-5, 1687-9, 1702, 1705, 1799-1803, 1805-14, 1816-67, 1869, 1873 **NLW**

CLYNDERWEN gweler/see CLUNDERWEN

COEDCANLAS   *SD*
A small ancient parish, its church was rebuilt 1718 after being a ruin for half a century, and was
    again a ruin by the 1920s. PR included in those of Martletwy and Lawrenny

COSHESTON   *SD*
C 1723-42, 1752-1944   M 1723-40, 1754, 1761-1970 (Banns 1755-99, 1882-1967)   B 1723-42,
    1752-1891 **Pemb RO**
BT 1799-1886 **NLW**

CRINOW gweler/see CRYNWEDD

CRONWERN/CRUNWEAR   *SD*
PR CB 1725-83 M 1725-53 recorded in 1831 apparently lost
C 1783-1979   M 1754-1969   B 1783-1978 **Pemb RO**   Fac 1725-62 **NLW**
BT 1799-1839, 1841-91, 1893-1900 **NLW**

CRYNWEDD/CRINOW   *SD*
M 1757-72, 1776, 1786-8, 1792, 1815-36, 1838-1970 **NLW**   CB 1813- incumbent
BT 1829-30, 1832-9, 1841-55, 1857-72 **NLW**

DALE   *SD*
C 1723-1887   MB 1723-1958 **NLW**
BT 1799-1800, 1802-78 **NLW**

DINAS   *SD*
PR 1678- recorded in 1933 apparently lost
C 1804-12   M 1755-91   B 1781, 1804-12 **NLW**
BT 1675-6, 1678, 1680, 1682-6, 1688-9, 1699, 1702-3, 1799-1809, 1811-37, 1839-45, 1848-58, 1865,
    1867-81 **NLW**
Cop ms PR CMB 1676-1812 **NLW**

DINBYCH-Y-PYSGOD/TENBY   *SD*
C 1711-1930   M 1711-1971 (Banns 1823-1963)   B 1711-1971 **Pemb RO**   Fac 1711-28 **NLW**
BT 1685, 1762, 1799-1804, 1806-7, 1811-51, 1853-94 **NLW**

DOC PENFRO/PEMBROKE DOCK   *SD*
‹Penfro/Pembroke St. Mary 1844
C 1844-1927 Garrison 1856-1906 Dockyard 1875-1926 Pennar 1895-1934   M 1848-1932 (Banns
   1848-1955)   B 1844-1931 Garrison 1861-1922 **Pemb RO**
BT 1844-86 **NLW**

EAST WILLIAMSTON
An ancient chapelry whose PR are included in those of Begeli/Begelly

EGLWYS LWYD, YR/LUDCHURCH   *SD*
CB 1732-1812   M 1732-1837   Fac C 1813-1968 **NLW**
BT 1799-1839, 1842-54, 1857-60, 1865-77 **NLW**

EGLWYS WEN/WHITECHURCH   *SD*
PR M 1755-1812 recorded in 1831 apparently lost
CB 1704-1812   M 1704-53, 1813-38 **NLW**
BT 1674-5, 1678, 1680, 1683, 1685-90, 1699, 1701-3, 1799-1800, 1803-39, 1844-6, 1851-60, 1863,
   1865, 1869-70, 1872-80, 1882, 1885, 1890 **NLW**

EGLWYSWRW   *SD*
PR CMB 1731-9 recorded in 1831 apparently lost. Diocesan records suggest that *c.* 1790 this parish
   had registers going back to 1685
CMB 1740-1812 **NLW**
BT 1674, 1676, 1680, 1683-7, 1689, 1703, 1799-1863, 1865-7, 1869-74, 1879-80 **NLW**

EGLWYS WYTHWR/MONINGTON   *SD*
Diocesan records suggest that *c.* 1790 this parish had registers going back to 1751
M 1773-1809, 1816-33 **NLW**
BT 1674-6, 1679-81, 1686-7, 1689, 1697, 1703, 1799-1800, 1802-24, 1826-40, 1842, 1844-7, 1849-54,
   1860, 1865-9, 1871-3, 1875 **NLW**
Cop ts PR (extracts) C 1818-44 B 1802-87 **NLW**

FFORD, Y/FORD   *SD*
Odd entries CMB 1801-49 with PR Treamlod/Ambleston and Casnewydd-bach/Little Newcastle
C 1885-1944   M 1837-1963   B 1866-1945 **Pemb RO**
BT 1839-42, 1844-54, 1856-65, 1875, 1885 **NLW**

*FISHGUARD/ABERGWAUN   *SD*
Diocesan records suggest that *c.* 1790 this parish had a register going back to 1761
C 1799-1912   M 1785-1837 (Banns 1902-40)   B 1799-1854 **NLW**
BT 1685, 1799-1829, 1831-47, 1863-4 **NLW**
Cop ms PR C 1783-1854 M 1785-1837 B 1799-1854 **NLW**

FREYSTROP   *SD*
C 1729-1876   M 1740-3, 1754-84, 1813-1969 (Banns 1863-1947)   B 1729-1891 **Pemb RO**
BT 1799-1801, 1804-7, 1809-70, 1883-5 **NLW**

GARN, Y/ROCH   *SD*
C 1677-1737, 1763-1974   M 1677-1737, 1754-1922   B 1677-1737, 1783-1901 **Pemb RO**   Fac
   C 1813-1974   M 1837-1922 **NLW**
BT 1799-1800, 1802-63, 1865-8, 1871-86 **NLW**
Cop ts PR CB 1677-1737, 1763-1812 M 1677-1737, 1783-1812 **NLW**

*GOODWICK/WDIG   *SD*
‹Llanwnda
M 1913-74 (Banns 1923-74) **Pemb RO**

*GRANSTON/TREOPERT   *SD*
Diocesan records suggest that *c.* 1790 the registers went back to 1727
C 1793-1812   M 1778-1970 (Banns 1778-1814, 1828-1908)   B 1793-1805 **Pemb RO**
BT 1799-1843, 1846, 1865-7 **NLW**
Cop ms PR C 1785-1811 M 1778-1813 B 1784-1813   ts PR (extracts) CB 1785-1902 M 1778-1817
    NLW

GUMFRESTON   *SD*
C 1647-1966   M 1655-1970 (Banns 1813-21, 1843-1949)   B 1654-1954 **Pemb RO**
BT 1799-1831, 1833-50, 1853-9, 1861-73 **NLW**

HAROLDSTON ST. ISSELLS   *SD*
PR CMB 1765-[1812] recorded in 1933 apparently lost
M 1814-1969   B 1813-98   Mf C 1813-1980 **Pemb RO**
BT 1798-1802, 1807, 1809-57, 1859-70 **NLW**

HAROLDSTON WEST   *SD*
C 1748-1812   M 1751-86, 1813-1959   B 1750-1812   Mf C 1813-1976   B 1814-1977 **Pemb
RO**
BT 1800-1, 1803-18, 1820-46, 1849 **NLW**

HASGUARD   *SD*
PR C 1764-1812 M 1756-1812 B 1792-1812 recorded in 1831 apparently lost. M 1813-37 not
    recorded in 1933
C 1813-1968   M 1837-1957   B 1814-1969 **Pemb RO**
BT 1800-3, 1805-13, 1816-20, 1823-40, 1842, 1854-6, 1868-70, 1876-8 **NLW**

*HAVERFORDWEST/HWLFFORDD St. Martin   *SD*
C 1721-36, 1745-85, 1793-1887   M 1721-1917 (Banns 1813-1952)   B 1721-36, 1745-85, 1793-
    1974 **Pemb RO**
BT 1800-7, 1809-19, 1823-71 **NLW**
Cop ts PR (extracts) C 1722-1812 M 1729-1884 B 1721-1839   Mf cop ms PR CB 1745-73 M
    1745-72 (**Cardiff Central Library** MS. 2.116) **NLW**

*HAVERFORDWEST/HWLFFORDD St. Mary   *SD*
C 1602-43, 1678-1725, 1728-1955   M 1600-48, 1686, 1699-1706, 1716-23, 1728-1965 (Banns 1754-
    1967)   B 1590-1643, 1683-1706, 1716-24, 1728-1966 **Pemb RO**   Mf 1590-1644, 1713-25
    NLW
BT 1799-1801, 1804-6, 1808-82 **NLW**
Cop ms/ts PR 1590-1812 **NLW**   CMB 1754-72 **Soc Gen**

*HAVERFORDWEST/HWLFFORDD St. Thomas   *SD*
C 1714-1962   M 1714-1952   B 1710-1901 **Pemb RO**
BT 1813-18, 1823, 1825-73 **NLW**
Cop ts PR (extracts) C 1716-1907 M 1713-1892 B 1712-1879 **NLW**

*HAYSCASTLE/CAS-LAI   *SD*
PR C 1800-12 M 1810-37 B 1798-1812 recorded in 1933 and M 1787-1812 recorded in 1831
    apparently lost. Diocesan records suggest that *c.* 1790 the registers went back to 1764
M 1837-1968   B 1813-1941 **Pemb RO**   C 1813- incumbent
BT 1799-1808, 1810-66, 1872-89, 1891-6 **NLW**
Cop ts PR C 1800-12 M 1810 B 1798-1812 **NLW**

*HENRY'S MOAT/CASTELLHENRI   *SD*
M 1755-1837 **NLW**   CB 1813- incumbent
BT 1674-6, 1678-84, 1686, 1689, 1799, 1803-5, 1807-16, 1818-37, 1839-48, 1850, 1853, 1855, 1858-9, 1861-7, 1871, 1874, 1878-89, 1897-1906 **NLW**

HERBRANDSTON   *SD*
C 1717-20, 1729-1908   M 1729-1970 (Banns 1813-52)   B 1717-20, 1729-1812 **Pemb RO**
BT 1799-1804, 1806-63, 1865-70 **NLW**

HODGESTON   *SD*
CB 1766-1812   M 1755-1801, 1814-1961 (Banns 1755-1848) **Pemb RO**
BT 1686, 1799-1807, 1809-67, 1869-79, 1889-93, 1895 **NLW**

HUBBERSTON   *SD*
C 1702-1959   M 1702-1920 (Banns 1783-1869)   B 1702-1958 **NLW**   Mf **Pemb RO**
BT 1800, 1803-4, 1807-9, 1811-59, 1862-7 **NLW**

HUNDLETON   *SD*
‹Monkton
C 1897-1935   M 1954-70   B 1897-1959 **Pemb RO**

HWLFFORDD/HAVERFORDWEST St. Martin   *SD*
C 1721-36, 1745-85, 1793-1887   M 1721-1917 (Banns 1813-1952)   B 1721-36, 1745-85, 1793-1974 **Pemb RO**
BT 1800-7, 1809-19, 1823-71 **NLW**
Cop ts PR (extracts) C 1722-1812 M 1729-1884 B 1721-1839   Mf cop ms PR CB 1745-73 M 1745-72 (**Cardiff Central Library** MS.2.116) **NLW**

HWLFFORDD/HAVERFORDWEST St. Mary   *SD*
C 1602-43, 1678-1725, 1728-1955   M 1600-48, 1686, 1699-1706, 1716-23, 1728-1965 (Banns 1754-1967)   B 1590-1643, 1683-1706, 1716-24, 1728-1966 **Pemb RO**   Mf 1590-1644, 1713-25 **NLW**
BT 1799-1801, 1804-6, 1808-82 **NLW**
Cop ms/ts PR 1590-1812 **NLW**   CMB 1754-72 **Soc Gen**

HWLFFORDD/HAVERFORDWEST St. Thomas   *SD*
C 1714-1962   M 1714-1952   B 1710-1901 **Pemb RO**
BT 1813-18, 1823, 1825-73 **NLW**
Cop ts PR (extracts) C 1716-1907 M 1713-1892 B 1712-1879 **NLW**

JEFFREYSTON   *SD*
C 1695-1945   M 1695-1971   B 1695-1977 **NLW**
BT 1799-1876, 1879, 1881, 1885-6, 1888-9, 1903-4 **NLW**
Cop ts PR (extracts) 1715-1801 **NLW**

JOHNSTON   *SD*
C 1637-1804, 1813-1956   M 1637-1809, 1813-1971   B 1637-1803 **Pemb RO**
BT 1799-1801, 1804-7, 1809-12, 1814-66 **NLW**

*JORDANSTON/TREFWRDAN   *SD*
CB 1802-13   M 1803-51 (Banns 1812-96) **NLW**
BT 1799-1800, 1802-10, 1812-21, 1823-37, 1839-40, 1843-7, 1857-8, 1866.**NLW**
Cop ts PR (extracts) C1811-39 M 1834-9 B 1808-97 **NLW**

LAMBSTON   *SD*
C 1737-1812   M 1741-1968 (Banns 1755-1833)   B 1737-1957 **Pemb RO**
BT 1799-1804, 1806-41, 1843, 1845, 1849, 1868 **NLW**

*LAMPETER VELFREY/LLANBEDR FELFFRE   *SD*
PR CB 1779-1812 recorded in 1831 apparently lost
C 1813-1923   M 1755-1980 Princes Gate 1949-64 **Pemb RO**   B 1813- incumbent
BT 1677, 1679, 1681, 1686, 1698-9, 1720-2, 1724-5, 1727, 1729, 1735, 1737-43, 1763-70, 1774-6,
    1780, 1782-4, 1786-9, 1793-9, 1803-81, 1885-6 **NLW**

*LAMPHEY/LLANDYFÁI   *SD*
C 1776-1883   M 1755-1975   B 1776-1962 **Pemb RO**
BT 1799-1807, 1809-75, 1877-8, 1880-9 **NLW**

LAWRENNY
C 1708-1895   M 1717-1970 (Banns 1824-1919)   B 1717-1812 **Pemb RO**
BT 1685, 1800, 1808-9, 1811-16, 1818-37, 1839-60, 1862-4, 1866-9, 1871, 1873-5 **NLW**

*LETTERSTON/TRELETERT   *SD*
The earliest registers reputedly destroyed at the time of the French invasion 1797 (1831 survey).
    Diocesan records suggest that *c.* 1790 the registers went back only 36 years
C 1801-1975   M 1801-1970 (Banns 1801-1941)   B 1801-1976 **Pemb RO**
BT 1773, 1799, 1802-65, 1886-9, 1891 **NLW**
Cop ts PR (extracts) C 1813-70 **NLW**

*LITTLE NEWCASTLE/CASNEWYDD-BACH   *SD*
Civil register 1654-8 (**Cardiff Central Library** MS.4.44) Mf **NLW**
CB 1783-1813   M 1813-1966 **NLW**
BT 1679-80, 1685, 1799, 1801, 1803, 1805-9, 1811-79, 1885 **NLW**

LLANBEDR FELFFRE/LAMPETER VELFREY   *SD*
PR CB 1779-1812 recorded in 1831 apparently lost
C 1813-1923   M 1755-1980 Princes Gate 1949-64 **Pemb RO**   B 1813- incumbent
BT 1677, 1679, 1681, 1686, 1698-9, 1720-2, 1724-5, 1727, 1729, 1735, 1737-43, 1763-70, 1774-6,
    1780, 1782-4, 1786-9, 1793-9, 1803-81, 1885-6 **NLW**

LLANDDEWI FELFFRE/LLANDDEWI VELFREY   *SD*
C 1727-70, 1778-1812   M 1727-1970   B 1727-70, 1778-1812 **NLW**
BT 1676, 1680-7, 1689, 1697-9, 1702-3, 1705-8, 1713, 1717, 1724-6, 1728-30, 1732-85, 1790-6, 1798-
    1800, 1802-3, 1806-7, 1809-39, 1841-73, 1876-8, 1880 **NLW**

LLANDEILO   *SD*
The church was a ruin by 1930. The following note appears in Llangolman BT 1811 : 'I hereby
    certify that there are no registers in the parish of Llandilo and that all [CMB] were for these last
    twenty years entered in the register of the parish of Llangolman'
C 1814-60   M 1813-34   B 1814-45 **NLW**
BT see Llangolman

*LLANDELOY/LLAN-LWY   *SD*
CMB 1754-97 **NLW**   C 1796-1973   M 1796-1967   B 1796-1974 **Pemb RO**
BT 1799-1811, 1813-44, 1846-9, 1851-69, 1872-3 **NLW**
Cop ts PR (extracts) C 1813-72 M 1807-55 B 1813-89 **NLW**

*LLANDISSILIO/LLANDYSILIO (-YN-NYFED)   *SD*
CMB 1720-50 **NLW**   C 1751-1812   M 1783-1969   B 1751-1948   Fac CMB 1720-50 **Carm
   RO**   Mf CB 1720-51   M 1720-51, 1837-1969 **Pemb RO**
BT 1671-2, 1677-9, 1681-2, 1684-7, 1689-90, 1693-5, 1697-9, 1707, 1715, 1717, 1719-22, 1724-54,
   1756-90, 1792-4, 1796, 1798, 1802-36, 1841-3, 1847-8, 1850-4, 1863-70, 1875-6 **NLW**

LLANDUDOCH/ST. DOGMAELS   *SD*
PR CB 1713-77 M 1713-53 recorded in 1831 apparently lost
C 1778-1812   M 1754-62, 1778-1834   B 1778-1885 **NLW**
BT 1674-5, 1679-87, 1689, 1691-2?, 1703, 1705, 1757, 1799-1804, 1806-38, 1845-7, 1849-60, 1865-76
   NLW

LLANDYFÁI/LAMPHEY   *SD*
C 1776-1883   M 1755-1975   B 1776-1962 **Pemb RO**
BT 1799-1807, 1809-75, 1877-8, 1880-9 **NLW**

LLANDYSILIO (-YN-NYFED)/LLANDISSILIO   *SD*
CMB 1720-50 **NLW**   C 1751-1812   M 1783-1969   B 1751-1948   Fac CMB 1720-50 **Carm
   RO**   Mf CB 1720-51   M 1720-51, 1837-1969 **Pemb RO**
BT 1671-2, 1677-9, 1681-2, 1684-7, 1689-90, 1693-5, 1697-9, 1707, 1715, 1717, 1719-22, 1724-54,
   1756-90, 1792-4, 1796, 1798, 1802-36, 1841-3, 1847-8, 1850-4, 1863-70, 1875-6 **NLW**

LLANEILFYW/ST. ELVIS   *SD*
The church was a ruin by 1900
C 1784-1836   M 1791-1839 **Pemb RO**   B nil
BT 1813, 1817-22, 1824, 1829, 1833-7 **NLW**
Cop ts PR C 1784-1811 (extracts to 1824) M 1791-1811 (extracts to 1839) **NLW**

LLANFAIR NANT-GWYN   *SD*
PR M 1776-1812 recorded in 1933 apparently lost. Diocesan records suggest that *c.* 1790 this parish
   had 'no register of births and burials', and that it had been at one time united with Eglwys-
   wen/Whitechurch
CB 1795-1812   M 1813-37 **NLW**
BT 1674-5, 1678, 1680, 1683, 1685-90, 1699, 1701-3, 1800, 1803-9, 1812-37, 1839-40, 1844-53,
   1855-65, 1868, 1870-2, 1874-80, 1890 **NLW**

LLANFAIR NANT-Y-GOF   *SD*
Civil register 1655-8 (**Cardiff Central Library** MS.4.44)   Mf **NLW**
CB 1801-1975   M 1802-1969 (Banns 1823-1973) **Pemb RO**
BT 1681, 1799, 1802-7, 1809-40, 1843-4, 1846-53, 1855-64, 1886-91 **NLW**

LLANFALLTEG   *SD*
CB 1711-1978   M 1755-1969 **Pemb RO**   Mf CB 1711-1812   M 1759-1969 **Carm RO**
BT 1671-2, 1677-9, 1681-4, 1686-7, 1690-1, 1693, 1695-9, 1707, 1713, 1717, 1719, 1724-6, 1728-31,
   1733-1800, 1802-12, 1814-43 **NLW**

LLANFIHANGEL PENBEDW   *SD*
CB 1680-1812   M 1680-1836 **NLW**
BT 1676, 1678-81, 1683-8, 1701-3, 1799-1801, 1804-6, 1809-26, 1828-36, 1839, 1847-9, 1852-6, 1858,
   1860, 1865-6, 1870-3, 1875-6, 1878 **NLW**

LLANFYRNACH   *SD*
Diocesan records suggest that *c.* 1790 this parish had registers going back to 1714
CB 1765-1812   M 1754-1968 (Banns 1823-44, 1908-56) **Pemb RO**
BT 1675-6, 1678-83, 1685-8, 1703, 1799-1813, 1815-20, 1823-63, 1865-7, 1869-71, 1875-7 **NLW**

LLAN-GAN   *SD*
C 1768-93   M 1769-1963   B 1768-94 **Pemb RO**   Mf **Carm RO**
BT 1677-9, 1681-5, 1690-1, 1693-5, 1697-9, 1704-5, 1707-8, 1711, 1713, 1715-18, 1720-2, 1725-7,
    1729-83, 1785-92, 1794-5, 1805, 1807-31, 1833, 1837, 1840 **NLW**

LLANGOLMAN   *SD*
M 1755-1958 **NLW**   Mf C 1813-1971   M 1755-1958   B 1813-1977 **Pemb RO**
BT 1685-6, 1799-1807, 1809-37, 1840-52, 1854-9, 1861 **NLW**
Cop ts PR (extracts) C 1762-1812 M 1824-30 B 1776-1811 **NLW**

LLANGWM   *SD*
CB 1716-1949   M 1716-1966 (Banns 1811-18, 1865-1948) **Pemb RO**
BT 1799-1807, 1809-83 **NLW**

LLANHUADAIN/LLAWHADEN   *SD*
C 1653-1980   M 1653-1971 (Banns 1823-1930)   B 1653-1956 **NLW**
BT 1772, 1799, 1801-77, 1879-81, 1883 **NLW**
Cop ts PR M 1754-1837 **Soc Gen**

LLANHYWEL/LLANHOWEL   *SD*
CB 1797-1812   M 1796-1837   Carnhedryn C 1880-1921   M 1881-1906 **NLW**
BT 1799-1841, 1843-4, 1846, 1848-69, 1872-3 **NLW**
Cop ts PR (extracts) C 1838-94 M 1805-82 B 1826-1902 **NLW**

LLANISAN-YN-RHOS/ST. ISHMAELS   *SD*
C 1761-1946   M 1755-1970 (Banns 1855-1933)   B 1761-1926 **Pemb RO**
BT 1799, 1801-3, 1805-79 **NLW**

LLANLLAWERN/LLANLLAWER   *SD*
CB 1770-1968   M 1781-1837 **NLW**
BT see Llanychlwydog
Cop printed BT CMB 1674-5, 1680-9, 1699 & PR CB 1771-1812 M 1781-1812 (ed. Rev. J. Meredith
    Williams, Fishguard, 1925)

LLAN-LWY/LLANDELOY   *SD*
CMB 1754-97 **NLW**   C 1796-1973   M 1796-1967   B 1796-1974 **Pemb RO**
BT 1799-1811, 1813-44, 1846-9, 1851-69, 1872-3 **NLW**
Cop ts PR (extracts) C 1813-72 M 1807-55 B 1813-89 **NLW**

LLANRHEITHAN   *SD*
PR M 1786-98 recorded in 1831 apparently lost. Diocesan records suggest that *c.* 1790 the registers
    went back 25 years
C 1803-1968   M 1799-1952 (Banns 1799-1823)   B 1799-1977 **Pemb RO**
BT 1799, 1801-5, 1807-27, 1829-48, 1850-3, 1855-8, 1862-5, 1867, 1869, 1871-7 **NLW**
Cop ts PR (extracts) CMB 1799-1907 **NLW**

LLANRHIAN   *SD*
A few entries CMB 1686- included in earliest extant PR
C 1729-1812   M 1729-1905   B 1729-1881 **NLW**
BT 1739, 1798-1801, 1803, 1806-79 **NLW**
Cop ts PR C 1686-1812 (extracts to 1903) M 1729-1807 (extracts to 1862) B 1731-1812 (extracts to
    1880) **NLW**

LLANSTADWEL/LLANSTADWELL *SD*
C 1714-1904   M 1714-1892   B 1714-1903 **NLW**
BT 1800-3, 1805-7, 1809-13, 1818, 1820-57, 1860-1, 1866-7 **NLW**

LLANSTINAN *SD*
Diocesan records suggest that *c.* 1790 the registers went back 29 years; and that in 1814 there were
  extant C 1784-1812 M 1788-1812 B 1800-13
M 1797-1971 (Banns 1823-70) **NLW**   Mf C 1814-1977   M 1797-1971   B 1813-1976 **Pemb
  RO**
BT 1685-6, 1799-1804, 1806-7, 1810-35, 1841-53, 1855-67, 1871-6 **NLW**
Cop ms PR M 1779-1818 **NLW**

LLANTWYD/LLANTOOD *SD*
CB 1783-5   M 1813-37 **NLW**
BT 1674-6, 1678-81, 1684-7, 1700, 1703, 1705, 1799-1800, 1802-40, 1842, 1844-7, 1849-60, 1865-8,
  1870-5, 1896-7 **NLW**

LLANTYDEWI/ST. DOGWELLS *SD*
C 1718-1973   M 1718-53, 1756-1933, 1939-68 (Banns 1927-39)   B 1722-74, 1783-1966 **NLW**
BT 1799-1800, 1802-7, 1811-79, 1885 **NLW**

LLANWNDA *SD*
The earliest PR reputedly destroyed at the time of the French invasion 1797 (1831 survey).
  Diocesan records suggest that *c.* 1790 the register went back only as far as 1777
C 1813-1931   M 1813-1968 (Banns 1823-69, 1907-45, 1973-4)   B 1799-1942 **Pemb RO**
BT 1685, 1799-1806, 1808-46, 1864-72, 1877-81, 1883-4, 1887 **NLW**
Cop ms PR B 1799-1812   ts PR (extracts) CMB 1799-1896 **NLW**

LLAN-Y-CEFN *SD*
C 1816-1979   M 1813-1911, 1917-60   B 1816-1980 **NLW**
BT 1799-1805, 1807-11, 1813, 1816-37, 1844-6, 1849-57, 1861, 1863-5, 1871-80 **NLW**

LLANYCHÂR/LLANYCHAER *SD*
Civil register 1654-9 (**Cardiff Central Library** MS.4.44) Mf **NLW.** Diocesan records suggest
  that *c.* 1790 'the old register [was] lost. The existing register goes back only 2 years'
C 1788-1812   M 1787-1970 (Banns 1824-49)   B 1789-1812   Fac CB 1813-1985 **NLW**
BT 1676, 1678-83, 1685-6, 1689, 1705, 1799-1808, 1810-38, 1843-7, 1853-65 **NLW**
Cop printed PR C 1788-1812 M 1787-1811 B 1789-1812 (ed. Rev. J. Meredith Williams, Fishguard,
  [1924])

LLANYCHLWYDOG *SD*
CB 1770-1812   M 1781-1812 **NLW**   C 1813-1927   M 1814-1961   B 1813-1965 **Pemb
  RO**
BT 1674-6, 1678-83, 1685-9, 1799-1804, 1806-7, 1809-44, 1874 **NLW**
Cop printed BT CMB 1674-5, 1680-9, 1699 & PR C 1770-1803 M 1780-1812 B 1770-1812 (ed. Rev.
  J. Meredith Williams, Fishguard, 1925)

*LLAWHADEN/LLANHUADAIN *SD*
C 1653-1980   M 1653-1971 (Banns 1823-1930)   B 1653-1956 **NLW**
BT 1772, 1799, 1801-77, 1879-81, 1883 **NLW**
Cop ts PR M 1754-1837 **Soc Gen**

LLYS-Y-FRÂN   *SD*
CB 1728-1803   M 1728-1803, 1813-1903, 1924-63 **NLW**
BT 1799-1820, 1822-37, 1839-41, 1843-4, 1846-52, 1855, 1858-63, 1865-6, 1868-9 **NLW**

LOVESTON   *SD*
CB 1791-1977   M 1783-1957 **Pemb RO**
BT 1799-1820, 1823-36, 1838-64, 1866-9, 1871-3, 1876, 1878, 1880, 1884-5, 1888, 1890-1, 1893-9,
    1901-2, 1907-9 **NLW**

*LUDCHURCH/YR EGLWYS LWYD   *SD*
CB 1732-1812   M 1732-1837   Fac C 1813-1968 **NLW**
BT 1799-1839, 1842-54, 1857-60, 1865-77 **NLW**

MAENCLOCHOG   *SD*
CB 1770-1812   M 1770-1970 **NLW**   Fac M 1813-1970   Mf CB 1770-1812 **Pemb RO**
BT 1685, 1799, 1801-36, 1839-52, 1854-61, 1865 **NLW**
Cop ts PR (extracts) C 1771-1832 M 1779-1877 B 1770-1888 **NLW**

MAENORBŶR/MANORBIER   *SD*
C 1761-1950   M 1755-1971   B 1761-1888 **Pemb RO**   Fac C 1813-70   M 1755-1837   B
    1813-87 **NLW**
BT 1685-6, 1799-1804, 1806-21, 1823-85 **NLW**

MAENORDEIFI   *SD*
CB 1724-70, 1780-1812   M 1724-1837 **NLW**
BT 1674-6, 1678-9, 1681-2, 1684, 1686-9, 1702-3, 1705, 1799-1856, 1859-75 **NLW**
Cop ts PR CB 1724-70 M 1725-53 **Soc Gen**

MANORBIER gweler/see MAENORBŶR

MANOROWEN (MARNAWAN)   *SD*
PR C 1783-1812 M 1786-96 B 1785-1800 recorded in 1831 apparently lost
M 1779-85, 1797-1970 (Banns 1797-1818, 1927-67, 1973-4)   Mf C 1813-1978   B 1813-1977
    Pemb RO
BT 1799-1800, 1802-4, 1806-48, 1865, 1868, 1870-81, 1883-4, 1887 **NLW**
Cop ms PR M 1779-1814 (Banns 1797-1818)   ts PR (extracts) C 1817-1903 M 1779-1801 B 1813-
    1906 **NLW**

MARLOES   *SD*
C 1749-51, 1771-1876   M 1749-1969   B 1749-51, 1771-1924 **Pemb RO**
BT 1799-1836, 1838-75, 1877 **NLW**

MARTLETWY   *SD*
C 1728-31, 1739-45, 1754-8, 1760-1850   M 1728-31, 1739-45, 1754-8, 1762-80, 1813-1971 (Banns
    1824-78)   B 1728-31, 1739-45, 1754-8, 1762-85, 1809-11, 1813-95 **Pemb RO**
BT 1799-1803, 1805-47, 1849-60, 1862-75, 1877-8, 1880-4, 1886-8 **NLW**

MATHRI/MATHRY   *SD*
PR CMB 1729-1812 recorded in 1831 apparently lost
C 1810-12   M 1813-1969 (Banns 1778-1916)   B 1810-1940 **Pemb RO**
BT 1799-1853, 1855-62, 1864-9, 1875-6 **NLW**
Cop ts PR C 1729-1810 (extracts to 1904) M 1729-54 (extracts 1814-35) B 1729-1810 (extracts to
    1873) **NLW**

MELINE *SD*
CB 1702-1812   M 1702-1836 **NLW**
BT 1674-6, 1679-81, 1683-4, 1686-7, 1689-90, 1692, 1700, 1799-1809, 1811-17, 1819-30, 1832-40, 1842, 1844-7, 1849-52, 1855, 1857-9, 1862-4, 1869, 1873-4, 1876, 1878-9 **NLW**
Cop ms PR CB 1702-1812 M 1702-54 **NLW**

*MILFORD HAVEN/ABERDAUGLEDDAU   *SD*
‹Steynton 1891. Consecrated 1808
C 1808-33, 1860-1960   M 1891-1975   B 1877-1955 **Pemb RO**
BT see Steynton

*MINWEAR/MYNWAR   *SD*
C 1753-81, 1813-1971   M 1757-1810, 1813-1935   B 1753-1807, 1813-1975 **Pemb RO**
BT 1799-1818, 1820-1, 1823-41, 1844, 1849, 1851-3, 1855-9, 1872, 1874-6, 1879-81 **NLW**
Cop ms PR C 1795-1812 B 1784-1812 **Pemb RO**

*MONINGTON/EGLWYS WYTHWR   *SD*
Diocesan records suggest that *c.* 1790 this parish had registers going back to 1751
M 1773-1809, 1816-33 **NLW**
BT 1674-6, 1679-81, 1686-7, 1689, 1697, 1703, 1799-1800, 1802-24, 1826-40, 1842, 1844-7, 1849-54, 1860, 1865-9, 1871-3, 1875 **NLW**
Cop ts PR (extracts) C 1818-44 B 1802-87 **NLW**

MONKTON (PENFRO/PEMBROKE St. Nicholas)   *SD*
CMB 1711-50 **NLW**   C 1748-1966   M 1748-1970 (Banns 1917-36)   B 1748-1900 **Pemb RO**
BT 1685, ?1774, 1799-1807, 1809-82 **NLW**

MORFIL/MORVIL   *SD*
Civil register 1653-8 (**Cardiff Central Library** MS.4.44) Mf **NLW.** Diocesan records suggest that *c.* 1790 this parish had a register only 'begun in the year 1789'
M 1814-1953 **Pemb RO**   CB 1813- incumbent
BT 1674, 1676, 1678-88, 1699, 1804-11, 1813-16, 1819-20, 1823-37, 1839-40 **NLW**

MOT, Y/NEW MOAT   *SD*
CB 1755-1812   M 1754-1969 **Pemb RO**
BT 1799-1800, 1803, 1805, 1809-21, 1823-31, 1833-70, 1878-81, 1884 **NLW**

MOUNTON   *SD*
A small parish long associated with Arberth/Narberth and apparently without its own PR

*MOYLGROVE/TREWYDDEL   *SD*
C 1769-1812   M 1770-7, 1781-1837   B 1769-1909 **NLW**
BT 1675-6, 1678-86, 1688-9, 1702-3, 1708, 1799-1801, 1803-19, 1821-75, 1877-9 **NLW**
Cop ts PR (extracts) C 1770-1818 M 1771-1833 B 1770-1815 **NLW**

MYNACHLOG-DDU   *SD*
PR C 1802-12 recorded in 1831 apparently lost. M 1813-37 not recorded in 1933. Diocesan records suggest that *c.* 1790 the registers went back to 1758
M 1837-1951 (Banns 1890-1951)   Mf CB 1813-1977 **Pemb RO**
BT 1674, 1676, 1678-9, 1681-2, 1685-9, 1705, 1799-1800, 1802-3, 1806-42, 1845, 1848-51, 1865-6, 1871-6, 1878-9 **NLW**

MYNWAR/MINWEAR   *SD*
C 1753-81, 1813-1971   M 1757-1810, 1813-1935   B 1753-1807, 1813-1975 **Pemb RO**
BT 1799-1818, 1820-1, 1823-41, 1844, 1849, 1851-3, 1855-9, 1872, 1874-6, 1879-81 **NLW**
Cop ms PR C 1795-1812 B 1784-1812 **Pemb RO**

*NARBERTH/ARBERTH   *SD*
C 1676-1703, 1762-1918   M 1676-1703, 1779-1805, 1811-1964 (Banns 1811-42, 1896-1966)   B
   1676-1703, 1762-1898 **Pemb RO**   Fac 1676-1845 **NLW**
BT 1799-1801, 1803, 1805, 1807-67, 1872-3 **NLW**
Cop ts PR (extracts) C 1681-1844, 1854-84 M 1756-1837 **NLW**

NASH with UPTON   *SD*
C 1742-1959   M 1744-1969   B 1742-1976 **Pemb RO**
BT 1696, 1800-7, 1809-11, 1813-80, 1882-1903 **NLW**

*NEVERN/NYFER (NANHYFER)   *SD*
The earliest PR 1663-1710 is an early 19th century copy
C 1663-1910   M 1663-1837   B 1663-1869 **NLW**
BT 1634, 1674-6, 1678-80, 1682-7, 1689, 1702, 1799-1800, 1802-70, 1878-83, 1885-9 **NLW**
Cop ms PR 1663-1812   ts PR (extracts) 1663-1850 **NLW**

*NEW MOAT/Y MOT   *SD*
CB 1755-1812   M 1754-1969 **Pemb RO**
BT 1799-1800, 1803, 1805, 1809-21, 1823-31, 1833-70, 1878-81, 1884 **NLW**

*NEWPORT/TREFDRAETH   *SD*
PR CMB 1741-62 recorded in 1831 apparently lost
C 1765-71, 1799-1800, 1807-71   M 1765-1940 (Banns 1824-1962)   B 1765-71, 1799-1800, 1805-
   1930 **Pemb RO**
BT 1674-6, 1680-2, 1684-9, 1699, 1702-3, 1800, 1806-73, 1875 **NLW**
Cop ms/ts PR C 1765-1812 M 1778-1895 B 1766-1847 **NLW**

NEWTON NORTH (LLYS PRAWST)   *SD*
The church was a ruin by 1900. CB 1784-1812 M 1757-1812 recorded in 1831 apparently lost
C 1816-90   M 1814-53   B 1815-60 **Pemb RO**
BT 1813-17, 1819, 1821-3, 1825, 1827-30, 1832-3, 1843, 1856-9 **NLW**

NOLTON   *SD*
PR earliest date given as 1695 in 1831
CB 1704-1812   M 1704-1924 **Pemb RO**   Fac M 1814-1924 **NLW**
BT 1685-6, 1799-1800, 1802-5, 1807-61, 1863-8, 1871-85 **NLW**
Cop ts PR CB[1695]-1736, 1751-1812 M[1695]-1736, 1781-1812 **NLW**

NYFER(NANHYFER)/NEVERN   *SD*
The earliest PR 1663-1710 is an early 19th century copy
C 1663-1910   M 1663-1837   B 1663-1869 **NLW**
BT 1634, 1674-6, 1678-80, 1682-7, 1689, 1702, 1799-1800, 1802-70, 1878-83, 1885-9 **NLW**
Cop ms PR 1663-1812   ts PR (extracts) 1663-1850 **NLW**

*PEMBROKE/PENFRO St. Mary   *SD*
C 1711-1961   M 1711-1915   B 1711-1950 **NLW**   Mf **Pemb RO**
BT 1799-1807, 1809-88 **NLW**

*PEMBROKE/PENFRO St. Michael   *SD*
   C 1711-1901   M 1711-1930   B 1711-1929 **NLW**   Mf **Pemb RO**
   BT 1799-1807, 1809-81 **NLW**

PEMBROKE/PENFRO St. Nicholas gweler/see MONKTON

*PEMBROKE DOCK/DOC PENFRO   *SD*
   ‹Penfro/Pembroke St. Mary 1844
   C 1844-1927 Garrison 1856-1906 Dockyard 1875-1926 Pennar 1895-1934   M 1848-1932 (Banns
      1848-1955)   B 1844-1931 Garrison 1861-1922 **Pemb RO**
   BT 1844-86 **NLW**

PENALUN/PENALLY   *SD*
   C 1738-86, 1792-1885   M 1739-51, 1754-1966   B 1738-86, 1792-1940 **Pemb RO**   Fac C
      1738-86   M 1738-1890   B 1738-86, 1813-1936 **NLW**
   BT 1799-1806, 1809-73, 1875, 1877, 1890-2 **NLW**

PENFRO/PEMBROKE St. Mary   *SD*
   C 1711-1961   M 1711-1915   B 1711-1950 **NLW**   Mf **Pemb RO**
   BT 1799-1807, 1809-88 **NLW**

PENFRO/PEMBROKE St. Michael   *SD*
   C 1711-1901   M 1711-1930   B 1711-1929 **NLW**   Mf **Pemb RO**
   BT 1799-1807, 1809-81 **NLW**

PENFRO/PEMBROKE St. Nicholas gweler/see MONKTON

PENRHYDD/PENRITH   *SD*
   PR CB 1771-97 M 1755-1812 recorded in 1831 apparently lost
   M 1813-36 **NLW**   CB 1813- incumbent
   BT 1674, 1676, 1679-85, 1688-9, 1702-3, 1705, 1799, 1802-13, 1815-29, 1832-6, 1838-9, 1842-59,
      1866, 1869-71, 1876-80, 1882 **NLW**

*PONTVANE/Y BONT-FAEN   *SD*
   Diocesan records suggest that *c.* 1790 this parish had registers going back to 1748
   M 1815-1971 **Pemb RO**   CB 1813- incumbent
   BT 1676, 1678-9, 1681-4, 1686, 1800-13, 1815-19, 1821-40, 1845-7, 1850, 1853, 1855 **NLW**

PRENDERGAST   *SD*
   C 1696-1864   M 1696-1837 (Banns 1825-49)   B 1696-1840 **NLW**   Mf **Pemb RO**
   BT 1777, 1801-13, 1815-61, 1865-73 **NLW**

*PUNCHESTON/CAS-MAEL   *SD*
   Civil register 1653-9 (**Cardiff Central Library** MS.4.44) Mf **NLW**. PR M 1813-37 recorded in
      1933 apparently lost
   CB 1789-1807   M 1797-1810, 1838-1967 **NLW**
   BT 1675-6, 1678-83, 1686, 1688, 1799, 1801-4, 1806-7, 1809-11, 1813-43, 1845-8, 1852-9 **NLW**

PWLLCROCHAN   *SD*
   C 1695-1976   M 1695-1811, 1815-36, 1839-1956 (Banns 1886-1940)   B 1695-1812 **NLW**
   BT 1799-1810, 1812-21, 1823-91 **NLW**

REDBERTH   *SD*
CMB to 1807 entered in PR Caeriw/Carew. Separate register of CMB 1807-12 recorded in 1831
    apparently lost
CMB 1813- incumbent
BT 1802-3, 1805-7, 1809-28, 1830-8, 1840-76, 1884-90, 1896-9, 1901-2, 1905 **NLW**

REYNOLDSTON (REYNALTON)   *SD*
C 1786-1977   M 1786-1948   B 1786-1953 **NLW**
BT 1799-1800, 1802-4, 1806-76, 1879, 1881, 1903-4 **NLW**

RHOSCROWDDER/RHOSCROWTHER   *SD*
CB 1731-1812   M 1731-1970 (Banns 1813-32) **NLW**
BT 1799-1807, 1809, 1811-93 **NLW**

RHOSFARCED/ROSEMARKET   *SD*
PR CB 1777-1804 recorded in 1831 apparently lost. Diocesan records suggest that *c.* 1790 the
    registers went back to 1754
C 1804-12, 1826-89   M 1772-1812, 1837-1969 (Banns 1823-1978)   B 1804-89 **Pemb RO**
BT 1799, 1801-31, 1833-6, 1838, 1840-2, 1844-50, 1853-5, 1858 **NLW**
Cop ms PR (extracts) C 1761-1803 **Pemb RO**

ROBESTON WATHEN   *SD*
PR CB 1737-89 M [1737-54], 1800-5 recorded in 1831 apparently lost. The 1935 return claims that
    a ms copy of PR 1750-1812 made in 1902-3 was kept at the parish church of Arberth/Narberth
C 1790-1812   M 1814-1970   B 1790-1968 **Pemb RO**
BT 1799-1801, 1803-7, 1809-10, 1812, 1814-67 **NLW**
Cop ts PR (extracts) M 1756-1837 **NLW**

ROBESTON WEST   *SD*
CB 1731-1812   M 1731-1836 **NLW**
BT 1799, 1801-7, 1809-10, 1813-21, 1823-36, 1840-7, 1849-67, 1869 **NLW**
Cop ts PR C 1731-1812 M 1742-1812 B 1743-1812 **NLW**

*ROCH/Y GARN   *SD*
C 1677-1737, 1763-1974   M 1677-1737, 1783-1922   B 1677-1737, 1783-1901 **Pemb RO**   Fac
    C 1813-1974   M 1837-1922 **NLW**
BT 1799-1800, 1802-63, 1865-8, 1871-86 **NLW**
Cop ts PR CB 1677-1737, 1763-1812 M 1677-1737, 1783-1812 **NLW**

*ROSEMARKET/RHOSFARCED   *SD*
PR CB 1777-1804 recorded in 1831 apparently lost. Diocesan records suggest that *c.* 1790 the
    registers went back to 1754
C 1804-12, 1826-89   M 1772-1812, 1837-1969 (Banns 1823-1978)   B 1804-89 **Pemb RO**
BT 1799, 1801-31, 1833-6, 1838, 1840-2, 1844-50, 1853-5, 1858 **NLW**
Cop ms PR (extracts) C 1761-1803 **Pemb RO**

RUDBAXTON   *SD*
C 1735-1950   M 1736-1970 (Banns 1755-1836)   B 1735-1812   Mf B 1813-1976 **Pemb RO**
BT 1799-1807, 1809-50, 1852-86 **NLW**
Cop ts PR (extracts) CMB 1735-1810 **NLW**

SAIN FFRED/ST. BRIDES   *SD*
CB 1725-1813   M 1725-1970 **Pemb RO**
BT 1800-1, 1803, 1805-15, 1825-77 **NLW**
Cop ts PR M 1725-1812 (extracts to 1836) **NLW**

SAIN PEDROG/ST. PETROX   *SD*
CB 1640-1812   M 1640-1836 **NLW**
BT 1685, 1799-1802, 1804-7, 1809, 1811-19, 1821-59, 1861-96 **NLW**

ST. BRIDES gweler/see SAIN FFRED

*ST. DAVID'S/TYDDEWI   *SD*
C 1724-1984   M 1724-1966 (Banns 1808-50, 1878-1963)   B 1724-1963 **NLW**
BT 1813-56, 1864, 1866, 1872-4 **NLW**
Cop ts PR C 1724-1858 M 1724-1837 B 1724-1812 (extracts to 1906) **NLW**

*ST. DOGMAELS/LLANDUDOCH   *SD*
PR CB 1713-77 M 1713-53 recorded in 1831 apparently lost
C 1778-1812   M 1754-62, 1778-1834   B 1778-1885 **NLW**
BT 1674-5, 1679-87, 1689, 1691-2?, 1703, 1705, 1757, 1799-1804, 1806-38, 1845-7, 1849-60, 1865-76
   NLW

*ST. DOGWELLS/LLANTYDEWI   *SD*
C 1718-1973   M 1718-53, 1756-1933, 1939-68 (Banns 1927-39)   B 1722-74, 1783-1966 **NLW**
BT 1799-1800, 1802-7, 1811-79, 1885 **NLW**

SAINT EDRENS   *SD*
Diocesan records suggest that *c.* 1790 the registers went back to 1770
C 1791-1959   M 1800-1932 (Banns 1809-18)   B 1788-1887 **Pemb RO**
BT 1799-1813, 1815-45 **NLW**
Cop ts PR (extracts) C 1785-1829 B 1789-1886 **NLW**

*ST. ELVIS/LLANEILFYW   *SD*
The church was a ruin by 1900
C 1784-1836   M 1791-1839 **Pemb RO**   B nil
BT 1813, 1817-22, 1824, 1829, 1833-7 **NLW**
Cop ts PR C 1784-1811 (extracts to 1824) M 1791-1811 (extracts to 1839) **NLW**

ST. FLORENCE   *SD*
C 1763-1920   M 1755-1836   B 1763-1957 **Pemb RO**
BT 1799-1890, 1892 **NLW**

SAINT ISHEL/ST. ISSELLS   *SD*
PR CB 1753-66 recorded in 1831 apparently lost
C 1766-83, 1787-1922   M 1778-1938   B 1766-75, 1783-1908 **NLW**
BT 1685-6, 1775, 1799-1837, 1839-89, 1892, 1895-8 **NLW**
Cop ts PR (extracts) CMB 1766-1829 **Pemb RO**

*ST. ISHMAELS/LLANISAN-YN-RHOS   *SD*
C 1761-1946   M 1755-1970 (Banns 1855-1933)   B 1761-1926 **Pemb RO**
BT 1799, 1801-3, 1805-79 **NLW**

ST. ISSELLS gweler/see SAINT ISHEL

ST. LAWRENCE   *SD*
CB 1767-99   M 1766-1970 (Banns 1799-1944) **Pemb RO**   Mf C 1814-47   M 1800-37 (Banns
   1799-1944)   B 1813-1946 **NLW**
BT 1799, 1802-54, 1866, 1871-4 **NLW**
Cop ts PR (extracts) C 1770-1897 M 1767-1869 B 1767-1811 **NLW**

*ST. NICHOLAS/TREMARCHOG   *SD*
PR 1758- in poor condition in 1933 apparently lost. Diocesan records suggest that *c.* 1790 the
   registers went back to 1727
CB 1793-1812   M 1779-1971 (Banns 1780-1817, 1907) **Pemb RO**
BT see Treopert/Granston
Cop ms/ts PR C 1783-1874 M 1782-1899 B 1783-1898 **NLW**   ts PR (extracts) C 1810-74
   M 1782-1899 B 1799-1898 **Pemb RO**

*ST. PETROX/SAIN PEDROG   *SD*
CB 1640-1812   M 1640-1836 **NLW**
BT 1685, 1799-1802, 1804-7, 1809, 1811-19, 1821-59, 1861-96 **NLW**

ST. TWYNNELLS   *SD*
PR CB 1729-1812 M 1729-71 recorded in 1831 and CB 1760-1812 recorded in 1933 apparently lost
C 1813-1922   M 1774-1835 **NLW**   B 1813- incumbent
BT 1799-1807, 1809-71, 1874-8, 1882, 1889-90, 1899 **NLW**

SLEBETS/SLEBECH   *SD*
C 1788-1806, 1813-1925   M 1762-1957, 1960-71 (Banns 1941-3)   B 1782-1807, 1813-1972
   NLW   Mf **Pemb RO**
BT 1799-1818, 1820-44, 1846-59, 1861-81 **NLW**

SOLFACH/SOLVA gweler/see TRE-GROES/WHITCHURCH

SPITAL/SPITTAL   *SD*
CB 1754-1812   M 1783-1971 (Banns 1806-79) **Pemb RO**
BT 1803, 1813-16, 1818-19, 1823-7, 1849-66 **NLW**

STACKPOLE ELIDIR/STACKPOLE ELIDOR   *SD*
CB 1724-1812   M 1724-1837 **NLW**
BT 1685-6, 1799-1802, 1804-37, 1839-43, 1845-74, 1878-96 **NLW**

STEYNTON   *SD*
C 1637-1917   M 1637-1970 (Banns 1901-58)   B 1637-1899 **Pemb RO**
BT 1799-1804, 1806-7, 1809-10, 1812-67 **NLW**

TALBENNI/TALBENNY   *SD*
C 1764-1813   M 1764-1958 (Banns 1791-1833, 1922)   B 1764-1812 **Pemb RO**
BT 1799-1807, 1809-10, 1812-58, 1865, 1874 **NLW**

TEMPLETON (TREDEML)   *SD*
‹Arberth/Narberth 1862
CMB 1862- incumbent
BT 1863, 1865-7 **NLW**

*TENBY/DINBYCH-Y-PYSGOD   *SD*
C 1711-1930   M 1711-1971 (Banns 1823-1963)   B 1711-1971 **Pemb RO**   Fac 1711-28 **NLW**
BT 1685, 1762, 1799-1804, 1806-7, 1811-51, 1853-94 **NLW**

TREAMLOD/AMBLESTON   *SD*
CB 1765-1974   M 1776-1968 **NLW**
BT 1685, 1799-1862, 1864 **NLW**

TREFDRAETH/NEWPORT   *SD*
PR CMB 1741-62 recorded in 1831 apparently lost
C 1765-71, 1799-1800, 1807-71   M 1765-1940 (Banns 1824-1962)   B 1765-71, 1799-1800, 1805-
1930 **Pemb RO**
BT 1674-6, 1680-2, 1684-9, 1699, 1702-3, 1800, 1806-73, 1875 **NLW**
Cop ms/ts PR C 1765-1812 M 1778-1895 B 1766-1847 **NLW**

TREFELEN/BLETHERSTON   *SD*
CB 1653-1980   M 1653-1971 **NLW**
BT 1772, 1799, 1801-38, 1840-57, 1859-70, 1872-3, 1875-9, 1881-3 **NLW**

TREFGARN/TREFFGARNE   *SD*
Odd entries CMB 1803-12 with PR Treamlod/Ambleston
C 1727-1975   M 1727-1962   B 1727-1819 **Pemb RO**
BT 1799-1804, 1806-9, 1811-19, 1821-56, 1858-9 **NLW**

TREFWRDAN/JORDANSTON   *SD*
CB 1802-13   M 1803-51 (Banns 1812-96) **NLW**
BT 1799-1800, 1802-10, 1812-21, 1823-37, 1839-40, 1843-7, 1857-8, 1866 **NLW**
Cop ts PR (extracts) C 1811-39 M 1834-9 B 1808-97 **NLW**

TRE-GROES/WHITCHURCH   *SD*
Diocesan records suggest that *c.* 1790 the registers went back to 1731
C 1753-1974   M 1772-1969 (Banns 1772-1874, 1877-94) Solfach/Solva 1908-70   B 1752-1957
   Pemb RO
BT 1799-1800, 1802-7, 1809-82, 1886, 1889-91, 1898-9, 1902-4 **NLW**
Cop ts PR C 1753-94 M 1772-1812 B 1752-94 (extracts CMB to 1907) **NLW**

TRELETERT/LETTERSTON   *SD*
The earliest registers reputedly destroyed at the time of the French invasion 1797 (1831 survey).
   Diocesan records suggest that *c.* 1790 the registers went back only 36 years
C 1801-1975   M 1801-1970 (Banns 1801-1941)   B 1801-1976 **Pemb RO**
BT 1773, 1799, 1802-65, 1886-9, 1891 **NLW**
Cop ts PR (extracts) C 1813-70 **NLW**

TREMARCHOG/ST. NICHOLAS   *SD*
PR 1758- in poor condition in 1933 apparently lost. Diocesan records suggest that *c.* 1790 the
   registers went back to 1727
CB 1793-1812   M 1779-1971 (Banns 1780-1817, 1907) **Pemb RO**
BT see Treopert/Granston
Cop ms/ts PR C 1783-1874 M 1782-1899 B 1783-1898 **NLW**   ts PR (extracts) C 1810-74 M 1782-
   1899 B 1799-1898 **Pemb RO**

TREOPERT/GRANSTON   *SD*
Diocesan records suggest that *c.* 1790 the registers went back to 1727
C 1793-1812   M 1778-1970 (Banns 1778-1814, 1828-1908)   B 1793-1805 **Pemb RO**
BT 1799-1843, 1846, 1865-7 **NLW**
Cop ms PR C 1785-1811 M 1778-1813 B 1784-1813   ts PR (extracts) CB 1785-1902 M 1778-1817
   NLW

TREWYDDEL/MOYLGROVE   *SD*
C 1769-1812   M 1770-7, 1781-1837   B 1769-1909 **NLW**
BT 1675-6, 1678-86, 1688-9, 1702-3, 1708, 1799-1801, 1803-19, 1821-75, 1877-9 **NLW**
Cop ts PR (extracts) C 1770-1818 M 1771-1833 B 1770-1815 **NLW**

TYDDEWI/ST. DAVID'S   *SD*
C 1724-1984   M 1724-1966 (Banns 1808-50, 1878-1963)   B 1724-1963 **NLW**
BT 1813-56, 1864, 1866, 1872-4 **NLW**
Cop ts PR C 1724-1858 M 1724-1837 B 1724-1812 (extracts to 1906) **NLW**

UPTON gweler/see NASH

UZMASTON   *SD*
C 1720-1959   M 1733-79, 1788-1984 (Banns 1827, 1855, 1878)   B 1723-1972 **Pemb RO**   Mf
   CMB 1720-1812 **NLW**
BT 1799-1810, 1812-16, 1818-70 **NLW**

WALTON EAST   *SD*
CB 1721-1974   M 1721-1971 **NLW**
BT 1799-1807, 1809-44, 1846, 1848-52, 1854-5, 1857-69, 1871, 1875 **NLW**

WALTON WEST   *SD*
PR M 1755-1812 recorded in 1831 apparently lost. M 1813-37 not recorded in 1933
C 1763-1882   M 1838-1970 (Banns 1824-1946)   B 1763-1953 **Pemb RO**
BT 1800-4, 1809-65, 1873-4 **NLW**

*WALWYN'S CASTLE/CASTELL GWALCHMAI   *SD*
CMB 1755-1813 **NLW**
BT 1772, 1801-6, 1809-14, 1818-74 **NLW**

WARREN   *SD*
PR M 1755-76 recorded in 1831 and CB 1760-1812 M 1774-1812 recorded in 1933 apparently lost
C 1813-1968   M 1813-35, 1840-1966 (Banns 1825-1966) **NLW**   B 1813- incumbent
BT 1799-1805, 1807-71, 1873-8, 1882, 1888-90 **NLW**

WDIG/GOODWICK   *SD*
‹Llanwnda
M 1913-74 (Banns 1923-74) **Pemb RO**

*WHITCHURCH/TRE-GROES   *SD*
Diocesan records suggest that *c.* 1790 the registers went back to 1731
C 1753-1974   M 1772-1969 (Banns 1772-1874, 1877-94) Solfach/Solva 1908-70   B 1752-1957
   Pemb RO
BT 1799-1800, 1802-7, 1809-82, 1886, 1889-91, 1898-9, 1902-4 **NLW**
Cop ts PR C 1753-94 M 1772-1812 B 1752-94 (extracts CMB to 1907) **NLW**

*WHITECHURCH/EGLWYS WEN   *SD*
PR M 1755-1812 recorded in 1831 apparently lost
CB 1704-1812   M 1704-53, 1813-38 **NLW**
BT 1674-5, 1678, 1680, 1683, 1685-90, 1699, 1701-3, 1799-1800, 1803-39, 1844-6, 1851-60, 1863,
   1865, 1869-70, 1872-80, 1882, 1885, 1890 **NLW**

*WISTON/CAS-WIS   *SD*
C 1653-66, 1715-1878   M 1653-66, 1715-1970   B 1653-66, 1715-1921 **NLW**
BT 1799-1806, 1808-82 **NLW**

YERBESTON   *SD*
PR none before 1813 to be found in 1831, and CB 1791-1812 recorded in 1933 as being in poor
   condition now apparently lost. Diocesan records suggest that in 1814 there were extant PR C
   1786-1812 M 1778-1811 B 1787-1812
CB 1813-1976   M 1813-1968 **Pemb RO**
BT 1799-1831, 1833-5, 1840, 1843-7, 1849, 1851-73, 1875-8, 1880-6, 1888-91, 1893-5, 1898-1902,
   1904-9 **NLW**

TREFALDWYN
MONTGOMERYSHIRE

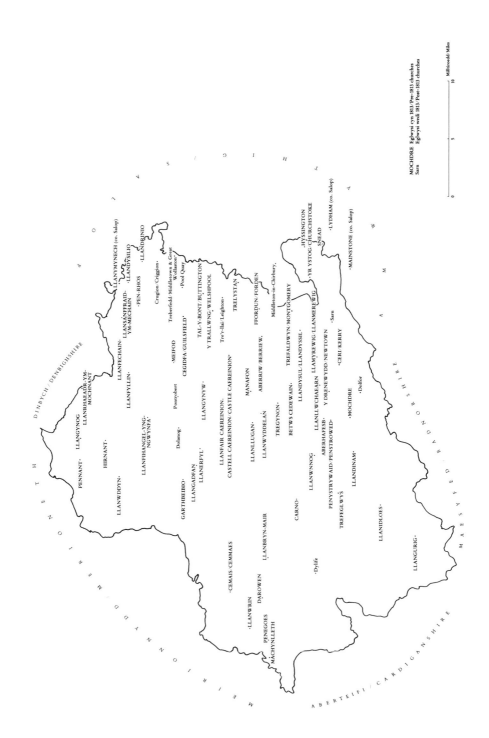

MOCHDRE Eglwysi cyn 1813 / Pre-1813 churches
Sarn Eglwysi wedi 1813 / Post-1813 churches

ABERHAFESB *SA*
PR CMB 1721-7 recorded in 1936 apparently lost
C 1578-1601, 1623-5, 1630-51, 1726-1812   M 1579-1602, 1623-4, 1628, 1633-42, 1644, 1648, 1726-
   1837   B 1578-82, 1584-7, 1590, 1603, 1619, 1623-6, 1640-6, 1726-1902 **NLW**
BT 1665-8, 1670, 1672-3, 1676-8, 1680-1, 1683-8, 1698-1701, 1703, 1705-17, 1719-1834 **NLW**
   Mf 1676-1834 **CROH & CROR**

ABERRIW/BERRIEW *SA*
C 1596-1628, 1685-1888   M 1596-8, 1600-3, 1607-9, 1616-26, 1685-1907   B 1596-1628, 1683-
   91, 1693-1923 **NLW**
BT 1662-6, 1668-74, 1676-8, 1681-5, 1687-96, 1698-1700, 1702-10, 1713-1848, 1850-4 **NLW**   Mf
   1673-1854 **CROH & CROR**

ASTON gweler/see LYDHAM

BERRIEW gweler/see ABERRIW

BETWS CEDEWAIN *SA*
C 1661-1956   M 1662-1836   B 1662-1857 **NLW**
BT 1662-8, 1670-4, 1676-83, 1685-8, 1690-6, 1698-1718, 1720-1853 **NLW**   Mf **CROH &
   CROR**

*BUTTINGTON/TAL-Y-BONT** *SA*
PR CMB 1723-35 recorded in 1936 apparently lost
C 1736-1948   M 1736-1971 (Banns 1824-1900)   B 1736-1953 **NLW**
BT 1638, 1660-1, 1663-1734, 1736-1833, 1836-48 **HRO**   1849-62 **NLW**   Mf 1854-62 **CROH
   & CROR**   Fac 1638-1848 **NLW**

CARNO *B*
C 1638-47, 1661-87, 1699-1716, 1718-24, 1736-1809   M 1638-47, 1661-86, 1699-1724, 1736-1837
   (Banns 1823-1975)   B 1638-47, 1661-86, 1699-1724, 1736-1809, 1813-1916 **NLW**
BT 1677, 1680, 1683, 1685-6, ?1688, 1689-90, 1692-3, 1695-1700, 1703, 1705, 1708-9, 1711-13, 1717-
   21, 1723-32, 1734, 1737, 1739-56, 1758-80, 1782-1837 **NLW**
Cop ms PR (extracts) M 1757-1809 **NLW**

CARREGHWFA/CARREGHOFA gweler/see LLANYMYNECH

CASTELL CAEREINION/CASTLE CAEREINION *SA*
C 1689-1732, 1734-1856   M 1689-1732, 1734-1971 (Banns 1810-1943)   B 1689-1732, 1734-1877
   NLW
BT 1663, 1665-9, 1672-3, 1676-9, 1681, 1685-91, 1693-5, 1698-1709, 1713-14, 1717-23, 1725-7,
   1729-31, 1733-5, 1737-1843 **NLW**   Mf **CROH & CROR**

CASTLEWRIGHT gweler/see MAINSTONE

CEGIDFA/GUILSFIELD *SA*
C 1572-1642, 1696-1895   M 1572-1642, 1696-1878   B 1572-1642, 1696-1875 **NLW**
BT 1667-8, 1670, 1672-3, 1675-85, 1687-95, 1697-1700, 1702-1859 **NLW**   Mf **CROH & CROR**
Cop ms PR CMB 1575-1608 **NLW**

CEMAIS/CEMMAES　　　　*B*
C 1711-45, 1751-1927　　M 1711-45, 1749-1970 (Banns 1823-1918)　　B 1711-45, 1749-1863 **NLW**
BT 1668, 1670-4, 1676-8, 1680-4, 1686-9, 1692, 1694-6, 1700-4, 1706-7, 1709-15, 1717-18, 1720-3,
　1725-32, 1734-5, 1737-1837, 1851 **NLW**
Cop ms PR/BT C 1668-1867 M 1668-1885 B 1668-1863　　ms BT (extracts) CMB 1668-1750 **NLW**

CERI/KERRY　　　　*SA*
C 1602-6, 1609-1915　　M 1602-6, 1609-1961 (Banns 1823-1936)　　B 1602-6, 1609-1860 **NLW**
BT 1705, 1707-8, 1710, 1713-40, 1742-95, 1797-1810, 1813-47 **NLW**
Cop PR CMB 1602-1812 *Montgomeryshire Collections,* 39 (1915-20)　　ts PR CMB 1602-1812 **Soc
Gen**

*CHURCHSTOKE/YR YSTOG　　　　*H*
Included townships of Brompton and Rhiston, co. Salop
C 1558-1853　　M 1558-1812　　B 1558-1812 **SRO**
BT 1660, 1663-1718, 1720-54, 1756-87, 1789-1833, 1836-53, 1855-8, 1861 **HRO**

CRUGION/CRIGGION　　　　*SA*
‹Alberbury (Llanfihangel-yng-Ngheintyn), co. Salop 1864. PR for Alberbury CMB 1564-1812 are
　in Local Studies Department, Shropshire Libraries, Shrewsbury; C 1813-1908 M 1813-1958
　B 1813-51 are in SRO. BT for Alberbury 1660-1864 with gaps are in HRO. Cop PR for Alber-
　bury CMB 1564-1812 are in Shropshire Parish Register Society, Hereford, 6-7 (1902)
C 1829-　　M 1865-　　B 1843- incumbent

DAROWEN　　　　*B*
C 1633-50, 1658-61, 1663-5, 1669-72, 1675-82, 1684-9, 1708-34, 1736-1876　　M 1633-50, 1658-60,
　1673, 1675-82, 1684-9, 1708-34, 1736-1837 (Banns 1824-44)　　B 1633-50, 1658-60, 1670-1, 1673,
　1675-82, 1684-9, 1708-34, 1736-1871 **NLW**
BT ?1669, 1670-2, 1674, 1676-8, 1681-7, 1691-6, 1698, 1700, 1702-6, 1708-13, 1716-17, 1719,
　1729-31, 1733-8, 1740-1854, 1905 **NLW**
Cop ms PR CMB 1633-1771 (partly indexed)　　ms BT (extracts) CMB 1670-1757 **NLW**

DOLANOG (PONTDOLANOG)　　　　*SA*
‹Llanfair Caereinion, Llanfihangel-yng-Ngwynfa, Llanerfyl & Llangynyw 1856
C 1856-　　B 1865- incumbent　　M 1862-1970 **NLW**

DOLFOR　　　　*SA*
‹Ceri/Kerry 1851
C 1852-　　B 1853- incumbent　　M 1867-1968 **NLW**

DRENEWYDD, Y/NEWTOWN　　　　*SA*
C 1660-75, 1679-1971　　M 1660-75, 1679-1958 (Banns 1887-1971)　　B 1660-75, 1679-1915 **NLW**
BT 1662, 1665-8, 1671-4, 1676-84, 1686-96, 1698-1841 **NLW**　　Mf 1665-1841 **CROH & CROR**

DYLIFE　　　　*B*
‹Llanbryn-mair, Darowen, Penegoes & Trefeglwys 1856
C 1856-1926 **NLW**　　B 1857- incumbent　　Fac B 1857-1980 **NLW**
BT 1882, 1890-4 **NLW**

FFORDUN/FORDEN　　　　*SA*
C 1598-1748, 1751-1807, 1813-78　　M 1598-1748, 1751-1930　　B 1598-1748, 1751-1807, 1813-1920
　House of Industry C 1795-1863　　B 1795-1864 **NLW**
BT 1638, 1660, 1663-1833, 1836-63 **HRO**

GARTHBEIBIO *SA*
PR M 1754-1837 recorded as missing in 1936, although CB 1760-1812 includes M entries to 1795
C 1710-1925   M 1722-95, 1837-1917, 1919-41   B 1710-1903 **NLW**
BT 1667-76, 1678, ?1680-2, 1684-9, ?1691-4, 1696, 1698-1700, 1702-3, 1705, 1707-8, 1718, 1721-4,
    1726-1836, 1850-5 **NLW**   Mf **CROH & CROR**
Cop ms PR C 1710-59 M 1722-59 B 1715-59 **CROR**

GREAT WOLLASTON gweler/see TREBERFEDD/MIDDLETOWN

*GUILSFIELD/CEGIDFA   *SA*
C 1572-1642, 1696-1895   M 1572-1642, 1696-1878   B 1572-1642, 1696-1875 **NLW**
BT 1667-8, 1670, 1672-3, 1675-85, 1687-95, 1697-1700, 1702-1859 **NLW**   Mf **CROH & CROR**
Cop ms PR CMB 1575-1608 **NLW**

HIRNANT   *SA*
C 1600-1, 1614-15, 1620-36, 1640-7, 1651, 1653-7, 1662, 1673-7, 1680-2, 1685-1706, 1720-1812   M
    1601, 1614-15, 1620-36, 1640-7, 1653, 1656, 1688-1706, 1720-1971   B 1600-1, 1614-15, 1620-36,
    1640-7, 1653-7, 1662, 1673-7, 1680-2, 1685-1706, 1720-1812 **NLW**
BT 1667, 1670, 1672, 1674, 1682-3, 1685-96, 1698-1702, 1705-7, 1711-14, 1716, 1718-39, 1741-54,
    1756-71, 1773-1845, 1851-4 **NLW**   Mf 1674-1854 **CROH & CROR**
Cop ms/ts PR C 1720-1912 M 1720-1837 B 1720-1909 **CROR**

HYSSINGTON   *H*
Included township of Mucklewick, co. Salop, transferred to Shelve 1884
CMB 1701- incumbent
BT 1598-9, 1605, 1610, 1613, 1638, 1660-1, 1663-97, 1699-1702, 1704-54, 1756-1833, 1836-47,
    1849-63, 1865, 1867, 1869-70 **HRO**

*KERRY/CERI   *SA*
C 1602-6, 1609-1915   M 1602-6, 1609-1961 (Banns 1823-1936)   B 1602-6, 1609-1860 **NLW**
BT 1705, 1707-8, 1710, 1713-40, 1742-95, 1797-1810, 1813-47 **NLW**
Cop PR CMB 1602-1812 *Montgomeryshire Collections*, 39 (1915-20)   ts PR CMB 1602-1812 **Soc
Gen**

*LEIGHTON/TRE'R-LLAI   *H*
‹Worthen, co. Salop, 1853. PR for Worthen C 1558-1931 M 1558-1972 B 1558-1965 are in SRO
C 1854-   B 1864- incumbent   M 1855-1971 **SRO**

LLAMYREWIG/LLANMEREWIG   *SA*
C 1661, 1663-6, 1670-4, 1676-85, 1688-1899   M 1670-4, 1676-85, 1688-1971   B 1663-6, 1670-4,
    1676-85, 1688-1823 **NLW**
BT 1665, 1667-8, 1670-4, 1676-7, 1679-89, 1691-5, 1699-1703, 1705-25, 1728-59, 1761-6, 1768-1837
    NLW   Mf **CROH & CROR**
Cop ms PR CMB 1661-1761 **NLW**

LLANBRYN-MAIR   *B*
C 1663-1899   M 1663-1934   B 1663-1884 **NLW**   Fac C 1899-1979   B 1884-1981 **NLW**
BT 1670-4, 1676-82, 1685-7, 1689-93, 1695-6, 1699-1702, 1704-23, 1725-1837, 1882, 1905-7 **NLW**
Cop ms PR CB 1663-1812 M 1663-1837   ms PR (extracts) CMB 1665-1780 **NLW**

LLANDINAM			*B*
C 1587-1634, 1636-75, 1678, 1685-6, 1689-90, 1703-6, 1712-71, 1774, 1783, 1787, 1789, 1793-6		M
	1591-1633, 1636-75, 1678, 1685-6, 1689-90, 1703-6, 1712-71		B 1587-1614, 1636-75, 1678,
	1685-6, 1689-90, 1703-6, 1712-71 **NLW**
BT 1671, 1677-80, 1685-7, 1689-93, 1695-1700, 1703-9, 1711-13, 1716-24, 1726-34, 1737-57,
	1759-60, 1762-80, 1782-1839, 1850, 1864 **NLW**
Cop ms PR (extracts) M 1753-1836 **NLW**

LLANDRINIO			*SA*
PR M 1813-37 recorded in 1936 apparently lost
C 1662-8, 1674-1898		M 1664-5, 1675-86, 1688-1812, 1837-1971		B 1662-7, 1687-97, 1709-18,
	1728-74, 1781-1812 **NLW**
BT 1668, 1674, 1677-96, 1698-1703, 1705-6, 1708-1813, 1815-33 **NLW**		Mf **CROH & CROR**

LLANDYSILIO			*SA*
C 1662-1735, 1737, 1740-1963		M 1663-1735, 1740-1971 (Banns 1919-75)		B 1662-1733, 1740-
	1872 **NLW**
BT 1663, 1668, 1674, 1677, 1680-96, 1698-1701, 1703-9, 1711-43, 1745-51, 1753-1848 **NLW**		Mf
	CROH & CROR

LLANDYSUL/LLANDYSSIL			*SA*
C 1689-1889	M 1689-1971	B 1689-1960 **NLW**
BT 1671-2, 1674, 1677, 1682-90, 1692, 1694-6, 1698-1835, 1850-7 **NLW**		Mf **CROH & CROR**

LLANERFYL			*SA*
C 1626-40, 1643-5, 1648, 1660, 1662-71, 1674-1857		M 1626-36, 1663-70, 1674-1837		B 1626-45,
	1652-3, 1660, 1662-71, 1674-1812 **NLW**
BT 1667, 1679, 1682, 1686-94, 1696, 1698-1718, 1720-1836 **NLW**		Mf 1667-1836 **CROH &
	CROR**

LLANFAIR CAEREINION			*SA*
C 1608-22, 1624-66, 1669-76, 1680-1702, 1723-1892		M 1608-22, 1624-43, 1662-6, 1670-6,
	1680-1702, 1723-1955		B 1608-22, 1624-67, 1670-6, 1680-1702, 1723-1901 **NLW**
BT 1662, 1665-8, 1678, 1680, 1682-93, 1695-6, 1698, 1700-3, 1705-9, 1711-22, 1724-6, 1728-32,
	1734-1852 **NLW**		Mf **CROH & CROR**

LLANFECHAIN			*SA*
C 1603-1705, 1707-1863		M 1603-1705, 1707-1837		B 1603-1705, 1707-1880 **NLW**
BT 1667, 1671-3, 1678, 1680-7, 1689, 1691-4, 1696, 1698-1703, 1705-15, 1717-19, 1721-1850 **NLW**
	Mf **CROH & CROR**

LLANFIHANGEL-YNG-NGWYNFA			*SA*
C 1663-7, 1688-98, 1708-1869		M 1663-7, 1688-93, 1708-1968 (Banns 1823-1961)		B 1663-7,
	1688-98, 1708-1864 **NLW**
BT 1662, 1673, 1676, 1678, 1680-91, 1693, 1703, 1708-10, 1712, 1715-16, 1722, 1724-1857 **NLW**
	Mf **CROH & CROR**
Cop ts PR C 1663-1761 M 1663-1753 B 1663-1762 **CROR**

LLANFYLLIN			*SA*
C 1654, 1660-1, 1664-1875		M 1669-1708, 1711-1939 (Banns 1871-1963)		B 1665-1956 **NLW**
BT 1667-8, 1672, 1677-81, 1684-92, 1694-5, 1716-19, 1723-1840, 1842, 1846 **NLW**		Mf **CROH
	& CROR**

LLANGADFAN *SA*

PR CMB 1630-41 recorded in 1831 apparently lost. PR B ends in 1873, but burials 1831-1920 are in a separate cemetery register, kept in Welsh, which gives location of grave as well as dates of death and burial, and deceased's age and abode

C 1673-96, 1700-5, 1717-1879   M 1673-96, 1700-5, 1717-1811, 1813-37 (Banns 1823-1950) B 1673-96, 1700-5, 1717-1920 **NLW**

BT 1663-5, 1669-72, 1674, 1676-8, 1680-96, 1698, 1703, 1705, 1707-15, 1717-26, 1728-1836 **NLW** Mf **CROH & CROR**

LLANGURIG *B*

C 1687-91, 1694-1702, 1707-1861   M 1683-1837 (Banns 1827-1958)   B 1686-1756, 1758-1875 **NLW**

BT 1677, 1683, 1685, 1687, 1689, 1691-3, 1695-1713, 1716-28, 1730-5, 1737, 1739-1867, 1883-5 **NLW**

LLANGYNOG *SA*

C 1720-1870   M 1720-61, 1763-1971 (Banns 1824-66)   B 1720-1885 **NLW**

BT 1662-5, 1668, 1673, 1676-82, 1684-6, 1691-2, 1694, 1696, 1702, 1704, 1708-13, 1715-16, 1719-26, 1728-1842, 1849-56, 1859 **NLW**   Mf **CROH & CROR**

LLANGYNYW *SA*

C 1584-90, 1593-1683, 1729-1914   M 1584-90, 1593-1649, 1661-83, 1729-1837   B 1584-90, 1594-1683, 1729-1895 **NLW**

BT 1662-71, 1673-4, 1676, 1679-96, 1698-1703, 1705-13, 1715-34, 1737-1839 **NLW**   Mf **CROH & CROR**

LLANIDLOES *B*

C 1616-49, 1654-5, 1658, 1660-1830   M 1614-49, 1662-83, 1687-90, 1695-7, 1711-1835   B 1614-44, 1647-8, 1661-87, 1692-1840 **NLW**

BT 1677, 1683, 1685-93, 1695-9, 1703-5, 1707-8, 1711-13, 1716-21, 1724-34, 1737, 1739-56, 1758-1840 **NLW**

Cop ms PR C 1616-1812 (extracts to 1830) M 1614-1812 (extracts to 1836) B 1614-1818 (extracts to 1839) **NLW**   ms PR CM 1711-18 with index **Soc Gen**

LLANLLUGAN *SA*

CB 1603-33, 1670, 1672, 1676, 1679-1702, 1731-1812   M 1603-33, 1670, 1672, 1676, 1679-1702, 1731-1971 **NLW**   Fac C 1813-1982   B 1813-1981 **NLW**

BT 1663, 1668, 1670, 1672-4, 1676-7, 1679, 1681-4, 1687, 1691-5, 1698-1703, 1705-42, 1744-66, 1768-1807, 1809-50 **NLW**   Mf **CROH & CROR**

Cop PR/BT CMB 1603-1790 *Montgomeryshire Collections,* 34-35 (1907-10)   ms PR/BT CMB 1603-1790 **NLW**

LLANLLWCHAEARN *SA*

C 1658-1948   M 1658-1975 (Banns 1823-1932)   All Saints M 1891-1971 (Banns 1891-1949) B 1658-1904 **NLW**

BT 1662-8, 1670-4, 1676-9, 1681-96, 1698-1754, 1756-61, 1763-1835, 1837-9, 1850 **NLW**   Mf **CROH & CROR**

*LLANMEREWIG/LLAMYREWIG *SA*

C 1661, 1663-6, 1670-4, 1676-85, 1688-1899   M 1670-4, 1676-85, 1688-1971   B 1663-6, 1670-4, 1676-85, 1688-1823 **NLW**

BT 1665, 1667-8, 1670-4, 1676-7, 1679-89, 1691-5, 1699-1703, 1705-25, 1728-59, 1761-6, 1768-1837 **NLW**   Mf **CROH & CROR**

Cop ms PR CMB 1661-1761 **NLW**

LLANRHAEADR-YM-MOCHNANT gweler/see Sir Ddinbych/Denbighshire

LLANSANFFRAID-YM-MECHAIN   *SA*
PR CB 1757-1813 printed in 1962-6 apparently lost
C 1582-1615, 1653-4, 1656, 1665, 1680, 1712-50, 1813-1911   M 1582-1615, 1674-1750, 1754-1837
   B 1582-1615, 1666, 1668-1750, 1813-51 **NLW**
ET 1666-73, 1681-3, 1686-96, 1698-1701, 1705-52, 1754-1844 **NLW**   Mf **CROH & CROR**
Cop PR B 1759-66, 1772-4, 1780-91 *Montgomeryshire Collections,* 57-59 (1962-6)

LLANWDDYN   *SA*
C 1624-44, 1649-59, 1662-3, 1665-80, 1684-91, 1693, 1695-1888   M 1624-30, 1666-79, 1683-4,
   1695, 1701-1968   B 1623-45, 1647, 1649-51, 1653-4, 1656-7, 1664, 1666-79, 1681-92, 1695-1881
   NLW
BT 1669, 1676-80, 1682-8, 1690-2, 1694-6, 1698-9, 1701-2, 1704-5, 1707-19, 1721-33, 1735-1851
   NLW   Mf **CROH & CROR**
Cop ts PR C 1624-93 M 1624-95 B 1623-1700 **CROR**

LLANWNNOG   *B*
C 1668-1775, 1783-1873   M 1668-1911 (Banns 1823-49, 1875-99)   B 1668-1882 **NLW**
BT 1677, 1679-80, 1685-6, 1690-2, 1695-1700, 1707-13, 1716-21, 1723-37, 1739-56, 1758-73, 1775-
   1852 **NLW**
Cop ms PR C 1668-1812 M 1754-85 B 1668-1850 M (extracts) 1670-1820 **NLW**

LLANWRIN   *B*
C 1671-90, 1695-1812   M 1671-90, 1695-1837 (Banns 1824-59)   B 1671-90, 1695-1917   Fac C
   1813-1976 **NLW**
BT ?1667, 1670-2, 1674, 1677, 1680-1, 1683-4, 1686, 1689, 1695-1702, 1704-18, 1720-3, 1725-1858,
   1906-7, 1910-11 **NLW**
Cop ms BT CMB 1667-1722 **NLW**

LLANWYDDELAN   *SA*
PR CMB 1664-1779 recorded in 1936 apparently lost
C 1783-1808, 1813-1944   M 1784-1971   B 1783-1808 **NLW**
BT 1662-3, 1665-8, 1670-1, 1673, 1676-7, 1679-86, 1688-96, 1698-1727, 1729-1846 **NLW**   Mf
   CROH & CROR

LLANYMYNECH   *L*
Parish comprising the townships of Llwyntidman/Llwyntidmon and Treprennal, co. Salop, and
   Carreghwfa/Carreghofa (formerly a detached part of Denbighshire), co. Montgomery
C 1666-1867   M 1666-1943   B 1666-1898 **SRO**
BT 1662-1857 with gaps **Lichfield JRO**
Cop PR CMB 1666-1812 Shropshire Parish Register Society, St. Asaph, 8 (1917)

LYDHAM   *H*
Shropshire parish including the detached township of Aston, co. Montgomery
C 1596-1660, 1691-1980   M 1596-1660, 1691-1837   B 1596-1660, 1679-88, 1691-1981 **SRO**
BT 1638, 1660-1702, 1704-52, 1754-1833, 1836-9, 1845-6, 1850 **HRO**
Cop PR CMB 1596-1812 Shropshire Parish Register Society, Hereford, 3 (1903)

MACHYNLLETH   *B*
C 1684-1722, 1731-1889   M 1684-1722, 1731-1894   B 1684-1722, 1731-1863 **NLW**   Fac C
    1889-1948 **NLW**
BT 1662, 1666-8, 1670-4, 1676-81, 1683-96, 1699-1706, 1711, 1719, 1723, ?1726, 1728-1857, 1889-90
    NLW
Cop ms PR/BT CB 1662-1782 M 1662-1812 B (extracts) 1782-1812 **NLW**

MAINSTONE   *H*
Shropshire parish including township of Castlewright, co. Montgomery
C 1590-1867   M 1590-1956   B 1590-1812 **SRO**
BT 1638, 1660-85, 1688-1833, 1836-78 **HRO**

MANAFON   *SA*
C 1596-1665, 1678-1891   M 1654, 1678-1971 (Banns 1813-38)   B 1596-1667, 1678-1930 **NLW**
BT 1662-3, 1665-8, 1670-4, 1676-96, 1698-1836, 1838-50 **NLW**   Mf **CROH & CROR**

MEIFOD   *SA*
C 1597, 1600, 1602, 1604-22, 1624-6, 1628-32, 1634-42, 1647-1880   M 1602, 1605-18, 1620-6,
    1628-31, 1634-7, 1640-2, 1649-1837 (Banns 1838-1917)   B 1600, 1602-26, 1628-32, 1634-42,
    1647-1922 **NLW**
BT 1662-3, 1665-8, 1670, 1672-3, 1675-7, 1679-82, 1684-96, 1698, 1700-1830, 1832-6 **NLW**   Mf
    1667-1822 **CROH & CROR**

MIDDLETON-IN-CHIRBURY   *H*
‹Chirbury, co. Salop, & Yr Ystog/Churchstoke, co. Montgomery, 1846
C 1846-96   M 1846-1970   B 1847-1972 **SRO**

*MIDDLETOWN/TREBERFEDD & GREAT WOLLASTON   *H*
‹Alberbury (Llanfihangel-yng-Ngheintyn) 1864 [see entry for Crugion/Criggion]. Includes the
    Montgomeryshire townships of Treberfedd/Middletown and Ucheldre/the Heldre
C 1829-1908   M 1864-1970 **SRO**   B 1872- incumbent

MOCHDRE   *SA*
C 1682, 1685-1714, 1717-18, 1722-6, 1729-1866   M 1729-1971 (Banns 1824-1976)   B 1695-1715,
    1723-4, 1729-1878 **NLW**
BT 1700, 1706-8, 1712-18, 1720-1, 1723-9, 1731-47, 1751-95, 1797-1810, 1813-38, 1840-51 **NLW**
Cop ms PR CMB 1682-1812 **NLW**

*MONTGOMERY/TREFALDWYN   *SA*
C 1574-1641, 1645-8, 1650-3, 1656-91, 1694-1972   M 1575-1641, 1645-7, 1651, 1653, 1656-91,
    1694-1981   B 1574-1641, 1645-7, 1652-3, 1656-91, 1694-1966 **NLW**
BT 1663-1772, 1774-1826, 1829-33, 1836-72 **HRO**

*NEWTOWN/Y DRENEWYDD   *SA*
C 1660-75, 1679-1971   M 1660-75, 1679-1958 (Banns 1887-1971)   B 1660-75, 1679-1915 **NLW**
BT 1662, 1665-8, 1671-4, 1676-84, 1686-96, 1698-1841 **NLW**   Mf 1665-1841 **CROH & CROR**

PENEGOES   *B*
C 1679-1812   M 1679-1970 (Banns 1823-77)   B 1679-1869 **NLW**
BT 1667, 1673-4, 1681-4, 1686, 1689-96, 1698-1702, 1704-6, 1715-16, 1718-19, 1721, 1726, 1728-36,
    1738-9, 1741-3, 1745-1852, 1856-8, 1861-4 **NLW**
Cop ms BT CMB 1667-1743 & PR C 1679-1812 (extracts to 1827) M 1679-1837 B 1679-1865 **NLW**

PENNANT (PENNANT MELANGELL)   *SA*
C 1680-3, 1685, 1689-1713, 1720-1812   M 1685-6, 1691-1713, 1720-1971   B 1680-6, 1689-1713,
   1720-1812 **NLW**
BT 1662, 1667-8, 1672-3, 1676-8, 1680-2, 1684-7, 1689-96, 1698-1719, 1721-4, 1727-1847, 1850-3
   NLW   Mf **CROH & CROR**
Cop ms/ts PR C 1680-1908 M 1680-1837 B 1680-1909 **CROR**

PEN-RHOS (TRINITY CHAPEL)   *SA*
‹Llandrinio, Llansanffraid-ym-Mechain, Meifod & Cegidfa/Guilsfield 1844. PR CB 1695-1804
   M 1701-54 recorded in 1936 apparently lost
C 1805-46   M (Banns) 1846-1935   B 1805-1963 **NLW**
BT see Llandrinio

PENYSTRYWAID/PENSTROWED   *B*
C 1628-47, 1661-1812   M 1628-47, 1661-1837   B 1628-47, 1661-1812 **NLW**
BT 1676-7, 1679-80, 1683, 1685-7, 1689, 1691-3, 1695-1700, 1703-5, 1707-9, 1712-13, 1716-19, 1721,
   1724-6, 1728-34, 1737, 1739-50, 1752-6, 1758-65, 1768-80, 1782-93, 1795-1837, 1864, 1868-9, 1872
   NLW

PONTDOLANOG gweler/see DOLANOG

PONTROBERT   *SA*
‹Meifod, Llangynyw & Llanfihangel-yng-Ngwynfa 1854
C 1853-   B 1857- incumbent   M 1853-1970 **NLW**

POOL QUAY   *SA*
‹Cegidfa/Guilsfield & Y Trallwng/Welshpool 1863
C 1863-1978   B 1863-1978 **NLW**   M 1864- incumbent

RHOS-GOCH gweler/see TRELYSTAN

SARN   *H*
‹Ceri/Kerry & Yr Ystog/Churchstoke
C 1860-   M 1861-   B 1860- incumbent

SNEAD   *H*
C 1665-1812   M 1665-1952   B 1665-1812 **SRO**
BT 1605, 1608, 1614, 1631, 1660-1, 1663-1833, 1836, 1838-9, 1841-60 **HRO**

TAL-Y-BONT/BUTTINGTON   *SA*
PR CMB 1723-35 recorded in 1936 apparently lost
C 1736-1948   M 1736-1971 (Banns 1824-1900)   B 1736-1953 **NLW**
BT 1638, 1660-1, 1663-1734, 1736-1833, 1836-48 **HRO**   1849-62 **NLW**   Mf 1854-62 **CROH**
   & CROR   Fac 1638-1848 **NLW**

TRALLWNG, Y/WELSHPOOL   *SA*
C 1634-1703, 1708-1945   M 1634-1703, 1708-1953   B 1634-1703, 1708-1944 **NLW**
BT 1662-3, 1681-2, 1684-5, 1690-1, 1693-5, 1698-1705, 1708-1859, 1861-8 **NLW**   Mf 1662-1845
   CROH & CROR
Cop PR CMB 1634-1736 (extracts) *Montgomeryshire Collections*, 36 (1912)

TREBERFEDD/MIDDLETOWN & GREAT WOLLASTON   *H*
‹Alberbury (Llanfihangel-yng-Ngheintyn) 1864 [see entry for Crugion/Criggion]. Includes the
   Montgomeryshire townships of Treberfedd/Middletown and Ucheldre/the Heldre
C 1829-1908   M 1864-1970 **SRO**   B 1872- incumbent

TREFALDWYN/MONTGOMERY   *SA*
C 1574-1641, 1645-8, 1650-3, 1656-91, 1694-1972   M 1575-1641, 1645-7, 1651, 1653, 1656-91,
   1694-1981   B 1574-1641, 1645-7, 1652-3, 1656-91, 1694-1966 **NLW**
BT 1663-1772, 1774-1826, 1829-33, 1836-72 **HRO**

TREFEGLWYS   *B*
C 1626, 1630-8, 1660-89, 1695-1812   M 1660-89, 1695-1812   B 1632-9, 1661-90, 1695-1812
   NLW
BT 1677, 1680, 1683-7, 1689-93, 1695-1700, 1703-5, 1707-9, 1711-13, 1715-21, 1723-34, 1737,
   1739-43, 1745-56, 1758-1836 **NLW**
Cop PR C 1626-1723 M 1661-1723 B 1632-1722 *Montgomeryshire Collections,* 32-33 (1902-4)
   CMB 1695-6 Sir Thomas Phillips, *Register of the Baptisms, Marriages and Burials of the Parish of
   Tref Eglwys...1695-6* (Middle Hill Press, *c.* 1867)   ms PR C 1626-1836 (extracts to 1856)
   M 1661-1850 (extracts to 1858) B 1632-1812 (extracts to 1873) **NLW**

TREGYNON   *SA*
C 1689-1891   M 1680-4, 1689, 1695-1838 (Banns 1823-1938)   B 1677-81, 1685, 1689-1864
   NLW
BT 1666-8, 1670, 1672, 1674, 1677, 1679, 1681-95, 1699-1724, 1726-97, 1799-1839, 1851-4 **NLW**
   Mf 1666-1839 **CROH & CROR**

TRELYSTAN (WOLSTONMYND)   *H*
‹Worthen, co. Salop, 1853. Formerly a chapelry comprising the Montgomeryshire townships of
   Trelystan, Tre'r-llai/Leighton and Rhosgoch with Mulsop
C 1660-1961   M 1660-1796, 1815-1955   B 1660-1814 **SRO**
BT 1638, 1660, 1663-1827, 1829-33, 1836-7, 1840-3, 1845-6, 1849-87 **HRO**

TRE'R-LLAI/LEIGHTON   *H*
‹Worthen, co. Salop, 1853. PR for Worthen C 1558-1931 M 1558-1972 B 1558-1965 are in SRO
C 1854-   B 1864- incumbent   M 1855-1971 **SRO**

TRINITY CHAPEL gweler/see PEN-RHOS

*WELSHPOOL/Y TRALLWNG   *SA*
C 1634-1703, 1708-1945   M 1634-1703, 1708-1953   B 1634-1703, 1708-1944 **NLW**
BT 1662-3, 1681-2, 1684-5, 1690-1, 1693-5, 1698-1705, 1708-1859, 1861-8 **NLW**   Mf 1662-1845
   CROH & CROR
Cop PR CMB 1634-1736 (extracts) *Montgomeryshire Collections,* 36 (1912)

WOLSTONMYND gweler/see TRELYSTAN

YSTOG, YR/CHURCHSTOKE   *H*
Included townships of Brompton and Rhiston, co. Salop
C 1558-1853   M 1558-1812   B 1558-1812 **SRO**
BT 1660, 1663-1718, 1720-54, 1756-87, 1789-1833, 1836-53, 1855-8, 1861 **HRO**

MYNEGAI : INDEX